Entrepreneurship in a Regional Context

Enterprise and entrepreneurship are of strong interest to policy-makers because new and small firms can be key contributors to job and wealth creation. However, this contribution varies spatially, with some areas in a country having new firm formation rates that are up to three or four times higher than others. The vast majority of these new firms begin in the geographical area in which the founder lives, works or was born, emphasising that entrepreneurship is a local event. The book documents a diversity of research approaches to examining the regional determinants of entrepreneurship in countries as contrasting as India and Sweden. The Editor's call is for scholars to better understand the long run factors that influence enterprise at the local and regional level. For policy-makers the Editor's challenge is for them to be much clearer about the targets for their policies. Is it new firms, new jobs, or productivity and does it matter where these targets are delivered?

This book was published as a special issue of *Regional Studies*.

Michael Fritsch is Professor of Economics and Chair of Business Dynamics, Innovation, and Economic Change at the Friedrich Schiller University Jena, Germany. His main fields of research are new business formation processes and their impact on economic development, innovation systems, economic development strategies, as well as markets and market failure.

David J. Storey, OBE, is Professor in the School of Business Management and Economics at the University of Sussex. He is interested in the financing and performance of new firms and the public policy environment in which such firms can thrive.

Regions and Cities

Series Editor in Chief
Susan M. Christopherson, *Cornell University, USA*

Editors
Maryann Feldman, *University of Georgia, USA*
Gernot Grabher, *HafenCity University Hamburg, Germany*
Ron Martin, *University of Cambridge, UK*
Martin Perry, *Massey University, New Zealand*

In today's globalised, knowledge-driven and networked world, regions and cities have assumed heightened significance as the interconnected nodes of economic, social and cultural production, and as sites of new modes of economic and territorial governance and policy experimentation. This book series brings together incisive and critically engaged international and interdisciplinary research on this resurgence of regions and cities, and should be of interest to geographers, economists, sociologists, political scientists and cultural scholars, as well as to policy-makers involved in regional and urban development.

For more information on the Regional Studies Association visit www.regionalstudies.org

There is a **30% discount** available to RSA members on books in the ***Regions and Cities*** series, and other subject related Taylor and Francis books and e-books including Routledge titles. To order just e-mail alex.robinson@tandf.co.uk, or phone on +44 (0) 20 7017 6924 and declare your RSA membership. You can also visit www.routledge.com and use the discount code: **RSA0901**

88. Entrepreneurship in a Regional Context
Edited by Michael Fritsch and David J. Storey

87. The London Olympics and Urban Development
The mega-event city
Edited by Gavin Poynter, Valerie Viehoff and Yang Li

86. Making 21st Century Knowledge Complexes
Technopoles of the world revisited
Edited by Julie Tian Miao, Paul Benneworth and Nicholas A. Phelps

85. Soft Spaces in Europe
Re-negotiating governance, boundaries and borders
Edited by Philip Allmendinger, Graham Haughton, Jörg Knieling and Frank Othengrafen

84. Regional Worlds: Advancing the Geography of Regions
Edited by Martin Jones and Anssi Paasi

83. Place-making and Urban Development
New challenges for contemporary planning and design
Pier Carlo Palermo and Davide Ponzini

82. Knowledge, Networks and Policy
Regional studies in postwar Britain and beyond
James A. Hopkins

81. Dynamics of Economic Spaces in the Global Knowledge-based Economy
Theory and East Asian cases
Sam Ock Park

80. Urban Competitiveness
Theory and practice
Daniele Letri and Peter Kresl

79. Smart Specialisation
Opportunities and challenges for regional innovation policy
Dominique Foray

78. The Age of Intelligent Cities
Smart environments and innovation-for-all strategies
Nicos Komninos

77. Space and Place in Central and Eastern Europe
Historical trends and perspectives
Gyula Horváth

76. Territorial Cohesion in Rural Europe
The relational turn in rural development
Edited by Andrew Copus and Philomena de Lima

75. The Global Competitiveness of Regions
Robert Huggins, Hiro Izushi, Daniel Prokop and Piers Thompson

74. The Social Dynamics of Innovation Networks
Edited by Roel Rutten, Paul Benneworth, Dessy Irawati and Frans Boekema

73. The European Territory
From historical roots to global challenges
Jacques Robert

72. Urban Innovation Systems
What makes them tick?
Willem van Winden, Erik Braun, Alexander Otgaar and Jan-Jelle Witte

71. Shrinking Cities
A global perspective
Edited by Harry W. Richardson and Chang Woon Nam

70. Cities, State and Globalization
City-regional governance
Tassilo Herrschel

69. The Creative Class Goes Global
Edited by Charlotta Mellander, Richard Florida, Bjørn Asheim and Meric Gertler

68. Entrepreneurial Knowledge, Technology and the Transformation of Regions
Edited by Charlie Karlsson, Börje Johansson and Roger Stough

67. The Economic Geography of the IT Industry in the Asia Pacific Region
Edited by Philip Cooke, Glen Searle and Kevin O'Connor

66. Working Regions
Reconnecting innovation and production in the knowledge economy
Jennifer Clark

65. Europe's Changing Geography
The impact of inter-regional networks
Edited by Nicola Bellini and Ulrich Hilpert

64. The Value of Arts and Culture for Regional Development
A Scandinavian perspective
Edited by Lisbeth Lindeborg and Lars Lindkvist

63. The University and the City
John Goddard and Paul Vallance

62. Re-framing Regional Development
Evolution, innovation and transition
Edited by Philip Cooke

61. Networking Regionalised Innovative Labour Markets
Edited by Ulrich Hilpert and Helen Lawton Smith

60. Leadership and Change in Sustainable Regional Development
Edited by Markku Sotarauta, Ina Horlings and Joyce Liddle

59. Regional Development Agencies: The Next Generation?
Networking, knowledge and regional policies
Edited by Nicola Bellini, Mike Danson and Henrik Halkier

58. Community-based Entrepreneurship and Rural Development
Creating favourable conditions for small businesses in Central Europe
Matthias Fink, Stephan Loidl and Richard Lang

57. Creative Industries and Innovation in Europe
Concepts, measures and comparative case studies
Edited by Luciana Lazzeretti

56. Innovation Governance in an Open Economy
Shaping regional nodes in a globalized world
Edited by Annika Rickne, Staffan Laestadius and Henry Etzkowitz

55. Complex Adaptive Innovation Systems
Relatedness and transversality in the evolving region
Philip Cooke

54. Creating Knowledge Locations in Cities
Innovation and integration challenges
Willem van Winden, Luis de Carvalho, Erwin van Tujil, Jeroen van Haaren and Leo van den Berg

53. Regional Development in Northern Europe
Peripherality, marginality and border issues
Edited by Mike Danson and Peter De Souza

52. Promoting Silicon Valleys in Latin America
Luciano Ciravegna

51. Industrial Policy Beyond the Crisis
Regional, national and international perspectives
Edited by David Bailey, Helena Lenihan and Josep-Maria Arauzo-Carod

50. Just Growth
Inclusion and prosperity in America's metropolitan regions
Chris Benner and Manuel Pastor

49. Cultural Political Economy of Small Cities
Edited by Anne Lorentzen and Bas van Heur

48. The Recession and Beyond
Local and regional responses to the downturn
Edited by David Bailey and Caroline Chapain

47. Beyond Territory
Edited by Harald Bathelt, Maryann Feldman and Dieter F. Kogler

46. Leadership and Place
Edited by Chris Collinge, John Gibney and Chris Mabey

45. Migration in the 21st Century
Rights, outcomes, and policy
Kim Korinek and Thomas Maloney

44. The Futures of the City Region
Edited by Michael Neuman and Angela Hull

43. The Impacts of Automotive Plant Closures
A tale of two cities
Edited by Andrew Beer and Holli Evans

42. Manufacturing in the New Urban Economy
Willem van Winden, Leo van den Berg, Luis de Carvalho and Erwin van Tuijl

41. Globalizing Regional Development in East Asia
Production networks, clusters, and entrepreneurship
Edited by Henry Wai-chung Yeung

40. China and Europe
The implications of the rise of China as a global economic power for Europe
Edited by Klaus Kunzmann, Willy A Schmid and Martina Koll-Schretzenmayr

39. Business Networks in Clusters and Industrial Districts
The governance of the global value chain
Edited by Fiorenza Belussi and Alessia Sammarra

38. Whither Regional Studies?
Edited by Andy Pike

37. Intelligent Cities and Globalisation of Innovation Networks
Nicos Komninos

36. Devolution, Regionalism and Regional Development
The UK experience
Edited by Jonathan Bradbury

35. Creative Regions
Technology, culture and knowledge entrepreneurship
Edited by Philip Cooke and Dafna Schwartz

34. European Cohesion Policy
Willem Molle

33. Geographies of the New Economy
Critical reflections
Edited by Peter W. Daniels, Andrew Leyshon, Michael J. Bradshaw and Jonathan Beaverstock

32. The Rise of the English Regions?
Edited by Irene Hardill, Paul Benneworth, Mark Baker and Leslie Budd

31. Regional Development in the Knowledge Economy
Edited by Philip Cooke and Andrea Piccaluga

30. Regional Competitiveness
Edited by Ron Martin, Michael Kitson and Peter Tyler

29. Clusters and Regional Development
Critical reflections and explorations
Edited by Bjørn Asheim, Philip Cooke and Ron Martin

28. Regions, Spatial Strategies and Sustainable Development
David Counsell and Graham Haughton

27. Sustainable Cities
Graham Haughton and Colin Hunter

26. Geographies of Labour Market Inequality
Edited by Ron Martin and Philip S. Morrison

25. Regional Innovation Strategies
The challenge for less-favoured regions
Edited by Kevin Morgan and Claire Nauwelaers

24. Out of the Ashes?
The social impact of industrial contraction and regeneration on Britain's mining communities
Chas Critcher, Bella Dicks, David Parry and David Waddington

23. Restructuring Industry and Territory
The experience of Europe's regions
Edited by Anna Giunta, Arnoud Lagendijk and Andy Pike

22. Foreign Direct Investment and the Global Economy
Corporate and institutional dynamics of global-localisation
Edited by Jeremy Alden and Nicholas F. Phelps

21. Community Economic Development
Edited by Graham Haughton

20. Regional Development Agencies in Europe
Edited by Charlotte Damborg, Mike Danson and Henrik Halkier

19. Social Exclusion in European Cities
Processes, experiences and responses
Edited by Judith Allen, Goran Cars and Ali Madanipour

18. Metropolitan Planning in Britain
A comparative study
Edited by Peter Roberts, Kevin Thomas and Gwyndaf Williams

17. Unemployment and Social Exclusion
Landscapes of labour inequality and social exclusion
Edited by Sally Hardy, Paul Lawless and Ron Martin

16. Multinationals and European Integration
Trade, investment and regional development
Edited by Nicholas A. Phelps

15. The Coherence of EU Regional Policy
Contrasting perspectives on the structural funds
Edited by John Bachtler and Ivan Turok

14. New Institutional Spaces
TECs and the remaking of economic governance
Martin Jones, Foreword by Jamie Peck

13. Regional Policy in Europe
S. S. Artobolevskiy

12. Innovation Networks and Learning Regions?
James Simmie

11. British Regionalism and Devolution
The challenges of state reform and European integration
Edited by Jonathan Bradbury and John Mawson

10. Regional Development Strategies
A European perspective
Edited by Jeremy Alden and Philip Boland

9. Union Retreat and the Regions
The shrinking landscape of organised labour
Ron Martin, Peter Sunley and Jane Wills

8. The Regional Dimension of Transformation in Central Europe
Grzegorz Gorzelak

7. The Determinants of Small Firm Growth
An inter-regional study in the United Kingdom 1986–90
Richard Barkham, Graham Gudgin, Mark Hart and Eric Hanvey

6. The Regional Imperative
Regional planning and governance in Britain, Europe and the United States
Urlan A. Wannop

5. An Enlarged Europe
Regions in competition?
Edited by Louis Albrechts, Sally Hardy, Mark Hart and Anastasios Katos

4. Spatial Policy in a Divided Nation
Edited by Richard T. Harrison and Mark Hart

3. Regional Development in the 1990s
The British Isles in transition
Edited by Ron Martin and Peter Townroe

2. Retreat from the Regions
Corporate change and the closure of factories
Stephen Fothergill and Nigel Guy

1. Beyond Green Belts
Managing urban growth in the 21st century
Edited by John Herington

Entrepreneurship in a Regional Context

Edited by
Michael Fritsch and David J. Storey

LONDON AND NEW YORK

First published 2015 by Routledge

2 Park Square, Milton Park, Abingdon, Oxon OX14 4RN
711 Third Avenue, New York, NY 10017, USA

Routledge is an imprint of the Taylor & Francis Group, an informa business

First issued in paperback 2017

British Library Cataloguing in Publication Data
A catalogue record for this book is available from the British Library

ISBN 13: 978-1-138-91209-0 (hbk)
ISBN 13: 978-1-138-08531-2 (pbk)

Typeset in Bembo
by RefineCatch Limited, Bungay, Suffolk

Publisher's Note
The publisher accepts responsibility for any inconsistencies that may have arisen during the conversion of this book from journal articles to book chapters, namely the possible inclusion of journal terminology.

Contents

Citation Information

The chapters in this book were originally published in *Regional Studies*, volume 48, issue 6 (June 2014). When citing this material, please use the original page numbering for each article, as follows:

Chapter 1
Entrepreneurship in a Regional Context: Historical Roots, Recent Developments and Future Challenges
Michael Fritsch and David J. Storey
Regional Studies, volume 48, issue 6 (June 2014) pp. 939–954

Chapter 2
The Long Persistence of Regional Levels of Entrepreneurship: Germany, 1925–2005
Michael Fritsch and Michael Wyrwich
Regional Studies, volume 48, issue 6 (June 2014) pp. 955–973

Chapter 3
Start-ups and Local Entrepreneurial Social Capital in the Municipalities of Sweden
Hans Westlund, Johan P. Larsson and Amy Rader Olsson
Regional Studies, volume 48, issue 6 (June 2014) pp. 974–994

Chapter 4
Regional Social Legitimacy of Entrepreneurship: Implications for Entrepreneurial Intention and Start-up Behaviour
Ewald Kibler, Teemu Kautonen and Matthias Fink
Regional Studies, volume 48, issue 6 (June 2014) pp. 995–1015

Chapter 5
Entrepreneurship as an Urban Event? Empirical Evidence from European Cities
Niels Bosma and Rolf Sternberg
Regional Studies, volume 48, issue 6 (June 2014) pp. 1016–1033

Chapter 6
Population Change and New Firm Formation in Urban and Rural Regions
Heike Delfmann, Sierdjan Koster, Philip McCann and Jouke van Dijk
Regional Studies, volume 48, issue 6 (June 2014) pp. 1034–1050

Chapter 7
The Significance of Entry and Exit for Regional Productivity Growth
Udo Brixy
Regional Studies, volume 48, issue 6 (June 2014) pp. 1051–1070

Chapter 8
Spatial Determinants of Entrepreneurship in India
Ejaz Ghani, William R. Kerr and Stephen O'Connell
Regional Studies, volume 48, issue 6 (June 2014) pp. 1071–1089

Chapter 9

Is Entrepreneurship a Route Out of Deprivation?
Julian S. Frankish, Richard G. Roberts, Alex Coad and David J. Storey
Regional Studies, volume 48, issue 6 (June 2014) pp. 1090–1107

Chapter 10

Regional Effect Heterogeneity of Start-up Subsidies for the Unemployed
Marco Caliendo and Steffen Künn
Regional Studies, volume 48, issue 6 (June 2014) pp. 1108–1134

Please direct any queries you may have about the citations to
clsuk.permissions@cengage.com

Entrepreneurship in a Regional Context: Historical Roots, Recent Developments and Future Challenges

MICHAEL FRITSCH* and DAVID J. STOREY†
*School of Economics and Business Administration, Friedrich Schiller University Jena, Jena, Germany.
†School of Business Management and Economics, University of Sussex, Falmer, Brighton, UK.

FRITSCH M. and STOREY D. J. Entrepreneurship in a regional context: historical roots, recent developments and future challenges, *Regional Studies*. This paper reviews research on regional new business formation published in four special issues of *Regional Studies* over a period of 30 years. It is observed that over those decades there has been a heightened recognition of the role of both formal institutions and 'soft' factors such as social capital and a culture of entrepreneurship. However, the core challenge is to explain why, in several high-income countries, despite these claimed cultural changes, the relative position of regions with regard to new business formation exhibits little or no variation over long periods of time.

Entrepreneurship New business formation Regional characteristics

FRITSCH M. and STOREY D. J. 区域脉络中的创业精神：历史根源、晚近的发展与未来的挑战，*区域研究*。本文回顾发表于区域研究期刊三十年间的四个特刊中，有关区域新企业形成的研究。本文观察到，这数十年来，增加了对于正式制度与诸如社会资本及创业精神文化等'软性'因素的承认。然而核心的挑战，在于解释为何在部分高所得国家中，儘管宣称具有上述的文化变迁，但区域之于新企业形成的相对位置，长期下来却几乎没有变动、甚至是完全相同。

创业精神 新企业形成 区域特徵

FRITSCH M. et STOREY D. J. L'esprit d'entreprise dans un contexte régional: les racines historiques, les développements récents et les défis à venir, *Regional Studies*. Cet article examine les travaux de recherche sur la création de nouvelles entreprises sur le plan régional qui ont été publiés dans quatre numéros spéciaux de *Regional Studies* sur une période de 30 années. Il est à noter que sur ces décennies il y a eu une reconnaissance accrue du rôle des institutions officielles et des facteurs 'doux', tels le capital social et une culture d'entrepreneuriat. Cependant, le défi primordial consiste à expliquer pourquoi, dans plusieurs pays à revenu élevé, en dépit des prétendus changements culturels, la situation relative des régions quant à la création de nouvelles entreprises montre peu ou pas de variation au fil des années.

Esprit d'entreprise Création de nouvelles entreprises Traits régionaux

FRITSCH M. und STOREY D. J. Entrepreneurship im regionalen Kontext – historische Wurzeln, neuere Entwicklungen und zukünftige Herausforderungen, *Regional Studies*. Wir geben einen Überblick über die Entwicklung der Forschung über das regionale Gründungsgeschehen anhand von vier Special Issues von *Regional Studies*, die über einen Zeitraum von dreißig Jahren erschienen sind. Über die Jahre wurde die Bedeutung sowohl von formalen Institutionen als auch von 'weichen' Faktoren wie etwa Sozialkapital und einer regionalen 'Kultur' unternehmerischer Selbständigkeit zunehmend erkannt. Eine wesentliche Herausforderung für zukünftige Forschung besteht darin, zu erklären, wieso in einer Reihe von entwickelten Ländern die relative Position von Regionen in Bezug auf das Gründungsgeschehen über lange Perioden weitgehend konstant geblieben ist, obwohl sich sowohl das Niveau der Gründungsaktivitäten als auch die allgemeine Einstellung zu unternehmerischer Selbständigkeit über die Zeit wesentlich verändert hat.

Entrepreneurship Gründungsgeschehen Regionale Gegebenheiten

FRITSCH M. y STOREY D. J. Espíritu empresarial en un contexto regional: raíces históricas, desarrollos recientes y retos futuros, *Regional Studies*. En este artículo presentamos una sinopsis de los estudios sobre la creación de nuevos negocios de ámbito regional publicados en cuatro números especiales de *Regional Studies* durante un periodo de 30 años. Observamos que durante estos decenios ha habido un mayor reconocimiento del papel de las instituciones formales y los factores 'blandos' tales como el capital social y la cultura del empresariado. Sin embargo, el reto fundamental es explicar por qué en varios países con ingresos altos pese a los cambios culturales afirmados, la posición relativa de las regiones con respecto a la creación de nuevos negocios muestra poca o ninguna variación durante largos periodos de tiempo.

Espíritu empresarial Creación de nuevas empresas Características regionales

INTRODUCTION AND HISTORICAL CONTEXT

Following its inception in 1967, *Regional Studies* published several important articles on regional new business formation (FIRN and SWALES, 1978; JOHNSON and CATHCART, 1979b), but it was not until 1982 that a decision was taken to formulate a special issue devoted specifically to this topic. This special issue appeared in 1984[1] and became the forerunner of subsequent issues appearing in 1994 and 2004. The current special issue follows in that tradition.

This article begins by reviewing the history and evolution of research in the field of regional entrepreneurship, taking the three previous special issues of *Regional Studies* as well as this issue as cornerstones. It is acknowledged that interest in regional new business formation has three motivations. The first reflects an expectation that the creation of new businesses enhances job creation, raises productivity and incomes, and lowers unemployment (ACS and STOREY, 2004). The second is that, within the same country, there are wide variations in rates of new business formation and that in many, but not all, instances it is the more prosperous regions that have higher formation rates. The simple inference is that raising rates of new business formation in regions where these are low generates economic benefits. A third motivation is based on the observation that most new businesses are set up by local people so that they can be regarded as an element of a region's endogenous economic potential (FIGUEIREDO *et al.*, 2002; STAM, 2007; DAHL and SORENSON, 2009). Strengthening this endogenous potential by stimulating regional entrepreneurship can be regarded as a complementary strategy to the widespread mobility orientation of regional policy that tries to attract businesses from outside the region (EWERS and WETTMANN, 1980).

In practice, many of the papers included in the special issues of 1984, 1994 and 2004 have questioned these simple inferences. The last decade has seen scholarly understanding of entrepreneurship develop considerably, partly because of the availability of better data but also because of the greater diversity of disciplinary approaches – and the current papers reflect these developments. The changes are set out in the third section; a brief review of the papers is provided in the fourth section, with the fifth section setting out the authors' personal observations of current uncertainties and hence directions for further work. The paper concludes by offering evidence-based guidance to those tasked with seeking economic improvement through enterprise promotion at a regional level.

SPATIAL VARIATIONS IN NEW AND SMALL BUSINESSES IN ECONOMIC DEVELOPMENT: A REVIEW OF THE 1984, 1994 AND 2004 SPECIAL ISSUES OF *REGIONAL STUDIES*

The special issue of 1984: context and findings

Although work on new businesses in the Strathclyde region of Scotland (FIRN and SWALES, 1978) and Northern England (JOHNSON and CATHCART, 1979b) had been published in *Regional Studies*, it was the 1979 contribution of David Birch in the United States – and the controversy this generated (for coverage, see LANDSTROM, 2005) – that transformed the subject.

At the aggregate or national level, BIRCH (1979) was interpreted as showing that two-thirds of the increase in employment in the United States between 1969 and 1976 was in businesses with fewer than 20 workers (STOREY and JOHNSON, 1987a). His second finding, highly relevant for regions, was that the contribution of job losses to employment change was broadly invariant across regions. Regions with a high net increase in employment were therefore those where new jobs were created – rather than those losing the fewest; in contrast, regions with small, zero or negative net new jobs were those where the contribution of new and small businesses was small. Since job creation was delivered primarily by new and small businesses, the interpretation was that poor-performing regions needed to raise new business formation and hence create jobs.

Those contributing to the first special issue of *Regional Studies* in 1984 were keenly aware of the Birch findings. The six papers were described by the editor as 'position statements by leading researchers interested in the subject of small firms and regional economic development' (STOREY, 1984, p. 187). Thirty years later the vocabulary, the geographical and sectoral coverage of the firms, the data sources, and the analytical approaches used in these papers have, perhaps inevitably, a somewhat dated 'feel' to them. The changing vocabulary is reflected in that five of the six papers use the term 'new firm formation' or 'new firm'. Conspicuous by their absence are the terms 'entrepreneur' or 'entrepreneurship', which are not only absent from the titles of any of the papers, but also appear only once in the text of each of three papers and are completely absent from the text of the other three papers. The geographical coverage is concentrated heavily on the British Isles, with only one paper making a comparison with the United States.[2] Four of the papers examined only manufacturing firms. The data used were, in three cases (GOULD and KEEBLE, 1984; GUDGIN and FOTHERGILL, 1984; LLOYD and MASON, 1984), taken from the records of the UK Factory Inspectorate – a source that had been used by industrial economists such as BEESLEY (1955) virtually 30 years previously. In the other papers the data sources were the fledgling official UK data used by WHITTINGTON (1984); official Ireland data used by O'FARRELL and CROUCHLEY (1984) and personal survey data used by OAKEY (1984).

The analytical approaches were very basic by modern standards. Only three papers (GUDGIN and FOTHERGILL, 1984; WHITTINGTON, 1984; O'FARRELL and CROUCHLEY, 1984) used ordinary least squares (OLS) regressions, with the others simply providing tabulations. Despite their analytical limitations, what clearly emerged was 'real differences between regions in terms of the numbers of small firms, birth rates, performance and potential contribution to economic development' (STOREY, 1984, p. 187). As ever it was the differences, rather than the areas of consensus, that provided the impetus for continuing research.

The 'explanations', or at least the emphasis placed upon them by the authors, were very different. WHITTINGTON (1984), for example, placed emphasis on home ownership (as a proxy for access to capital) and occupational structure (as a proxy for human capital). For both GUDGIN and FOTHERGILL (1984) and O'FARRELL and CROUCHLEY (1984) the influences differed starkly between urban and rural areas, with formation rates being higher in urban areas. A third key influence was firm size: geographical areas where average firm size was small had high rates of new business formation (GOULD and KEEBLE, 1984). It remained, however, unclear how far this firm size-effect was due to differences in the sectoral composition of the regional economy (FRITSCH and FALCK, 2007).

As will become clear, several of these explanations continue to be seen as important by the scholars of today, but they are incomplete. They failed to take into account the full range of potential influences upon new business formation rates at a regional level that could be identified, even from the limited research evidence available at the start of the 1980s. Table 1, amended from STOREY (1982), identifies five groups of influences and ten associated metrics that prior work had shown to influence new business formation rates at a regional level. By producing a simple, unweighted, collation of these metrics Storey generated a regional new business formation 'league table' of UK regions. Verification of this 'league table' came later

Table 1. Factors influencing variations in UK new firm formation, 1982

Factor	Rationale	Evidence	Metric(s)
Firm size in locality	Individuals working in small firms are more likely to start a (small) business than those working in large firms, primarily because of greater awareness of the enterprise 'option' and experience of what was required	JOHNSON and CATHCART (1979a)	Percentage of manufacturing employment in small plants Percentage of manufacturing employment in large plants
Human capital	Individuals with more human capital are more likely to create a successful business, although not necessarily more likely to start a new business	CROSS (1981)	Percentage of population with degree(s)
	The higher success rate was because, in part, ownership generally required some literary and numerical skills provided by formal education	NICHOLSON and BRINKLEY (1979)	Percentage with no qualifications
	The ambiguity over the link between education and formation rates was because education also enhanced the earnings of an individual as an employee		Percentage in administration and management Percentage manual workers
Access to finance	Business creation normally requires some access to finance and so regions where finance is more plentiful will have more new firms	COOPER (1973) LITVAK and MAULE (1972)	Personal savings Home ownership House prices
Barriers to entry	Given that individuals are most likely to start a firm in the sector in which they were (most recently) employed and because it is more difficult to start a firm in sectors where large firms dominate, then regions with more employment in such sectors are likely to have fewer new firms	GUDGIN (1978)	Percentage of manufacturing employment in four large firm-dominated sectors: shipbuilding, metal manufacturing, chemicals, and mechanical engineering
Demand-side influences	New business formation is likely to be stimulated by local spending power since most new firms sell (very) locally	LLOYD (1980)	Regional disposable income

Source: STOREY (1982).

when value added tax (VAT) data (WHITTINGTON, 1984) and information about public policy expenditure (STOREY and JOHNSON, 1987b) became available.

Therefore, summarizing the stock of knowledge on this topic in the early 1980s it is fair to say that in the UK there were real regional variations in new business formation. There were also a range of possible explanations for these variations. What was needed was a clearer understanding of the role played by these, and possibly other, influences. This began to be addressed a decade later.

The 1994 special issue: coordinated research in high-income countries

The inability of researchers in 1984 to agree on the explanations for the observed regional differences in new business formation was, in part, because the sources of data used to make the comparisons were so diverse. It was noted above that even though these data were UK based – and three of them even came from the same source: Factory Inspectorate – valid comparisons were hindered by inconsistency over definitions, time periods and sectoral limitations. A second cause was that the analytical approaches varied considerably. A third problem was omitted variable bias.

The 1994 special issue set out to address these three limitations explicitly. It was also able to benefit from establishment data becoming available in several high-income countries (FRITSCH, 1993, for West Germany; and REYNOLDS and MAKI, 1990, for the United States). But in doing so, it introduced the international component as a new source of variation. Instead of being limited primarily to the British Isles (the UK and Ireland), the 1994 special issue covered France, Germany (West), Italy, Sweden and the United States. As REYNOLDS *et al.* (1994a) state:

> To provide partial compensation for this variation and enhance the potential for cross-national comparisons, two procedures were employed to increase standardization. First, the same conceptual framework was used for all analyses – there was harmonization of the abstract models. This meant that each country team made an attempt to incorporate indicators of the same set of regional factors, even if the measures were different. Second, the same analysis procedure was employed in all of the studies – ordinary least squares regression analysis with forced entry of all independent variables.
>
> (p. 344)

A third change, compared with 1984, was the first formal attempt to introduce a measure of policy. This was meant to capture the recognition that, by the mid-1990s, policy-makers at national and regional levels had become aware that new enterprises could play an important role in stimulating job and wealth creation and had introduced policies to enhance firm formation rates (STOREY, 1994). It was therefore reasonable to assume that those areas that had introduced policies might have been expected to have formation rates above those in otherwise similar regions that had not introduced such policies.

To reflect these developments the five key influences on new business formation noted in Table 1 were expanded and developed and are shown in Table 2. Consistent evidence was found across all countries that urban regions had higher rates of new firm formation than rural regions; that regions with a relatively high proportion of its firms defined as small had higher rates than regions with a low proportion of small firms; that in-migration and population and income growth were also associated with higher new business formation rates. The factors examined, and the results obtained, are captured in Table 2 and taken from REYNOLDS *et al.* (1994b).

Despite confirming many of the findings from 1984, from a policy point of view key uncertainties remained. It appeared that the main influences on new business formation were 'set in stone' and not easily amenable to public policy change. Second, the unemployment result was ambiguous – implying that in some regions low unemployment appeared to be associated with high rates of new business formation, whereas in other regions it was the opposite. Thirdly, it was difficult to point to clear evidence of enterprise policies – or even the political composition of regions – exerting a direct influence on new business formation.

This was frustrating for politicians who, as noted above, were keenly aware of research telling them that new firms were a crucial source of economic dynamism. However, the regional research implied that, even if such a relationship existed, the strongest influences on formation rates were not easily amenable to change at the regional or local levels – such as educational attainment, firm size, population density and existing economic buoyancy. REYNOLDS *et al.* (1994a) summarized it thus: 'This research programme suggests that regional characteristics are a major factor affecting variation in firm births. The ability of governments to affect regional characteristics is an open question' (p. 346). The key analytical limitation of the 1994 papers was that they all used only cross-section OLS regression. This was primarily because time-series data for most countries provided insufficient observations for fixed-effects panel regression techniques to take account of unobserved region-specific fixed effects.

The 2004 special issue: broadening the perspectives

The key starting point for the 2004 special issue was the policy void left by REYNOLDS *et al.* (1994a, 1994b). Could researchers say what, if anything, local politicians could do to stimulate enterprise in the hope that it would lead to enhanced economic development? To address this, the seven papers in the 2004 special issue sought to be a development in four respects. The first

Table 2. Factors influencing variations in new business formation (NBF): results of the 1994 special issue

Processes included	1994 Reynolds *et al.* results
Demand growth	
In-migration/population growth	Clear evidence of a positive impact on both service and manufacturing NBF rates
Growth in gross domestic product (GDP)	
Urbanization/agglomeration	
Percentage 25–44 years old	Clear evidence of a positive impact on both service and manufacturing NBF rates
Percentage secondary housing	
Population density	
Percentage with higher education	
Percentage managers in workforce	
R&D personnel	
Unemployment	
Unemployment level	Some evidence of a positive impact on manufacturing NBF – but mixed positive and negative impact for services NBF
Change in unemployment	
Personal household wealth	
Household income	Some evidence of a positive impact on manufacturing NBF but no clear impact for services
Dwelling prices	
Percentage owner-occupied dwellings	
Land prices	
Access to finance	
Small firms/specialization	
Proportion autonomous workers/self-employed	Clear positive impact for both manufacturing and services NBF
Proportion small firms	
Industry specialization index	
Political ethos	
Socialist voters	Some evidence that left-wing regions have higher NBF
Labour laws	
Government spending/policies	
Local government expenditures	No evidence that expenditures or individual government programmes influence NBF
Government assistance programmes	

Source: REYNOLDS *et al.* (1994b).

was to widen the disciplinary approaches beyond its existing heavy focus upon economics and geography. The second was to draw upon cross-section as well as the, now more available, longer time-series data, without which it was difficult to draw conclusions about the direction of causation. A third advance was to analyse the effect of new business formation on regional economic development more widely (AUDRETSCH and KEILBACH, 2004; FRITSCH and MUELLER, 2004; VAN STEL and STOREY, 2004). Finally, it took the first steps in linking creativity with entrepreneurship (LEE *et al.*, 2004).

The overall effect was again to confirm many of the relationships identified earlier (Tables 1 and 2), but with important provisos concerning the link between entrepreneurship and the economic performance of regions. These provisos are highly relevant for the 2014 papers.

The first is the role of time lags. FRITSCH and MUELLER (2004) showed the impact of entrepreneurship on employment could be considered as having three effects over time. The first was consistently positive – reflecting the additional economic activity/employment created by the new firm. However, the next effect, at a later point in time, was to remove the less efficient economic incumbents. A 'third round' effect was to stimulate improved performance amongst surviving incumbents. This model emphasized that entrepreneurship/new business formation was capable of being either positive or negative, depending on whether the destructive effect was outweighed by the two positive contributions. It was also clear these effects were far from instantaneous and pointed to the importance of examining these relationships by taking full account of time lags. Evidence of the role of time lags and their ambiguity for UK regions was provided by VAN STEL and STOREY (2004) and later by MUELLER *et al.* (2008) pointing to entrepreneurship having a positive effect in existing prosperous regions but a negligible, or even negative, effect in low-income regions where there was the greatest need for new firms to contribute to job creation.

However, the paper that generated the greatest policy interest was by LEE *et al.* (2004) who documented a correlation between enterprise and cultural creativity.

ACS and STOREY (2004) interpret their results as showing that 'areas having disproportionate numbers of authors, designers, musicians, composers are associated with entrepreneurship as is the so-called "Melting Pot Index", which measures the proportion of the population that is foreign-born' (p. 875). This provided an incentive to policy-makers in many areas to support the greater diversification of its population on the grounds that this would enhance entrepreneurship and hence economic development.

However, despite its superficial attraction, the policy implications were more opaque. This was because, although there clearly was a spatial correlation between the presence of 'bohemians' and rates of new business formation, it was less clear how areas that were 'un-creative' could transform themselves. Moreover, the causal relationship underpinning this correlation between artistic culture and new business formation remained unclear. As GLAESER (2004) pointed out, the regional share of people in creative occupations is also highly correlated with a range of other indicators capturing the formal qualifications of the regional workforce. Hence it is unclear whether the creativity indicator captures only creativity, or more generic educational qualifications. If it is the latter, then enhancing these is likely to be possible only in the (very) long run and for reasons only partly related to entrepreneurship.

This reflected a wider concern that, although associations were observed between structural variables such as education, wealth, in-migration etc. and new business formation, the direction of causation was open to question. In short, were high rates of new business formation a cause of economic development or an outcome? The issue of endogeneity therefore became centre stage in the discussions.

THE CONTEXT FOR THE 2014 PAPERS

The authors of the 2014 papers have three advantages over their predecessors. They have access to considerably better data, at least for high-income countries. They can also draw upon a wider range of disciplinary perspectives to identify factors other than the 'usual suspects' that may explain regional variations in business formation rates. Finally, the analytical tools that can be used to test hypotheses have advanced considerably.

Better data

During the last decade there has been a huge leap forward in the quality and availability of entrepreneurship data. These include:

- More precise measurement of self-employment and the more accurate identification of start-ups. For many countries data on start-ups are available by industry and by types (e.g., those owned by females, high growth enterprises, own-account workers), and by survival rates (ORGANISATION FOR ECONOMIC CO-OPERATION AND DEVELOPMENT (OECD), 2013).
- The availability of longitudinal data at the micro-level of firms and at the level of regions. These longer time-series facilitate fixed-effect panel analysis accounting for unobserved influences (e.g., FRITSCH and FALCK, 2007; SUTARIA and HICKS, 2004).
- More longitudinal data about individuals such as the Panel Study of Entrepreneurial Dynamics (PSED) (REYNOLDS and CURTIN, 2011; DAVIDSSON and GORDON, 2012) and diverse household panels (e.g., the German Socio-Economic Panel or the British Household Panel Survey – BHPS). This enables entrepreneurial choice to be more accurately modelled.
- More broadly comparable data about new business formation and business ownership across countries. This includes the Global Entrepreneurship Monitor (GEM) (BOSMA, 2013) and the COMPENDIA database for a number of OECD countries (VAN STEL, 2008). This enables researchers to take account of factors that apply nationwide such as macro-economic conditions and the role of formal institutions when examining regional variations across national borders (NAUDÉ, 2011; VIVARELLI, 2013).

The last decade has also seen new and better data become available on the independent variables that are expected to influence new business formation rates at the regional level. This has enabled the inclusion of a more diverse range of influences on new business formation rates. These include measures of social capital (e.g., WESTLUND and ADAM, 2010; WESTLUND *et al.*, in this issue) or the values of the population (e.g., KIBLER *et al.*, in this issue).[3]

However, despite these clear improvements one issue remains unresolved. It is that virtually all these datasets relate *either* to the founder *or* to businesses. Data linking the two are far less common yet vital,[4] since businesses can be owned by multiple individuals, and individuals may own multiple businesses,[5] so it is likely that a different picture emerges depending upon which metric is chosen.

Entrepreneurship and institutions as a focus of research

Differences in observed rates of entrepreneurship across countries are frequently attributed to differences in the scale and nature of both formal and informal institutions. The role played by formal institutions such as entry regulations or labour laws for the emergence and the development of new businesses is extensively documented (BAUMOL, 1990; BOETTKE and COYNE, 2009; HENREKSON, 2007; NYSTROM, 2008; VAN STEL *et al.*, 2007). This is valuable context for making international comparisons, but because most of these formal institutions apply nationwide, with only modest variation across regions, their effect is primarily to provide context for regional variations (KLAPPER *et al.*, 2006, HENREKSON, 2005). However, in countries undergoing major political change, the effect of a radically changed institutional framework – such as in the former socialist countries of Central and Eastern Europe – on entrepreneurship is likely to be considerable (ESTRIN and MICKIEWICZ, 2011; FRITSCH *et al.*, 2014; KSHETRI, 2009; SMALLBONE and WELTER, 2001).

It is not only formal institutions that influence behaviour, but also the unwritten 'rules of the game' (NORTH, 1994) such as norms, values and codes of conduct (WILLIAMSON, 2000; FREYTAG and THURIK, 2007). A number of empirical studies show that informal institutions differ significantly between regions (BEUGELSDIJK and NOORDERHAVEN, 2004; BEUGELSDIJK, 2007; BOSMA and SCHUTJENS, 2011; OBSCHONKA *et al.*, 2013; WAGNER and STERNBERG, 2004). Such differences may then lead to more or less entrepreneurship-friendly policies at the regional level. Although several studies find a statistical relationship between personality traits and personal attitudes of the regional population and the level of entrepreneurship, they are unable to identify the causality of these effects. Do specific value-sets amongst the population of a region bring about relatively high or low levels of entrepreneurship or is it entrepreneurship that causes the expression of these values? Such analyses are further hampered by entrepreneurial regions becoming attractive to in-migrants.

One approach to addressing this problem of endogeneity is to draw upon long-run historical data. FRITSCH and WYRWICH (in this issue) and GLAESER *et al.* (2012) use this approach as an instrument for the historical level of entrepreneurship.

Knowledge and innovation: entrepreneurship as economic creativity

During the last 20 years knowledge and innovation have increasingly been seen as closely linked with entrepreneurship at both the national and regional levels. The most direct link is reflected in the commercialization of knowledge through the creation of a new enterprise. This relationship lies at the heart of the 'knowledge spillover theory of entrepreneurship' (ACS *et al.*, 2009). From this it follows that the knowledge conditions in the respective industry or technological field are of importance (AUDRETSCH, 2007). In so far as industries follow a life cycle, new business formation plays a role in the early phases that tend to be characterized by a so-called 'entrepreneurial technological regime', in contrast with latter stages which have a more 'routinised regime' (AUDRETSCH, 1995).

Since knowledge tends to be 'sticky' in space, the regional knowledge-base becomes a determinant of regional start-ups, particularly for innovative new businesses. This regional knowledge may have different sources, including the educational attainment of the workforce, the presence of private and public research in the locality, as well as the work experience of the population that is related to the regional industry structure (HELFAT and LIEBERMAN, 2002). It is not only a main source of entrepreneurial opportunities but also may be a determinant of important capabilities such as the recognition of entrepreneurial opportunities and the absorptive capacity for new knowledge (QIAN and ACS, 2013).

Entrepreneurship as a process of individual development in its regional context

Another potentially promising approach for improving our understanding of regional entrepreneurship is to investigate individual behaviour in its regional and its wider (sectoral, national) context. Entrepreneurship is then primarily seen as a development process at the individual level. Many contributors to this approach come from academic disciplines such as sociology and psychology, but also from the natural sciences (for an overview, see OBSCHONKA and SILBEREISEN, 2012). Examples of this research include:

- *Identifying the entrepreneurial personality*, i.e. finding those personality traits that are conducive, and those that are unfavourable, to starting and running a business (ZHAO and SEIBERT, 2006; ZHAO *et al.*, 2010; RAUCH and FRESE, 2007, CALIENDO *et al.*, 2014). Much of this research draws upon the concept of the 'Big Five': a comprehensive personality taxonomy comprising five dimensions which are associated with entrepreneurial behaviour.[6] These are, however, very general patterns that, to become valuable, would, as a minimum, have to recognize that different personality profiles are likely to be required in different entrepreneurial circumstances.
- *The intergenerational transmission of entrepreneurship.* Entrepreneurship research has consistently found that children and grandchildren of parents who ran a business have a significantly higher probability of being entrepreneurs themselves (e.g., CHLOSTA *et al.*, 2012; DUNN and HOLTZ-EAKIN, 2000; LASPITA *et al.*, 2012). However, there are at least four explanations for this intergenerational transmission: peer effects of being close to entrepreneurs, so acquiring knowledge and the 'taste for entrepreneurship'; transfer of valid personality characteristics and entrepreneurial skills from parents (SCHMITT-RODERMUND, 2007); direct inheritance of existing businesses; and direct financial support from parents (NICOLAOU *et al.*, 2008; KOELLINGER *et al.*, 2010; LINDQUIST *et al.*, 2012). Currently it is unclear which are dominant.
- *Education, choices and experiences made during the professional career.* The link between educational

attainment and subsequent business ownership has been examined extensively. The relationship is, however, by no means consistently positive (STOREY and GREENE, 2011).[7] Generally, education enhances the individuals' skills making them more able to be either an employee or a business owner. Somewhat more robust is the evidence positively linking business performance with educational attainment – at least at the aggregate level of regions (FOTOPOULOS, 2013; ACS and ARMINGTON, 2004).

- Another item, identified in Table 1, that receives more consistent empirical support in recent research is *prior employment in a small firm* (ELFENBEIN *et al.*, 2010) or *in a professional environment where self-employment is relatively frequent* (SORGNER and FRITSCH, 2013). In both cases it appears to enhance the likelihood of an individual starting in business. Disagreement with an employer is also frequently an important driver of spin-offs (ACS *et al.*, 2009; KLEPPER, 2009), but the regional dimension of this has yet to be explored.

Regional differences in new business formation clearly reflect differences in the composition and contribution of these groups of factors across regions. So, for example, regions with a high share of entrepreneurial personalities (OBSCHONKA *et al.*, 2013) or of people working in small firms would be expected to have higher new business formation rates. However, such simple explanations that are based on the correlation between two variables are only a part of the story because individual behaviour can also be significantly shaped by the regional environment. Hence, people with identical characteristics may act differently when located in different places; equally, 'identical' firms can be more successful in some regions than in others (e.g., STUETZER *et al.*, 2014). In addition, people are mobile across regions and may self-select into certain spatial environments. For example, founders have a strong tendency to locate their businesses close to their place of residence (FIGUEIREDO *et al.*, 2002; STAM, 2007; DAHL and SORENSON, 2009), so that spatial mobility during the career path has an important effect on the regional distribution of new businesses. Alternatively, certain regions may attract people with specific characteristics, implying that their potential or talent is lost for their 'home' region (for a review, see LEVIE, 2007). Therefore, explaining new business formation and firm behaviour also requires explanations that account for the effect of the regional environment on individual behaviour and mobility.

This view of entrepreneurship as a development process at the individual level supplements our understanding of new business formation at the regional level. It acknowledges that because individual development and behaviour take place in a certain location and in an environment that is partly region specific, then outcomes are also linked to the region. One therefore needs an improved understanding of how regional conditions shape individual decisions and developments.[8] As far as these decisions then feed back into the region-specific, it has to be regarded as an evolutionary process not only at the individual level but also at the level of regions (BOSCHMA and FRENKEN, 2011).

MINNITI (2005) provides an illustrative example of these relationships by modelling the interplay between individual decisions and their regional context. The mutually reinforcing nature of entrepreneurship is reflected in a regional environment in which one person's decision to start a business – and be demonstrably successful – encourages others to follow, meaning that high levels of regional entrepreneurship can be self-reinforcing. This process also works in reverse with low enterprise regions continuing in that manner over long periods of time.

The effect of new business formation on regional development

It was noted above that, for 30 years or more, politicians have been persuaded there is research-based evidence that new business formation promotes economic growth. Hence many countries, and regions within those countries, have introduced policies aimed at stimulating the formation of new firms.

From a theory perspective, the basic mechanism that transforms new business formation into growth is competition between entries and incumbent firms (for an overview, see FRITSCH, 2013). Hence the new business constitutes a challenge to incumbents leading to increased competition. This process is strongly influenced by both industry-specific conditions and the regional environment. As a result, the contribution of new businesses to employment across regions varies markedly and can, as noted above, even be negative (MUELLER *et al.*, 2008). Theory suggests the effect of new business formation on regional growth is influenced by three factors: the quality of the newcomers in terms of the competitive pressure they exert on incumbents; how incumbent firms react to this competition; and the characteristics of the competitive process. In the latter instance the legislative environment plays a vital role in either promoting or inhibiting both entry and exit, so influencing the number of competitors, demand conditions and technological developments.

In short, the evidence increasingly questions the prevalence of an automatic and positive link between new firm formation and economic development. So, although the link may be present, its strength and even its sign depend heavily upon a wide range of other factors.

The persistence of regional entrepreneurship over time

The long-term persistence of regional levels and structures of self-employment and new business formation has been documented in several recent papers (FRITSCH and MUELLER, 2007; ANDERSSON and KOSTER, 2011; FOTOPOULOS, 2013; FRITSCH and WYRWICH, in this issue). It appears that in Germany, Sweden and the UK the cross-regional structure of entrepreneurship remains broadly constant over time – even when there are considerable changes at national level and when countries undergo striking political change. ANDERSSON and KOSTER (2011) and FRITSCH and WYRWICH (in this issue) attribute this stability to a regional culture of entrepreneurship that, as an informal institution, changes only slowly (NORTH, 1994; WILLIAMSON, 2000). Nevertheless key questions remain unresolved:

- What are the main constituents of a regional entrepreneurship culture?
- How does it emerge?
- How it is transferred across generations and over longer periods of time despite, in some instances, massive external shocks and migration flows?
- Why is there stability in a region's relative position with regards to the level of entrepreneurship, an entrepreneurship culture, when, at a national level, many high-income countries have experienced a considerable increase in new business formation rates (AUDRETSCH *et al.*, 2011) – implying that a 'cultural' change has taken place?

The link with unemployment, deprivation and disadvantage

Despite the range of 'health warnings' over assuming a direct causative link between increased enterprise, job creation and the reduction in unemployment (for a recent summary, see VIVARELLI, 2013) the simplistic notion that unemployment can be reduced by converting the unemployed into self-employed business owners remains widespread. This theme, linking enterprise with promoting social inclusion, is also captured in a greater focus on social – as well as for-profit – enterprises (HAUGH, 2007). It is therefore no surprise that the political emphasis upon entrepreneurship rises sharply when economic conditions deteriorate and in localities in which there is deprivation (FRANKISH *et al.*, in this issue).

In practice, evidence examining the role of unemployment in influencing new business formation at a regional level has a long history of generating mixed results. It will be recalled from Table 2 summarizing the 1994 results that these were conflicting – perhaps in part because the institutional setting in, for example, the United States and Sweden differed sharply. PARKER (2009) summarizes the position admirably by saying:

> there is really no economic reason why unemployment and entrepreneurship need to be related at all. The extent to which they are related probably reflects rigidities in the economy. These rigidities are likely to diminish over time as governments adjust their tax-benefit systems to make their economies more flexible.
>
> (p. 146)

On these grounds it would seem unlikely that evidence would emerge that entrepreneurship could become a tool in the armoury of those seeking to reduce unemployment and the social and economic costs this imposes on individuals and society more widely. However, as will be shown, two of the papers in this volume reopen that issue.

OVERVIEW OF THE PAPERS IN THIS ISSUE

This section briefly describes the papers included in this special issue and links their findings to the existing stock of knowledge described above. FRITSCH and WYRWICH (in this issue) analyse the persistence of self-employment and new business formation in German regions over longer periods of time. As noted above, several studies found the regional 'league table' of start-up rates varied little over time (FRITSCH and MUELLER, 2007; ANDERSSON and KOSTER, 2011; FOTOPOULOS, 2013). This might have been expected if there had been few changes over time in factors influencing new firm formation rates, then these rates would also have been expected to be stable. The novelty of the FRITSCH and WYRWICH (in this issue) paper is that this regional stability is found in East Germany over a period of time when it experienced seismic shocks such as the Second World War and four decades of a socialist regime that sought to eliminate private businesses. Fritsch and Wyrwich attribute this long-term persistence to the presence of a regional culture of entrepreneurship.

WESTLUND *et al.* (in this issue) investigate the relationship between social capital and self-employment in Swedish municipalities. Based on survey data, they find clear differences in public attitudes towards entrepreneurship. Those living in metropolitan regions say they view entrepreneurship positively, whereas this is much less the case amongst those living in traditional manufacturing municipalities with only one or very few dominant employers. Their multivariate analysis shows that areas reporting more positive public attitudes towards entrepreneurship also have higher new business formation.

KIBLER *et al.* (in this issue) deal with a closely related topic. They provide a detailed analysis of how social acceptance of entrepreneurship in the spatial environment – the regional social legitimacy of entrepreneurship – affects new business formation. Using survey data for selected regions of Austria and Finland, they positively link the regional social legitimacy of entrepreneurship with both entrepreneurial intentions and the likelihood of realizing these intentions by engaging in a start-up. They conclude that social legitimacy 'can compensate for economic restrictions in the local environment and can give those with entrepreneurial intentions the final impulse needed to turn their intentions into actual start-up behaviour'.

BOSMA and STERNBERG (in this issue) examine whether urban areas have higher rates of new firm formation than other types of region. Using GEM data for 47 urban areas in 22 European countries they find no such effect, so contradicting the REYNOLDS *et al.* (1994a, 1994b) finding shown in Table 2. Instead, what they find is that the 'type' of entrepreneurship varies, with urban areas having more opportunity entrepreneurship. Further analysis of a subsample of urban areas reveals a positive relationship between GEM indicators of entrepreneurial activity and many of the variables noted in Table 2 such as high education levels, prior growth, household income as well as diversity of economic activities. This confirms the link between a regional environment characterized by economic prosperity and one conducive to the emergence and the realization of entrepreneurial opportunities. Again, however, the direction of causation has to be left open.

DELFMANN *et al.* (in this issue) focus on the effect of regional population change, particularly a decline of population, on entrepreneurship. The issue is important because many regions in Europe will shortly be faced with this problem. Their analysis for the Netherlands shows the effect of population change on the level and structure of new business formation varies markedly between urban and rural areas. Population decline in urban areas lowers new business formation. In contrast, in rural regions the effect can even be positive as a result of responding to the need to provide minimum levels of services and activities even when population falls. This is compatible with seeing entrepreneurship in regions with a declining population as more driven by necessity, whereas in regions with population growth there is a greater emphasis upon opportunity-based entrepreneurship.

BRIXY (in this issue) deals with the effect of entries and the turnover of establishments on regional total factor productivity (TFP) and employment in Germany. The paper theorizes that it is longer-lived, rather than the total numbers of, entrants that influence TFP because only the former constitute a credible threat to incumbents. Brixy finds support for this, with even short-term survivors exerting a more powerful influence on TFP than the overall number of start-ups. A second important result points to sectoral differences. While new business formation has a positive effect on employment growth in both manufacturing and services, the effect is significantly greater in manufacturing.

Finally, one of the key limitations of prior special issues was their exclusive focus upon high-income countries. In part this reflected an absence of good data, so it is pleasing to see this addressed by GHANI *et al.* (in this issue) who examine regional entrepreneurship in India. They emphasize the distinction between the formal and the informal – or unorganized sectors. They find new business formation is higher in areas where the quality of physical infrastructure and workforce education is also higher. Stringent labour laws appear to lower formal new business formation while household banking access appears to be conducive to the emergence of start-ups particularly in the service sector, and in unorganized manufacturing.

The final two papers have a strong policy focus, which has been a consistent theme throughout previous special issues. FRANKISH *et al.* (in this issue) examine whether those living in low-income areas benefit from entrepreneurship more than those in employment living in the same location. This is an important issue since if it is the case then there is some justification for governments encouraging enterprise amongst the disadvantaged. The core result of the paper is that over a five-year period business owners living in deprived areas are more likely than employees to move their main residence to a more prosperous area – implying increased wealth. However, the paper finds this is also the case in prosperous areas – implying that entrepreneurship 'pays' wherever you live. A third, less surprising, result is that the 'returns' to entrepreneurship are strongly linked to business performance. Broadly, the business owner is only more likely to move their main residence to a more prosperous location when their business survives and its sales rise by more than one-third over five years.

CALIENDO and KÜNN (in this issue) analyse regional differences in the effectiveness of two publicly funded programmes that support start-ups by the unemployed in Germany. Both programmes are shown to be effective by enhancing the probability that participants will re-enter employment and with higher income. The interesting finding is that these effects differ in regions with different economic conditions. While the Bridging Allowance programme appears to be more effective in regions with disadvantaged economic conditions, the pattern is less pronounced for the Start-up Subsidy programme. The authors conclude that the two programmes have been successful in effectively helping participants to overcome labour demand restrictions and integrating them in the labour market, but particularly in areas with poor economic conditions.

OBSERVATIONS, LIMITATIONS AND AREAS FOR FURTHER WORK

Over the last three decades, although there has been a striking improvement in understanding and quantifying new business formation – and why it varies between regions – many important issues remain unresolved. This section highlights these issues as the basis for further work, with the ultimate intention of being able to offer better evidence-based recommendations to regional policy-makers.

The emergence, quality and performance of new businesses in regional context

The emergence of new businesses is a development process at the individual and the regional levels.

Unfortunately our ability to offer guidance on the design of policy instruments is limited by our imperfect knowledge of the determinants of individuals' decisions to start and run their own business and how this process is shaped by region-specific factors.

The case of innovative start-ups demonstrates why it is important to analyse new business formation in this way. Several empirical studies have shown that most innovative founders have at least some academic background (STUETZER *et al.*, 2012) and that, after finishing university, they then work as dependent employees before starting their own firm.[9] Some of these individuals are spatially mobile during their career and so are at least partly motivated by the availability of attractive jobs (CHEN and ROSENTHAL, 2008; DAHL and SORENSON, 2010). When asked, such individuals frequently report that being able to start their business close to their place of residence was a powerful factor in making this choice (LARSSON *et al.*, 2003).

This suggests that there are at least four factors that determine the emergence of an innovative start-up: first, the personal background and personality of the founder; second, education at a more or less 'entrepreneurial' university; third, geographical labour market mobility and experience acquired in dependent employment;[10] and fourth, the conditions for start-up in the region of residence. Empirical analyses that regress the number of innovative start-ups on regional characteristics (e.g., FRITSCH and AAMOUCKE, 2013; BADE and NERLINGER, 2000) find a strong positive correlation between innovative start-ups and the presence of universities and other public research institutes.

What is less clear is which of the four factors are dominant, in part because of data limitations. In addition to detailed information about regional characteristics, such an analysis requires representative longitudinal microdata about individuals that includes information on location, family background, education, employment and, in the case of founders, about their respective firm and its development. Several of the Nordic countries have access to this type of data and our expectation is that, for this reason, these countries are likely to take the lead in this strain of research.

Cultures, regional persistence of entrepreneurship and the league table phenomenon

The availability of time-series data on national and regional measures of entrepreneurship that stretch back many decades provides new insights, but also new challenges. The challenges stem from very different emphases being placed on observing and analysing the data. For AUDRETSCH (2007) the key change is the clear move towards an entrepreneurial society. In contrast, others see an almost eerie long-term stability in the regional ranking of rates of new business formation in Sweden, the UK and Germany, respectively (ANDERSSON and KOSTER, 2011; FOTOPOULOS, 2013; FRITSCH and WYRWICH, in this issue). The third key long-term characteristic is, perhaps alongside this long-term stability, considerable short-term volatility – both in the creation and in the survival of new firms and in their performance.

This combination of long-term stability – in this case at a national level – and short-term volatility is reflected in Fig. 1. It shows quarterly data on new firm registrations and de-registrations in the UK over the period 2000–11. The stability is reflected in new registrations in Q1 2000 being approximately 50 000, which is virtually the same as more than a decade later. In contrast, the temporal variations are considerable, with the recession of 2007–09 seeing new registrations falling by 50% and de-registrations more than doubling in less than two years.

This concurrence of short-term fluctuations and regional long-term persistence might suggest that the

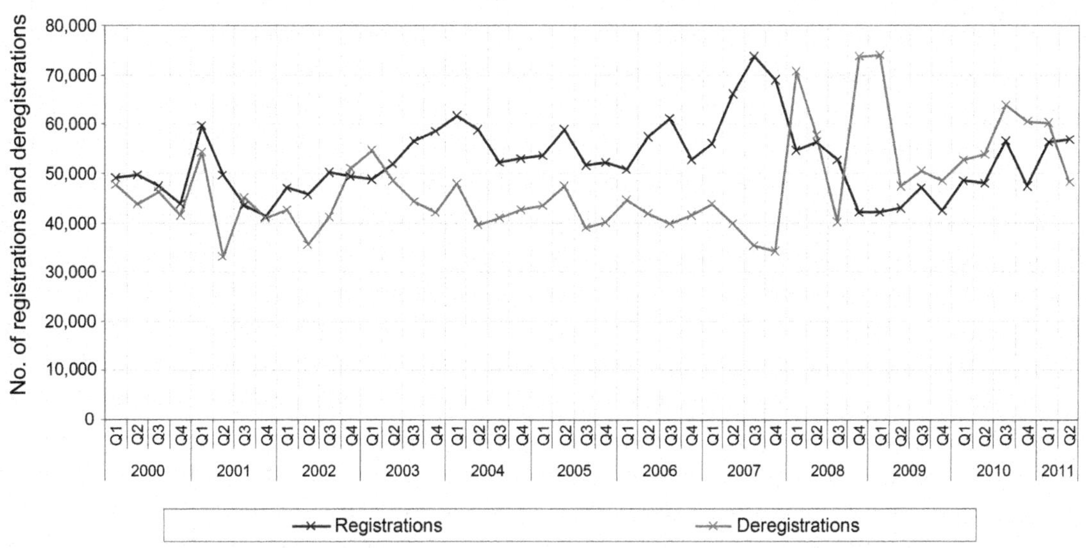

Fig. 1. Business registrations and de-registrations at the end of the quarter in the UK, 2000–11

factors explaining temporal variations in the national rate differ from those that determine long-term trends at a regional level. So, for example, the drivers of short-run temporal changes are (KOELLINGER and THURIK, 2012; PARKER, 2009; SARIDAKIS *et al.*, 2014) interest rates and immediate personal economic circumstances – most notably unemployment, job insecurity and income levels. In contrast, the factors influencing enterprise in the longer-term, such as attitudes, culture and psychological factors, family, human capital, education, sectoral structure etc. may change at a national level but the relative position of regions with regard to these factors can remain stable.

Yet even this distinction is not wholly satisfactory. First, it does not explain why enterprise rates vary so markedly between regions in the same country when some variables – such as interest rates – play a powerful role at national level, but vary only very marginally between regions in the country. Second, it fails to recognize that regions are, to different degrees, sensitive in their response to national influences. This could, for example, mean that people in regions with high levels of entrepreneurship are more likely to set up and own a business when becoming unemployed as compared with people in less entrepreneurial regions. Hence the same factors could have very different influences in different regions. A third criticism is that regions reflect relative positions in a league table, whereas the national data reflect overall change. So, in a sports league, if the standards of all the clubs participating go up (or down) this does not automatically imply a change in the league position of the clubs that participate. Yet even this is somewhat counter-intuitive since expansion and decline are not normally consistent. We are therefore faced with a challenge to understand the processes at work when the same explanations for entrepreneurial activity are offered when this rises, often considerably, at a national level, yet the regions that comprise that national total seem to make the same relative contribution (FOTOPOULOS, 2013).

The still largely unfulfilled promise of regional entrepreneurship research: policy guidance

The paper concludes by exploring the implications raised by the persistence of regional entrepreneurship rankings, when combined with short-term volatility. What can be done to improve regional entrepreneurship if, in the medium-term, so much appears to be predetermined by history? Can regions lagging behind in entrepreneurship be helped to move up, and remain high, in the national league table?

The central starting point is to recognize that moving up the regional league table, other than on a temporary basis, is likely to take perhaps several decades – unless the region is fortunate in terms of having a discovery of natural resources or the growth of a major employer. It then has to recognize that there is no simple and automatic link between new business formation and job creation (FRITSCH, 2013) implying that policies simply to 'get more enterprise' are likely to be no more successful than the Scottish Business Birth Rate strategy referred to by VAN STEL and STOREY (2004). As a minimum, policies need to be clear on what they are expected to achieve. BRIXY (in this issue) shows that the factors influencing productivity at a regional level are different from those that influence direct employment creation. Politicians therefore have to make decisions on what economic factors they wish to address. The papers also point to the importance of recognizing that policies may impact rural and urban areas, prosperous and less prosperous, and growing and declining regions very differently (BOSMA AND STERNBERG, in this issue; DELFMANN *et al.*, in this issue; CALIENDO and KÜNN, in this issue). Policy therefore needs to reflect these differences and has to be tailored to local circumstances.

Once the duration and the need for clarity of objectives and for regionally tailored policies are recognized, the papers point to the potential returns from such measures. FRANKISH *et al.* (in this issue) show that disadvantaged individuals who make the transition to business ownership do benefit more than others. Policies to ease that transition are therefore valuable. GHANI *et al.* (in this issue) find that infrastructure, labour laws and access to finance can promote enterprise, whilst CALIENDO and KÜNN (in this issue) provide a broadly positive assessment of public programmes seeking to encourage the unemployed to become business owners.

What remains less tractable is seeking to address directly attitudes towards entrepreneurship which both WESTLUND *et al.* (in this issue) and KIBLER *et al.* (in this issue) show vary considerably by region and are associated with actual entrepreneurial activity. The policy response fundamentally depends on whether attitudes are a cause or an outcome. If they are a cause then they should be addressed directly – perhaps through awareness-raising of the benefits of entrepreneurship. If, instead, they are an outcome then the valid policy response is to address issues of economic disadvantage – health, education and knowledge, infrastructure etc. – so improving economic conditions directly. During the next decade researchers have to shed more light on this association if policy is to move forward based on evidence.

Acknowledgements – The authors are indebted to the Editors of *Regional Studies*, and to Arnoud Lagendijk in particular, for their support and encouragement in the preparation of this special issue.

NOTES

1. These papers in the special issues were supplemented by others on this topic in a separate book (STOREY, 1985).

2. In the associated edited volume (STOREY, 1985) two chapters relate to the United States (SHAFFER and PULVER, 1985; MARKUSEN and TEITZ, 1985).
3. The European Value Study (http://www.europeanvaluesstudy.eu/) also provides such information at a regional level. Unfortunately, in some regions it has insufficient observations.
4. A notable exception is the Nordic countries. For example, DAHL and SORENSON (2012) draw upon the Danish IDA database to track individuals and their enterprises. They conclude that new firms performed better when their owners had lived for a longer period in the region in which they start a business.
5. For example, GREENE *et al.* (2008) find that about one in four new business owners also own another business. The earlier work by ROSA and SCOTT (1999) – albeit restricted to limited companies – found half had only a single director but that 10% had more than three.
6. OBSCHONKA *et al.* (2013) find evidence that people with an entrepreneurial personality are not evenly spread over space but are clustered in certain regions.
7. PARKER (2009, p. 380) is more positive about the positive strength of this relationship and attributes much of the inconsistency to the lack of econometric sophistication in the approaches used by some researchers.
8. This corresponds to the distinction between 'nature' (an individual's innate qualities) and 'nurture' (personal experiences made) that can be particularly found in the psychological literature (WHITE *et al.*, 2007; OBSCHONKA and SILBEREISEN, 2012).
9. The average age of an innovative founder in Germany is about 41 years (METZGER *et al.*, 2010; MUELLER, 2010). Assuming that an average founder has finished his or her university education at the age of 25, this means that he or she has worked as a dependent employee for a period of a little more than 15 years before starting their own firm.
10. ROBERTS and EESLEY (2011) by assessing the employment effects of new businesses set up by alumni of the Massachusetts Institute of Technology (MIT) find that only about one-third of the jobs created in these firms are located in Massachusetts.

REFERENCES

ACS Z. J. and ARMINGTON C. (2004) The impact of geographic differences in human capital on service firm formation rates, *Journal of Urban Economic* **56**, 244–278.

ACS Z. J. and STOREY D. J. (2004) Introduction: entrepreneurship and economic development, *Regional Studies* **38**, 871–877.

ACS Z. J., BRAUNERHJELM P., AUDRETSCH D. B. and CARLSSON B. (2009) The knowledge spillover theory of entrepreneurship, *Small Business Economics* **32**, 15–30.

ANDERSSON M. and KOSTER S. (2011) Sources of persistence in regional start-up rates – evidence from Sweden, *Journal of Economic Geography* **11**, 179–201.

AUDRETSCH D. B. (1995) *Innovation and Industry Evolution*. MIT Press, Cambridge, MA.

AUDRETSCH D. B. (2007) *The Entrepreneurial Society*. Oxford University Press, Oxford.

AUDRETSCH D. B. and KEILBACH M. (2004) Entrepreneurship capital and economic performance, *Regional Studies* **38**, 949–959.

AUDRETSCH D. B., THURIK R. and STAM E. (2011) *Unraveling the Shift to the Entrepreneurial Economy*. EIM Research Reports No. H201113. EIM, Zoetermeer.

BADE F.-J. and NERLINGER E. (2000) The spatial distribution of new technology based firms: empirical results for West Germany, *Papers in Regional Science* **79**, 155–176.

BAUMOL W. J. (1990) Entrepreneurship: productive, unproductive and destructive, *Journal of Political Economy* **98**, 893–921.

BEESLEY M. (1955) The birth and death of industrial establishments: experience in the West Midlands conurbation, *Journal of Industrial Economics* **4**, 45–61.

BEUGELSDIJK S. (2007) Entrepreneurial culture, regional innovativeness and economic growth, *Journal of Evolutionary Economics* **17**, 187–210.

BEUGELSDIJK S. and NOORDERHAVEN N. (2004) Entrepreneurial attitude and economic growth: a cross-section of 54 regions, *Annals of Regional Science* **38**, 199–218.

BIRCH D. (1979) *The Job Generation Process*. Mimeo. MIT, Cambridge, MA.

BOETTKE P. J. and COYNE C. J. (2009) Context matters: institutions and entrepreneurship, *Foundations and Trends in Entrepreneurship* **5**, 135–209.

BOSCHMA R. and FRENKEN K. (2011) The emerging empirics of evolutionary economic geography, *Journal of Economic Geography* **11**, 295–307.

BOSMA N. (2013) The global entrepreneurship monitor (GEM) and its impact on entrepreneurship research, *Foundations and Trends in Entrepreneurship* **9**, 1–108.

BOSMA N. and SCHUTJENS V. (2011) Understanding regional variation in entrepreneurial activity and entrepreneurial attitude in Europe, *Annals of Regional Science* **47**, 711–742.

BOSMA N. and STERNBERG R. (2014) Entrepreneurship as an urban event? Empirical evidence from European cities, *Regional Studies* **48**. http://dx.doi.org/10.1080/00343404.2014.904041

BRIXY U. (2014) The significance of entry and exit for regional productivity growth, *Regional Studies* **48**. http://dx.doi.org/10.1080/00343404.2014.895804

CALIENDO M. and KÜNN S. (2014) Regional effect heterogeneity of start-up subsidies for the unemployed. *Regional Studies* **48**. http://dx.doi.org/10.1080/00343404.2013.851784

CALIENDO M., FOSSEN F. and KRITIKOS A. (2014) Personality characteristics and the decision to become and stay self-employed, *Small Business Economics* **42**, 787–814. DOI 10.1007/s11187-013-9514-8

CHEN Y. and ROSENTHAL S. S. (2008) Local amenities and life cycle migration: do people move for jobs or fun?, *Journal of Urban Economics* **65**, 519–537.

CHLOSTA S., PATZELT H., KLEIN S. B. and DORMANN C. (2012) Parental role models and the decision to become self-employed: the moderating effect of personality, *Small Business Economics* **38**, 121–138.

COOPER A. C. (1973) Technical entrepreneurship: what do we know?, *R&D Management* **3**, 59–64.

CROSS M. (1981) *New Firms and Regional Economic Development.* Gower, Farnborough.

DAHL M. S. and SORENSON O. (2009) The embedded entrepreneur, *European Management Review* **6**, 172–181.

DAHL M. S. and SORENSON O. (2010) The migration of technical workers, *Journal of Urban Economics* **67**, 33–45.

DAHL M. S. and SORENSON O. (2012) Home sweet home: entrepreneurs location choices and the performance of their ventures, *Management Science* **58**, 1059–1071.

DAVIDSSON P. and GORDON S. R. (2012) Panel studies of new venture creation: a methods-focused review and suggestions for future research, *Small Business Economics* **39**, 853–876.

DELFMANN H., KOSTER S., MCCANN P. and VAN DIJK J. (2014) Population change and new firm formation in urban and rural regions, *Regional Studies* **48**. http://dx.doi.org/10.1080/00343404.2013.867430

DUNN T. and HOLTZ-EAKIN D. (2000) Financial capital, human capital, and the transition to self-employment: evidence from intergenerational links, *Journal of Labor Economics* **18**, 282–305.

ELFENBEIN D. W., HAMILTON B. H. and ZENGER T. R. (2010) The small firm effect and the entrepreneurial spawning of scientists and engineers, *Management Science* **56**, 659–681.

ESTRIN S. and MICKIEWICZ T. (2011) Entrepreneurship in transition economies: the role of institutions and generational change, in MINNITI M. (Ed.) *The Dynamics of Entrepreneurship: Evidence from the Global Entrepreneurship Monitor Data*, pp. 181–208. Oxford University Press, Oxford.

EWERS H.-J. and WETTMANN R. W. (1980) Innovation-oriented regional policy, *Regional Studies* **14**, 161–179. http://dx.doi.org/10.1080/09595238000185171

FIGUEIREDO O., GUIMARAES P. and WOODWARD D. (2002) Home-field advantage: location decisions of Portuguese entrepreneurs, *Journal of Urban Economics* **52**, 341–361.

FIRN J. K. and SWALES J. K. (1978) The formation of new manufacturing establishments in the Central Clydeside and West Midlands conurbations 1963–1972: a comparative analysis, *Regional Studies* **12**, 199–213.

FOTOPOULOS G. (2013) On the spatial stickiness of UK new firm formation rates, *Journal of Economic Geography* DOI 10.1093/jeg/lbt011

FRANKISH J. S., ROBERTS R. G., COAD A. and STOREY D. J. (2014) Is entrepreneurship a route out of deprivation?, *Regional Studies* **48**. http://dx.doi.org/10.1080/00343404.2013.871384

FREYTAG A. and THURIK R. (2007) Entrepreneurship and its determinants in a cross-country setting, *Journal of Evolutionary Economics* **17**, 117–131.

FRITSCH M. (1993) Regional differences in new firm formation: evidence from West Germany, *Regional Studies* **26**, 233–241.

FRITSCH M. (2013) New business formation and regional development – a survey and assessment of the evidence, *Foundations and Trends in Entrepreneurship* **9**, 249–364.

FRITSCH M. and AAMOUCKE R. (2013) Regional public research, higher education, and innovative start-ups – an empirical investigation, *Small Business Economics* **41**, 865–885.

FRITSCH M. and FALCK O. (2007) New business formation by industry over space and time: a multi-dimensional analysis, *Regional Studies* **41**, 157–172.

FRITSCH M. and MUELLER P. (2004) The effects of new firm formation on regional development over time, *Regional Studies* **38**, 961–975.

FRITSCH M. and MUELLER P. (2007) The persistence of regional new business formation-activity over time – assessing the potential of policy promotion programs, *Journal of Evolutionary Economics* **17**, 299–315.

FRITSCH M. and WYRWICH M. (2013) The long persistence of regional levels of entrepreneurship: Germany 1925–2005, *Regional Studies* **48**. http://dx.doi.org/10.1080/00343404.2013.816414

FRITSCH M., BUBLITZ E., SORGNER A. and WYRWICH M. (2014) How much of a socialist legacy? The re-emergence of entrepreneurship in the East German transformation to a market economy, *Small Business Economics*. DOI 10.1007/s11187-014-9544-x

GHANI E., KERR W. R. and O'CONNELL S. (2013) Spatial determinants of entrepreneurship in India, *Regional Studies* **48**. http://dx.doi.org/10.1080/00343404.2013.839869

GLAESER E. L. (2004) Review of Richard Florida's the rise of the creative class, *Regional Science and Urban Economics* **35**, 593–596.

GLAESER E. L., KERR S. P. and KERR W. R. (2012) *Entrepreneurship and Urban Growth: An Empirical Assessment with Historical Mines.* Harvard Business School Working Paper No. 13-015. Cambridge, MA.

GOULD A. and KEEBLE D. (1984) New firms and rural industrialization in East Anglia, *Regional Studies,* **18**, 189–201.

GREENE F. J., MOLE K. F. and STOREY D. J. (2008) *Three Decades of Enterprise Culture: Entrepreneurship, Economic Regeneration and Public Policy*. Palgrave, Basingstoke.

GUDGIN G. (1978) *Industrial Location Processes and Regional Employment Growth.* Saxon House, Farnborough.

GUDGIN G. and FOTHERGILL S. (1984) Geographical variation in the rate of formation of new manufacturing firms, *Regional Studies* **18**, 203–206.

HAUGH H. (2007) Community-led social venture creation, *Entrepreneurship Theory and Practice* **31**, 161–182.

HELFAT C. E. and LIEBERMAN M. B. (2002) The birth of capabilities: market entry and the importance of pre-history, *Industrial and Corporate Change* **11**, 725–760.

HENREKSON M. (2005) Entrepreneurship: a weak link in the welfare state?, *Industrial and Corporate Change* **14**, 437–467.

Henrekson M. (2007) Entrepreneurship and Institutions, *Comparative Labor Law and Policy Journal* **28**, 717–742.

Johnson P. S. and Cathcart D. G. (1979a) The founders of new manufacturing firms: a note on the size of their 'incubator' plants, *Journal of Industrial Economics* **28**, 29–224.

Johnson P. S. and Cathcart D. G. (1979b) New manufacturing firms and regional development: some evidence from the Northern region, *Regional Studies,* **13**, 269–280.

Kibler E., Kautonen T. and Fink M. (2014) Regional social legitimacy of entrepreneurship: implications for entrepreneurial intention and start-up behaviour, *Regional Studies* **48**. http://dx.doi.org/10.1080/00343404.2013.851373

Klapper L., Laeven L. und Rajan R. (2006) Entry regulation as a barrier to entrepreneurship, *Journal of Financial Economics* **82**, 591–629.

Klepper S. (2009) Spinoffs: a review and synthesis, *European Management Review* **6**, 159–171.

Koellinger P. and Thurik A. R. (2012) Entrepreneurship and the business cycle, *Review of Economics and Statistics* **94**, 1143–1156.

Koellinger P., van der Loos M. J. H. M., Groenen P. J. F., Thurik A. R., Rivadeneira F., van Rooij F. J. A., Uitterlinden A. G. and Hofman A. (2010) Genome-wide association studies in economics and entrepreneurship research: promises and limitations, *Small Business Economics* **35**, 1–18.

Kshetri N. (2009) Entrepreneurship in post-socialist economies: a typology and institutional contexts for market entrepreneurship, *Journal of International Entrepreneurship* **7**, 236–259.

Landstrom, H. (2005) *Pioneers in Entrepreneurship and Small Business Research*. Springer, New York, NY.

Larsson E., Hedelin L. and Gärling T. (2003) Influence of expert advice on expansion goals of small businesses in rural Sweden, *Journal of Small Business Management* **41**, 205–212.

Laspita S., Breugst N., Heblich S. and Patzelt H. (2012) Intergenerational transmission of entrepreneurial intentions, *Journal of Business Venturing* **27**, 414–435.

Lee S. Y., Florida R. and Acs Z. J. (2004) Creativity and entrepreneurship: a regional analysis of new firm formation, *Regional Studies* **38**, 879–891.

Levie J. (2007) Immigration, in-migration, ethnicity and entrepreneurship in the United Kingdom, *Small Business Economics* **28**, 143–169.

Lindquist M. J., Sol J. and van Praag M. (2012) *Why Do Entrepreneurial Parents have Entrepreneurial Children?* IZA Discussion Paper No. 6740. Institute for the Study of Labor (IZA), Bonn.

Litvak I. A. and Maule C. J. (1972) Managing the entrepreneurial Enterprise, *Business Quarterly* **37**, 42–50.

Lloyd P. E. (1980) *New Manufacturing Enterprises in Greater Manchester and Merseyside*. Working Paper No. 12. North West Industry Research Unit, Manchester University, Manchester.

Lloyd P. E. and Mason C. M. (1984) Spatial variations in new firm formation in the United Kingdom: comparative evidence from Merseyside, Greater Manchester and South Hampshire, *Regional Studies* **18**, 207–220.

Markusen A. R. and Teitz M. B. (1985) The world of small business: turbulence and survival, in Storey D. J. (Ed.) *Small Firms in Regional Economic Development: Britain, Ireland and the United States*, pp. 193–218. Cambridge University Press, London.

Metzger G., Heger D., Hoewer D. and Licht G. (2010) *High-Tech- Gründungen in Deutschland* [High-tech Start-ups in Germany]. Center for European Economic Research (ZEW), Mannheim.

Minniti M. (2005) Entrepreneurship and network externalities, *Journal of Economic Behavior and Organization* **57**, 1–27.

Mueller K. (2010) Academic spin-off's transfer speed – analyzing the time from leaving university to venture, *Research Policy* **39**, 189–199.

Mueller P., van Stel A. and Storey D. J. (2008) The effects of new firm formation on regional development over time: the case of Great Britain, *Small Business Economics* **30**, 59–71.

Naudé W. (2011) *Entrepreneurship and Economic Development*. Palgrave Macmillan, Houndmills.

Nicholson B. and Brinkley I. (1979) *Entrepreneurial Characteristics and the Development of New Manufacturing Enterprises*. Centre for Environmental Studies, London.

Nicolaou N., Shane S., Cherkas L., Hunkin J. and Spector T. D. (2008) Is the tendency to engage in entrepreneurship genetic?, *Management Science* **54**, 167–179.

North D. C. (1994) Economic performance through time, *American Economic Review* **84**, 359–368.

Nystrom K. (2008) The institutions of economic freedom and entrepreneurship: evidence from panel data, *Public Choice* **136**, 269–282.

Oakey R. P. (1984) Innovation and regional growth in small high-technology firms. Evidence from Britain and the USA, *Regional Studies* **18**, 237–251.

Obschonka M. and Silbereisen R. K. (2012) Entrepreneurship from a developmental science perspective, *International Journal of Developmental Science* **6**, 107–115.

Obschonka M., Schmitt-Rodermund E., Gosling S. D. and Silbereisen R. K. (2013) The regional distribution and correlates of an entrepreneurship-prone personality profile in the United States, Germany, and the United Kingdom: a socioecological perspective, *Journal of Personality and Social Psychology* **105**, 104–122. DOI 10.1037/a0032275

O'Farrell P. N. and Crouchley R. (1984) An industrial and spatial analysis of new firm formation in Ireland, *Regional Studies* **18**, 221–236.

Organisation for Economic Co-operation and Development (OECD) (2013) *Entrepreneurship at a Glance*. OECD, Paris.

Parker S. C. (2009) *The Economics of Entrepreneurship*. Cambridge University Press, London.

Qian H. and Acs Z. J. (2013) An absorptive capacity theory of knowledge spillover entrepreneurship, *Small Business Economics* **40**, 185–197.

RAUCH A. and FRESE M. (2007) Let's put the person back into entrepreneurship research: a meta-analysis on the relationship between business owners' personality traits, business creation, and success, *European Journal of Work and Organizational Psychology* **16**, 353–385.

REYNOLDS P. D. and CURTIN R. T. (2011) United States: panel study of entrepreneurial dynamics I, II; overview, in REYNOLDS P. D. and CURTIN R. T. (Eds) *New Business Creation: An International Overview*, pp. 255–294. Springer, New York, NY.

REYNOLDS P. D. and MAKI W. (1990) *Business Volatility and Economic Growth.* Final Report. Small Business Administration, Washington, DC.

REYNOLDS P. D., STOREY D. J. and WESTHEAD P. (1994a) Cross national comparison of the variation in new firm formation rates: an editorial overview, *Regional Studies* **28**, 343–346.

REYNOLDS P. D., STOREY D. J. and WESTHEAD P. (1994b) Cross national comparison of the variation in new firm formation rates, *Regional Studies* **28**, 443–456.

ROBERTS E. B. and EESLEY C. E. (2011) Entrepreneurial impact: the role of MIT, *Foundations and Trends Entrepreneurship* **7**, 1–149.

ROSA P. and SCOTT M. (1999) The prevalence of multiple owners and directors in the SME sector: implications for our understanding of start-up and growth, *Entrepreneurship and Regional Development* **11**, 21–37.

SARADAKIS G., MARLOW S. and STOREY D. J. (2014) Do different factors explain male and females self-employment rates?, *Journal of Business Venturing* **29**, 345–362.

SCHMITT-RODERMUND E. (2007) The long way to entrepreneurship: personality, parenting, early interests and competencies as precursors for entrepreneurial activity among the 'termites', in SILBEREISEN R. K. and LERNER R. M. (Eds) *Approaches to Positive Youth Development*, pp. 205–224. Sage, Thousand Oaks, CA.

SHAFFER R. E. and PULVER C. C. (1985) Regional variations in capital structure of new businesses: the Wisconsin case, in STOREY D. J. (Ed.) *Small Firms in Regional Economic Development: Britain, Ireland and the United States*, pp. 166–192. Cambridge University Press, London.

SMALLBONE D. and WELTER F. (2001) The distinctiveness of entrepreneurship in transition economies, *Small Business Economics* **16**, 249–262.

SORGNER A. and FRITSCH M. (2013) *Occupational Choice and Self-Employment – Are They Related?* Jena Economic Research Papers No. 001-2013. Friedrich Schiller University and Max Planck Institute of Economics, Jena.

STAM E. (2007) Why butterflies don't leave: locational behaviour of entrepreneurial firms, *Economic Geography* **83**, 27–50.

STOREY D. J. (1982) *Entrepreneurship and the New Firm.* Croom-Helm, London.

STOREY D. J. (1984) Editorial, *Regional Studies* **18**, 187–188.

STOREY D. J. (1985) *Small Firms in Regional Economic Development.* Cambridge University Press, Cambridge.

STOREY D. J. (1994) *Understanding the Small Business Sector.* Routledge, London.

STOREY D. J. and GREENE F. J. (2011) *Small Business and Entrepreneurship.* Pearsons, London.

STOREY D. J. and JOHNSON S. (1987a) *Job Generation and Labour Market Change.* Macmillan, Basingstoke.

STOREY D. J. and JOHNSON S. (1987b) Regional variations in entrepreneurship in the UK, *Scottish Journal of Political Economy* **34**, 161–173.

STUETZER M., GOETHNER M. and CANTNER U. (2012) Do balanced skills help nascent entrepreneurs to make progress in the venture creation process?, *Economic Letters* **117**, 186–188.

STUETZER M., OBSCHONKA M., BRIXY U. and STERNBERG R. (2014) Regional characteristics, opportunity perception and entrepreneurial activities, *Small Business Economics* **42**, 221–244. DOI 10.1007/s11187-013-9488-6

SUTARIA V. and HICKS D. A. (2004) New firm formation: dynamics and determinants, *Annals of Regional Science* **38**, 241–262.

VAN STEL A. (2008) The COMPENDIA database: COMParative Entrepreneurship Data for International Analysis, in CONGREGADO E. (Ed.) *Measuring Entrepreneurship: Building a Statistical System*, pp. 65–84. Springer, New York, NY.

VAN STEL A. and STOREY D. J. (2004) The link between firm births and job creation: is there a Upas tree effect?, *Regional Studies* **38**, 893–909.

VAN STEL A., STOREY D. J. and THURIK R. (2007) The effect of new business regulations on nascent and young business entrepreneurship, *Small Business Economics,* **28**, 171–186.

VIVARELLI M. (2013) Is entrepreneurship necessarily good? Microeconomic evidence from developed and developing countries, *Industrial and Corporate Change* **22**, 1453–1495.

WAGNER J. and STERNBERG R. (2004) Start-up activities, individual characteristics, and the regional milieu: lessons for entrepreneurship support policies from German micro data, *Annals of Regional Science* **38**, 219–240.

WESTLUND H. and ADAM F. (2010) Social capital and economic performance: a meta-analysis of 65 Studies, *European Planning Studies* **18**, 893–919.

WESTLUND H., LARSSON J. P. and OLSSON A. R. (2014) Start-ups and local entrepreneurial social capital in the municipalities of Swedish, *Regional Studies* **48**. http://dx.doi.org/10.1080/00343404.2013.865836

WHITE R. E., THORNHILL S. and HAMPSON E. (2007) A biosocial model of entrepreneurship: the combined effect of nurture and nature, *Journal of Organizational Behavior* **28**, 451–466.

WHITTINGTON R. C. (1984) Regional bias in new firm formation in the UK, *Regional Studies* **18**, 253–256.

WILLIAMSON O. (2000) The new institutional economics: taking stock, looking ahead, *Journal of Economic Literature* **38**, 595–613.

ZHAO H. and SEIBERT S. E. (2006) The big-five personality dimensions and entrepreneurial status: a meta-analytical review, *Journal of Applied Psychology* **91**, 259–271.

ZHAO H., SEIBERT S. E. and LUMPKIN G. T. (2010) The relationship of personality to entrepreneurial intentions and performance: a meta-analytic review, *Journal of Management* **36**, 381–404.

The Long Persistence of Regional Levels of Entrepreneurship: Germany, 1925–2005

MICHAEL FRITSCH*† and MICHAEL WYRWICH*
*Friedrich Schiller University Jena, School of Economics and Business Administration, Jena, Germany.
†German Institute for Economic Research (DIW-Berlin), Berlin, Germany

FRITSCH M. and WYRWICH M. The long persistence of regional levels of entrepreneurship: Germany, 1925–2005, *Regional Studies*. This paper investigates the persistent levels of self-employment and new business formation in different time periods and under different framework conditions. The analysis shows that regional differences regarding the level of self-employment and new business formation tend to be persistent for periods as long as eighty years, despite abrupt and drastic changes in the political–economic environment. This pronounced persistence demonstrates the existence of regional entrepreneurship culture that tends to have long-lasting effects.

Entrepreneurship Self-employment New business formation Persistence Culture

FRITSCH M. and WYRWICH M. 长期存在的区域层级创业精神：德国，1925 年至 2005 年，*区域研究*。本文探讨在不同时程阶段、不同架构条件之下，自雇与新兴企业形成的续存程度。研究分析显示，自雇以及新兴企业形成程度的区域差异，倾向持续存在长达八年之久，儘管政治经济环境时有突发性与剧烈的改变。此一深厚的持续性，证明了区域创业精神文化的存在，该文化倾向拥有长期的影响。

创业精神 自雇 新兴企业形成 持续性 文化

FRITSCH M. et WYRWICH M. La persistance de longue durée des niveaux régionaux de l'esprit d'entreprise: l'Allemagne de 1925 jusqu'à 2005, *Regional Studies*. Cet article examine les niveaux de travail indépendant et la création de nouvelles entreprises à des périodes différentes et dans des conditions-cadres différentes. L'analyse montre que les différences régionales pour ce qui est du niveau de travail indépendant et de la création de nouvelles entreprises ont tendance à persister pendant des périodes aussi longues que quatre-vingts années, en dépit des changements inattendus du milieu politico-économique. Cette persistance marquée démontre la présence d'une culture entrepreneuriale qui a tendance à avoir des effets à long terme.

Esprit d'entreprise Travail indépendant Création de nouvelles entreprises Persistance Culture

FRITSCH M. und WYRWICH M. Die Persistenz regionalen Unternehmertums: Deutschland, 1925–2005, *Regional Studies*. Wir analysieren die Persistenz von unternehmerischer Selbständigkeit und des regionalen Gründungsgeschehens in verschiedenen Zeiträumen und unter unterschiedlichen Rahmenbedingungen. Es zeigt sich, dass regionale Unterschiede im Niveau unternehmerischer Selbständigkeit und des Gründungsgeschehens Zeiträume von bis zu 80 Jahren überdauern, auch wenn es zu plötzlichen und tiefgreifenden Veränderungen des politisch-ökonomischen Umfeldes kommt. Diese ausgeprägte Persistenz belegt die Existenz einer regionalen Kultur unternehmerischer Selbständigkeit, die über lange Zeiträume fortwirkt.

Entrepreneurship Selbständigkeit Unternehmensgründungen Persistenz Kultur

FRITSCH M. y WYRWICH M. La larga persistencia del empresariado regional: Alemania, 1925–2005, *Regional Studies*. En este artículo investigamos el nivel persistente del empleo autónomo y la formación de nuevas empresas en diferentes periodos de tiempo y bajo diferentes condiciones estructurales. El análisis muestra que, pese a los cambios bruscos y drásticos en el entorno político y económico, las diferencias regionales con respecto al nivel de empleo autónomo y la formación de nuevas empresas tienden a ser persistentes durante periodos de hasta ochenta años. Esta persistencia pronunciada demuestra la existencia de una cultura empresarial de ámbito regional que suele tener efectos de larga duración.

Espíritu empresarial Empleo autónomo Formación de nuevas empresas Persistencia Cultura

INTRODUCTION

Studies of established market economies such as West Germany (FRITSCH and MUELLER, 2007), the Netherlands (VAN STEL and SUDDLE, 2008), Sweden (ANDERSSON and KOSTER, 2011), the United Kingdom (MUELLER *et al.*, 2008), and the United States (ACS and MUELLER, 2008) show that regional start-up rates tend to be relatively persistent and path dependent over periods of one or two decades. Hence, regions that have a relatively high level of entrepreneurship and start-up activity today can be expected also to experience high levels in future. One main reason for this strong persistence could be that region-specific determinants of entrepreneurship also remain relatively constant over time, or, as stated by MARSHALL (1920), *natura non facit saltum* (nature does not make jumps). Another explanation could be the existence of a regional entrepreneurship culture which is reflected, for instance, by informal institutions, that is, norms, values and codes of conduct in a society (NORTH, 1994) that are in favour of entrepreneurship. An entrepreneurial culture should, at least to some degree, be independent of socio-economic conditions and may, therefore, even survive considerable shocks to the socio-economic environment, such as serious economic crises, devastating wars and drastic changes of political regimes (NORTH, 1994; WILLIAMSON, 2000).

The persistence of regional entrepreneurship is analysed in three different scenarios, each with a specific degree of change in economic conditions. In contrast to extant work that studies time periods of up to ten to twenty years (for example, ANDERSSON and KOSTER, 2011), the present paper investigates persistence of regional entrepreneurship for periods as long as eighty years. Moreover, while work to date has studied the persistence of entrepreneurship under stable socio-economic conditions, the examples include different kinds of disruptive changes or 'jumps' in the conditions for entrepreneurship. Hence, the persistence of regional entrepreneurship found under such dramatically changing conditions cannot be caused by persistence of the determinants of entrepreneurial activity, but must be due to other reasons, such as a regional culture of entrepreneurship. This is particularly remarkable in the third scenario involving East Germany, a region that has been under a socialist regime for forty years that more or less tried to extinguish private firms and entrepreneurship completely. The findings can be regarded as a strong indication for the existence of a regional entrepreneurial culture that survived even drastic and long-lasting changes to the socio-economic environment.

The next section reviews the previous research on the persistence of regional entrepreneurship and discusses the concept of an entrepreneurial culture or entrepreneurship capital. The third section explains the empirical strategy in more detail and gives an overview on the three scenarios used for the analysis. The following sections then analyse the persistence of entrepreneurship in these scenarios. The final (sixth) section discusses the results, draws policy conclusions and proposes avenues for further research.

PERSISTENCE IN REGIONAL ENTREPRENEURSHIP: BEYOND STABILITY IN CONTEXT

Studies of a number of established market economies have found that the regional level of new business formation tends to be rather constant over periods of ten to twenty years (ACS and MUELLER, 2008; ANDERSSON and KOSTER, 2011; FRITSCH and MUELLER, 2007; MUELLER *et al.*, 2008; VAN STEL and SUDDLE, 2008). One obvious explanation for this phenomenon could be that regional determinants of new business formation and their effects are relatively stable over time. Indeed, variables that have been shown to be conducive to the emergence of new firms, such as qualification of the regional workforce or employment share in small firms (FRITSCH and FALCK, 2007), do tend to remain fairly constant over successive years. Some authors have claimed, however, that the persistence of start-up rates may indicate the presence of an entrepreneurial culture (ANDERSSON and KOSTER, 2011), sometimes referred to as 'entrepreneurship capital' (AUDRETSCH and KEILBACH, 2004).

An entrepreneurial culture is typically understood 'as a positive collective programming of the mind' (BEUGELSDIJK, 2007, p. 190) or an 'aggregate psychological trait' (FREYTAG and THURIK, 2007, p. 123) in the regional population oriented toward entrepreneurial values such as individualism, independence and motivation for achievement (also ANDERSSON and KOSTER, 2011; AOYAMA, 2009; AUDRETSCH and KEILBACH, 2004; BEUGELSDIJK, 2007; BEUGELSDIJK and NOORDERHAVEN, 2004; DAVIDSSON, 1995; DAVIDSSON and WIKLUND, 1997; FORNAHL, 2003; MINNITI, 2005; LAFUENTE *et al.*, 2007). ETZIONI (1987) argues that one important aspect of entrepreneurial culture is spatial variation in social acceptance of entrepreneurs and their activities. According to Etzioni, the degree of societal legitimacy when it comes to entrepreneurship may be higher in some regions than in others. As a consequence, the more entrepreneurship is regarded as legitimate, the higher the demand for it and the more resources are dedicated to such activity. This social acceptance of entrepreneurship can be regarded as an informal institution, which is defined as codes of conduct as well as norms and values within a society (NORTH, 1994), issues that can be well subsumed under the notion of 'culture'. According to WILLIAMSON (2000), it belongs to the level of social structure that is deeply embedded in a population and that tends to change very slowly over long periods of time. Formal institutions, governance structures and resource allocation undergo much more frequent changes and can be regarded as being embedded in the informal institutional framework.[1]

In an approach inspired by social psychology, FORNAHL (2003) conceptualizes how a specific regional attitude toward entrepreneurship may emerge via the presence of positive local examples or role models. The main idea of this approach is that an individual's perception of entrepreneurship – the cognitive representation – is shaped by observing entrepreneurial role models in the social environment. This leads to learning from the role models, increasing the social acceptance of entrepreneurial lifestyles and raising the likelihood of adopting entrepreneurial behavior. With respect to learning, SORENSON and AUDIA (2000) argue that observing successful entrepreneurs enables potential entrepreneurs to organize the resources and activities required for starting and running one's own venture and increases individual self-confidence, in the sense of 'if they can do it, I can, too' (p. 443). Accordingly, having a relatively high number of entrepreneurs in a region is conducive to new business formation probably because it provides opportunities to learn about entrepreneurial tasks and capabilities.[2]

These findings suggest that regional entrepreneurship might become self-reinforcing, as MINNITI (2005) puts it. Minniti provides a theoretical model that, based on the above-mentioned regional role model effects, can explain why regions with initially similar characteristics may end up with different levels of entrepreneurial activity. Chance events at the outset of such a process may induce entrepreneurial choice among individuals that leads to different levels of regional entrepreneurship. The presence of entrepreneurial role models in the social environment reduces ambiguity for potential entrepreneurs and may help them acquire necessary information and entrepreneurial skills. In this way, entrepreneurship creates a sort of perceptual non-pecuniary externality that spurs additional start-up activity and makes entrepreneurship self-reinforcing.[3] In Minniti's model, this self-reinforcing effect of entrepreneurship depends critically on the ability of individuals 'to observe someone else's behavior and the consequences of it' (p. 5). Thus, regional social capital, the properties of regional networks and, particularly, regional entrepreneurial history play a role in the region's level of entrepreneurship. In the same sense, FORNAHL (2003) argues that self-augmenting processes may lead to the emergence of cognitive representation in favour of entrepreneurship, which translates into an increasing number of entrepreneurs in the region and a specific regional entrepreneurial attitude. Therefore, according to the findings of WAGNER and STERNBERG (2004) and BOSMA and SCHUTJENS (2011), spatial variation with respect to entrepreneurial attitudes should be expected. Further, ANDERSSON and KOSTER (2011), in an empirical analysis of Swedish regions, find that the positive effect of past start-up activities on the present level of new business formation is particularly pronounced in regions with relatively high start-up rates in previous years. This suggests that persistence and self-augmentation of a regional entrepreneurship culture may require a certain 'threshold-level'.

A regional culture of entrepreneurship, however, may need more than societal legitimacy of entrepreneurship, individuals able and willing to start firms, role models, networks, and peer effects. An infrastructure of supporting services, particularly the availability of competent consulting as well as investing financial institutions (AUDRETSCH and KEILBACH, 2004), may also be necessary. Similarly, there are regional differences with respect to the prevalence of entrepreneurship-facilitating social capital represented, for instance, by networks aiming at stimulating new firms, and a vital local culture of venture capital financing (WESTLUND and BOLTON, 2003). In short, there are many aspects of the regional environment that may be, to different degrees, conducive to new business formation (DUBINI, 1989).[4]

There is considerable empirical evidence that points towards a long-term persistence of informal institutions in general. BECKER *et al.* (2010), for instance, compare Eastern European regions that had been affiliated with the Habsburg Empire that existed until 1918 with regions that had not. They show that having been part of the Habsburg Empire in the past increases current trust and reduces corruption of police and courts compared with other regions with the same formal institutions but no past association with the Habsburg Empire. A very long persistence of regional informal institutions is vividly illustrated by VOIGTLAENDER and VOTH (2012), who show that German regions that experienced anti-Semitic violence in the fourteenth century also had higher levels of violence against Jews in the 1920s and 1930s. If such attitudes can survive for centuries, it seems possible that other attitudes, such as those toward entrepreneurship, might also be long-term characteristics of a region, persisting even such disruptive events such as world wars or institutional upheavals like the transition from communism to a market economy in East Germany, which involved a rapid change of the norms and values that underlie economic activity (NEWMAN, 2000). But also the forty years of a socialist regime in the regions of East Germany might have left considerable traces. An indication for such longer-term effects is the study by ALESINA and FUCHS-SCHUENDELN (2007) who find that East German citizens who were exposed to the socialist regime are much more in favour of redistribution and state intervention than their West German counterparts.

The reasons for such a long-term persistence of values in a region are largely unclear. A main mechanism that may explain regional persistence of entrepreneurial values and attitudes may be their transmission from parents or grandparents to their children that has been found to be a significant effect in several empirical studies (for example, CHLOSTA *et al.*, 2012; DOHMEN *et al.*, 2012; LASPITA *et al.*, 2012).

To summarize the literature, a regional entrepreneurial culture may exist and persist for mainly three reasons: the presence of peer effects and the intergenerational transmission of entrepreneurial role models and values; social acceptance of entrepreneurship; and the existence of entrepreneurial supporting services and institutions (for example, financing and advice). These factors have a pronounced positive effect on the level of entrepreneurial activity. Because these factors change only gradually over time as well as due to the self-reinforcing effects mentioned above, a regional culture of entrepreneurship should not only take a considerable time to develop, but also be long-lasting, so that it may be regarded as a certain kind of 'capital'. Moreover, even if supportive institutional infrastructure for entrepreneurship has been destroyed by a rigorous anti-entrepreneurship policy, as was the case in East Germany under its socialist regime, the regional population's positive attitude towards entrepreneurship might continue to prevail for some time.

EMPIRICAL STRATEGY

The persistence of regional entrepreneurship is analysed in three scenarios that relate to different time periods and regions. Particularly, the three scenarios are characterized by rather different degrees of stability in the political–economic environment. The idea behind this approach is to identify how long entrepreneurship can persist depending on the length of the time period and the turbulence of the framework conditions.

The first scenario (Scenario I) presents regional entrepreneurship in West Germany from 1984 to 2005, a period characterized by relatively stable conditions without any major shocks to the socio-economic environment.

For the second scenario (Scenario II) the period of analysis is extended to cover eighty years and regional entrepreneurship in West German regions in 1925 is compared with the level of entrepreneurial activity in the period 1984–2005. A number of considerable disruptions occurred during this period, including the world economic crisis of the late 1920s, the Second World War, occupation by the Allied powers, massive in-migration, the introduction of a new constitutional base and political system, as well as reconstruction of the economy. If persistence of regional entrepreneurship in the second scenario is found, it can be viewed as an indication that this must have reasons other than persisting structural characteristics that are effective even in the face of severe ruptures in the past. Moreover, since the entire adult population is replaced over a long·period of eighty years, the persistence of relatively high or low levels of entrepreneurship would indicate an intergenerational transfer of the attitude towards entrepreneurial behavior.

The final scenario (Scenario III) investigates the persistence of regional entrepreneurship in East Germany from 1925 to 2005. After the end of the Second World War, East Germany experienced considerably more severe shocks than West Germany. By the end of the war, this part of the country was occupied by the Soviet Army. In contrast to West Germany where the Western Allies soon began to assist in the reconstruction of the economy, the Soviets dismantled existing machinery and transferred it for productive use in the USSR. Moreover, they quickly installed a socialist regime with a centrally planned economic system. In 1949, an East German state – the German Democratic Republic (GDR) – was founded which was part of the Soviet Bloc. As a consequence of political pressure and severe economic problems, there was massive out-migration of East Germans into the West until the closing of the East German border in 1961. Throughout the GDR period a reshaping of regional structures was enforced by different industrialization policy campaigns (BERENTSEN, 1992).

The socialist East German state collapsed in late 1989 and East and West Germany were reunified in 1990. The following transformation process of the East German economy to a market economic system was a 'shock treatment' where the ready-made formal institutional framework of West Germany was adopted practically overnight (for example, BREZINSKI and FRITSCH, 1995; HALL and LUDWIG, 1995). This development rapidly induced massive structural change accompanied by a rather complete replacement of the incumbent firms. Between 1989 and 1991, the share of manufacturing employment in East Germany dropped from 48.7% to 16.0% (HALL and LUDWIG, 1995) and unemployment rose from virtually zero in 1989 to more than 15% in 1992 (BURDA and HUNT, 2001). In the course of the transformation process, the regions again experienced massive out-migration, especially that of young and qualified workers (HUNT, 2006). Even now, more than twenty years after this transformation process began, nearly all East German regions lag considerably behind their West German counterparts.

East Germany's forty years of socialist regime after the Second World War are of particular interest for the analysis because during this period the region was host to a great deal of policies intended to eradicate entrepreneurship. In the socialist regime, collectivist values were strongly favoured and entrepreneurship was perceived as a bourgeois anachronism (for example, PICKEL, 1992; THOMAS, 1996). Hence, the adoption of a rigorous anti-entrepreneurship policy strategy that included massive socialization of private enterprises and the suppression of any remaining private-sector activity (for details, see BREZINSKI, 1987; PICKEL, 1992). This policy was operated with a particular focus on those regions that could be regarded as strongholds of entrepreneurship characterized by high levels of self-employment (EBBINGHAUS, 2003, pp. 75–89).

The massive migration from former German territories at the end of the Second World War as well as the out-migration of East Germany during and after the socialist regime might have shaped regional cultures. This can be expected because migration tends to be selective with regards to age, qualification (for example, HUNT, 2006), and certain personality characteristics that could be regarded as pro-entrepreneurial (for example, BONEVA and FRIEZE, 2001; JOKELA, 2009). Unfortunately, there is not sufficient information available that would allow for such effects to be controlled. It can, however, be said that immigration from former German territories at the end of the war has been hardly selective since almost the entire German population was forced to leave. Moreover, these expellees had limited choice in where they were settled by authorities. Empirical evidence suggests that the placement of expellees was mainly determined by the availability of food and housing, that is, they were settled in more rural locations with less wartime destruction (BURCHARDI and HASSAN, 2013). Given the limited locational choice of expellees after the war, it appears rather unlikely that those with a more entrepreneurial personality shaped regional cultures by selecting themselves into regions with high levels of entrepreneurship. In the case of East Germany, (Scenario III) out-migration of entrepreneurial people due to the anti-entrepreneurial pressure of the socialist GDR regime should have weakened the remaining regional culture of entrepreneurship. Therefore, if persistence after the breakdown of the socialist regime is still found, this can be regarded a relatively strong indication for the long-term effect of entrepreneurial culture.

The analyses use the self-employment rate and the regional start-up rate as indicators for regional entrepreneurship. These two measures are well accepted in entrepreneurship research and are the only reasonable indicators available at a regional basis for relatively long time periods.[5]

SCENARIO I: PERSISTENCE OF REGIONAL ENTREPRENEURSHIP IN A STABLE ENVIRONMENT – WEST GERMANY, 1984–2005

The analysis of the persistence of regional entrepreneurship begins by looking at the rather stable environment of West Germany, which has already been investigated by FRITSCH and MUELLER (2007). The same data source as that paper is used, but the period of analysis (1984–2005) is slightly extended to more than twenty years. Moreover, not only does this paper investigate the correlation of regional start-up rates over time, but also it analyses the effect of the regional self-employment rate on the level of start-ups in order to make the analysis compatible with Scenarios II and III. The analysis is at the level of seventy-one planning regions,[6] which represent functional spatial units. The data on start-up activity are obtained from the German Social Insurance Statistics. This dataset contains every German establishment that employs at least one person obliged to pay social insurance contributions (SPENGLER, 2008). The start-up rate is measured in accordance with the labour market approach (AUDRETSCH and FRITSCH, 1994), whereby the number of annual start-ups in the private sector is divided by the sum (in thousands) of employees in the private sector plus registered unemployed persons.[7] The regional self-employment rate is the number of establishments in a region's non-agricultural private-sector industries divided by the regional workforce (including registered unemployed persons). Fig. 1 shows the regional start-up rates in Germany today.

There are considerable regional differences in the levels of new business formation in Germany at the end of the observation period: the year 2005.[8] Fig. 1 reveals that start-up rates tend to be higher in West Germany compared with East Germany.[9] The lower level of start-ups with at least one employee in East Germany probably has to do with problems of transitioning to a market economy after having been under a socialist regime for forty years. Due to this legacy, East Germany can be regarded as a distinct regional growth regime (FRITSCH, 2004).

Regional start-up rates and self-employment rates are highly correlated over time (Table 1; for descriptive statistics, see Tables A1 and A2 in Appendix A). The self-employment rate reflects the stock of entrepreneurs, whereas the start-up rate indicates new entries. The relationship is not as close for years that are farther apart, but even over a twenty-year period, the value of the correlation coefficient always remains above 0.85 for the self-employment rate and 0.70 for the start-up rate. This correlation is presumably stronger for the self-employment rate because it is mainly determined by the already existent stock of self-employed and to a low degree by start-up activity in one year. Figs 2 and 3 illustrate the high degrees of variation across regions, as well as the high persistence of regional levels of new business formation and self-employment over time.

For a more in-depth analysis, the current regional start-up rate is regressed on its lagged values and on some other variables intended to control for relevant characteristics of the regional environment (Table 2). In order to compare the effects of past start-up activities, all variables are standardized to a mean of zero and a standard deviation (SD) of 1.[10] The control variables include regional population density, which represents a 'catch-all' variable of regional characteristics, the employment share of research and development (R&D) personnel,[11] which may indicate the level of innovative entrepreneurial opportunities available in a region, and the local unemployment rate (for a discussion of these variables, see FRITSCH and MUELLER,

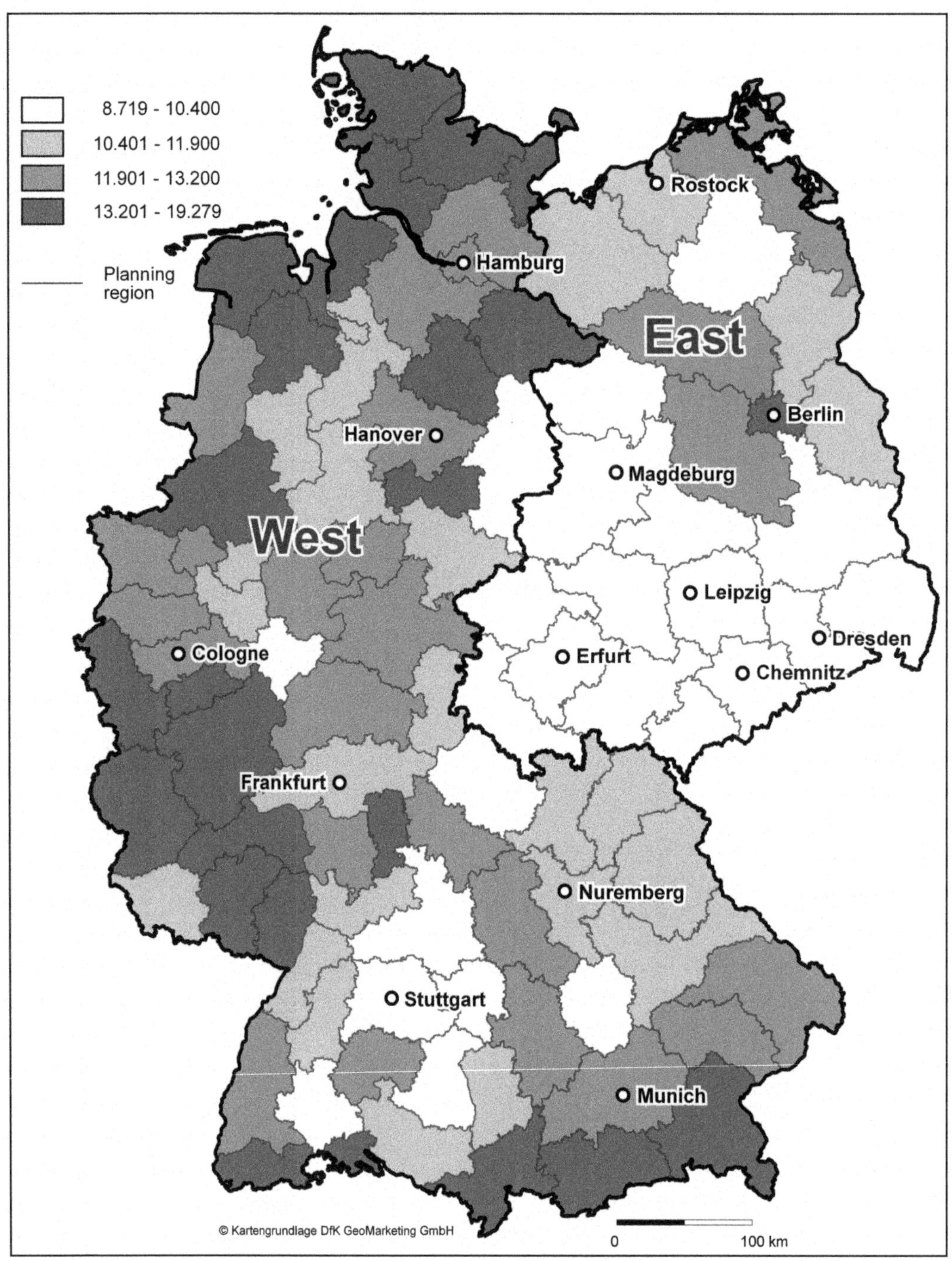

Fig. 1. Start-up rates in German planning regions, 2005

2007). Federal state dummies were included to capture the effects of different political conditions and spatial autocorrelation.[12] Robust standard errors are employed to account for heteroskedasticity (WHITE, 1980). The model is run for the period 1984–2005, but also the results of a model restricted to the years 2000–2005 are shown for reasons of comparability with the analysis performed for East Germany in the fifth section.

Table 1. Correlation of self-employment rates and start-up rates over time – West Germany, 1984–2005

	$t-1$	$t-5$	$t-10$	$t-15$	$t-20$
Self-employment rate $t = 0$	0.995***	0.97***	0.93***	0.86***	0.87***
Start-up rate $t = 0$	0.95***	0.90***	0.85***	0.76***	0.72***

Note: ***Statistically significant at the 1% level.

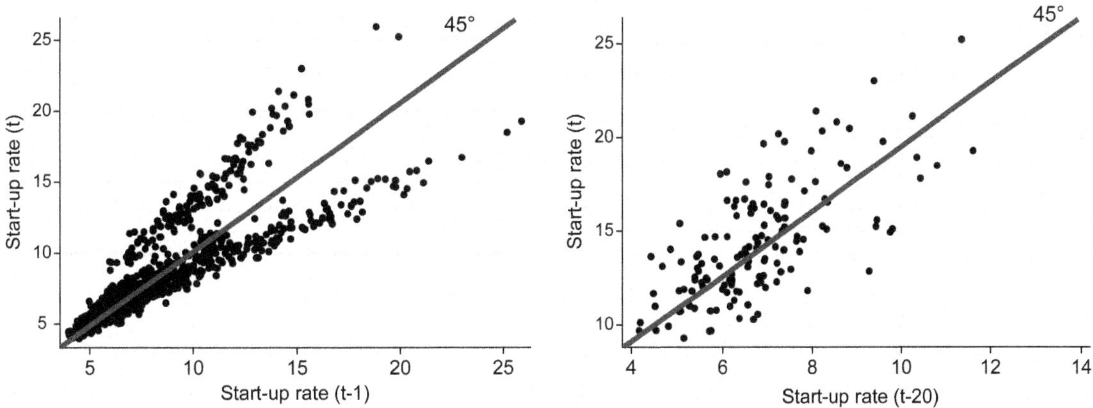

Fig. 2. Relationship between start-up rate (per 1000 individuals) in t and t – 1 (left) and t and t – 20 (right)
Note: The 'split' in the upper part in the left panel results from observations of the period 2003–2005. For these years the Social Insurance Statistics reports a higher number of start-ups due to changes in the reporting system. The number of observations on the right side is considerably lower because the data contain only two years with information about the lagged start-up rates for $t - 20$ (2004 and 2005). The restriction to the years 2004 and 2005 in the right panel results in a different scaling of the x- and y-axes because observations after the change in the reporting system are compared with data points before this change occurred. The persistence suggested by the figures in the right-hand panel indicates that the 'jump' in the recorded number of start-ups was not region specific

The results indicate a highly significant positive effect of new business formation in previous periods on current start-up rates (Table 2). The effect in Model I is strongest for the start-up rate in $t - 1$, which is in line with previous research. Using more than one lagged start-up rate implies the problem of multicollinearity. In order to rule out this issue and to demonstrate that the previous level of new business formation has not only a short-term effect, the start-up rate of the period $t - 3$ is included in Model II. This lagged start-up rate is highly significant as well. As in the previous analysis of regional persistence of entrepreneurship in Germany by FRITSCH and MUELLER (2007), it is found that the share of R&D personnel has a significant positive effect on the level of regional new business formation, whereas the effect of population density is significantly negative in two of the three models.[13] The effect of the local unemployment rate varies considerably with the period under inspection. This variation can be explained with intensified policy programmes after 2002 for promoting start-ups by unemployed people. These programmes obviously had the effect that the statistical relationship between the regional unemployment rate and new business formation is significantly positive when this period is included, while it tends to be negative in other periods.[14] Altogether, the results show the same persistency pattern of start-up activity as found by FRITSCH and MUELLER (2007) for a slightly extended period of analysis. Looking at the over-time variation in the determinants of new business formation, a high degree of stability is also found (see Table A3 in Appendix A). This indicates that the persistence of regional start-up rates in West Germany in the 1984–2005 period may be well explained by rather stable framework conditions.

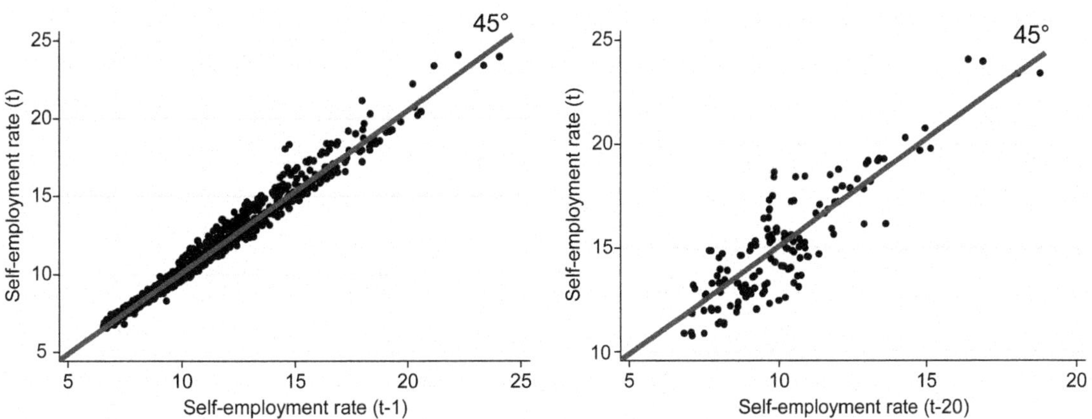

Fig. 3. Relationship between self-employment rate (%) in t and in t – 1 (left) and in t and in t – 20 (right)

Table 2. Effect of past start-up rates on the current start-up rate in West Germany, 1984–2005[a]

	I	II	III
	1984–2005		2000–2005
Start-up rate (t – 1)	0.432*** (0.0213)	–	0.656*** (0.0461)
Start-up rate (t – 2)	0.0972*** (0.00774)	–	–
Start-up rate (t – 3)	0.113*** (0.00992)	0.243*** (0.0236)	–
Population density (log) (t – 1)	–0.0408* (0.0222)	–0.107*** (0.0382)	–0.154*** (0.0394)
Share of R&D personnel (t – 1)	0.0425** (0.0197)	0.129*** (0.0285)	0.128*** (0.0281)
Unemployment rate (t – 1)	0.0276* (0.0154)	0.0660** (0.0286)	0.170*** (0.0474)
Federal state dummies	**	**	**
Constant	–0.238*** (0.0601)	–0.264** (0.110)	–0.0396 (0.118)
Number of observations	1349	1349	355
F-value	274.38***	114.32***	38.97***
Adjusted R^2	0.793	0.592	0.459

Notes: Dependent variable: regional start-up rate in t_0. Pooled ordinary least squares (OLS) regressions. Newey–West standard errors are given in parentheses. ***Statistically significant at the 1% level; and **statistically significant at the 5% level. Newey–West standard errors were used to control for potential autocorrelation of the lagged dependent values with the residuals. A lag of 3 was specified. Running the models with the Huber–Sandwich–White procedure leads only to rather small changes of the standard errors. Potential effects of changes in the reporting system in the years 1999 and 2003 are controlled for by year dummies. Running models I and II only for the 1984–1998 period does not qualitatively change the effect of lagged start-up rates.

[a]Lagrange Multiplier tests indicate some remaining spatial autocorrelation in some of the models of the first and second scenarios even when the federal state dummies are included. The results are, however, robust when running spatial lag and spatial error models. The results are presented with federal state dummies because this model is also used for the quantile regressions (see Fig. 4). Performing the analysis with different control variables suggests that the spatial autocorrelation does not pertain to the start-up or the self-employment rates but is caused by some of the control variables. Accordingly, the Lagrange Multiplier test does not indicate any spatial autocorrelation if the model is run without the control variables. In alternative specifications, the stock of start-ups in past years was used and average start-up rates were lagged as independent variables. Both indicators significantly affect start-up activity.

Table 3. Effect of past self-employment rates on the current start-up rate in West Germany, 1984–2005

	I	II	III
	1984–2005		2000–2005
Self-employment rate (t – 1)	1.118*** (0.0815)	–	0.606*** (0.0413)
Self-employment rate (t – 2)	–0.811*** (0.0772)	–	–
Self-employment rate (t – 3)	0.251*** (0.0520)	0.539*** (0.0339)	–
Population density (log) (t – 1)	–0.0126 (0.0327)	–0.0274 (0.0430)	–0.0511 (0.0444)
Share of R&D personnel (t – 1)	0.220*** (0.0272)	0.300*** (0.0324)	0.182*** (0.0321)
Unemployment rate (t – 1)	0.206*** (0.0294)	0.273*** (0.0349)	0.360*** (0.0521)
Federal state dummies	n.s.	n.s.	n.s.
Constant	–0.107 (0.115)	–0.175 (0.149)	–0.0298 (0.113)
Number of observations	1349	1349	355
F-value	112.01***	55.31***	35.76***
Adjusted R^2	0.381	0.296	0.560

Note: Dependent variable: regional start-up rate in t_0. Pooled ordinary least squares (OLS) regressions. Newey–West standard errors are given in parentheses. ***Statistically significant at the 1% level; and **statistically significant at the 5% level. Newey–West standard errors were used to control for potential autocorrelation of the lagged dependent values with the residuals. A lag of 3 was specified. Running the models in accordance with the Huber–Sandwich–White procedure leads only to rather small changes of the standard errors. Potential effects of change in the reporting system in the years 1999 and 2003 are controlled for by year dummies. Running models I and II only for the 1984–1998 period does not qualitatively change the effect of lagged self-employment rates.

Since the historical data used in the analyses of Scenarios II and III provide only information about self-employment but not on start-up rates, the regressions for the past self-employment rate (Table 3) are also performed in order to be compatible with these scenarios. As could have been expected, it is found that the past regional self-employment rate has a strongly significant effect on the current level of start-ups. This effect is particularly pronounced for the self-employment rate lagged by one year. While population density is not statistically significant, a strong relationship between the start-up rate and the regional level of R&D employment is again found. Also, the unemployment rate proves to be statistically significant.

In a further step, the work of ANDERSSON and KOSTER (2011) is followed and quantile regressions are run. The idea behind this analysis is that the effect of a culture of entrepreneurship that leads to persistence of start-up rates should be particularly strong in regions with relatively high levels of new business formation. Due to the extremely high correlation between start-up rates in successive years, the model is restricted to the start-up rate in t – 3 and the control variables (Tables 2 and 3).[15] It is indeed found that the estimated marginal effect of previous levels of new business formation tends to be the stronger the higher is the past level of new business formation (Fig. 4) and self-employment (Fig. 5). This relationship is considerably more pronounced if the start-up rate is used as indicator for the past level of entrepreneurial activity (Fig. 4). All in all, the results indicate that persistence of start-up activity is especially reinforced in those regions that have experienced high levels of self-employment and new business formation in the past.[16] Whether this

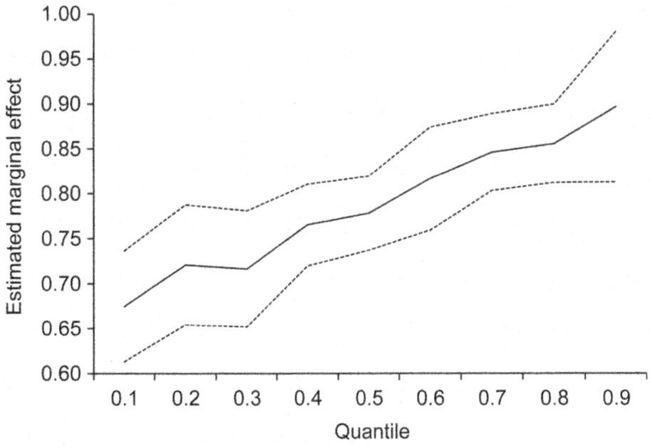

Fig. 4. Estimated marginal effect of the start-up rate in $t-3$ on the start-up rates in t_0 in West Germany (dotted lines indicate upper and lower confidence intervals; bootstrapped standard errors with 1000 replications)

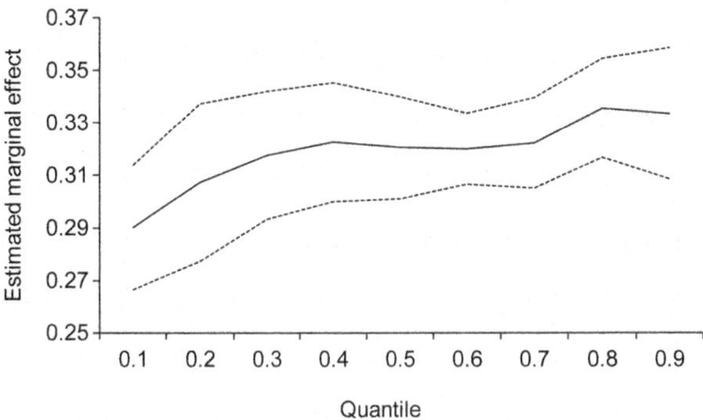

Fig. 5. Estimated marginal effect of the self-employment rate in $t-3$ on the start-up rates in t_0 in West Germany (dotted lines indicate upper and lower confidence intervals; bootstrapped standard errors with 1000 replications)

pattern of persistency of regional entrepreneurship is mainly caused by the relatively stable framework conditions during this period or whether persistence can be found over a longer period that includes some drastic changes in the economic and political environment is investigated in the following scenarios.

SCENARIO II: PERSISTENCE OF REGIONAL ENTREPRENEURSHIP IN THE FACE OF A WORLD WAR FOLLOWED BY MASSIVE IN-MIGRATION – WEST GERMANY, 1925–2005

The second scenario is characterized by considerable disruptions: the world economic crisis of 1929, the advent of the Nazi regime in 1933, the devastating Second World War, occupation by the Allied powers, massive in-migration of refugees from former territories (particularly from the East), separation into East and West Germany, reconstruction of the country, and German Reunification. The indicator for the presence of regional entrepreneurship prior to the shock events is the self-employment rate in 1925. This is the number of self-employed persons in non-agricultural private sectors divided by all employees. The historical data are based on a comprehensive survey conducted in 1925 (STATISTIK DES DEUTSCHEN REICHS, 1927). The definition of administrative districts at this time is much different from what is defined as a district today. Nevertheless, it is possible to assign the historical districts to the current planning regions. The self-employment rate in 1925 measures the share of role models within the total regional employment, thereby reflecting how widespread self-employment was across regions prior to the disruptive shock events.[17]

Fig. 6 shows the distribution of self-employment rates across the regions of Germany in 1925. A first observation is that these self-employment rates were, on average, higher in regions that became West Germany after the war. Regions with relatively high self-employment rates are especially to be found around the urban centres of Hamburg, Frankfurt, Cologne, Munich and Nuremberg. Also, the south-western part of Germany, which is known for its innovative spirit and entrepreneurial culture (for example, BATEN *et al.*, 2007), had high levels of self-employment in 1925. Regions with relatively low self-employment rates in West Germany include the Ruhr area north of Cologne, which is characterized by a high concentration of large-scale industries such as mining and steel processing, and a number of rural regions in the east and the south-east.

Correlation coefficients between the self-employment rate in 1925 and self-employment as well as start-up rates for the 1984–2005 period show a highly significant positive relationship (Table 4; for descriptive statistics, see Tables A4 and A5 in Appendix A). Regressing the start-up rates for the years 1984–2005 on the self-employment rate in 1925 reveals a significant positive effect (Table 5). Controlling for the industry structure in 1925 does not change this pattern.[18] The effect of the employment share of R&D personnel is significantly positive, like in the analysis of Scenario I, whereas population density is now insignificant. A difference to the results for Scenario I is the significantly negative effect of the unemployment rate that is in line with the analysis of FRITSCH and MUELLER (2007) for the 1984–2002 period.[19] The significant effect of the self-employment rate strongly indicates the persistence of regional differences in start-up activity over longer time periods which include several disruptive shocks to environmental conditions.

For Scenario II, quantile regressions were again applied. The aim is to discover how the effect of historical self-employment rates differs across quantiles

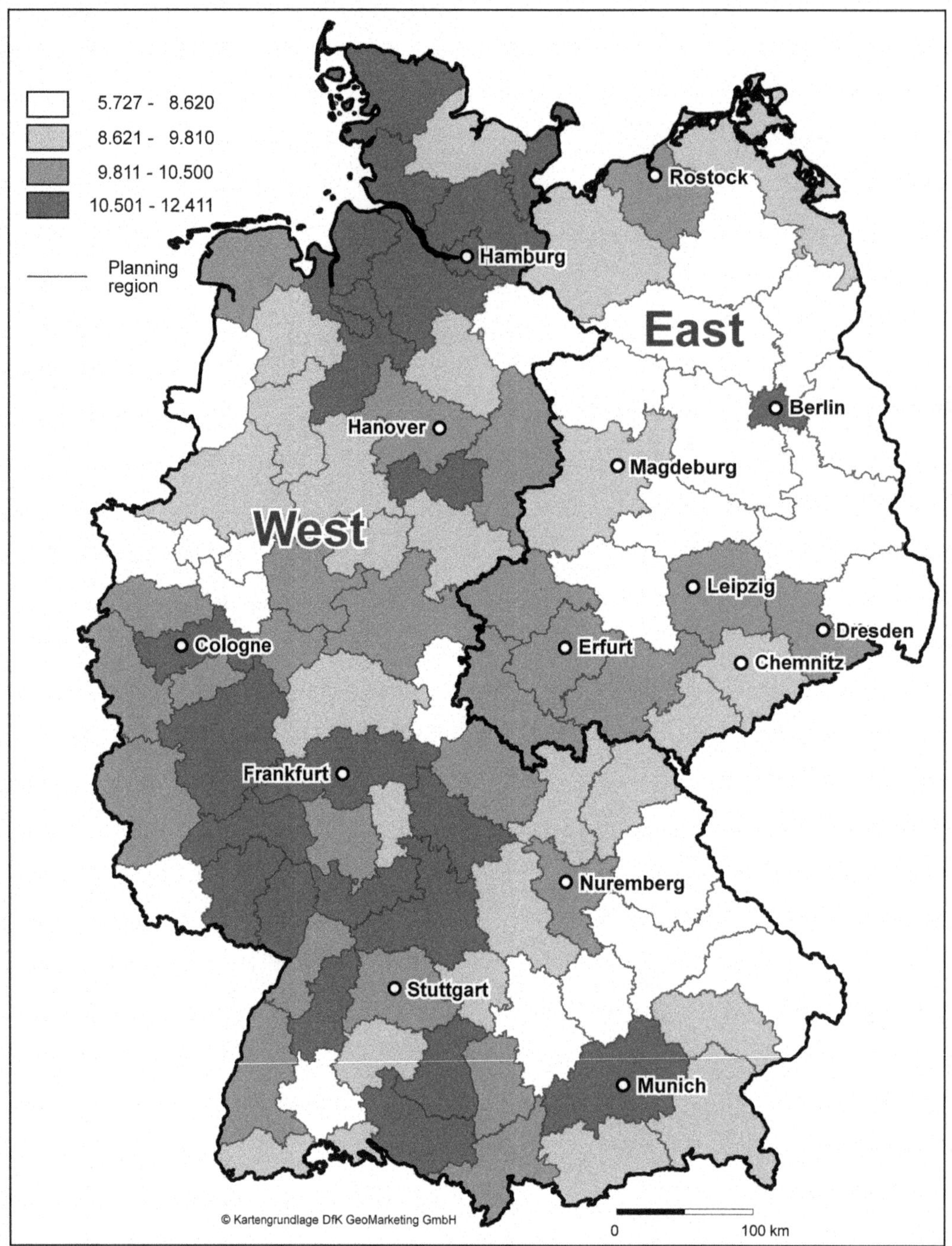

Fig. 6. Share of self-employed persons in non-agricultural sectors in total employment in German regions, 1925

(Fig. 7). The highest marginal effect can be found for the upper quartiles of the distribution. Thus, persistence is particularly pronounced in those regions that had high levels of self-employment prior to the disruptive historical shocks that characterized this scenario. Furthermore, there seems to be a threshold value around the median with respect to the estimated marginal effect. This may indicate that there is a critical value for the self-reinforcing effect of entrepreneurial culture.

SCENARIO III: PERSISTENCE OF REGIONAL ENTREPRENEURSHIP IN THE FACE OF A WORLD WAR, FORTY YEARS OF A SOCIALIST REGIME, A SHOCKING TRANSFORMATION PROCESS AND MASSIVE OUT-MIGRATION – EAST GERMANY, 1925–2005

As a result of the massive anti-entrepreneurship policy of the socialist period in East Germany, the self-employment rate

Table 4. Correlation of self-employment rate in 1925 with self-employment rates and start-up rates over time – West Germany, 1984–2005

		I	II	III
I	Self-employment rate, 1984–2005	1		
II	Start-up rate, 1984–2005	0.853***	1	
III	Self-employment rate, 1925	0.153***	0.085***	1

Note: ***Statistically significant at the 1% level.

Table 5. Effect of the self-employment rate in 1925 on regional start-up rates in West Germany, 1984–2005

	I	II	III
	Start-up rate		
Self-employment rate, 1925	0.0286**	0.0619***	0.0362**
	(0.0142)	(0.0148)	(0.0153)
Population density (log) (t – 1)	–	–	0.00537
			(0.0224)
Share R&D personnel (t – 1)	–	–	0.0608***
			(0.0188)
Unemployment rate (t – 1)	–	–	–0.0564***
			(0.0170)
Industry structure 1925	–	***	***
Federal state dummies	***	***	***
Constant	–0.430***	–0.513***	–0.482***
	(0.0590)	(0.0624)	(0.0617)
Number of observations	1349	1349	1349
F-value	209.35***	210.89***	186.20***
Adjusted R^2	0.782	0.802	0.806

Note: Dependent variable: Regional start-up rate in t_0. Pooled ordinary least squares (OLS) regressions. Robust standard errors are given in parentheses. ***Statistically significant at the 1% level; **statistically significant at the 5% level; and *statistically significant at the 10% level. There are jumps in the number of start-ups and changes in the reporting system for years after 1998, which are controlled for by employing year dummies. Running the models only for the 1984–1998 period does not lead to any significant change of the effect of the historical self-employment rate.

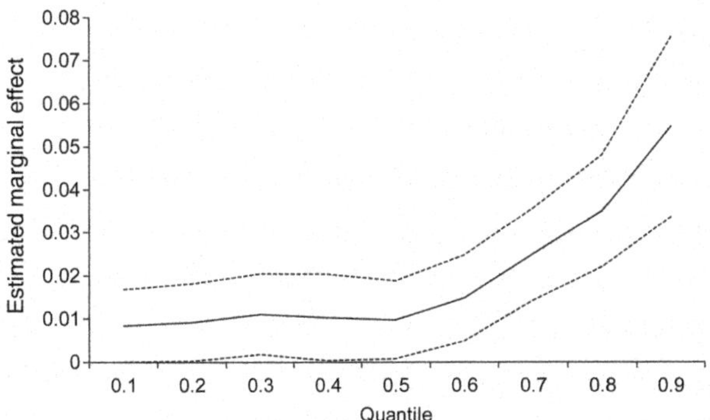

Fig. 7. Estimated marginal effect of the self-employment rate in 1925 on the start-up rates in West Germany (dotted lines indicate upper and lower confidence intervals; bootstrapped standard errors with 1000 replications)

at the end of the GDR regime in 1989 was only about 1.8% compared with 10.5% in West Germany. The few private firms in existence were primarily found in those small trades ill-served by inflexible centrally planned state firms. Remarkably, the remaining levels of self-employment were particularly high in those regions that had a pronounced entrepreneurial tradition in pre-socialist times. Further, the socialist regime was not able to crowd out self-employment equally effective across the GDR. This is, for instance, indicated by the finding that in regions with a pronounced entrepreneurial tradition, a higher share of craftsmen abstained from joining socialist handicraft cooperatives (WYRWICH, 2012).[20] Thus, regional variation in private-sector activity in 1989 can be regarded as mainly a result of variation in private initiative or of different levels of resistance to political attempts to abolish private firms. This persistence of regional entrepreneurial cultures during forty years of a socialist regime is particularly remarkable because the anti-entrepreneurial policy should have created relatively high incentives for people with an entrepreneurial mindset to leave the GDR which, in turn, certainly led to an entrepreneurial blood-letting in these regions.

With the transformation to a market economy system, new business formation in East Germany started to boom, particularly in the services and construction sectors. However, it took until 2005 – fifteen years – before the self-employment rate in East Germany matched that of West Germany. Despite the now similar levels of self-employment, however, characteristics of the new businesses in terms of industry affiliation, survival and number of employees are quite different between the two regions. Start-ups in East Germany since 1990 have been much more concentrated in sectors characterized by a small minimum efficient size, particularly construction, tourism and consumer services. They have lower survival rates (FRITSCH *et al.*, 2013) and, on average, fewer employees than new businesses set up in West Germany during the same period. In short, East Germany did not become a carbon copy of West Germany but is instead, due to its socialist legacy, a distinct regional growth regime (FRITSCH, 2004).

Analysing the persistence of East German start-up rates in successive years is limited by the relatively short time series of available data and by the turbulence of the transformation process, which was particularly pronounced during the 1990s. Therefore, this analysis is restricted to start-up rates for 2000–2005 and include only the start-up rate of the previous period (t – 1) so as not to lose too many observations. The spatial framework consists of the twenty-two East German planning regions. The region of Berlin is excluded since the data do not allow one to distinguish between the eastern and western part of the city, the latter of which was not under socialist regime. Information on the self-employment rate in 1925, the self-employment rate at the end of the socialist period in 1989,[21] and the start-up rates during the 2000–2005 period is used.

A first result is that there is a significant positive relationship between the regional self-employment rates for 1925, 1989 and 2000–2005, indicating high levels of persistence of entrepreneurship despite a number of severe shocks (Table 6). The significantly positive correlation of self-employment in 1925 with that in 1989, which marks the demise of the GDR regime, is particularly remarkable. This statistical relationship indicates that the policy of crowding out private firms during the socialist regime had weaker effects in areas with high levels of self-employment before the Second World War. This may be regarded as an indication of regional differences in resistance to anti-entrepreneurship policies that are reflective of strong entrepreneurial intentions and the strength of a regional entrepreneurship culture. High levels of continuing self-employment are found in regions that had a relatively strong tradition in the manufacturing sector prior to the war, such as Chemnitz and Dresden (Fig. 8) (for a more detailed description, see WYRWICH, 2012). One way how entrepreneurial culture may have survived is intergenerational transmission via parental or grand parental role models in self-employment (for

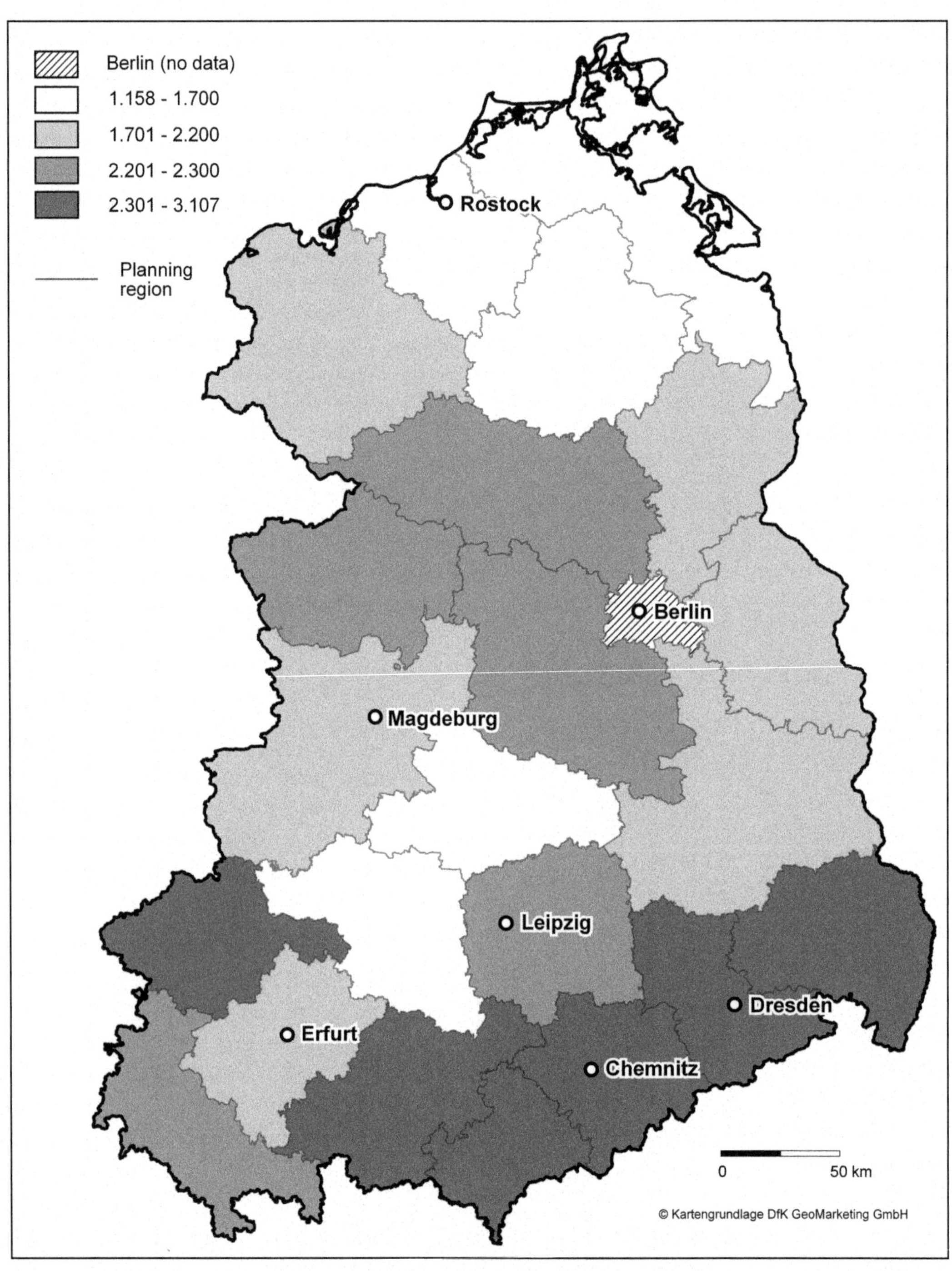

Fig. 8. Self-employment rates in East German regions, 1989

Table 6. Correlation between self-employment rates in 1925, 1989 and 2000–2005, and start-up rates in 2000–2005 in East German regions

		I	II	III
I	Self-employment rates, 2000–2005	1		
II	Start-up rates, 2000–2005	0.486***	1	
III	Self-employment rate, 1925	0.290***	–0.105	1
IV	Self-employment rate, 1989	0.391***	–0.235***	0.308***

Note: ***Statistically significant at the 1% level.

example, CHLOSTA *et al.*, 2012; DOHMEN *et al.*, 2012; LASPITA *et al.*, 2012). Furthermore, there might have been a favourable collective memory about the merits of entrepreneurship in areas where it played an important role for economic prosperity in the past.

During the 2000–2005 period, the correlation coefficient between the start-up rate in year t and in $t-1$ in East German regions is 0.846, indicating a high level of persistence. However, the relationship between the self-employment rate of 1989 and the start-up rates of the 2000–2005 period is significantly negative (Table 6). This result is most certainly driven by transition-specific effects, such as the booming new business formation particularly in the construction sector and in small-scale consumer services, a sector that was highly underdeveloped in the GDR economy. Many of these service-sector start-ups occurred out of necessity due to a lack of other job opportunities available. This interpretation is consistent with the significantly negative correlation between the unemployment rate with the self-employment rates in 1925 and 1989 (see Table A5 in Appendix A). This indicates that regions with high remnants of entrepreneurial culture experienced a comparatively positive labour market development after transition. In any case, the level of local unemployment that was mainly caused by the transition to a market economy might confound a positive effect of the historical self-employment rate on start-up activity. Accordingly, a significantly positive effect of the historical self-employment rates is found when controlling for local unemployment in a multivariate framework (Table 7).

Table 7. Effect of self-employment rates in 1925 and 1989 on current levels of new business formation in East Germany, 2000–2005 (Scenario III)[a]

	I	II	III	IV	V
			Start-up rate		
Start-up rate ($t-1$)	0.365***	–	–	–	–
	(0.0789)				
Self-employment rate, 1925	–	0.145**	0.147**	0.260***	–
		(0.0600)	(0.0624)	(0.0856)	
Self-employment rate, 1989	–	–	–	–	0.247**
					(0.0953)
Population density (log) ($t-1$)	–0.157**	–	–	–0.111	0.134
	(0.0728)			(0.111)	(0.104)
Share R&D personnel ($t-1$)	0.264***	–	–	0.117	0.0627
	(0.0846)			(0.108)	(0.100)
Unemployment rate ($t-1$)	0.0818*	–	–	0.134**	0.107**
	(0.0456)			(0.0590)	(0.0537)
Industry structure, 1925	–	–	***	***	***
Federal state dummies	***	***	***	***	***
Constant	–0.441***	–0.652***	–0.712***	–0.844***	–0.764***
	(0.0953)	(0.100)	(0.148)	(0.174)	(0.199)
Number of observations	110	110	110	110	110
F-value	9.16***	9.44***	9.00***	7.47***	6.67***
Adjusted R^2	0.433	0.341	0.404	0.444	0.420

Notes: Dependent variable: regional start-up rate in t_0. Pooled ordinary least squares (OLS) regressions. Robust standard errors are given in parentheses. ***Statistically significant at the 1% level; **statistically significant at the 5% level; and *statistically significant at the 10% level. Newey–West standard errors for Model I were alternatively employed since the lagged start-up rate was used in this specification. The resulting standard errors are hardly different.

[a]Lagrange Multiplier tests reveal that there is no spatial autocorrelation in the models of Scenario III. The opening of the West Berlin economy may have had a special impact on start-up activity in the adjacent regions that comprise the planning regions of the federal state of Brandenburg. Such an effect is controlled for in the regression by the respective federal state dummy. There is an additional dummy control variable indicating planning regions that are adjacent to West Berlin because the effect of regional integration might be more pronounced there. Abstaining from this distinction only slightly changes the results. Since East Germany (excluding Berlin for reasons explained in the text) consists of five federal states, the regressions for East Germany include four dummies for federal states (plus a reference category and the dummy indicating co-location with West Berlin).

The regression analysis for East Germany shows a considerable persistence of regional start-up rates in the 2000–2005 period (Model I in Table 7). Also, the share of R&D personnel, population density and the unemployment rate are statistically significant with the expected signs. Models II–IV also show a significant positive effect of the self-employment rate of 1925, and the self-employment rate of 1989 also proves to have a highly significant positive effect (Model V). The results strongly indicate persistence of regional entrepreneurship. Interestingly, the coefficient for the standardized self-employment rate in 1925 in Model IV is not smaller but even slightly (but not statistically significant) higher than the coefficient for the self-employment rate in 1989 employed in Model V. This can be regarded a further indication for the strong long-term influence of entrepreneurial culture. Quantile regressions using Model IV show that the effect of the self-employment rate in 1925 on current start-up activity is strongest for those regions with the highest levels of self-employment eighty years earlier (Fig. 9). Remarkably, the increase of the marginal effect with rising historical self-employment rates is not as straightforward as in Scenario II. This might be explained by the much more intensive disruptive shocks in East Germany that might have damaged the entrepreneurial culture.

The findings for Scenario III demonstrate that there is significant persistence of regional differences in entrepreneurship over long periods of time and they have even survived four decades of socialism characterized by a massive anti-entrepreneurship policy. That regional entrepreneurship has sustained under these hostile circumstances suggests that a regional entrepreneurship culture, once established, may be rather robust.

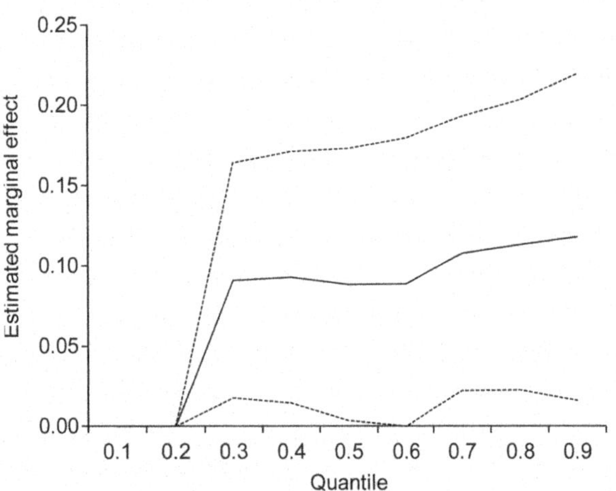

Fig. 9. Estimated marginal effect of the self-employment rate in 1925 on the start-up rates in East Germany (dotted lines indicate upper and lower confidence intervals; bootstrapped standard errors with 1000 replications)

DISCUSSION AND CONCLUSIONS

This empirical investigation has revealed pronounced persistence of self-employment and start-up rates in German regions over long periods of time, which is a strong indication for the presence of a regional entrepreneurship culture that has long-lasting effects. The fact that such a regional culture of entrepreneurship can survive even abrupt and harsh changes in environmental conditions, such as, in the case of East Germany, the Second World War and forty years of a socialist regime (Scenario III), shows that persistence of entrepreneurship is only partially due to stability in the regional determinants of entrepreneurship. It turns out that a regional culture of entrepreneurship can survive the destruction of supportive infrastructure, as was the case in East Germany during forty years of its socialist regime. The findings for East Germany are particularly strong evidence that peer effects and regional norms and values can create an entrepreneurship-friendly 'mental software' in the regional population that is not forgotten in times of hostile environmental conditions. This result is even more remarkable given the massive migration into West German regions and out of East German regions after the Second World War. Obviously, a regional culture of entrepreneurship is a strong force that, once developed, can survive and influence regional development for long periods of time. This finding is in accordance with other research that shows a high stability of informal institutions over time (NORTH, 1994; WILLIAMSON, 2000). History matters!

The high level of persistence of regional entrepreneurship found implies not only long-term effects once an entrepreneurial culture has developed, but also the stability of regional levels of self-employment and new business formation strongly suggests that the establishment of an entrepreneurial culture may require long periods of time and considerable political effort. Hence, trying to build a regional entrepreneurial culture can be regarded as an investment in a kind of capital stock that may have a main effect only in the long run, but which will be a long-lasting one.

The results give rise to a number of important questions. The first question concerns the sources of a regional entrepreneurship culture. How does a regional culture of entrepreneurship emerge and what can policy do to stimulate the development of such a culture? Analyses of historical examples of the emergence of an entrepreneurship culture may be particularly helpful for answering these questions. Knowledge about the emergence of high levels of regional entrepreneurship is currently rather limited, leaving much room for speculation. In many regions the sources of an entrepreneurship culture may be deeply rooted in economic history. Perhaps the type of agriculture that prevailed in a region, for example, large-scale farming with many employees (like in northeast Germany) versus small family-run farms (such as are found in the German region Baden-Wuerttemberg), plays a role. Differences in the structure of agriculture may be based in socio-political reasons, but they may also have to do with the quality of the soil or with certain social practices, such as the mode of inheritance. If, for example, it has been common practice in a region to divide the land among the beneficiaries in real terms (*Realteilung*), the resulting small lots created an incentive to shift economic activity toward some type of craft business, perhaps first as a secondary occupation that later became the main source of income. This is an often-heard explanation for the emergence of an economic structure characterized by relatively many small firms in some regions in the south of Germany. This type of economic shift would not have been so likely to occur, however, if land was cohesively transferred to one beneficiary only (*Anerberecht*), as was the case in other regions of Germany. Such examples suggest that attempts to explain the emergence of a regional entrepreneurship culture will need to reach far back into the economic history of regions.

A second important question is how a culture of entrepreneurship, once established, is transmitted across generations and can persist through severe changes in environmental conditions. Recent research has demonstrated the importance of role models and peer-effects that may partly explain the persistence of such a culture (BOSMA *et al.*, 2012; CHLOSTA *et al.*, 2012; DOHMEN *et al.*, 2012; LASPITA *et al.*, 2012). There is compelling evidence that high levels of regional new business formation can be an important source of growth (for an overview, see FRITSCH, 2013). There may, however, be further factors that are important for the persistence that should be subject to further research.[22]

A third question not touched on in this paper but which is left for further analysis is the effect of a regional culture of entrepreneurship on regional development. Given the compelling empirical evidence showing a positive contribution of new business formation to regional growth, it should be expected that regions with such a culture can draw long-term benefits and are better able to cope with the challenges of their external environment. Hence, the analysis of long-term growth trajectories may reveal the full effects of entrepreneurial culture.

Acknowledgements – This paper is based on research conducted within the framework of the Collaborative Research Center 'Social Developments in Post-Socialist Societies – Discontinuity, Tradition, Structural Formation' at the universities of Halle and Jena, Germany. The authors are indebted to the German Research Foundation (DFG) for financial support. Special thanks are extended to Martin Andersson, Robert Gold, Sierdjan Koster and the anonymous referees for helpful comments on earlier versions of this paper.

APPENDIX A

Table A1. *Descriptive statistics for West Germany*

	Mean	Median	Minimum	Maximum	SD
Self-employment rate, 1984–2005	0.091	0.086	0.055	0.205	0.021
Start-up rate (per 1000 individuals), 1984–2005	7.932	6.838	3.981	25.901	3.096
Self-employment rate, 1925	0.097	0.098	0.057	0.124	0.012
Population density (log), 1987–2005	5.426	5.288	4.279	7.125	0.662
Share of research and development (R&D) personnel, 1987–2005	0.027	0.024	0.007	0.078	0.012
Unemployment rate, 1987–2005	0.087	0.083	0.030	0.177	0.028

Note: SD, standard deviation.

Table A2. *Correlation matrix for West Germany*

		I	II	III	IV	V
I	Self-employment rate, 1987–2005	1				
II	Start-up rate, 1984–2005	0.838***	1			
III	Self-employment rate, 1925	0.150***	0.081***	1		
IV	Population density (log), 1987–2005	–0.359***	–0.056*	–0.097***	1	
V	Share of research and development (R&D) personnel, 1987–2005	–0.202***	–0.022	0.214***	0.539***	1
VI	Unemployment rate, 1987–2005	–0.048*	0.157***	–0.151***	0.183***	–0.107***

Note: ***Statistically significant at the 1% level; **statistically significant at the 5% level; and *statistically significant at the 10% level.

Table A3. Correlations for the persistence of potential determinants of new business formation in East and West Germany over time

	$t-1$	$t-5$	$t-10$	$t-15$	$t-20$
West Germany, 1984–2005					
Population density t_0	1.000***	0.9995***	0.999***	0.998***	0.996***
Share of R&D personnel t_0	0.998***	0.980***	0.955***	0.941***	0.907***
Unemployment rate t_0	0.985***	0.924***	0.866***	0.842***	0.745***
East Germany, 2001–2005					
Population density t_0	1.000***	0.999***	–	–	–
Share of R&D personnel t_0	0.893***	0.955***	–	–	–
Unemployment rate t_0	0.949***	0.889***	–	–	–

Notes: ***Statistically significant at the 1% level.
R&D, research and development.

Table A4. Descriptive statistics for East Germany

	Mean	Median	Minimum	Maximum	SD
Self-employment rate, 2000–2005	0.092	0.092	0.077	0.105	0.006
Start-up rate (per 1000 individuals), 2000–2005	10.516	10.382	7.918	14.525	1.397
Self-employment rate, 1925	0.090	0.089	0.078	0.102	0.008
Self-employment rate, 1989	0.021	0.022	0.012	0.031	0.005
Population density (log), 2001–2005	4.795	4.776	3.876	5.704	0.517
Share of research and development (R&D) personnel, 2001–2005	0.025	0.024	0.010	0.051	0.008
Unemployment rate, 2001–2005	0.197	0.197	0.128	0.260	0.026

Note: SD, standard deviation.

Table A5. Correlation matrix for East Germany

		I	II	III	IV	V	VI
I	Self-employment rate, 2000–2005	1.000***					
II	Start-up rate, 2000–2005	0.489***	1.000***				
III	Self-employment rate, 1925	0.293***	–0.150	1.000***			
IV	Self-employment rate, 1989	0.391***	–0.268***	0.308***	1.000***		
V	Population density (log), 2001–2005	0.087	–0.330***	0.536***	0.569***	1.000***	
VI	Share of research and development (R&D) personnel, 2001–2005	–0.148	–0.209**	0.233**	0.247***	0.589***	1.000***
VII	Unemployment rate, 2001–2005	–0.375***	0.123	–0.491***	–0.454***	–0.366***	–0.339***

Note: ***Statistically significant at the 1% level; and **statistically significant at the 5% level.

NOTES

1. Although formal and informal institutions are related, other factors may play a rather significant role. This is evidenced by the observation that the extent of an entrepreneurship culture can strongly vary across regions within a country that are characterized by the same framework of formal institutions (for example, ANDERSSON, 2012; BEUGELSDIJK, 2007; DAVIDSSON, 1995; DAVIDSSON and WIKLUND, 1997; ETZIONI, 1987; WESTLUND and BOLTON, 2003).
2. This is an implication of the highly significantly positive effect of the small business employment share on the regional level of start-ups (for example, FRITSCH and FALCK, 2007) because such a high share of employment in small businesses indicates the presence of relatively many firms and entrepreneurs.
3. '[I]n addition to economic circumstances, the local amount of entrepreneurial activity is itself an important variable in determining individual decisions whether to act upon a recognized opportunity. In other words, I argue that entrepreneurship creates a "culture" of itself that influences individual behavior in its favor' (MINNITI, 2005, p. 3).
4. DUBINI (1989) distinguishes between munificent and sparse entrepreneurial environments. A munificent entrepreneurial environment is characterized by a large number of entrepreneurial role models, an efficient infrastructure, well-established capital markets, and the availability of opportunities and incentives for starting entrepreneurial ventures. A sparse entrepreneurial environment lacks not only the values, culture and tradition of entrepreneurship, but also the necessary infrastructure, well-functioning capital markets and innovation activities that may generate entrepreneurial opportunities, as well as government incentives. Hence, incentives for starting firms in such an environment are rather low.

5. If available, alternative indicators for new business formation and self-employment from other sources tend to be highly correlated with the data used here.
6. There are actually seventy-four West German planning regions. For administrative reasons, the cities of Hamburg and Bremen are defined as planning regions even though they are not functional economic units. To avoid distortions, the official definition of planning regions was adjusted by merging these two cities with adjacent planning regions. Therefore, Hamburg was merged with the region of Schleswig-Holstein South and Hamburg-Umland South. Bremen was merged with Bremen-Umland. Thus, the number of regions in the sample was seventy-one.
7. Start-ups in agriculture were not considered in the analysis because self-employment in this sector must be regarded a special case and shaped by factors rather different from those relevant in other parts of the economy. Further, this sector is characterized by a high employment contribution of helping family members who are not captured in the Social Insurance Statistics.
8. The highest regional start-up rates (over twenty start-ups per 1000 workforces) are more than five times larger than the lowest start-up rates (about four start-ups per 1000 workforce).
9. According to a different database – the German Micro Census – that measures the number of founders instead of the number of start-ups and which also comprises new businesses without employees, the East German start-up rate reached the West German level in 2004 and has been slightly above the value for West Germany since 2005 (FRITSCH *et al.*, 2012). This clearly indicates a higher share of start-ups without any employee in East Germany, many of them probably founded out of necessity due to relatively high unemployment rates in this part of the country.
10. This procedure was also applied for the analyses of the second and third scenarios.
11. R&D employees over total employment. R&D employees are defined as those with tertiary degrees working as engineers or natural scientists (source: German Social Insurance Statistics).
12. The German federal states (*Laender*) are an important level of policy-making. Germany consists of sixteen federal states: West Germany comprises ten federal states and East Germany consists of six federal states (including Berlin). As mentioned above, the planning regions for the cities of Hamburg and Bremen, each representing a federal state, were merged with surrounding planning regions that belong to other federal states. Since these two newly created regions do not represent their own political units, they were used as a reference category when including dummy variables for federal states.
13. Population density (as well as alternative measures such as employment density or market size in terms of population) and the share of R&D personnel are highly correlated ($r = 0.54$). The correlation between population density and employment density is 0.98. The correlation between the number of population and population density is 0.68. Excluding the share of R&D personnel makes the effect of population density insignificant. This suggests that density as such does not have a significant effect.
14. FRITSCH and MUELLER (2007) found a negative effect of the local unemployment rate. Restricting the period to the years analysed by Fritsch and Mueller makes the unemployment rate significantly negative in Model I and insignificant in Model II.
15. Running the model with the start-up rate in $t-1$, $t-2$ or $t-4$ does not lead to any significant changes in the results. The same pattern emerges if the model is run without the control variables that are included in the models presented in Table 2.
16. The quantile regressions were restricted to the period 1984–1998 because including the years 1999–2005 leads to somewhat fuzzy results that are obviously caused by an abrupt increase of the recorded level of start-up activity between 1998 and 1999. This jump in the data is probably due to some post-1998 changes in the reporting system of the Social Insurance Statistics.
17. Unfortunately, the historical data do not contain information about the number of start-ups. Furthermore, there is only limited information on the planning region that comprises the federal state of Saarland since parts of this area did not belong to Germany in 1925. The information on the remaining districts is used. Excluding these areas (which equals omitting one observation per year) does not change the results.
18. The employment shares of three large economic sectors – construction, manufacturing and other industries – in 1925 were used to control for the economic structure of the regional economy. This will avoid the fact that the self-employment rate mainly reflects the industry structure in that year.
19. As mentioned in the fourth section, the positive effect for the regional unemployment rate found in the framework of Scenario I (Tables 2 and 3) is presumably shaped by programmes for promoting start-ups by unemployed people that have been introduced after 2002. If the years 2003–2005 are excluded, the coefficient for the unemployment rate is always negative.
20. This may be regarded as an indication that the attempts of the socialist GDR regime to battle entrepreneurship particularly in regions with high levels of self-employment has been of rather limited success.
21. The information on self-employment in 1989 was obtained from the GDR Statistical Office and adjusted to the actual definition of spatial units (for details, see KAWKA, 2007). The self-employment rate in 1989 is the number of self-employed divided by the number of all employees. Unfortunately, the available data do not provide information about the economic sectors of the businesses.
22. Another factor that can contribute to persistence is path dependency. If new business formation has a positive effect on regional development, then high levels of growth may lead to high start-up rates in future periods making new business formation not only a source, but also a symptom of growth (ANYADIKE-DANES *et al.*, 2011). However, given the severe external shocks that German regions have experienced in the period under inspection in this paper, particularly the destruction of the country in the Second World War, such an explanation can be hardly regarded as plausible for the German example that has been analysed herein.

REFERENCES

ACS Z. and MUELLER P. (2008) Employment effects of business dynamics: mice, gazelles and elephants, *Small Business Economics* **30**, 85–100.

ALESINA A. and FUCHS-SCHUENDELN N. (2007) Good-bye Lenin (or not?): the effect of communism on people's preferences, *American Economic Review* **97**, 1507–1528.

ANDERSSON M. (2012) Start-up rates, entrepreneurship culture and the business cycle – Swedish patterns from national and regional data, in BRAUNERHJELM P. (Ed.) *Entrepreneurship, Norms and the Business Cycle – Swedish Economic Forum Report 2012*, pp. 91–110. Entreprenörskapsforum, Stockholm.

ANDERSSON M. and KOSTER S. (2011) Sources of persistence in regional start-up rates – evidence from Sweden, *Journal of Economic Geography* **11**, 179–201.

ANYADIKE-DANES M., HART M. and LENIHAN H. (2011) New business formation in a rapidly growing economy: the Irish experience, *Small Business Economics* **36**, 503–516.

AOYAMA Y. (2009) Entrepreneurship and regional culture: the case of Hamamatsu and Kyoto, Japan, *Regional Studies* **43**, 495–512.

AUDRETSCH D. B. and FRITSCH M. (1994) On the measurement of entry rates, *Empirica* **21**, 105–113.

AUDRETSCH D. B. and KEILBACH M. (2004) Entrepreneurship capital and economic performance, *Regional Studies* **38**, 949–959.

BATEN J., SPADAVECCHIA A., STREB J. and YING S. (2007) What made southwest German firms innovative around 1900? Assessing the importance of intra- and inter-industry externalities, *Oxford Economic Papers* **59**, 105–126.

BECKER S. O., BOECKH K., HAINZ C. and WOESSMANN L. (2010) *The Empire is Dead, Long Live the Empire! Long-Run Persistence of Trust and Corruption in Bureaucracy.* CEPR Discussion Paper Number 8288. Centre for Economic Policy Research (CEPR), London.

BERENTSEN W. H. (1992) The socialist face of the GDR: Eastern Germany's landscape – past, present, and future, *Landscape and Urban Planning* **22**, 137–151.

BEUGELSDIJK S. (2007) Entrepreneurial culture, regional innovativeness and economic growth, *Journal of Evolutionary Economics* **17**, 187–210.

BEUGELSDIJK S. and NOORDERHAVEN N. (2004) Entrepreneurial attitude and economic growth: a cross-section of 54 regions, *Annals of Regional Science* **38**, 199–218.

BONEVA B. S. and FRIEZE I. H. (2001) Toward a concept of a migrant personality, *Journal of Social Issues* **57**, 477–491.

BOSMA N., HESSELS J., SCHUTJENS V., VAN PRAAG M. and VERHEUL I. (2012) Entrepreneurship and role models, *Journal of Economic Psychology* **33**, 410–424.

BOSMA N. and SCHUTJENS V. (2011) Understanding regional variation in entrepreneurial activity and entrepreneurial attitude in Europe, *Annals of Regional Science* **47**, 711–742.

BREZINSKI H. (1987) The second economy in the GDR – pragmatism is gaining ground, *Studies in Comparative Communism* **20**, 85–101.

BREZINSKI H. and FRITSCH M. (1995) Transformation: the shocking German way, *Moct-Most* **5(4)**, 1–25.

BURCHARDI K. B. and HASSAN T. A. (2013) The economic impact of social ties: evidence from German reunification, *Quarterly Journal of Economics* **128(3)**, 1219–1271.

BURDA M. C. and HUNT J. (2001) From reunification to economic integration: productivity and the labor market in Eastern Germany, *Brookings Papers on Economic Activity* **2**, 1–92.

CHLOSTA S., PATZELT H., KLEIN S. B. and DORMANN C. (2012) Parental role models and the decision to become self-employed: the moderating effect of personality, *Small Business Economics* **38**, 121–138.

DAVIDSSON P. (1995) Culture, structure and regional levels of entrepreneurship, *Entrepreneurship and Regional Development* **7**, 41–62.

DAVIDSSON P. and WIKLUND J. (1997) Values, beliefs and regional variations in new firm formation rates, *Journal of Economic Psychology* **18**, 179–199.

DOHMEN T., FALK A., HUFFMAN D. and SUNDE U. (2012) The intergenerational transmission of risk and trust attitudes, *Review of Economic Studies* **79**, 645–677.

DUBINI P. (1989) The influence of motivations and environments on business start-ups: some hints for public policy, *Journal of Business Venturing* **4**, 11–26.

EBBINGHAUS F. (2003) *Ausnutzung und Verdrängung: Steuerungsprobleme der SED-Mittelstandspolitik 1955–1972.* Duncker & Humblot, Berlin.

ETZIONI A. (1987) Entrepreneurship, adaptation and legitimation, *Journal of Economic Behavior and Organization* **8**, 175–199.

FORNAHL D. (2003) Entrepreneurial activities in a regional context, in FORNAHL D. and BRENNER T. (Eds) *Cooperation, Networks, and Institutions in Regional Innovation Systems*, pp. 38–57. Edward Elgar, Cheltenham.

FREYTAG A. and THURIK R. (2007) Entrepreneurship and its determinants in a cross-country setting, *Journal of Evolutionary Economics* **17**, 117–131.

FRITSCH M. (2004) Entrepreneurship, entry and performance of new businesses compared in two growth regimes: East and West Germany, *Journal of Evolutionary Economics* **14**, 525–542.

FRITSCH M. (2013) New business formation and regional development – a survey and assessment of the evidence, *Foundations and Trends in Entrepreneurship* **9**, 249–364.

FRITSCH M. and FALCK O. (2007) New business formation by industry over space and time: a multi-dimensional analysis, *Regional Studies* **41**, 157–172.

Fritsch M., Kritikos A. and Rusakova A. (2012) *Who Starts a Business and Who is Self-Employed in Germany?* Jena Economic Research Papers Number 001-2012. Friedrich Schiller University and Max Planck Institute of Economics, Jena.

Fritsch M. and Mueller P. (2007) The persistence of regional new business formation-activity over time – assessing the potential of policy promotion programs, *Journal of Evolutionary Economics* **17**, 299–315.

Fritsch M., Noseleit F. and Schindele Y. (2013) *Surviving Against the Tide: The Role of Region and Industry Performance for New Business Survival.* Mimeo, Jena and Groningen.

Hall J. B. and Ludwig U. (1995) German unification and the 'market adoption' hypothesis, *Cambridge Journal of Economics* **19**, 491–507.

Hunt J. (2006) Staunching emigration from East Germany: age and the determinants of migration, *Journal of the European Economic Association* **4**, 1014–1037.

Jokela M. (2009) Personality predicts migration within and between U.S. states, *Journal of Personality Research* **43**, 79–83.

Kawka R. (2007) Regional disparities in the GDR: do they still matter?, in Lentz S. (Ed.) *German Annual of Spatial Research and Policy: Restructuring Eastern Germany*, pp. 111–122. Springer, Berlin.

Lafuente E., Vaillant Y. and Rialp J. (2007) Regional differences in the influence of role models: comparing the entrepreneurial process of rural Catalonia, *Regional Studies* **41**, 779–795.

Laspita S., Breugst N., Heblich S. and Patzelt H. (2012) Intergenerational transmission of entrepreneurial intentions, *Journal of Business Venturing* **27**, 414–435.

Marshall A. (1920) *Principles of Economics*, 8th Edn. Macmillan, London.

Minniti M. (2005) Entrepreneurship and network externalities, *Journal of Economic Behavior and Organization* **57**, 1–27.

Mueller P., van Stel A. and Storey D. J. (2008) The effect of new firm formation on regional development over time: the case of Great Britain, *Small Business Economics* **30**, 59–71.

Newman K. L. (2000) Organizational transformation during institutional upheaval, *Academy of Management Review* **25**, 602–619.

North D. C. (1994) Economic performance through time, *American Economic Review* **84**, 359–368.

Pickel A. (1992) *Radical Transitions: The Survival and Revival of Entrepreneurship in the GDR.* Westview, Boulder, CO.

Sorenson O. and Audia P. G. (2000) The social structure of entrepreneurial activity: geographic concentration of footwear production in the United States, 1940–1989, *American Journal of Sociology* **106**, 424–462.

Spengler A. (2008) The establishment history panel, *Schmollers Jahrbuch/Journal of Applied Social Science Studies* **128**, 501–509.

Statistik des Deutschen Reichs (1927) *Volks-, Berufs- und Betriebszählung vom 16. Juni 1925: Die berufliche und soziale Gliederung der Bevölkerung in den Ländern und Landesteilen. Band*, pp. 403–405. Reimar Hobbing, Berlin.

Thomas M. (1996) How to become an entrepreneur in East Germany: conditions, steps and effects of the constitution of new entrepreneurs, in Brezinski H. and Fritsch M. (Eds) *The Economic Impact of New Firms in Post-Socialist Countries – Bottom Up Transformation in Eastern Europe*, pp. 227–232. Edward Elgar, Cheltenham.

Van Stel A. and Suddle K. (2008) The impact of new firm formation on regional development in the Netherlands, *Small Business Economics* **30**, 31–47.

Voigtlaender N. and Voth H.-J. (2012) Persecution perpetuated: the medieval origins of anti-Semitic violence in Nazi Germany, *Quarterly Journal of Economics* **127**, 1339–1392.

Wagner J. and Sternberg R. (2004) Start-up activities, individual characteristics, and the regional milieu: lessons for entrepreneurship support policies from German micro data, *Annals of Regional Science* **38**, 219–40.

Westlund H. and Bolton R. (2003) Local social capital and entrepreneurship, *Small Business Economics* **21**, 77–113.

White H. (1980) A heteroskedasticity-consistent covariance matrix estimator and a direct test for heteroskedasticity, *Econometrica* **48**, 817–838.

Williamson O. (2000) The new institutional economics: taking stock, looking ahead, *Journal of Economic Literature* **38**, 595–613.

Wyrwich M. (2012) Regional entrepreneurial heritage in a socialist and a post-socialist economy, *Economic Geography* **88**, 423–445.

Start-ups and Local Entrepreneurial Social Capital in the Municipalities of Sweden

HANS WESTLUND*†, JOHAN P. LARSSON† and AMY RADER OLSSON*
**KTH, Royal Institute of Technology, Department of Urban Planning and Environment, Stockholm, Sweden.*
†Jönköping International Business School, JIBS, Jönköping, Sweden.

WESTLUND H., LARSSON J. P. and OLSSON A. R. Start-ups and local entrepreneurial social capital in the municipalities of Sweden, *Regional Studies*. This paper contains one of the first empirical attempts to investigate the influence of local entrepreneurial social capital (ESC) on start-up propensity. A unique database, including not only total start-ups but also data on start-ups divided into six sectors, is used to study the impact of ESC on start-ups per capita. The results support the hypothesis that social capital, measured both as (1) firm perception of local public attitudes to entrepreneurship and (2) the share of small businesses influences start-up propensity in Swedish municipalities. The findings also support previous results suggesting that social capital has a somewhat stronger influence in rural areas than in urban areas.

Social capital   Entrepreneurship   Start-ups   Attitudes

WESTLUND H., LARSSON J. P. and OLSSON A. R. 瑞典城市中的新创企业与地方创业社会资本，*区域研究*。本文包含探讨地方创业社会资本（ESC）对新创企业倾向之影响的初步经验性尝试。本研究运用不仅涵盖所有新创企业、更包含依据六大部门划分数据的特殊数据集，研究地方创业社会资本对新创企业的平均影响。研究结果支持以下假说：同时做为（1）企业对于地方对创业精神的公众态度之认知，以及（2）小型企业比例的社会资本，影响着瑞典城市中新创企业的倾向。研究发现同时支持过去主张社会资本在乡村地区较城市地区更具有影响力之研究结果。

社会资本   创业精神   新创企业   态度

WESTLUND H., LARSSON J. P. et OLSSON A. R. La création d'entreprises et le capital social entrepreneurial local dans les municipalités suédoises, *Regional Studies*. Cet article comprend l'une des premières tentatives empiriques d'étudier l'impact du capital social entrepreneurial local (entrepreneurial social capital; ESC) sur la propension à créer une entreprise. On emploie une banque de données unique, y compris non seulement la création d'entreprises globale mais aussi des données sur la création d'entreprises ventilées en fonction de six secteurs, pour étudier l'impact de l'ESC sur la création d'entreprises par tête. Les résultats confirment l'hypothèse que le capital social, interprété à la fois comme (1) le point de vue des entreprises quant aux réactions du public vis-à-vis de l'esprit d'entreprise et (2) la part des petites entreprises, influence la propension à créer une entreprise dans les municipalités suédoises. Les conclusions confirment aussi les résultats antérieurs qui laissent supposer que le capital social exerce un peu plus d'influence en milieu rural qu'en zone urbaine.

Capital social   Esprit d'entreprise   Création d'entreprises   Attitudes

WESTLUND H., LARSSON J. P. und OLSSON A. R. Firmengründungen und lokales unternehmerisches Sozialkapital in schwedischen Gemeinden, *Regional Studies*. Dieser Beitrag enthält einen der ersten empirischen Versuche einer Untersuchung des Einflusses von lokalem unternehmerischem Sozialkapital auf die Neigung zur Firmengründung. Anhand einer eindeutigen Datenbank, die nicht nur die Gesamtanzahl von Firmengründungen, sondern auch nach sechs Sektoren aufgegliederte Daten über neu gegründete Firmen enthält, untersuchen wir die Auswirkungen von lokalem unternehmerischem Sozialkapital auf die Anzahl der Firmengründungen pro Einwohner. Die Ergebnisse bekräftigen die Hypothese, dass sich das Sozialkapital – gemessen als (1) die Auffassung der Firmen hinsichtlich der vor Ort vorhandenen öffentlichen Einstellung zum Unternehmertum sowie als (2) der Anteil von Kleinbetrieben – auf die Neigung zur Firmengründung in schwedischen Gemeinden auswirkt. Ebenso bekräftigen die Ergebnisse frühere Resultate, die auf einen etwas größeren Einfluss des Sozialkapitals in ländlichen im Vergleich zu städtischen Gegenden schließen ließen.

Sozialkapital   Unternehmertum   Firmengründungen   Einstellungen

WESTLUND H., LARSSON J. P. y OLSSON A. R. Empresas emergentes y capital social empresarial de ámbito local en los municipios de Suecia, *Regional Studies*. Este artículo contiene uno de los primeros intentos empíricos de analizar la influencia del capital social empresarial de ámbito local en cuanto a la tendencia de crear nuevos negocios. A partir de una base de datos única, en la que se incluyen no solamente las empresas emergentes sino también datos sobre las nuevas empresas clasificadas en función de seis sectores, estudiamos el impacto del capital social empresarial en las nuevas empresas per cápita. Los resultados apoyan la hipótesis de que el capital social, medido como (1) la percepción de las empresas en cuanto a las actitudes públicas locales hacia las actividades empresariales y (2) la participación de pequeñas empresas, influye en la tendencia a crear nuevos negocios en los municipios de Suecia. Los resultados también respaldan resultados anteriores en los que se sugiere que el capital social tiene en cierta medida mayor influencia en zonas rurales que en zonas urbanas.

Capital social Empresariado Creación de empresas Actitudes

INTRODUCTION

'Entrepreneurship' has become a buzzword in contemporary policy and public debate. Policies promoting entrepreneurship in the form of start-ups are being given high priority all over the world and at all government levels. In Sweden, measures supporting entrepreneurship are among the most prioritized in the Regional Growth Programs (*Regionala Tillväxtprogram*, RTP). Recent research has shown that local governments in Sweden also adopt a broad spectrum of measures to promote local entrepreneurship (RADER OLSSON and WESTLUND, 2011). At the municipal level, public expenditures for business promotion activities were on average about €30 per inhabitant in 2009, with a variation between €0 and €490.[1]

Although entrepreneurship is generally defined as the foundation of new businesses, the concept of entrepreneurship is increasingly being defined and applied in several contexts outside its 'core' (WESTLUND, 2011). Nevertheless, the present paper limits itself to analysing entrepreneurship in the form of start-ups.

The bulk of the entrepreneurship literature focuses on its determinants or its effects, and studies the emergence and growth of firms. Although a substantial body of literature addresses the spatial dimension of entrepreneurship, this constitutes only a small proportion of all work on entrepreneurship. GREK *et al.* (2011) point out that location factors are neglected in most studies trying to explain variations in entrepreneurship. Empirical studies of the determinants of spatial variations in start-up rates are most often based on regional data, since the availability of comparable national data is far more limited (GRIES and NAUDÉ, 2009). Early contributions in this area focused on describing regional variations in start-ups (JOHNSON, 1983; KEEBLE, 1993) and their causes (STOREY and JOHNSON, 1987). Later important contributions are by, for example, FRITSCH and FALCK (2007) and STERNBERG (2009).

Entrepreneurship is considered by many to be a highly individual choice. However, several recent contributions to the entrepreneurship literature reflect an ongoing dialogue between scholars of entrepreneurship, social capital and institutional change, including SAXENIAN (1994) and JOHANNISSON (2000). These authors argue that that the individual entrepreneur requires a network of supporters and, moreover, propose that entrepreneurship involves mobilizing a support community. This suggests that social capital has an impact on entrepreneurship. Social capital is most often defined as social networks and the norms and values distributed within and between these networks (PUTNAM, 1993; ORGANISATION FOR ECONOMIC CO-OPERATION AND DEVELOPMENT (OECD), 2001; WESTLUND, 2006). The norm and value aspect of social capital is closely connected to the concept of culture, although culture, as a general, unspecified concept, is a much broader term (WESTLUND, 2006). More specified expressions of the concept of culture, as, for example, 'entrepreneurship culture', are harder to distinguish clearly from the norm and value side of social capital, since culture in this respect mainly means norms, values and attitudes towards entrepreneurship, and their expressions in habits and actions.

In this spirit it can be argued that regional variations in the rate of start-ups are connected to variations in their entrepreneurial social capital (ESC) (WESTLUND and BOLTON, 2003). In this perspective, the propensity to start new firms is (among other things) a function of local ESC, a space-bound asset that contributes to the 'place surplus' (BOLTON, 2002; WESTLUND, 2006) of a place or a region, which spurs entrepreneurship and makes the place attractive for investors, migrants and visitors.

Research on the determinants of entrepreneurship has traditionally focused on the individual qualities of the entrepreneur, or a *dispositional* approach (THORNTON, 1999; AUTIO and WENNBERG, 2009). However, during the last ten to 15 years a *contextual* approach, strongly connected to what some scholars call 'institutional factors' (RAPOSO *et al.*, 2008; LAFUENTE *et al.*, 2007), seems to have strengthened its position considerably (e.g., ALDRICH, 1999; SØRENSEN, 2007).

Due to lack of register data, the main bulk of empirical research using both the dispositional and the contextual approaches has been based on samples of individual firms and data collected using interviews and questionnaires. However, recent Swedish research utilizes detailed, de-identified register data on individual self-employed/employers and their environments (e.g., DELMAR *et al.*, 2008; EKLUND and VEJSIU, 2008). A spatial perspective has generally been lacking in these studies. One exception is the study by ELIASSON and WESTLUND (2013), which distinguishes between urban and rural areas in Sweden. Another Swedish contribution is the study by PETTERSSON *et al.* (2010), which investigates the effects of agricultural sector start-ups on the rest of the economy.

In contrast to most of the existing international literature on entrepreneurship at the regional or national levels, the focus in this paper is on the local government (municipal) level. This might seem a surprising choice, given that economic change is more aptly associated with the spatial scale of a region or labour market. However, considerable variation is seen in entrepreneurship rates within Swedish regions and labour markets, more variation than can be explained by current wisdom regarding the relative advantages of size, density and accessibility. There would appear to be local-level factors that promote the necessary interaction within innovation systems that, in turn, propels local economic development.

This study does not attempt to gauge the effectiveness of expenditures on business promotion (at any level). However, consider the fact that many expenditures are in fact what LUNDSTRÖM *et al.* (2013) describe as 'broad' costs; they support new firms or small and medium-sized enterprises in general. Other studies directly address the development effect of entrepreneurship investments and policies that promote infrastructure, education and training, or access to finance for new firm creation (LUNDSTRÖM *et al.*, 2013; LUNDSTRÖM and STEVENSON, 2005). But many regional-, national- and European-level programmes are in fact produced within a single municipality or as a cooperative effort involving a few local governments. It can be argued that if these are successful, they contribute not only to the individual firms that have enjoyed tax credits, subsidies or training opportunities, but also to the local business climate (here described as 'entrepreneurial social capital' and discussed in the third section). Local social capital is often measured at the municipal level (see the third section), and it is argued that ESC is thus also better measured at the municipal level than at the regional or national levels.

In other words, the focus of this study is not on the way in which the source or size of entrepreneurship supporting expenditure can affect local support for entrepreneurship; there are several important studies of this type already in the literature including a recent study using Swedish regional and national data (LUNDSTRÖM *et al.*, 2013). Rather, the contention here is that whatever the source of funding, programmes are often produced in cooperation with local governments and that they contribute to local ESC. By focusing on the municipalities, greater focus is made at the level where entrepreneurship policies 'touch ground'.

An alternative would have been to focus on labour market areas, based on commuting patterns. However, labour market areas are rarely the spatial level at which policy measures are implemented. A labour market area approach would also mean merging urban and rural municipalities, which would hinder the analysis of possible urban–rural differences that is done in this paper. The role of the labour market is nevertheless present in the present analysis, since the particular categorization of urban and rural municipal types employed in the model used here, and the accessibility measure for each municipality, reflects the relative position of individual municipalities within a regional labour market.

REGIONAL DETERMINANTS OF NEW BUSINESS FORMATION

In a special issue of *Regional Studies*, REYNOLDS *et al.* (1994) summarize the findings of coordinated studies of determinants of new business formation in five European countries and the United States. Seven entrepreneurial processes were selected and measured according to a number of factors. Certain factors, albeit measured in somewhat different ways, explained a large share of the regional variations in start-up rates within the six countries. Growth in demand, measured as in-migration/population growth, showed a positive, significant impact in most countries. Urbanization/agglomeration in the form of population density also showed positive effects, as did the share of small firms in total firms. Of other tested variables, it should be noted that unemployment gave mixed or insignificant effects, as did local political majority, and government spending and assistance programmes were insignificant. The percentage of the labour force with a higher education was significant in only one country.[2] In a study of the United States, REYNOLDS *et al.* (1995) present fairly similar results. An index of economic diversity, comprising measures of the diversity of occupations and the proportion of small firms, has a major impact on start-ups in the model. So does a 'career opportunity index' (which can be seen as a measure of human capital), industrial volatility, and personal wealth (a measure of access to financial capital). In another study of the United States, ARMINGTON and ACS (2002) find that industrial density, population, income growth and human capital explain variations in firm birth rates.

REYNOLDS *et al.* (1994) also note differences in their models' explanatory power when start-ups in all sectors are compared with start-ups in manufacturing. The models for all economic sectors explained a higher proportion of the variance in start-ups compared with the models for manufacturing start-ups. Other scholars, among them ARMINGTON and ACS (2002) and NYSTRÖM (2007), have also shown that regional determinants of new business formation differ among industries. ARMINGTON and ACS (2002, p. 43) suggest that 'manufacturing firms may behave differently from other sectors of the economy'. BAPTISTA and MENDONÇA (2010) find that local access to knowledge and human capital significantly influences the entry of knowledge-based firms.

In the Swedish literature on regional determinants of new firm formation, a major study of factors influencing start-up rates in 80 labour market areas provided by DAVIDSSON *et al.* (1994) forms a benchmark with which the results of this study can be compared. More recent research on the regional determinants of start-ups in Sweden has generally been based at the municipality level, with similar arguments for this choice of spatial level as those mentioned in the first section. ANDERSSON and KOSTER (2011) show a clear persistence in start-up rates at the municipal level. According to them, a partial explanation is differences in 'entrepreneurial climate', a factor that links conceptually to local ESC. KARLSSON and BACKMAN (2011) show that local accessibility to human capital has a positive impact on new firm formation in municipalities. KARLSSON and NYSTRÖM (2011) investigate the role of knowledge for entrepreneurship and find that municipal-level accessibility to company research and development (R&D) has a stronger impact on new firm formation than accessibility to university R&D. They also find that close knowledge interactions are more important for new firm formation than long-distance knowledge interactions. GREK *et al.* (2011) show that accessibility has a positive impact on both the entry and exit of firms, i.e. on the renewal of local business life.

EMPIRICAL RESEARCH ON SOCIAL CAPITAL AND ENTREPRENEURSHIP

In one of the very first published studies of social capital and entrepreneurship, WESTLUND and BOLTON (2003) suggest that social capital affects the propensity to start new businesses in several ways. They distinguish between entrepreneurial-facilitating social capital and social capital that has inhibiting effects on entrepreneurship, the latter observed already by SCHUMPETER (1934), albeit in other terms. Both as an individual and a collective resource, social capital enables or hinders entrepreneurial activities and thus exerts direct effects on entrepreneurship. Also, social capital affects entrepreneurship through its influence on supply costs, i.e. the sum of transaction costs, capital costs and other costs that the nascent entrepreneur faces.

WESTLUND and BOLTON (2003) mainly view social capital in the tradition of COLEMAN (1988, 1990), i.e. as a societal phenomenon of communities, groups, etc. that influence human behaviour, such as the decision to start a new firm. However, as shown below, most of the literature on business-related social capital has had its starting point in the (nascent) individual entrepreneur's social networks and considers them to be a resource at his or her disposal. This distinction of social capital as either a collective, societal phenomenon or as an individual resource was partly discussed in WESTLUND and ADAM's (2010) article on social capital and economic growth, but it has not been observed and discussed in the earlier literature on social capital and entrepreneurship.

In a meta-analysis of 65 studies of the impacts of social capital on economic performance, WESTLUND and ADAM (2010) show that the literature focused on economic growth of countries and regions predominantly used aggregated 'trust in other persons' or 'associational activity' as measures of social capital.[3] Studies using firms as their object of investigation employed a larger variety of social capital measures, such as firms' networks and relationships with various actors. The meta-analysis found that while a vast majority of the firm-level studies showed positive impacts of social capital on firm performance, the results for the regional and national levels were mixed. At the national level, a vast majority of the studies using 'trust' as a measure of social capital showed positive results, but studies using associational activity mainly showed negative impacts. At the regional level, most studies showed positive results for both trust and associations, but when the studies of Italy were excluded there was no preponderance of positive or negative impacts.

Just one of the 65 studies analysed by WESTLUND and ADAM (2010) uses the act of starting up a new venture as the dependent variable; others used sales (in the case of firms) or general economic indicators such as gross domestic product (GDP), income or investment per capita (when the studied objects were countries or regions). The exception was DE CLERK and ARENIUS (2003) who use data from the Global Entrepreneurship Monitor (GEM) surveys on individuals' social networks and find that knowing an entrepreneur had a positive impact on launching a new venture. Most other empirical studies of the impact of social capital on starting new firms are also based on survey data about individual entrepreneurs and their social networks. In a summary of the literature, SIMONI and LABORY (2006) refer to a number of such studies. DAVIDSSON and HONIG (2003) show that nascent entrepreneurs' social capital had a positive impact on starting a new business and on the start-ups' performance. GREENE (2000) provides similar evidence regarding self-employed women. Among others, ALBELL *et al.* (2001) find in a British study that having self-employed friends had a positive influence on the decision to become self-employed. In a recent study, KARLSSON and WIGREN (2012) use a sample of 7260 Swedish university employees and find that people with more social capital, such as having contact with external product development teams, were more likely to start new firms.

LIAO and WELSCH (2005) use US individual survey data (Panel Study of Entrepreneurial Dynamics (PSED) I data) to test for significant differences in social capital between nascent entrepreneurs and the general public (non-entrepreneurs). Based on NAHAPIET and GHOSHAL (1998), social capital was measured in three ways: structural (networks), relational (trust), and cognitive (shared norms). LIAO and WELSCH (2005) find no significant differences in the three forms of social capital between entrepreneurs and non-entrepreneurs, but nascent entrepreneurs seemed to have a higher ability than non-entrepreneurs to convert structural capital to relational capital and thereby gain access to various actors' support. Their findings suggest that it is primarily relational capital that contributes to new business formation. However, in a similar study, SCHENKEL *et al.* (2009), using newer US survey data (PSED II data) of the same type as the former study, find neither evidence of such transitions between the different forms of social capital during the entrepreneurial process nor support for a special role of relational capital among nascent entrepreneurs.

DOH and ZOLNIK (2011) use World Value Survey (WVS) data to study the impact of social capital on self-employment of 23 243 persons in 2005. They employ a similar division of social capital as the above-mentioned studies: trust, associational activity and civic norms, but also construct an index, based on the three social capital types. After controlling for country factors and individual characteristics (age, sex), they find that the social capital index was significantly correlated to self-employment. However, generalized trust (trust in other people) was negatively significantly connected to self-employment, while institutional trust (trust in government and institutions) had a positive, significant sign.

BAUERNSCHUSTER *et al.* (2010) study the effect of social capital, measured as self-employed individuals' membership in clubs, on the propensity to be self-employed one to five years earlier, using German individual survey data and comparing small and large communities (fewer than 5000 versus more than 5000 inhabitants). They find positive, significant values for social capital in both groups, but stronger in the small community group. Although the authors note that the positive relationship between club membership and self-employment might be a result of unobserved individual characteristics, the difference between small and large communities suggests that social capital has a stronger impact on becoming self-employed in small communities.[4] The authors interpret this as an indication that in small communities social capital substitutes for a lack of formal institutions.

However, in a study using another type of social capital data, SCHULTZ and BAUMGARTNER (2011) analyse the influence of the number of different types of volunteer organizations in 2009 on new firm foundation in the period 1996–2006 in 254 rural Swiss municipalities. Their main finding is that there was a generally positive relation between the number of organizations and start-ups, but that 'bonding' organizations, i.e. organizations focusing on internal issues, did not have that effect.

To sum up, only one of the above referred studies (BAUERNSCHUSTER *et al.*, 2010) has explicitly employed a spatial perspective and compared smaller and larger communities. Another and more important problem is that many studies seem to suffer from two shortcomings. First, they have an endogeneity problem, since the dependent variable (entrepreneurship) often precedes the independent variable (social capital). In other cases it is not made clear whether or not the social capital metric represents a period preceding the measure of entrepreneurship. In studies using the GEM surveys, entrepreneurship is measured as the number 'nascent' entrepreneurs that may be in the start-up phase, but may also have started their business up to 3.5 years before the survey. In SCHULTZ and BAUMGARTNER (2011), new firms are counted if they are created within the 13 years before the year for which social capital is measured. Even if it can be argued that social capital is a sluggish variable in a short or mid-term perspective (although this is not discussed in any of the studies), the hypothesis that the cause-and-effect chain points in the opposite direction cannot be rejected. Also, other types of endogeneities in the referred studies cannot be completely excluded, as, for example, a study offered by ALBELL *et al.* (2001) that found that having more self-employed friends was positively correlated to being self-employed; or the study by KARLSSON and WIGREN (2012) that found positive correlations between having contact with external product development teams and the propensity to start new firms. The endogeneity issue is not discussed in these studies. Second, in other studies entrepreneurship is measured by self-employment, which in principle can have lasted for decades. This too causes endogeneity problems. Moreover, at least from a Schumpeterian view, self-employment cannot be considered a valid measure of entrepreneurship.

The review of current research shows a few important gaps. First, most studies of the impact of social capital on start-up propensity are based on the individual entrepreneur's social networks, while few studies investigate the impact of the social environment that exists independently of the entrepreneur. Second, very few earlier studies have a spatial approach. Third, several studies do not address endogeneity issues, which is reflected by the fact that the dependent variable precedes the independent variables in time.

Against this background, this paper focuses on the role of non-individual social capital in the spatial environment of the nascent entrepreneur but existing independently of the entrepreneur. The overarching research question is whether or not local social capital supporting entrepreneurship (ESC) affects start-up rates in Swedish municipalities. Specifically, the study analyses the impact of ESC in 1999 and 2001 on the formation of genuinely new firms (start-ups per capita) in Swedish municipalities in the period 2002–08. The analysis is performed for all start-ups and for start-ups divided into six industry groups. Also, as a response to the lack of studies with a spatial approach, the analysis is conducted for all municipalities and also with the municipalities divided into two region types (urban and rural). The fourth section presents data and methods and a first test of the social capital measures. Specifically, it seeks to define these socio-environmental characteristics as ESC using municipal-level metrics that can be reliably collected annually and in all Swedish municipalities. The fifth section describes the empirical analysis of the impact of social capital and control variables on start-ups. The sixth section concludes.

DATA AND METHODS

Data sources

Data on start-ups were provided by the Swedish Agency for Growth Policy Analysis (*Tillväxtanalys*), the official source for statistics on start-ups of new firms and bankruptcies in Sweden. To avoid effects of coincidental occurrences in a given year, the data cover the period 2002–08. Only genuinely new firms are included, i.e. not mergers or acquisitions. As ARMINGTON and ACS (2002) and NYSTRÖM (2007) note, regional determinants of new firm formation differ among industries. Therefore, not only is the total number of start-ups per capita analysed, but also the start-ups divided into the following six sectors:[5]

- Manufacturing.
- Construction.
- Trade, hotels and restaurants.
- Transportation and communications.
- Financial and business services (excluding real estate service).
- Education, health and medical service, and other public and personal services.

Data measuring one aspect of local ESC (firm leaders' assessment of local public attitudes toward entrepreneurship; see below) were downloaded from the Swedish Confederation of Enterprise (*Svenskt Näringsliv*[6]). Data for the other ESC variable and for control variables were downloaded from Statistics Sweden.[7]

Fig. 1 shows the geographical distribution of start-up rates. The metropolitan regions, municipalities surrounding the metropolitan regions and tourism municipalities show the highest rates. The lowest rates are found in many of the manufacturing–industrial municipalities. Compared with a similar map presented in DAVIDSSON *et al.* (1994) using data for the period 1985–89, the present data show roughly the same pattern. A few exceptions are the very far north-east and the far south-east, where Davidsson *et al.* find pockets with the highest start-up rates compared with the national average. The fact that these areas show average or lower-than-average start-up rates in the present dataset may be due to the categories chosen for the reporting of the data, or to the fact that the dataset reports municipal rather than labour market area delimitations. However, these parts of Sweden are also those that have experienced long-term population decline and struggle to provide a dynamic business environment. Therefore, the data may be reflective of medium-term structural changes as well. In any case, this comparison lends credence to the idea that 'policies aimed at increased new firm formation by strengthening the environment' have strong 'natural forces' to fight against (DAVIDSSON *et al.*, 1994, p. 407).

What measure of social capital should be used?

As discussed above, WESTLUND and ADAM's (2010) meta-study has ambiguous results regarding social capital impacts on national, regional and firm economic performance. They conclude that one likely explanation of the contradictory results is that trust in other persons and associational activity in civil society are insufficient measures of social capital, particularly the social capital expected to influence economic growth. Instead, they argue, measures of networks, relations and trust connected to the business sphere should be developed. Such measures were used in the firm-level studies and showed with few exceptions significant, positive results. In the same journal issue, SCHUTJENS and VÖLKER (2010) study entrepreneurs' local ties and their relevance for firm success and find a positive relationship between social capital and firm performance. In a study of university spin-offs SOETANTO and VAN GEENHUIZEN (2010) find that they utilized tight, strong networks in their first phase of development, but that in later stages these spin-offs extend their social networks. They also find that network characteristics tend to influence growth mainly in years following the early stage, with a social capital exerting a positive influence on networks that were relatively open to new knowledge and information.

Following WESTLUND and ADAM (2010) and the abovementioned results, it seems reasonable to question to what extent trust and associational activities within civil society should have an impact on general, macroeconomic indicators. However, when it comes to a micro-level activity such as starting a new firm, it can be argued that the values and opinions of the (local) civil society should have a significant impact. SCHUMPETER (1934, p. 86) stressed, for example, 'the reaction of the social environment against one who wishes to do something new [...]' as an entrepreneurship-inhibiting

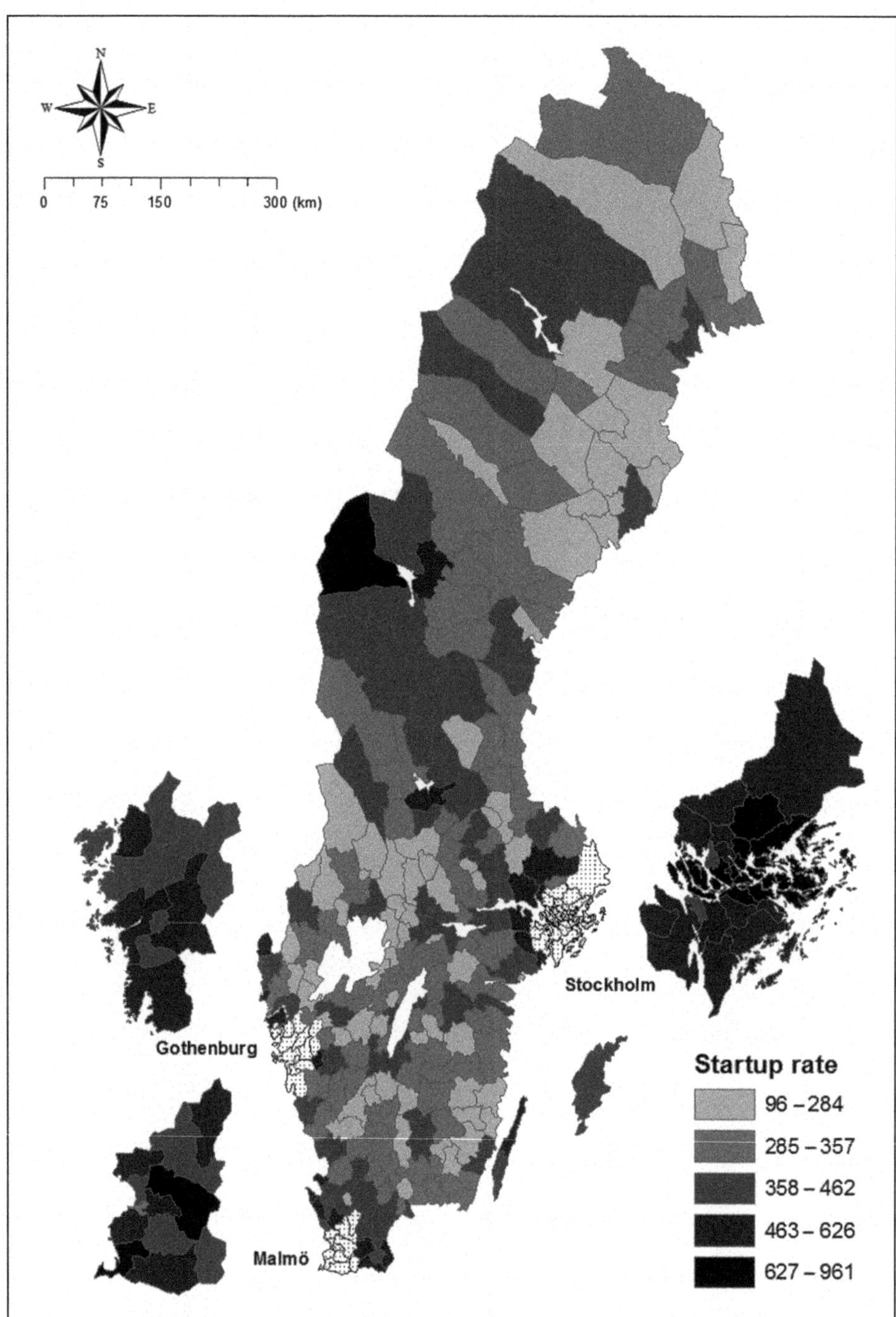

Fig. 1. Spatial distribution of start-up rates in Sweden, 2002–08, defined as the number of truly new firms per 10 000 inhabitants
Note: Observation units: municipalities (*N* = 290). The three metropolitan regions are enlarged: Gothenburg (upper left), Malmo (lower left) and Stockholm (right). Each category represents a quintile and contains 58 municipalities

factor. ETZIONI (1987) emphasizes the extent to which entrepreneurship is legitimized in a society as a decisive factor behind entrepreneurship's possible impact in this society. Reformulated, this begs the following question: do variations in local public opinion on entrepreneurship influence start-up rates? DAVIDSSON *et al.* (1994) remind us that our metrics for measuring the influence of a supportive local cultural environment for entrepreneurs have been crude at best, but that this does not mean they are not important causal factors explaining new firm formation. Other local factors that might have an impact on entrepreneurship could be attitudes to entrepreneurship among local public officials and politicians, existing firm initiatives to improve local business climate, and the status of the local business climate in general. As noted above, these environmental factors have rarely been used in studies of the impact of social capital on entrepreneurship.

The question of course arises: do such measures of local social capital that can be assumed to influence entrepreneurship really exist? The answer is yes – at least in Sweden. Since the year 2000 (yearly from 2002) the Federation of Swedish Enterprise (*Svenskt Näringsliv*) has surveyed at least 200 firms in each of Sweden's 290 municipalities.[8] Questions about the abovementioned factors are included in the survey. It should be noted that the survey only collects executives' opinions on these topics, and as such represents neither public opinion nor the attitudes of potential entrepreneurs. However, it can be argued that when analysing the impact of local social capital on starting new ventures, firm perception of public opinion is more important than actual public opinion. It can be recalled that other studies have attempted to measure the existence of an 'entrepreneurial culture' and have used metrics including political party majorities and the degree of regional autonomy. A review of these studies by DAVIDSSON *et al.* (1994) concludes that cultural variation may indeed be an important determinant of observed regional variation in entrepreneurship and economic development but that they are difficult to measure and that individual measures are likely correlated with each other.

The very best measure would of course be how potential entrepreneurs assess local public opinion, but such a measure is unfortunately not available. Similar arguments can be made regarding politicians' and officials' attitudes and the overall local business climate – the actual opinions of politicians and civil servants is less important than how these opinions are perceived by firms.

Table 1 shows a correlation matrix of five alternative measures of social capital from the survey 1999–2001 and average start-ups per year for 2002–08 in Sweden's 290 municipalities. (For descriptive statistics of the measures, see Table A3 in Appendix A.) All five social capital variables show significant correlations with entrepreneurship. Firm estimation of public support of entrepreneurship has the strongest correlation with 0.45 (0.00 significance). Three of the social capital measures are very strongly correlated: overall attitudes, and the attitudes of politicians and officials, respectively, while the two other variables (public attitudes to entrepreneurship and business' own initiatives to improve

Table 1. Correlations between various measures of entrepreneurial social capital (ESC) 1999/2001 and start-ups 2002–08 in Sweden's 290 municipalities

	(1)	(2)	(3)	(4)	(5)
(1) Start-ups/capita	1				
(2) Local government officials' attitudes	0.17	1			
(3) Local politicians' attitudes	0.20	0.95	1		
(4) Public attitudes	0.45	0.73	0.76	1	
(5) Business' own initiatives	0.13	0.62	0.64	0.64	1
(6) Overall judgment of the local business climate	0.22	0.93	0.94	0.83	0.74

business climate) show a lower correlation with the other three and with each other.

The results support the hypothesis that ESC measured in different ways in the survey is related to entrepreneurship. Also, the abovementioned assumption that it is firm *perception* of civil society support for entrepreneurship that has an impact on start-up rates is supported.[9]

Firm perception of attitudes among politicians and local officials correlated most strongly with the overall judgment, which indicates that the overall judgment of firms regarding support for entrepreneurship was primarily based on firm perception of politicians' and officials' attitudes and not on public opinion. A possible interpretation of this is that existing firms assess the business climate mostly based on their perception of local policies and government. The strongest correlation, between the perception of public opinion on entrepreneurship and start-ups, indicates that potential entrepreneurs are most affected by public opinion among the social capital variables. Based on the results in Table 1, the variable measuring firms' perception of public opinion regarding entrepreneurship is used as the measure of ESC of the *civil society* in the rest of this paper.

Fig. 2 shows the spatial distribution of civil society ESC. Here again, the municipalities of the metropolitan regions and tourism municipalities show high values. However, in contrast to the spatial distribution of start-up rates, the civil society ESC is also high in a large number of municipalities in southern Sweden, many of which are rural. Low scores are in particular found in traditional manufacturing municipalities with one or a few large employers. Communities with few large firms do not seem to be fertile ground for fostering positive public opinion towards entrepreneurship. This indicates a connection between the civil society ESC and the other measure of ESC: small firm traditions, expressed by the share of small firms of the total number of firms, which is discussed below.

Regional traditions, 'culture', social networks and path dependencies are factors that have been shown to have a long-term effect on variations in start-up rates (e.g., FRITSCH and MUELLER, 2007; FRITSCH and WYRWICH, 2014). JOHNSON and CATHCART (1979) show that small firms are more likely than large firms to have employees that start a business – a result that has been confirmed in many following studies (e.g., PARKER, 2009). The interpretation of JOHNSON and CATHCART (1979) in studies that followed was that this reflected pre-selection: those with a risk-averse mindset work in large firms that provide more secure employment. It can also be argued that workers in a small firm gain far more knowledge of what it takes to own and manage a firm. A possible basic economic explanation of the role of small firms for new firm formation might be that as a high share of new firms are

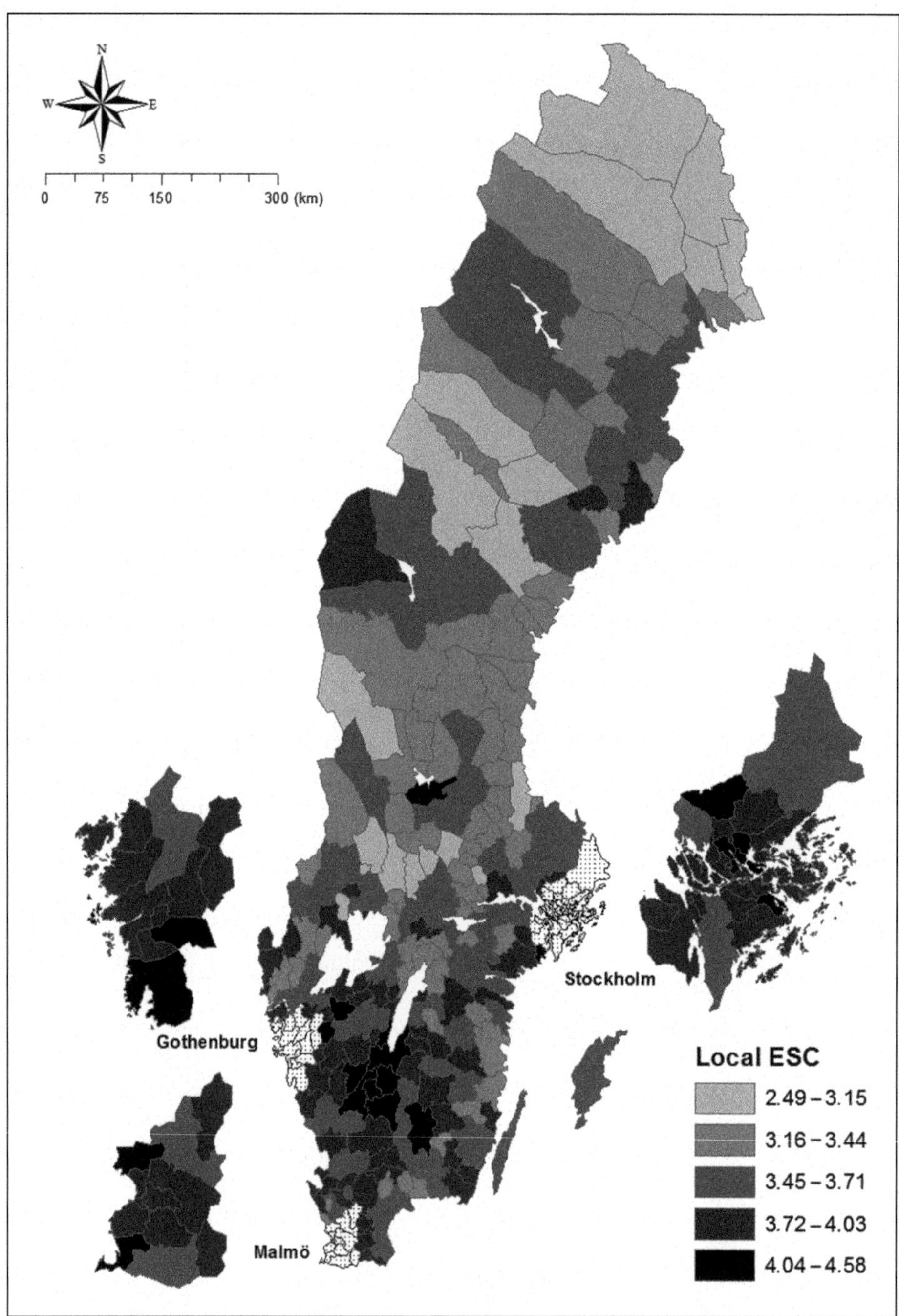

Fig. 2. Spatial distribution of civil society entrepreneurial social capital (ESC) in Sweden

Note: Observation units: municipalities (N = 290). The three metropolitan regions are enlarged: Gothenburg (upper left), Malmo (lower left) and Stockholm (right). Each category represents a quintile, and contains 58 municipalities

started in the sector where the founder was formerly employed, it can be more difficult for those working in large firms to create new firms, because new firms in these sectors might need more capital to achieve minimum efficient scale in the new enterprise. Also, in the results reported by REYNOLDS *et al.* (1994, 1995), the proportion of small firms was one of the most significant variables in explaining variations in start-up rates. REYNOLDS *et al.* (1994) refer to this variable as an expression of regional adaptability and 'flexible specialization', while REYNOLDS *et al.* (1995) consider it an expression of regional diversity. However, DAVIDSSON *et al.* (1994, p. 406) consider the proportion of small firms as important because these firms provide 'role models and experiences that facilitate individuals' decisions to found their own firms'. BOSMA *et al.* (2012) raise similar arguments when they discuss the importance of role models and peer effects. There are also other examples of studies of 'the culture of entrepreneurship' of which only a few are mentioned here. BEUGELSDIJK and NOORDERHAVEN (2004) show that regions differ in entrepreneurial attitude, and that a high score for entrepreneurial characteristics is correlated with a high rate of regional economic growth. FREYTAG and THURIK (2007) show that country-specific (cultural) variables seem to be able to explain the preference for entrepreneurship (but that they cannot explain actual entrepreneurship).

These examples indicate that the proportion of small firms reflects many determining factors: psychological, economic as well as cultural. Being aware of the multidimensional aspects of this variable, a focus is made on the cultural aspect, i.e. that the share of small firms at least partly is a reflection of regional culture and traditions – or expressed in other words, an expression of local, business-related social capital.

This variable is measured as the share of firms with fewer than 50 employees in the total number of firms. A high share indicates a community with a small firm tradition and thus lower barriers for start-ups to entry compared with communities dominated by one or a few large employers where the share of small firms is low and the barriers to entry are higher. The basic assumption here is that this small firm tradition is an expression of the historical, *business-related* ESC.

Control variables

Of course, many variables besides ESC are related to civil society and the business sector that influence start-up rates at the local level. Here, a focus is made on the variables found significant in REYNOLDS *et al.* (1994) and recent studies, albeit somewhat restructured:

- *Demand.* Two types of variables measuring demand are used. The first is local, regional and extra-regional accessibility to purchasing power (see below); the second is change in purchasing power parity (aggregated accessibility), 2002–08.
- *Urbanization/agglomeration.* This is measured by the number employed per square kilometre. A higher population density should mean higher access to both customers and inputs and thus facilitate entries of new firms.
- *Labour market participation.* The number employed in relation to the total number of people of working age. Assuming that starting up a new business is a substitute for unemployment, labour market participation (the inverted measure of 'total unemployment') can be expected to have a negative relation to start-ups per capita. Thus, municipalities with low labour market participation should have a higher rate of start-ups compared with those having a higher share.
- *Access to start-up capital.* One of the most important resources when starting a new business is start-up capital. Spatial differences in this respect cannot be measured in, for example, the density of bank offices. Instead, spatial variations in wealth can be assumed to influence access to start-up capital and the opportunity to get a loan. Spatial wealth variations are measured by average housing prices.
- *Age structure.* Following previous research (e.g., ELIASSON and WESTLUND, 2013) it is assumed that individuals of working age have a higher propensity to start new firms compared with young people and pensioners. This factor is measured by the number of people older than 65 and younger than 25 years in relation to the total population.
- *Human capital.* Human capital is measured by the share of the municipal labour force having three years or more of higher education in 2001. In today's knowledge economy, it can be assumed that the higher the share of higher educated in the labour force, the higher is the potential for the emergence of new firms in the fast-growing, knowledge-intense sectors. Even if one characteristic of the knowledge economy is increasing shares of knowledge workers in all sectors, there are clear differences in the knowledge contents of products from various sectors. Therefore, the expected effect of the human capital variable on start-ups in non-knowledge-intense sectors is less clear. It might even be the case that lower shares of labour with higher education promote start-ups in these sectors.
- *Municipal contracts.* This variable shows the share of the municipal activities by contract or direct sourced from private companies, associations and foundations, measured in as a percentage of total municipal expenditure. The primary aim of contracting/outsourcing municipal activities might be pure budget savings, but it should also be seen as a direct local policy measure to promote entrepreneurship. Furthermore, it is an indirect, inverted measure of local public employment. *Ceteris paribus*, the share of public employment of total local employment can be expected to have a negative impact on new firm formation, since the incentives for public employees to start a new firm should be lower than for the privately employed. Thus, the share of contracting/outsourcing is expected to have a positive impact on new firm formation.

The accessibility measure begs a more detailed explanation. The strength of demand is measured by municipalities' logarithmic accessibility to purchasing power (incomes in 2001). It can be assumed that higher accessibility to purchasing power spurs demand for more specialized goods and services and thereby increases incentives for starting new ventures. The accessibility measure used is the product of three market potential measures, each discounted by time-travelling distances. The three components are local, intra-regional and extra-regional accessibility:

$AW_{iL} = x_i \exp\{-\lambda_L t_{ii}\}$, internal accessibility to the total wage earnings of municipality i

$AW_{iR} = \sum_{r \in R_i} x_j \exp\{-\lambda_R t_{ij}\}$, intra-regional accessibility to the total wage earnings of municipality i

$AW_{iOR} = \sum_{r \notin R_i} x_k \exp\{-\lambda_{OR} t_{ik}\}$, extra-regional accessibility to the total wage earnings of municipality i

The summed-up measure used in the empirical analysis is defined as:

$$Accessibility_i = AW_{iL} + AW_{ir} + AW_{iOR}$$

where each municipality is situated in one of Sweden's 81 functional regions (R); and where time–distances t_{ii}, t_{ij} and t_{ik} measuring average commuting times within each municipality, within regions and outside of regions, respectively, are utilized. The distance-decay parameter λ is based on commuting flows and is estimated by JOHANSSON *et al.* (2003). The accessibility measure represents a continuous view of geography, and apart from capturing market potential originating outside of each municipality, it also alleviates the problems associated with using observational units of different sizes.

Spatial divisions

Earlier spatial–empirical explanations of new firm formation in Sweden indicate that municipalities that are centres of regional labour markets exhibit somewhat different determinants of start-up rates (KARLSSON and BACKMAN, 2011). This is taken into consideration by dividing the municipalities into two types: urban and rural. The division elaborated by economists at the Swedish Board of Agriculture is used, according to which the municipalities are classified into four different municipal types: (MT) 1, 2, 3 and 4. MT 1, metropolitan areas ($N = 46$); MT 2, urban areas ($N = 47$); MT 3, rural areas/countryside ($N = 164$); and MT 4, sparsely populated rural areas ($N = 33$). The four types of areas are defined as follows:

- Metropolitan areas (MT 1): include municipalities where 100% of the population lives within cities or within a 30-km distance from the cities. Using this definition, there are three metropolitan areas in Sweden: the Stockholm, Gothenburg and Malmo regions.
- Urban areas (MT 2): Municipalities with a population of at least 30 000 inhabitants and where the largest city has a population of 25 000 people or more. Smaller municipalities adjacent to these urban municipalities are included in a local urban area if more than 50% of the labour force in the smaller municipality commutes to a neighbor municipality. In this way, a functional-region perspective is adopted. In practice, this group is basically comprised of regional centres outside the metropolitan areas and their 'suburb municipalities'.
- Rural areas/countryside (MT 3): Municipalities not included in the metropolitan areas and urban areas are classified as rural areas/countryside, given they have a population density of at least five people/km^2.
- Sparse populated rural areas (MT 4): Municipalities that are not included in the three categories above and have fewer than five people/km^2.

Due to the relatively small number of municipalities in MT 1, 2 and 4, MT 1 and MT 2 are merged into one metropolitan/regional centre group, and MT 3 and MT 4 to a rural group. The regressions for these two groups are run separately in order to examine whether the explanatory variables vary in impact and strength between the two groups.

ANALYSIS

Table 2 shows the measure used in this study of start-up rates for urban and rural municipalities, here presented in relation to the national average (average = 100). Urban municipalities' total start-up rate is 27% higher than the national average. Rural municipalities have a start-up rate higher than average only in one sector: manufacturing. In three sectors rural municipalities are 6–8% below the average, but in the most knowledge-intense sector, financial and business services, rural municipalities are 27% below average. This is generally in line with the results of DAVIDSSON *et al.* (1994) who find that population size and especially population density are positively correlated with new firm birth rates.

Table 2. Relative start-up rates 2000–08 (average = 100) in total and divided into the six sectors in urban and rural municipalities

	Urban	Rural
Total	127	87
Manufacturing	91	103
Construction	113	92
Trade, hotels and restaurants	110	94
Transportation and communications	121	93
Financial and business services	156	73
Education, health and medical service, and other public and personal services	129	88

Note: Absolute differences in start-up rates across sectors of industry are presented in Table A2 in Appendix A.

Table 3. Descriptive statistics for variables used in the analysis

	Mean	Median	SD	Minimum	Maximum
Start-ups per 10 000 inhabitants	374.21	342.09	125.47	95.72	960.94
Civil society ESC	3.61	3.60	0.32	2.49	4.58
Accessibility to purchasing power (ln)	22.67	22.57	1.18	19.40	25.66
Share of university educated	0.12	0.11	0.04	0.06	0.35
Business-related ESC	0.98	0.98	0.01	0.95	0.99
Labour market participation	0.77	0.77	0.04	0.55	0.87
Percentage purchasing power growth	0.13	0.12	0.05	−0.07	0.23
Share of the population not of working age	0.48	0.48	0.02	0.40	0.55
Population density (municipality)	125.07	26.50	418.67	0.26	4030.56
Municipal contracts	6.54	5.17	4.95	.33	31.15

Note: ESC, entrepreneurial social capital; SD, standard deviation.

Descriptive statistics for the variables used in the analysis are shown in Table 3. It can be noted that the number of start-ups per 10 000 inhabitants is ten times higher in the municipality with the highest score compared with the one with the lowest. The variable with the largest span is population density.

Table 4 shows pairwise correlation of the variables. All independent variables have the expected signs, and in all cases but labour market participation the correlations are strong or fairly strong. Table 4 also shows that several of the independent variables are highly correlated.

Table 5 shows two models of the ordinary least squares (OLS) regressions for all sectors and for all municipalities and divided into the two spatial categories. In the first model all variables are significant for all municipalities and for urban municipalities. For the rural group, the only difference is that labour market participation is not significant. In the second model house prices are included. The inclusion of this variable makes population density and municipal contracts insignificant, while the other variables show similar results as for the first model. The only difference is that the share of university educated and the growth in purchasing power lose their significance in the rural group. The fact that the local policy variable, municipal contracts, becomes insignificant when house prices are included in the model should perhaps not be interpreted as meaning that municipal contracts have no influence on new firm formation. The correlation between contracts and house prices is very strong (0.81), which indicates that the two variables are very similar and that it should not be concluded that local municipal contracts are insignificant.

The model's explanatory value is clearly higher for the metro/urban municipalities. This might indicate that unemployment has a weak positive influence on start-up rates in metro/urban areas, but not in rural ones. One explanation for this may be the phenomenon that some new firms are started by urban professionals who retire full or part-time to attractive rural areas (KEEBLE and WALKER, 1994).

Overall, according to Model 2, a score of 1 increase in the civil society ESC index that ranges from 1 to 5 is associated with slightly fewer than 70 additional start-ups per 10 000 inhabitants, keeping all other factors constant. This number is not negligible and is in fact roughly equal to the start-up rate in the municipality that registered the lowest number. A somewhat naïve interpretation using the range of the index is that measured in this way civil society ESC can explain a cross-municipality variance of close to two start-ups per 100 inhabitants, albeit over a rather long time period, and disregarding the fact that the effect is heterogeneous across industries.

Table 4. Pairwise correlations for variables used in the analysis

	(1)	(2)	(3)	(4)	(5)	(6)	(7)	(8)	(9)	(10)	(11)
(1) Start-ups per 10 000 inhabitants	1										
(2) Civil society ESC	0.48	1									
(3) Accessibility to purchasing power (ln)	0.56	0.60	1								
(4) Share of university educated	0.65	0.38	0.65	1							
(5) Business-related ESC	0.24	−0.01	−0.11	−0.15	1						
(6) Labour market participation	0.07	0.53	0.33	−0.05	0.12	1					
(7) Percentage purchasing power growth	0.59	0.65	0.80	0.49	0.10	0.42	1				
(8) Share of the population not of working age	−0.61	−0.38	−0.75	−0.55	0.08	−0.17	−0.56	1			
(9) Population density (municipality)	0.53	0.27	0.50	0.54	−0.14	−0.04	−0.36	−0.48	1		
(10) Single-family home prices	0.82	0.57	0.76	0.78	0.04	0.19	0.69	−0.68	0.65	1	
(11) Municipal contracts	0.70	0.46	0.57	0.62	0.07	0.16	0.55	−0.51	0.58	0.81	1

Note: ESC, entrepreneurial social capital.

Table 5. Results of ordinary least squares (OLS) regressions for all municipalities and by municipality type

Variables/municipality type	All	Urban	Rural	All	Urban	Rural
Civil society ESC	83.85***	91.77**	70.66***	66.08***	70.40*	61.36***
	(17.42)	(40.64)	(19.61)	(16.84)	(39.74)	(19.10)
Accessibility to purchasing power (ln)	−32.68***	−41.45**	−48.75***	−35.89***	−46.42***	−37.06***
	(7.673)	(17.57)	(10.10)	(7.310)	(16.96)	(10.24)
Share of university educated	880.5***	801.7***	650.4***	490.8***	540.3**	311.6
	(134.9)	(211.6)	(217.4)	(145.8)	(223.1)	(228.3)
Business-related ESC	4306***	4986***	3994***	3689***	4454***	3568***
	(516.3)	−1105	(622.4)	(502.6)	−1077	(611.8)
Labour market participation	−360.2***	−625.1**	−190.1	−375.6***	−655.4**	−270.6*
	(125.6)	(259.2)	(163.3)	(119.4)	(249.0)	(159.2)
Purchasing power growth	498.3***	1026**	454.9***	383.2***	717.1*	218.5
	(146.5)	(412.1)	(157.2)	(140.6)	(410.4)	(164.2)
Share of the population not of working age	−2020***	−2009***	−1867***	−1637***	−2013***	−1229***
	(274.5)	(580.1)	(352.7)	(269.5)	(556.9)	(380.3)
Population density	0.0387***	0.0353**	1.005***	0.0180	0.0214	0.316
	(0.0122)	(0.0165)	(0.280)	(0.0122)	(0.0166)	(0.326)
Municipal contracts	5.425***	5.133***	4.315**	1.912	2.249	2.944
	(1.179)	(1.724)	(2.038)	(1.284)	(1.942)	(2.001)
Single-family house prices				0.0931***	0.0738***	0.132***
				(0.0167)	(0.0260)	(0.0350)
Constant	−2342***	−2693**	−1833**	−1769***	−1928*	−1888***
	(596.5)	−1101	(729.1)	(575.7)	−1091	(704.5)
Number of observations	289	93	196	289	93	196
R^2	0.742	0.767	0.501	0.768	0.788	0.537

Note: Standard errors are given in parentheses. ***$p < 0.01$, **$p < 0.05$ and *$p < 0.1$. Dependent variable: start-ups per 10 000 inhabitants (all industries). The model is estimated using an OLS estimator with robust standard errors. ESC, entrepreneurial social capital. Two different spatial econometric versions of the 'All' model were estimated for robustness purposes, the coefficients of which can be seen in Table A1 in Appendix A.

While the accessibility measure shows a positive correlation with start-ups in Table 4, it actually becomes negative when the other variables are controlled for. In other words, municipalities with better accessibility to purchasing power have lower start-up rates when other variables are kept constant. Three main explanations for these results are offered here. First, to the extent that entrepreneurial behaviour reflects economic growth, a negative market size variable may indicate convergence, and a catch-up effect by the smaller municipalities. Second, it may simply be the case that the local market plays a larger role, as reflected in the positive sign of the population density measure, which refers to the municipality rather than to the entire labour market region. Third, some effects that are often inferred when explaining the competitiveness of larger markets are already controlled for in this model. Two such effects are the sorting of workers with high human capital, as well as of workers in the early stages of their career. This third explanation is supported by the robustness of variables describing the share of university educated, and population not of working age across regressions. Further, it should be noted that *growth* in accessibility to purchasing power in the five years leading up to the reporting period is controlled for in the model. As seen in Table 4, the correlation between the level of purchasing power and its growth is as high as 0.8. This strong correlation probably means that all the positive effects of purchasing power are captured by the variable growth of purchasing power.

Even though the models are set up to handle spatial autocorrelation to the furthest extent possible, a standard Moran's *I*-test statistic using the inverse of time–travel distances between municipalities still indicates possible issues. A likely reason for the behaviour of these models is that the labour market regions are not as safely contained as indicated by time–travel distances and commuting behaviour. Table A1 in Appendix A displays the results from one spatial lag, and one spatial error model for each regression, in order to control for spatial autocorrelation. It presents the models for all municipalities, where the distance-weighting matrix takes into consideration all municipalities within a two-hour driving distance, as measured by average commuting times. As can be seen, the models are robust given such considerations.

Table 6 shows corresponding results with start-ups divided into the following six industry groups: manufacturing; construction; trade, restaurants and hotels; transportation and communications; business services; and education, health and medical service, and other public and personal services. Descriptive statistics on the split dependent variable are presented in Table A2 in Appendix A.

Table 6. Results of ordinary least squares (OLS) regressions by sector for all municipalities and by municipality type

	Manufacturing			Construction			Trade, hotels and restaurants			Transports and communications			Business services			Education, health and medical service, and other public and personal services		
	All	Urban	Rural	All	Urban	Rural	All	Urban	Rural	All	Urban	Rural	All	Urban	Rural	All	Urban	Rural
Civil society ESC	5.850**	−3.896	8.078**	−8.104*	−23.55**	0.282	27.74***	42.50***	21.81***	2.683	−1.069	3.903**	21.02***	35.27*	15.74**	8.682*	9.377	6.264
	(2.641)	(4.974)	(3.158)	(4.583)	(10.13)	(5.025)	(5.801)	(11.60)	(6.932)	(1.732)	(3.435)	(1.843)	(6.724)	(18.63)	(6.624)	(5.125)	(12.53)	(5.674)
Accessibility to purchasing power (ln)	−2.953***	−3.338	−3.219*	−7.036***	−13.35***	−1.848	−5.567**	−3.701	−10.05***	−1.847**	2.125	−3.758***	−12.86***	−18.27**	−12.91***	−6.215***	−11.35**	−3.365
	(1.136)	(2.101)	(1.682)	(1.971)	(4.280)	(2.677)	(2.494)	(4.901)	(3.693)	(0.744)	(1.451)	(0.980)	(2.891)	(7.867)	(3.529)	(2.204)	(5.292)	(3.023)
Share of university educated	−12.79	42.93	−74.84**	−108.2***	−131.8**	−86.61	−43.71	−93.25	−22.80	−0.709	−40.95**	29.46	454.8***	563.7***	319.4***	182.7***	199.2***	111.4
	(22.66)	(27.60)	(37.54)	(39.31)	(56.25)	(59.73)	(49.76)	(64.40)	(82.41)	(14.88)	(19.06)	(21.93)	(57.68)	(103.4)	(78.75)	(43.96)	(69.54)	(67.46)
Business-related ESC	376.3***	495.5***	400.9***	864.6***	712.8**	823.2***	707.9***	825.8**	574.7**	194.4***	16.40	235.3***	768.6***	1,211**	805.8***	550.9***	615.1*	576.0***
	(78.53)	(137.1)	(101.0)	(136.3)	(279.3)	(160.6)	(172.5)	(319.9)	(221.6)	(51.55)	(94.68)	(58.87)	(199.9)	(513.4)	(211.8)	(152.4)	(345.4)	(181.4)
Labour market participation	1.186	−2.011	8.849	−14.68	−26.50	−70.24*	−241.1***	−293.2***	−197.1***	−33.41***	−53.00**	−5.643	−7.228	−81.64	24.95	−52.54	−82.04	−46.19
	(18.62)	(31.62)	(26.15)	(32.30)	(64.42)	(41.60)	(40.89)	(73.77)	(57.39)	(12.20)	(21.84)	(15.21)	(47.39)	(118.4)	(54.84)	(36.12)	(79.65)	(46.98)
Percentage purchasing power growth	14.30	94.97*	3.486	271.4***	533.7***	151.5***	114.9**	194.5	97.13	2.006	75.01**	−19.41	−5.635	−110.5	24.09	66.56	117.5	12.72
	(22.16)	(51.86)	(27.25)	(38.45)	(105.7)	(43.35)	(48.67)	(121.0)	(59.81)	(14.52)	(35.82)	(15.88)	(56.41)	(194.2)	(57.15)	(42.99)	(130.7)	(48.96)
Share of the population not working age	−92.35**	41.90	−225.8***	−499.9***	−649.7***	−189.2*	−206.7**	−227.6	−65.48	−122.6***	−170.8***	−52.48	−324.0***	−523.9**	−400.7***	−360.1***	−370.5**	−229.0**
	(41.99)	(69.20)	(62.67)	(72.86)	(141.0)	(99.72)	(92.22)	(161.5)	(137.6)	(28.00)	(47.79)	(37.60)	(106.9)	(259.2)	(131.5)	(81.48)	(174.3)	(112.6)
Population density	0.00219	0.00259	0.0333	−0.00727**	−0.00642	−0.0688	−0.000499	0.00285	0.156	0.00198	−0.000626	0.0409	0.00981**	0.00864	0.161	0.00920**	0.0125**	−0.0771
	(0.00190)	(0.00206)	(0.0537)	(0.00329)	(0.00419)	(0.0855)	(0.00416)	(0.00480)	(0.118)	(0.00124)	(0.00142)	(0.0313)	(0.00483)	(0.00770)	(0.113)	(0.00368)	(0.00518)	(0.0965)
Municipal contracts	0.0858	0.114	0.216	0.0389	0.0846	0.476	−0.463	−0.133	−0.237	−0.0519	−0.0393	0.110	1.074**	0.660	1.165*	1.255***	1.666***	1.029*
	(0.199)	(0.240)	(0.329)	(0.346)	(0.490)	(0.523)	(0.438)	(0.561)	(0.722)	(0.130)	(0.166)	(0.191)	(0.507)	(0.901)	(0.690)	(0.387)	(0.606)	(0.591)
Single-family house prices	−0.00209	−0.00253	−0.00536	0.00650	0.00327	0.0261***	0.00979*	−0.00399	0.0245*	0.00342**	0.000751	0.00448	0.0711***	0.0748***	0.0578***	0.00715	0.00122	0.0300***
	(0.00259)	(0.00322)	(0.00576)	(0.00449)	(0.00656)	(0.00916)	(0.00568)	(0.00751)	(0.0126)	(0.00169)	(0.00222)	(0.00335)	(0.00659)	(0.0121)	(0.0121)	(0.00502)	(0.00811)	(0.0103)
Constant	−245.5***	−398.1***	−203.2*	−376.1**	24.67	−591.3***	−304.2	−458.4	−171.5	−61.21	69.17	−122.3*	−385.7*	−593.1	−375.1	−178.5	−100.8	−324.3
	(89.79)	(137.5)	(115.9)	(155.8)	(280.2)	(184.4)	(197.2)	(320.8)	(254.4)	(59.23)	(94.97)	(68.17)	(228.6)	(515.0)	(243.1)	(174.2)	(346.4)	(208.3)
Number of observations	287	92	195	287	92	195	287	92	195	286	92	194	287	92	195	287	92	195
R^2	0.154	0.259	0.200	0.499	0.645	0.438	0.295	0.307	0.288	0.286	0.498	0.293	0.881	0.883	0.588	0.625	0.648	0.318

Note: Dependent variable: start-ups per 10 000 inhabitants. Standard errors are given in parentheses. The model is estimated using an OLS estimator with robust standard errors. ***$p < 0.01$, **$p < 0.05$ and *$p < 0.1$. ESC, entrepreneurial social capital.

For all municipalities taken together, the model's explanatory power (in terms of variance explained by the right-hand-side variables) differs strongly among the sectors, from 83% for business services to 15% for manufacturing. There is a striking difference between the model's explanatory value for the two more knowledge-intense service groups (business services; and education, health and medical service, and other public and personal services) as compared with the other sectors. The explanatory value for manufacturing start-ups is particularly low. This supports the findings of, among others, REYNOLDS *et al.* (1994) and ARMINGTON and ACS (2002) that manufacturing start-ups differ from start-ups in other sectors, but it also indicates a more general gap between start-ups in knowledge-intense sectors and other sectors. As shown in Table 2, it is also in the two knowledge-intense sectors that the differences in start-up rates between urban and rural municipalities are highest. The model would appear to be best suited to explaining start-up rates in knowledge-intensive sectors. As an example, the share of workers with a university education is (intuitively) one of the most significant variables in explaining start-up behaviour in business services and education, health and medical service, and other public and personal services, while remaining insignificant, and in several estimations even *negative*, when explaining start-ups in the non-knowledge-intense sectors.

Business-related ESC, the share of small firms, is significant for all six sectors, while the civil society ESC shows generally significant results for all sectors except transport and communications (albeit negative for construction). When all municipalities are included, the main difference goes between the two more 'advanced' service groups, business services and education, health and medical service, and other public and personal services, on the one hand, and the other groups, on the other. Most variables are significant for the first two groups, whereas fewer variables are significant in the other groups. It can also be seen that municipal contracts have a strong positive impact on the two advanced service groups, in particular in education, health and medical service, and other public and personal services, but not in the other sectors.

When considering municipal types separately, civil society ESC is positively significant for four sectors in the rural areas, and for two sectors in the metro/city group. Business-related ESC is significant for all sectors in the rural municipalities and in five sectors in the urban ones. As for the estimates of civil society ESC for all municipalities across sectors, it is apparent that a large share of the overall effect shown in Table 5 is driven by business services and trade, hotels and restaurants where, intuitively, the effect is particularly strong in metropolitan regions.

Accessibility to purchasing power remains negative and significant in most cases with other variables held constant when the start-ups are divided into sectors. The growth in purchasing power is significant in some cases, in particular for construction. The share of university educated has strong significance in both urban and rural areas for the two knowledge-intense sectors, whereas the results for the other sectors are contradictory. Labour market participation is significant in transport and communications, and in the trade, hotels and restaurant sector. Age structure, or the population of non-working age, shows a clear and expected negative impact in most cases. Population density has the clearest impact in the two knowledge-intensive sectors. As pointed out, municipal contracts has a strong positive impact on the two advanced service sectors, in particular in education, health and medical service, and other public and personal services, but not in the other ones. The impact of house prices is strongest for business services, but is notable for some sectors in rural areas.

All in all, ESC, measured as (1) local firms' assessment of public attitudes to entrepreneurship and (2) by the share of small firms seems to exert a positive and significant influence on local start-up rates in both urban and rural municipalities in Sweden. When start-ups are divided into sectors, these two forms of ESC remain significant for ten of 12 sectors in rural areas, and for seven of 12 sectors in urban areas.

DAVIDSSON *et al.*'s (1994) study of new firm creation in Swedish regions found strong support for the idea that a 'supportive environment' was important to individual decisions to start firms. Davidsson *et al.* also noted that 'the attitudes towards entrepreneurship and self-employment [has become more favorable over the last decade [...]' (p. 407). Twenty years later the present study finds additional support for this conclusion. This study provides only a snapshot measure of ESC, but in future studies it may be useful to explore more thoroughly the relationship between ESC dynamics over time (which appear to change only slowly) and new firm formation (which is affected by both slow and more rapid business dynamics and structural change).

In sum, there would seem to be growing empirical support for the idea that observed entrepreneurship rates reflect the interaction of both slow- and fast-changing causal variables. It can be argued that start-up rates fluctuate much more than slowly changing norms supporting entrepreneurship, making causal links difficult to model. However, the results are basically in line with the literature described in the third section, suggesting that ESC may have a genuine influence on start-up rates. It may be that the relationship between ESC and start-up rates can be compared with the influence of human activity on observed global temperatures. If this is the case, then it provides insight as to why the local, regional, national and international investments often described as 'entrepreneurship policy' may fail to have significant or lasting impact on local start-up rates.

What then is the role of local policy in influencing ESC? The variable municipal contracts should have a direct effect on start-up propensity in sectors where public services are often outsourced to private providers in contemporary Sweden, such as education and elderly care. This is also reflected in the results, but with the exception of business services its influence on other sectors is insignificant.

Finally, there are two strong reasons to believe that the results are not driven by spatial autocorrelation. First, as noted by ANDERSSON and GRÅSJÖ (2009), the problem may itself be viewed as a symptom of the fact that the model lacks proper representation of some phenomena; these authors conclude that the inclusion of spatially lagged variables alleviates problems with spatial dependency. The accessibility measure and purchasing power growth measure used in the regressions in this paper are two such variables. Second, even though Moran's *I* indicates possible spatial dependency, neither spatial lag nor spatial error models produce results that contradict the general conclusions in this paper, as demonstrated in Table A1 in Appendix A.

CONCLUSIONS

Based on unique data representing civil society ESC and with spatially detailed data of genuinely new firms, the influence of local ESC on start-up rates was analysed, without any obvious endogeneity problems. Moreover, it was possible to analyse this influence in urban and rural municipalities, respectively, and in six sectors. To the authors' knowledge this has not been done before.

The results support the hypothesis that social capital, measured both as (1) firm perception of local public attitudes to entrepreneurship and (2) as the share of small businesses, influences start-up propensity in Swedish municipalities. The findings also support previous results suggesting that social capital has a somewhat stronger influence in rural areas than in urban areas. The results have, however, large variations in explanatory power for the various sectors, which confirms earlier research, particularly for manufacturing. Also, the results underscore clear differences between urban and rural municipalities. This suggests that further analyses should test sector-specific and region type-specific explanatory variables. Perhaps more importantly, if local social capital is indeed significant and is best articulated at the municipal level, these findings suggest that regional economic development models need to incorporate a higher degree of municipal-level data. It is well accepted that spatial characteristics affect business dynamics and there is growing evidence that social capital networks supporting new firm creation are locally generated and supported. Therefore, support is found for the idea that municipal characteristics, ESC in particular, may also be a determinant of new firm creation. In any case, the results underscore the need to understand better intra-regional variations in the support for entrepreneurship that cannot be explained by size or density alone.

It is, of course, also necessary to point out some weaknesses of the study. It covers only one country, and even if Sweden is in many ways a representative Western European country it cannot be assumed that the results can be transferred to other countries. This might be of special importance in the urban–rural context, since much Swedish territory is still rural. While urban municipalities in Sweden probably do not differ much from other Western European counterparts, the rural municipalities, with their very low population density compared with other European areas, might perhaps only be comparable with their counterparts in other Nordic countries. The study also relies on survey data regarding existing firm perceptions of attitudes towards entrepreneurship, which as noted are not necessarily the same as actual local public opinion or, more importantly, the perceptions of potential entrepreneurs. It also begs the question of how this perception differs among firms already in the region and those that may be persuaded to relocate there. Nevertheless, this study indicates that regional development science should not ignore the spatial dimension of entrepreneurship or the significance of local social capital.

Another issue for future research would be to investigate to what extent high start-up rates are coupled with high mortality rates among firms in general and start-ups in particular, and what the net result could be, i.e. which municipalities have the highest net result. Finally, this study uses linear modelling, but ideas are increasingly being developed in the literature about non-linear relationships between explanatory variables and new firm formation. This would be an interesting topic for future research.

Acknowledgements – The authors want to thank the editors of the special issue, Michael Fritsch and David Storey, for very valuable and insightful comments.

Funding – This work was partly financed by the research council Formas [grant number 2009-1192].

APPENDIX A: VARIABLES AND THEIR DEFINITIONS

- *Start-ups*: number of truly new firms per 10 000 inhabitants over the 2002–08 period, reported by municipality.
- *Civil society ESC*: firm leaders' opinion on local public attitudes toward entrepreneurship in 1999 and 2001 (average for the two years). It is measured by a questionnaire to 200 firm leaders in each municipality. Maximum score: 5.
- *Accessibility to purchasing power*: accessibility to purchasing power (wage earnings) based on average earnings and time–distances for commuting between all municipalities 2001. For details, see the fourth section.
- *Share of university educated*: number of employed workers with three years or more of higher education relative to the total number of employed workers in 2001.
- *Business-related ESC*: number of local firms with fewer than 50 employees relative to the total number of local firms in 2002.
- *Labour market participation*: number of people in employment relative to the total number of working-age individuals in 2002.
- *Purchasing power change*: change in purchasing power parity (summed up accessibility) over the 2002–08 period. Denominated in millions of Swedish kronas (SEK), 2008 prices.
- *Access to start-up capital*: average housing prices in 2001.
- *Age structure*: number of people in the municipality who are 65 years or older (the official retirement age) and younger than 25 years, relative to the population of the total municipality.
- *Population density 2002*: number of employed people relative to the municipality area in terms of square kilometres (km^2).
- *Municipal contracts 2001*: share of municipal activities by contract or direct sourced from private companies, associations and foundations measured as a percentage of total municipal expenditure.

Table A1. Results of spatial econometric regressions with lagged dependent variables and lagged error terms, with and without single-family home prices. Dependent variable: start-ups per 10 000 inhabitants (all industries)

Variables/spatial model type	Lag	Error	Lag	Error
Civil society ESC	95.78***	82.83***	80.82***	53.78***
	(15.80)	(17.39)	(15.99)	(17.03)
Accessibility to purchasing power (ln)	−37.63***	−39.47***	−39.00***	−46.04***
	(6.912)	(8.726)	(6.779)	(8.292)
Share of university educated	958.7***	967.8***	686.3***	543.2***
	(121.4)	(134.0)	(139.4)	(143.5)
Business-related ESC	3568***	3697***	3280***	3205***
	(473.0)	(489.3)	(469.7)	(466.1)
Employment share	−289.7**	−286.7**	−306.7***	−285.2**
	(113.4)	(130.5)	(111.2)	(122.5)
Purchasing power growth	227.9*	319.5**	210.5	273.6*
	(137.9)	(156.7)	(135.4)	(144.4)
Share of the population not of working age	−1557***	−1855***	−1397***	−1703***
	(255.1)	(278.4)	(253.7)	(262.0)
Population density	0.0344***	0.0349***	0.0210*	0.0157
	(0.0110)	(0.0114)	(0.0113)	(0.0112)
Municipal contracts	2.389**	4.606***	0.663	2.074*
	(1.142)	(1.251)	(1.211)	(1.232)
Single-family home prices			0.0621***	0.102***
			(0.0166)	(0.0166)
Constant	−1994***	−1707***	−1656***	−1060*
	(537.4)	(570.4)	(533.8)	(548.7)
Number of observations	288	288	288	288

Note: Models are estimated using a maximum likelihood estimator. 'Lag' refers to a spatial econometric model with lagged dependent variables; 'Error' refers to a model with lagged error terms. The rows and columns of the spatial weight matrix used are made up of the inverse of the time–travel distance between the respective municipalities. The number of observations is one less compared with Table 5, since one municipality (the island of Gotland) has no neighbours within a reasonable commute. ***$p < 0.01$, **$p < 0.05$ and *$p < 0.1$. ESC, entrepreneurial social capital.

Table A2. Descriptive statistics on start-ups per 10 000 inhabitants divided by industry sector

Industry sector	Mean	SD	Minimum	Maximum
Manufacturing	31.6	10.2	6.6	74.5
Construction	51.6	23.0	8.6	142.4
Trade, hotels and restaurants	88.7	24.5	19.4	220.7
Transport and communications	14.2	7.3	2.2	39.4
Business services	107.9	69.3	27.5	454.5
Education, health and medical service, and other public and personal services	80.3	29.7	25.8	237.5

Note: SD, standard deviation.

Table A3. Descriptive statistics on scores of survey questions that might be used as proxies for alternative measures of local entrepreneurial social capital (ESC)

Variable	Mean	Median	SD	Minimum	Maximum
Overall judgment of the local business climate	3.30	3.26	0.33	2.48	4.47
Local government officials' attitudes	3.32	3.30	0.32	2.47	4.44
Local politicians' attitudes	3.47	3.43	0.36	2.53	4.72
Business' own initiatives	3.52	3.50	0.20	2.93	4.26
Public attitudes (civil society ESC)	3.61	3.60	0.32	2.49	4.58

Notes: The table is based on the following survey questions:

- What is your overall judgment of the business climate in your municipality?
- What is your opinion on local government officials' attitudes towards entrepreneurship?
- What is your opinion on local politicians' attitudes towards entrepreneurship?
- What is your opinion on local business' own initiatives to strengthen local business climate?
- What is your opinion on local public attitudes towards entrepreneurship?

Scores: 1 = bad, 2 = not so good, 3 = good, 4 = very good, and 5 = excellent.
SD, standard deviation.

NOTES

1. See http://www.kolada.se/.
2. For details, see GARFOLI (1994).
3. Both measures were collected from the World Value Surveys (WVS) and similar, as, for example, the European Value Surveys (EVS).
4. This corresponds well to the results of ELIASSON *et al.* (2013), who investigated the impact of local business-related social capital on income growth per capita of the Swedish municipalities and found indications that the importance of local social capital decreases with increasing municipality size.
5. Comparable data for the primary sector were not available.
6. See http://foretagsklimat.svensktnaringsliv.se/start.do/.
7. See http://www.scb.se/.
8. The survey is conducted during September-November the year before they are presented, i.e. the data used in this study are collected between 1999 and 2001. The selection of companies is made by Statistics Sweden from its company register and is based on size classes. In larger municipalities the sample is higher than 200 firms; in Stockholm it is 1200. The survey comprises a number of questions on companies' opinion on the local business climate. Combined with statistics on start-ups, employment, size of private sector, etc. the survey forms the basis for a yearly ranking of the Swedish municipalities' business climate. Here, only the replies of certain questions are used.
9. From a critical perspective it can, of course, be argued that culture and economic behaviour are interrelated phenomena and that executives' views on local business climate not only have an impact on new firm formation but also are being influenced by the development of the local economy. This kind of endogeneity problem is increasingly being discussed in the literature, but is hard to solve. This paper uses the classical way to deal with possible endogeneity by using measures of the independent variables that are earlier in time than the measures of the dependent variables.

REFERENCES

ALBELL P., CHROUCHLEY R. and MILLS C. (2001) Social capital and entrepreneurship in Great Britain, *Enterprise and Innovation Management Studies* **2(2)**, 119–144.

ALDRICH H. E. (1999) *Organizations Evolving*. Sage, Newbury Park, CA.

ANDERSSON M. and GRÅSJÖ U. (2009) Spatial dependence and the representation of space in empirical models, *Annals of Regional Science* **43(1)**, 159–180.

ANDERSSON M. and KOSTER S. (2011) Sources of persistence in regional start-up rates – evidence from Sweden, *Journal of Economic Geography* **11(1)**, 179–201.

ARMINGTON C. and ACS Z. (2002) The determinants of regional variation in new firm formation, *Regional Studies* **36**, 33–45.

AUTIO E. and WENNBERG K. (2009) Social interactions and entrepreneurial activity. Paper presented at the Academy of Management Meeting, Chicago, IL, USA, 7–11 August 2009.

BAPTISTA R. and MENDONÇA J. (2010) Proximity to knowledge sources and the location of knowledge-based start-ups, *Annals of Regional Science* **45(1)**, 5–29.

BAUERNSCHUSTER S., FALCK O. and HEBLICH S. (2010) Social capital access and entrepreneurship, *Journal of Economic Behavior and Organization* **76**, 821–833.

BEUGELSDIJK S. and NOORDERHAVEN N. (2004) Entrepreneurial attitude and economic growth: a cross-section of 54 regions, *Annals of Regional Science* **38**, 199–218.

BOLTON R. E. (2002) Place surplus, exit, voice, and loyalty, in JOHANSSON B., KARLSSON C. and STOUGH R. R. (Eds) *Regional Policies and Comparative Advantage*, pp. 469–488. Edward Elgar, Cheltenham.

BOSMA N., HESSELS J., SCHUTJENS V. and VAN PRAAG M. (2012) Entrepreneurship and role models, *Journal of Economic Psychology* **33(2)**, 410–424.

COLEMAN J. S. (1988) Social capital in the creation of human capital, *American Journal of Sociology* **94(Suppl.)**, 95–120.

COLEMAN J. S. (1990) *Foundations of Social Theory*. Harvard University Press, Cambridge, MA.

DAVIDSSON P. and HONIG B. (2003) The role of social and human capital among nascent entrepreneurs, *Journal of Business Venturing* **18(3)**, 301–331.

DAVIDSSON P., LINDMARK L. and OLOFSSON C. (1994) New firm formation and regional development in Sweden, *Regional Studies* **28(4)**, 395–410.

DE CLERCQ D. and ARENIUS P. (2003) *Effects of Human Capital and Social Capital on Entrepreneurial Activity*. Babson College, Babson Kauffman Entrepreneurship Research Conference (BKERC), 2002–2006 (available at SSRN: http://ssrn.com/abstract=1782232).

DELMAR F., FOLTA T. and WENNBERG K. (2008) *The Dynamics of Combining Self-Employment and Employment*. Working Paper Number 2008:23. IFAU, Institute for Labour Market Evaluation, Uppsala.

DOH S. and ZOLNIK E. J. (2011) Social capital and entrepreneurship: an exploratory analysis, *African Journal of Business Management* **5(12)**, 4961–4975.

EKLUND S. and VEJSIU A. (2008) *Incentives to Self-Employment Decision in Sweden: A Gender Perspective*. Ministry of Industry, Stockholm.

ELIASSON K. and WESTLUND H. (2013) Attributes influencing self-employment propensity in urban and rural Sweden, *Annals of Regional Science* **50(2)**, 479–514.

ELIASSON K., WESTLUND H. and FÖLSTER S. (2013) Does social capital contribute to regional economic growth? Swedish experiences, in WESTLUND H. and KOBAYASHI K. (Eds) *Social Capital and Rural Development in the Knowledge Society*, pp. 113–126. Edward Elgar, Cheltenham.

ETZIONI A. (1987) Entrepreneurship, adaptation and legitimation, *Journal of Economic Behavior and Organization* **8**, 175–199.

FREYTAG A. and THURIK R. (2007) Entrepreneurship and its determinants in a cross-country setting, *Journal of Evolutionary Economics* **17**, 117–131.

FRITSCH M. and FALCK O. (2007) New business formation by industry over space and time: a multidimensional analysis, *Regional Studies* **41(2)**, 157–172.

FRITSCH M. and MUELLER P. (2007) The persistence of regional new business formation-activity over time – assessing the potential of policy promotion programs, *Journal of Evolutionary Economics* **17(3)**, 299–315.

FRITSCH M. and WYRWICH M. (2014) The long persistence of regional levels of entrepreneurship: Germany 1925 to 2005, *Regional Studies* (in this issue).

GARFOLI G. (1994) New firm formation and regional development: the Italian case, *Regional Studies* **28(4)**, 381–393.

GREENE P. (2000) Self-employment as an economic behavior: an analysis of self-employed women's human and social capital, *National Journal of Sociology* **12**, 1–55.

GREK J., KARLSSON C. and KLAESSON J. (2011) Determinants of entry and exit: the significance of demand and supply conditions at the regional level, in KOURTIT L., NIJKAMP P. and STOUGH R. R. (Eds) *Drivers of Innovation, Entrepreneurship and Regional Dynamics*, pp. 121–141. Springer, Berlin.

GRIES T. and NAUDÉ W. (2009) Entrepreneurship and regional economic growth: towards a general theory of start-ups, *European Journal of Social Science Research* **22(3)**, 309–328.

JOHANNISSON B. (2000) Modernising the industrial district – rejuvenation or managerial colonisation, in TAYLOR M. and VATNE E. (Eds) *The Networked Firm in a Global World: Small Firms in New Environments*, ch. 12. Ashgate, Aldershot.

JOHANSSON B., KLAESSON J. and OLSSON M. (2003) Commuters' non-linear response to time distances, *Journal of Geographical Systems* **5(3)**, 315–329.

JOHNSON P. S. (1983) New manufacturing firms in the U.K. regions, *Scottish Journal of Political Economy* **30(1)**, 75–79.

JOHNSON P. S. and CATHCART D. G. (1979) The founders of new manufacturing firms: a note on the size of their 'incubator' plants, *Journal of Industrial Economics* **28(2)**, 219–224

KARLSSON C. and BACKMAN M. (2011) Accessibility to human capital and new firm formation, *International Journal of Foresight and Innovation Policy* **7(1–3)**, 7–22.

KARLSSON C. and NYSTRÖM K. (2011) Knowledge accessibility and new firm formation, in DESAI S., NIJKAMP P. and STOUGH R. R. (Eds) *New Directions in Regional Economic Development: The Role of Entrepreneurship Theory and Methods, Practice and Policy*, pp. 174–197. Edward Elgar, Cheltenham.

KARLSSON T. and WIGREN C. (2012). Start-ups among university employees: the influence of legitimacy, human capital and social capital, *Journal of Technology Transfer* **37(3)**, 297–312.

KEEBLE D. (1993) Regional patterns of small firm development in the business services: evidence from the United Kingdom, *Environment and Planning A* **25**, 677–700.

KEEBLE D. and WALKER S. (1994) New firms, small firms and dead firms: spatial patterns and determinants in the United Kingdom, *Regional Studies* **28(4)**, 411–427.

LAFUENTE E., VAILLANT Y. and RIALP J. (2007) Regional differences in the influence of role models: comparing the entrepreneurial process of rural Catalonia, *Regional Studies* **41(6)**, 779–795.

LIAO J. and WELSCH H. (2005) Roles of social capital in venture creation: key dimensions and research implications, *Journal of Small Business Management* **43(4)**, 345–362.

LUNDSTRÖM A. and STEVENSON L. (2005) *Entrepreneurship Policy: Theory and Practice.* Kluwer, Boston, MA.

LUNDSTRÖM A., VIKSTRÖM P., FINK M., CRIJNS H., GŁODEK P., STOREY D. and KROKSGÅRD A. (2013) Measuring the costs and coverage of SME and entrepreneurship policy: a pioneering study entrepreneurship, *Entrepreneurship Theory and Practice*, Article first published online: 7 May 2013. DOI: 10.1111/etap.12037.

NAHAPIET J. and GHOSHAL S. (1998) Social capital, intellectual capital and the organizational advantage, *Academy of Management Review* **23**, 242–66.

NYSTRÖM K. (2006) *Entry and Exit in Swedish Industrial Sectors.* JIBS Dissertation Series Number 32, Jönköping International Business School, Jönköping.

NYSTRÖM K. (2007) An industry disaggregated analysis of the determinants of regional entry and exit, *Annals of Regional Science* **41(4)**, 877–896.

ORGANISATION FOR ECONOMIC CO-OPERATION AND DEVELOPMENT (OECD) (2001) *The Well-being of Nations: The Role of Human and Social Capital.* OECD, Paris.

PARKER S. C. (2009) Why do small firms produce the entrepreneurs?, *Journal of Socio-Economics* **38(3)**, 484–494.

PETTERSSON L., SJÖLANDER P. and WIDELL L. M. (2010) Do startups in the agricultural sector generate employment in the rest of the economy? – an Arellano–Bond dynamic panel study, in KOBAYASHI K., WESTLUND H. and YEHONG H. (Eds) *Social Capital and Development Trends in Rural Areas*, Vol. 6, pp. 255–273. MARG, Kyoto University, Kyoto.

PUTNAM R. D. (1993) *Making Democracy Work. Civic Traditions in Modern Italy.* Princeton University Press, Princeton, NJ.

RADER OLSSON A. and WESTLUND H. (2011) Measuring political entrepreneurship: an empirical study of Swedish municipalities. Paper presented at the 51st Congress of the European Regional Science Association, Barcelona, Spain, 30 August–3 September 2011.

RAPOSO M. L. B., MATOS FERREIRA J. J., FINISTERRA D. O., PACO A. M. and GOUVEIA RODRIGUES R. J. A. (2008) Propensity to firm creation: empirical research using structural equations, *International Entrepreneurship Management Journal* **4(4)**, 485–504.

REYNOLDS P., MILLER B. and MAKI W. R. (1995) Explaining regional variation in business births and deaths: U.S. 1976–88, *Small Business Economics* **7(4)**, 389–407.

REYNOLDS P., STOREY D. J. and WESTHEAD P. (1994) Cross-national comparisons of the variation in new firm formation rates, *Regional Studies* **28(4)**, 443–456.

SAXENIAN A. (1994) *Regional Advantage: Culture and Competition in Silicon Valley and Route 128.* Harvard University Press, Cambridge, MA.

SCHENKEL M. T., HECHAVARRIA D. M. and MATTHEWS C. H. (2009) The role of human and social capital and technology in nascent ventures, in REYNOLDS P. D. and CURTIN R. T. (Eds) *New Firm Creation in the United States*, pp. 157–183. Springer, Berlin.

SCHULTZ T. and BAUMGARTNER D. (2011) Volunteer organizations: odds or obstacle for small business formation in rural areas? Evidence from Swiss municipalities, *Regional Studies* **47(4)**, 597–612.

SCHUMPETER J. A. (1934) *The Theory of Economic Development.* Harvard University Press, Cambridge, MA.

SCHUTJENS V. and VÖLKER B. (2010) Space and social capital: the degree of locality in entrepreneurs' contacts and its consequences for firm success, *European Planning Studies* **18(6)**, 941–970.

SIMONI C. and LABORY S. (2006) The influence of social capital on entrepreneurial behaviour, in MINNITI M., ZACHARAKIS A., SPINELLI S., RICE M. P. and HABBERSHON T. G. (Eds) *Entrepreneurship: The Engine of Growth*, pp. 101–118. Praeger, Westport, CT.

SOETANTO D. P. and VAN GEENHUIZEN M. (2010) Social capital through networks: the case of university spin-off firms in different stages, *Tijdschrift voor Economische en Sociale Geografie* **101(5)**, 509–520.

SØRENSEN J. B. (2007) Bureaucracy and entrepreneurship: workplace effects on entrepreneurial entry, *Administrative Science Quarterly* **52(3)**, 387–412.

STERNBERG R. (2009) Regional dimensions of entrepreneurship, *Foundations and Trends in Entrepreneurship* **5(2)**, 211–340.

STOREY D. J. and JOHNSON S. (1987) Regional variations in entrepreneurship in the U.K., *Scottish Journal of Political Economy* **34(2)**, 161–173.

THORNTON P. A. (1999) The sociology of entrepreneurship, *Annual Review of Sociology* **25**, 19–46.

WESTLUND H. (2006) *Social Capital in the Knowledge Economy: Theory and Empirics.* Springer, Berlin.

WESTLUND H. (2011) Multidimensional entrepreneurship: theoretical considerations and Swedish empirics, *Regional Science Policy and Practice* **3(3)**, 199–218.

WESTLUND H. and ADAM F. (2010) Social capital and economic performance: a meta-analysis of 65 studies, *European Planning Studies* **18(6)**, 893–919.

WESTLUND H. and BOLTON R. E. (2003) Local social capital and entrepreneurship, *Small Business Economics* **21**, 77–113.

Regional Social Legitimacy of Entrepreneurship: Implications for Entrepreneurial Intention and Start-up Behaviour

EWALD KIBLER*¶, TEEMU KAUTONEN†‡ and MATTHIAS FINK†§

*Department of Management and Entrepreneurship, University of Turku, Turku, Finland.
†Institute for International Management Practice (IIMP), Anglia Ruskin University, Cambridge, UK.
‡Aalto University, School of Business, Aalto, Finland.
§Institute for Innovation(IFI), Johannes Kepler University Linz, Linz, Austria

KIBLER E., KAUTONEN T. and FINK M. Regional social legitimacy of entrepreneurship: implications for entrepreneurial intention and start-up behaviour, *Regional Studies*. A new understanding of the role of regional culture in the emergence of business start-up behaviour is developed. The focal construct is regional social legitimacy: the perception of the desirability and appropriateness of entrepreneurship in a region. The econometric analysis utilizes a combination of bespoke longitudinal survey data from 65 regions in Austria and Finland, and variables capturing regional socio-economic characteristics derived from official statistics. The study demonstrates that, and explains how, regional social legitimacy influences the relationships between individual entrepreneurial beliefs, intentions and start-up behaviour and how these interaction effects are conditioned by the socio-economic characteristics of the region.

Social legitimacy   Entrepreneurship   Institutions   Culture   Region   Psychology

KIBLER E., KAUTONEN T. and FINK M. 企业精神的区域社会正当性：创业企图以及草创行为，*区域研究*。本研究对区域文化在兴起的企业创业行为中的角色建立新的理解。核心的构想是区域社会正当性：亦即一个区域中对企业精神的期望与适切性的理解。本计量经济分析将运用奥地利与芬兰的六十五个区域的预定纵向调查资料组合，以及捕捉自正式统计衍生出的区域社会—经济特徵之变因。本研究证实并解释区域的社会正当性如何影响个别企业的信念、企图与草创行为之间的关联性，以及这些互动效应如何取决于该区域的社会经济特徵。

社会正当性   企业精神   制度   文化   区域   心理

KIBLER E., KAUTONEN T. et FINK M. La légitimité sociale régionale de l'entrepreneuriat: les conséquences pour les intentions entrepreneuriales et le comportement de démarrage, *Regional Studies*. On développe un nouveau sens du rôle de la culture régionale dans l'émergence du comportement de démarrage au moment de la création d'entreprises. Le point de mire est la légitimité sociale régionale: la façon de voir la nécessité et la pertinence de l'entrepreneuriat dans une région. L'analyse économétrique emploie une combinaison de données longitudinales sur mesure auprès de 65 régions en Autriche et en Finlande, et des variables qui captent des caractéristiques socio-économiques régionales et qui proviennent des statistiques officielles. L'étude démontre que, et explique comment, la légitimité sociale régionale influe sur les rapports entre les convictions entrepreneuriales individuelles, les intentions et le comportement de démarrage et comment ces effets d'interaction dépendent des caractéristiques socio-économiques de la région.

Légitimité sociale   Entrepreneuriat   Institutions   Culture   Région   Psychologie

KIBLER E., KAUTONEN T. und FINK M. Regionale soziale Legitimität des Unternehmertums: Auswirkungen auf unternehmerische Absichten und Firmengründungsverhalten, *Regional Studies*. Wir entwickeln ein neues Verständnis für die Rolle der regionalen Kultur beim auftretenden Verhalten während der Neugründung von Firmen. Im Mittelpunkt der Konstruktion steht die regionale soziale Legitimität: die Beurteilung der Erwünschtheit und Angemessenheit von Unternehmertum in einer Region. Für die ökonometrische Analyse kommen eine Kombination von maßgeschneiderten longitudinalen Erhebungsdaten aus 65 Regionen in Österreich und Finnland sowie Variablen zur Erfassung von aus offiziellen Statistiken gewonnenen regionalen sozioökonomischen Merkmalen zum Einsatz. Aus der Studie geht hervor, dass und wie sich regionale soziale Legitimität auf die Beziehungen zwischen den Überzeugungen, den Absichten und dem Firmengründungsverhalten der einzelnen Unternehmer auswirkt und wie diese Wechselwirkungen durch die sozioökonomischen Merkmale der Region bedingt werden.

Soziale Legitimität Unternehmertum Institutionen Kultur Region Psychologie

KIBLER E., KAUTONEN T. y FINK M. Legitimidad social regional del empresariado: implicaciones para la intención empresarial y la conducta en la creación de empresas, *Regional Studies*. Desarrollamos una nueva manera de entender el papel de la cultura regional para la aparición de una determinada conducta en la creación de empresas. La construcción focal es la legitimidad social de ámbito regional: la percepción de la conveniencia e idoneidad del empresariado en una región. En el análisis econométrico utilizamos una combinación de datos de un estudio longitudinal a medida para 65 regiones en Austria y Finlandia, así como variables que captan las características socioeconómicas regionales que proceden de estadísticas oficiales. Además de explicar de qué modo, en el estudio demostramos que la legitimidad social de ámbito regional influye en las relaciones entre las convicciones, las intenciones y la conducta en la creación de nuevas empresas por parte de cada empresario y cómo estos efectos de interacción están condicionados por las características socioeconómicas de la región.

Legitimidad social Empresariado Instituciones Cultura Región Psicología

INTRODUCTION

Research on the regional dimension of entrepreneurship complements the traditional focus on the individual in entrepreneurship research by demonstrating the crucial role entrepreneurship plays in regional development (FRITSCH and MUELLER, 2004; MUELLER *et al.*, 2008; VAN STEL and STOREY, 2004). It also identifies a range of regional features that influence entrepreneurial activity at the individual level (ARMINGTON and ACS, 2002; FRITSCH and FALCK, 2007; REYNOLDS *et al.*, 1994). In addition to the demographic, structural and economic characteristics of regions, scholars have increasingly devoted attention to investigating the role of the regional culture as a determinant of entrepreneurship (DAVIDSSON and WIKLUND, 1997; FRITSCH and WYRWICH, 2014; AOYAMA, 2009). The results of this nascent stream of research highlight the impact of regional cultural factors, especially in the early stages of new firm formation (BOSMA and SCHUTJENS, 2011; LAFUENTE *et al.*, 2007; VAILLANT and LAFUENTE, 2007).

This article adds to the knowledge of the influence of regional culture on individual entrepreneurial activity by focusing on the early stages of founding a new business: the formation of an intention to engage in starting a business and the subsequent translation of that intention into action (KAUTONEN *et al.*, 2015). More specifically, this study proposes that the *regional social legitimacy of entrepreneurship* – understood as a convergence of perceptions in a region that entrepreneurial activity is 'desirable, proper or appropriate' (SUCHMANN, 1995, p. 574) – reflects a core element of a region's entrepreneurship culture (ETZIONI, 1987; FRITSCH and WYRWICH, 2014) and shapes the way an individual's entrepreneurial beliefs influence the intention to start a business and the likelihood of the individual turning that intention into action. The hypothesis development builds upon the psychological foundations laid by the theory of planned behaviour (TPB) (AJZEN, 1991), which is complemented with institutional approaches to sociology (SCOTT, 1995; GREENWOOD *et al.*, 2011), economic geography (GERTLER, 2010; RODRIQUEZ-POSE, 2013), and regional entrepreneurship (LAFUENTE *et al.*, 2007; LANG *et al.*, 2013). The hypotheses are tested with two waves of survey data on working-age individuals (wave 1 = 2025; wave 2 = 984) from 65 regions in Austria and Finland. In order to advance the assessment of the regional knowledge base of social legitimacy that is developed in this research, a series of models are tested where each hypothesized relationship is interacted with a set of regional socio-economic factors suggested in the previous literature.

This research makes a number of contributions to the interface between regional studies and entrepreneurship. First, the study adds significant new empirical knowledge to the limited understanding of how regional social norms affect the formation of entrepreneurial intentions (LIÑÁN *et al.*, 2011) and of how regional features influence the translation of intentions into start-up behaviour (KIBLER, 2013). As such, the study further emphasizes entrepreneurship as a place-dependent (LANG *et al.*, 2013) process of emergence (STERNBERG, 2009) and responds to the call for longitudinal and multilevel research to establish causality and uncover the mechanisms through which regional social norms influence new firm formation (BOSMA and SCHUTJENS, 2011).

Second, this study introduces the concept of the regional social legitimacy of entrepreneurship, and develops and validates a corresponding measurement instrument. Hence, it addresses the lack of congruent concepts and measurement tools for the investigation of the regional cultural embeddedness of entrepreneurship (BOSMA *et al.*, 2008; TRETTIN and WELTER, 2011). Complementing the regional legitimacy concept and design with a psychological approach, it most notably provides a new understanding of how the impact of high (or low) levels of social legitimacy on an individual's entrepreneurial beliefs, intentions and actions varies depending on the regional socio-economic environment. Consequently, the – often self-evidently used – argument that social legitimacy increases the demand for entrepreneurship (ETZIONI, 1987) is critically developed here by offering a more nuanced regional knowledge base that explains: (1) which entrepreneurial beliefs are (not) supported by social legitimacy in a particular regional context; and (2) under what regional conditions social legitimacy strengthens (or weakens) the formation of entrepreneurial intention and its translation into start-up behaviour.

Third, based on the study, a number of regional implications for policy-makers and the enterprise community can be drawn regarding how they might promote entrepreneurship. In general, the regional social legitimacy of entrepreneurship has proven to be a feasible way of leveraging entrepreneurial intentions and action levels in a region. However, the findings reveal conditions that must be fulfilled in order for such interventions to be effective. Facilitating the formation of entrepreneurial intentions in a region through high levels of social legitimacy is only successful if the support measures explicitly address individuals' perceptions of entrepreneurship as a beneficial career path (entrepreneurial attitude). While this support is independent of the regional socio-economic context, measures that strengthen individuals' beliefs that they are 'fit' for entrepreneurship (perceived entrepreneurial ability), achieved via regional social legitimacy, are especially effective in rural regions. Interventions that strive to increase the likelihood of intentions turning into start-up behaviour by enhancing the social legitimacy of entrepreneurship are most suited to economically 'disadvantaged' regions. In regions where individuals perceive the social legitimacy of entrepreneurship as low, the translation of entrepreneurial intentions into actions can be supported by measures that help to build individuals' confidence that they are capable of starting and running businesses.

THEORY

Entrepreneurial intention and start-up behaviour

The conceptual foundation of the psychological processes leading to new firm formation is based on AJZEN's (1991) theory of planned behaviour (TPB). In the TPB, intention refers to 'a person's readiness to perform a given behavior' (AJZEN, 2011) and it is seen as the immediate antecedent of behaviour. A substantial amount of research in diverse behavioural domains demonstrates that intention is a good predictor of subsequent behaviour. Meta-analyses by ARMITAGE and CONNER (2001) and SHEERAN (2002) report mean correlations of 0.47 and 0.53 between intention and behaviour, respectively; and KAUTONEN *et al.* (2013, 2015) demonstrate that the TPB accounts for 31–39% of the variation in subsequent business start-up behaviour.

The formation of an intention is influenced by three antecedents: a favourable or unfavourable evaluation of the behaviour (*attitude*); beliefs concerning the expectations of important referent groups to perform or not perform the behaviour (*subjective norm*); and the perceived ability to perform the behaviour (*perceived behavioural control* – PBC). PBC not only predicts the formation of intentions, but also, by serving as a proxy for actual control, supports the prediction of actual behaviour (AJZEN, 1991).

Regional social legitimacy of entrepreneurship

Social legitimacy in institutional theory. The theoretical foundation of the regional social legitimacy of entrepreneurship and its effects on entrepreneurial intentions and behaviour is anchored in institutional theory, which has been suggested to be an appropriate framework for examining the influence of both cultural and spatial contexts on entrepreneurial activity (WELTER, 2011). Institutional economic and sociological theories share the assumption that individual beliefs and behaviours are structured by the rules and norms prevalent in the institutional environment, while acknowledging that institutional contexts can enable and constrain individual behaviours, while also depending upon them (GIDDENS, 1984; NORTH, 1990; SCOTT, 1995; HODGSON, 2006). The understanding of institutions in the present study follows the sociological work of SCOTT (1995), which defines institutions as 'social structures that have attained a high degree of resilience. [They] are composed of [three institutional pillars:] *cultural–cognitive*, *normative*, and *regulative* elements that, together with associated activities and resources, provide stability and meaning to social life' (p. 33). The regulative pillar is understood to guide behaviour through the force of formal rules and sanctions; normative institutions guide behaviour through social norms of acceptability and morality; and the cultural–cognitive institutions guide behaviour through 'deeply entrenched assumptions and conceptions of the "way the world is"' (SCOTT, 2010, p. 7).

Reflecting SCOTT's (1995) framework, sociological institutional scholars often stress the role of social legitimacy in economic behaviour (e.g. ALDRICH and FIOL, 1994; DIMAGGIO and POWELL, 1983; for an overview, see BITEKTINE, 2011), emphasizing a strong cultural dimension of legitimating processes and the social sanctions attached to them (BITEKTINE, 2011; DEEPHOUSE and SUCHMANN, 2008). While different theoretical constructs of social legitimacy have been developed, the concept is widely seen as 'a generalized perception or assumption that the actions of an entity are desirable, proper or appropriate' (SUCHMANN, 1995, p. 574). The present article's specific definition of social legitimacy reflects Scott's normative and cognitive institutional pillars, and particularly relies on SUCHMANN's (1995) conceptualization, which involves three dimensions of social legitimacy: *pragmatic*, *moral* and *cognitive* legitimacy. Applied to the entrepreneurial context, pragmatic legitimacy reflects self-interested calculations concerning entrepreneurship; moral legitimacy relies on normative evaluations of entrepreneurship; and cognitive legitimacy rests on taken-for-granted assumptions of entrepreneurship, irrespective of a negative, a positive or no valuation. Suchmann further refined this framework with two substantive foci of legitimacy, which in this context further distinguish between the perceived social legitimacy of what entrepreneurs do (*action*) and what values they represent (*essence*).

Regional perspective to social legitimacy. This study complements SUCHMANN's (1995) conceptualization with an institutional perspective on economic geography and regional entrepreneurship in order to emphasize the local dimension in the concept of social legitimacy. The extant literature contains a number of conceptualizations and empirical studies that provide direct or indirect information on social legitimacy as a regional phenomenon. For instance, GONZÁLEZ and HEALEY (2005) develop an institutional approach to regional economic activity that emphasizes the role of the social meanings that individuals attach to the region in which they are embedded. OSTROM's (2005) institutional framework suggests that economic processes in a region must be understood in the context of the common attributes and norms of behaviour prevalent in the regional community. She further argues that certain informal rules-in-use reflect the social expectations of the 'do's and don'ts' (p. 832) in a regional community that sanction its members' choices and behaviour. Inspired by the work of HOLMÉN (1995) and MARTIN (2000), HAYTER (2004, p. 107) underlines that regions develop specific region-bounded 'values, processes of valuations [and] modes of thought' over time that arguably reflect the core elements of social legitimacy. RAFIQUI (2009, p. 341) highlights the regional variability of social norms by emphasizing that 'varying physical environments and historical experiences means that beliefs [and] institutions [. . .] differ between places'. Supporting this argumentation, GERTLER's (2010) and RODRIQUEZ-POSE's (2013) recent work on institutional theory in economic geography suggests that regions cultivate distinctive institutional contexts over time, which leads to various social evaluations of economic activity.

In a similar vein, THORNTON and FLYNN (2003) and LANG *et al.* (2013) conclude that the geographic environment for entrepreneurial activity needs to be understood based on the social boundaries of local communities, reflecting the cognitive and culture-based shared meanings and valuations amongst the members of the community. Encapsulating Scott's view with a local perspective, MARQUIS and BATTILANA (2009, p. 294) further theorize 'that local communities are institutional arenas that have an enduring influence on organizational behaviour through regulative, normative, and cultural–cognitive processes'. These processes, in turn, are encoded in 'local' rules that are reflected in everyday expectations and practices, potentially affecting how members of the regional community perceive the social value of economic behaviours (GREENWOOD *et al.*, 2011; LANG and ROESSL, 2011). In line with ETZIONI's (1987) theorizations, the social legitimacy of entrepreneurship reflects one important aspect of the cultural and normative environment, which can support or hinder the emergence of entrepreneurial activity across different geographical contexts. Drawing upon these foundations, this study understands regional social legitimacy as the perceived normative rules-in-use concerning a particular behaviour in a regional community, which reflect the local understandings and beliefs concerning the social acceptance of that behaviour.

Influence of regional social legitimacy of entrepreneurship on new firm formation

While the concept of the regional social legitimacy of entrepreneurship is novel, prior studies provide indirect evidence on its relevance in the early stages of the firm formation process. For instance, DAVIDSSON and WIKLUND (1997) suggest that the prevalence of certain socio-cultural values affects regional levels of new firm formation. BOSMA and SCHUTJENS (2011) demonstrate that informal institutions at the regional level can play a stronger role in shaping entrepreneurial attitudes and behaviour than national institutional contexts. In addition, previous institutional entrepreneurship studies commonly suggest social acceptance of business failure and the presence of entrepreneurial role models in a region are potentially socio-cultural forces that influence early-stage entrepreneurship (LAFUENTE *et al.*, 2007; VAILLANT and LAFUENTE, 2007). As such, the recent literature highlights the importance of examining social values and norms affecting enterprising activity in a regional context. However, few studies address how specific regional cultural norms influence the psychological processes leading to the emergence of new firms.

To the best of the authors' knowledge, the only study to date that explicitly examines the cognitive mechanisms underpinning business start-up intentions in a regional cultural context is that by LIÑÁN *et al.* (2011), which combines an institutional approach with the TPB and shows that the influence of perceived societal values on individual entrepreneurial beliefs differs significantly between the two Spanish regions examined. Their study further proposes that examining the moderating role of the regional socio-cultural environment on entrepreneurial beliefs adds to the knowledge of how entrepreneurial intentions emerge. This concurs with the recent findings of KIBLER's

(2013) study, which demonstrate that different demographic, economic and structural features of a region can moderate the impact of entrepreneurial beliefs on the formation of entrepreneurial intention.

In addition to the aforementioned literature, the hypotheses in the present study are founded upon ETZIONI's (1987) and LIAO and WELSCH's (2005) investigations. ETZIONI (1987, p. 175) suggests that 'the extent to which entrepreneurship is legitimate, the demand for it is higher; the supply of entrepreneurship is higher; and more resources are allocated to the entrepreneurial function'. He adds that the 'acceptance of the risk taking involved will be much higher if entrepreneurship is legitimated' (p. 186). LIAO and WELSCH (2005) further emphasize that social legitimacy plays a particular role in new firm formation as it facilitates access by potential and nascent entrepreneurs to social capital and other external resources. Following these reflections, the present study's main theoretical argument is based on the assumption that the more an individual perceives entrepreneurship as socially legitimatized in a region, the more likely she or he evaluates a regional environment as benevolent and munificent for entrepreneurial activity. Accordingly, it is argued here that the regional social legitimacy of entrepreneurship has a positive influence on the beliefs leading to the formation of entrepreneurial intentions and to their translation into start-up behaviour.

Applying the regional interaction logic suggested by KIBLER (2013), it is specifically proposed here that a higher degree of regional social legitimacy of entrepreneurship strengthens an individual's certainty in their entrepreneurial beliefs – entrepreneurial attitude, perceived social support and perceived entrepreneurial ability – which, in turn, affects how strongly those beliefs affect the formation of entrepreneurial intention. Similarly, it is suggested that a higher level of regional social legitimacy, associated with a supportive and less risky environment for entrepreneurship (ETZIONI, 1987), can strengthen an individual's certainty of their intention and PBC, which increases the likelihood of intentions turning into action. Therefore, the specific research hypotheses offered for empirical testing are as follows:

Hypothesis 1 (H1): Regional social legitimacy of entrepreneurship strengthens the positive impact of (1) attitudes, (2) subjective norms and (3) perceived behavioural control (PBC) on entrepreneurial intentions.

Hypothesis 2 (H2): Regional social legitimacy of entrepreneurship strengthens the positive impact of (1) entrepreneurial intentions and (2) perceived behavioural control (PBC) on start-up behaviour.

Regional social legitimacy of entrepreneurship and the socio-economic context in the region

So far, the current study has hypothesized relationships that pertain to an individual's attitudes, perceptions, intentions and behaviours. This section outlines the argument that these relationships might vary depending on the specific socio-economic characteristics of the region where the individual lives. This argument is founded on recent studies that have emphasized the role of regional socio-economic factors in the nascent or pre-action phase of entrepreneurship (BOSMA and SCHUTJENS, 2011; KIBLER, 2013). However, since there is yet no direct evidence on the regional determinants of social legitimacy effects in the formation of entrepreneurial intention and its translation into start-up behaviour, this section omits formal hypotheses and instead offers a discussion that draws upon the existing regional entrepreneurship knowledge and provides a conceptual base to complement and assess the main hypotheses outlined above.

The literature suggests that urban, highly populated regions tend to support business start-up processes by providing more accessible market opportunities and entrepreneurial resources than rural, sparsely populated areas (KEEBLE and WALKER, 1994; REYNOLDS *et al.*, 1994; TÖDTLING and WANZENBÖCK, 2003). Often associated with urban contexts, a greater number of well-educated people in a region has often been found to raise entrepreneurial activity levels (ARMINGTON and ACS, 2002; AUDRETSCH and FRITSCH, 1994; BOSMA *et al.*, 2008). This is perhaps due to higher levels of creativity and innovation in the region (LEE *et al.*, 2004) and more established local, entrepreneurial networks (MAILLAT, 1995). When accompanied by higher education levels, 'younger' regional age compositions tend to induce a greater local potential of (high-growth) entrepreneurship (BOSMA *et al.*, 2008; BOSMA and SCHUTJENS, 2011), supported by the finding that (nascent) entrepreneurial activity levels are particularly high amongst people aged 25–44 years (REYNOLDS, 1997; PARKER, 2009). Subsequently, *regional demographic characteristics* also reflect how entrepreneurship is socially valued in the region (MARQUIS and BATTILANA, 2009), through co-determining the local availability of and access to entrepreneurial opportunities, networks and capital (AUDRETSCH and KEILBACH, 2004). In line with the evidence presented, regions with a high population density and a larger pool of young, well-educated workers may particularly strengthen local beliefs that entrepreneurship is appropriate and taken for granted, thus potentially conditioning the influence of social legitimacy on an individual's intention formation and start-up behaviour in the region.

Regional economic and *labour market characteristics* may also influence the way social legitimacy affects entrepreneurial intentions and actions. Previous research suggests that regions with higher income and wealth levels tend to provide favourable conditions for entrepreneurship. This influence has been ascribed to an increased spending capacity, higher demand for products, a greater supply of resources for business capitalization and lower borrowing costs (STAM, 2010). However, higher regional economic levels can make paid employment comparatively more attractive (BOSMA *et al.*, 2008) and potentially reflect the higher opportunity costs of becoming an entrepreneur in the region (ASHCROFT *et al.*, 1991). In addition, higher unemployment rates can indicate a lower demand for new businesses in the region (REYNOLDS *et al.*, 1994), but at the same time can increase the proportion of people being pushed towards entrepreneurship (AUDRETSCH and FRITSCH, 1994; BOSMA and SCHUTJENS, 2011). Furthermore, regions with a large share of service sector employment might indicate lower average business foundation costs (FRITSCH, 1997). Thus, contrary to the cost-intensive manufacturing sector, skills and educational references are the key to starting a business in a region dominated by the service sector (BRIXY and GROTZ, 2007). Such regions offer a local environment with more room to discover and exploit entrepreneurial opportunities (VAN STEL and STOREY, 2004). Accordingly, economic and labour market characteristics are relevant regional conditions for the emergence of entrepreneurship (STERNBERG, 2009), which in turn may relate to the extent to which regional social legitimacy affects the entrepreneurial process.

The previous research suggests that higher *regional entrepreneurship levels* in the past serve as an ongoing conduit for a positive entrepreneurial climate (ANDERSON and KOSTER, 2011), for instance, through increased innovation activities, knowledge spillovers, competition and firm diversity (AUDRETSCH and KEILBACH, 2004; FRITSCH and MUELLER, 2007). Moreover, higher levels of entrepreneurial activity can provide positive role models through showcasing successful firm formation stories (VAILLANT and LAFUENTE, 2007), which can foster local entrepreneurial learning processes (SORENSON and AUDIA, 2000) and thus the development of local perceptions favourable to entrepreneurship (FORNAHL, 2003; MINNITI, 2005). To this FRITSCH and WYRWICH's (2014) recent study adds that the establishment of a persistent regional entrepreneurship culture is rooted in higher entrepreneurial activity levels in certain periods in the past. Against this backdrop, higher business start-up rates help create a positive entrepreneurial climate in the region, thus arguably strengthening any recent influence on entrepreneurial beliefs and start-up behaviour exercised by the regional social legitimacy of entrepreneurship.

In summary, the available evidence suggests that demographic, economic, labour market characteristics and also past business start-up levels can have implications for individual enterprising activity. To what extent these socio-economic factors condition the way the regional social legitimacy of entrepreneurship influences the psychological processes that lead to the formation of entrepreneurial intentions and their subsequent translation into start-up behaviour is an empirical question in this study. Fig. 1 provides a summary of the relationships that will be examined in the following empirical analysis.

DATA AND VARIABLES

Data collection

The survey was conducted in two waves (in 2011 and 2012) in Austria and Finland by means of a postal

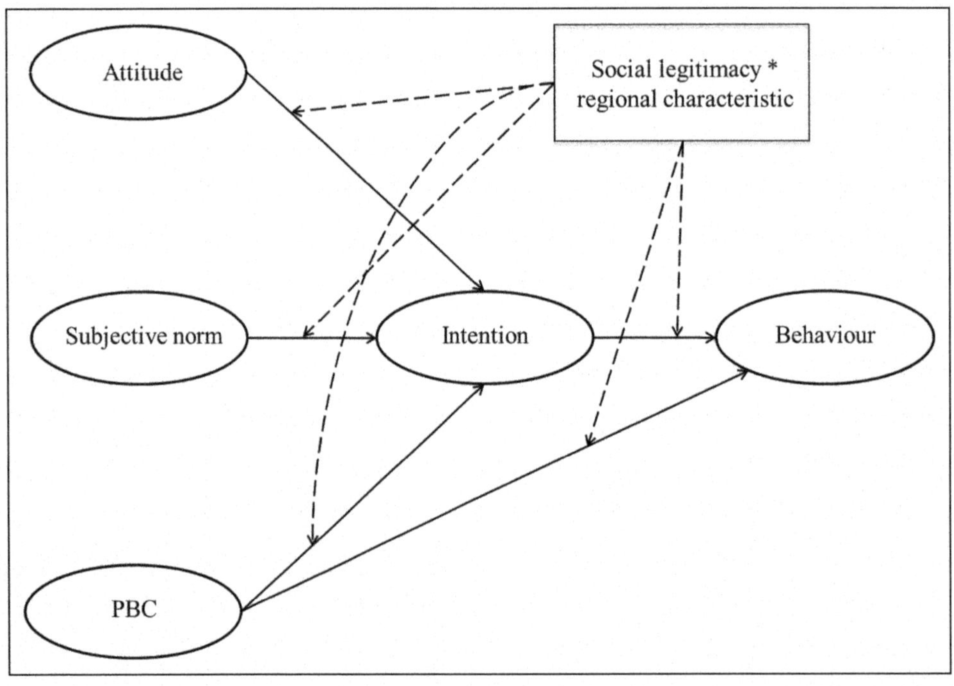

Fig. 1. Research model
Note: PBC, perceived behavioural control

survey targeting the working-age population (aged 20–64 years). Two countries were included in the research design in order to examine the robustness of the findings across different national environments.

In the first wave, 10 000 questionnaires were distributed in Finland and 15 000 in Austria. The questionnaires were sent to randomly selected respondents in a representative range of regions according to a strategy devised in consultation with statisticians at the Finnish Population Register Centre and Statistics Austria. The regions were selected randomly from a pool of 146 Austrian (with a population of more than 5000 people) and 193 Finnish municipalities (with a population of more than 3000 people) following a stratified sampling logic to ensure that the choice of municipalities represented different regional cultures and the three municipality types: urban, semi-urban and rural (STATISTICS AUSTRIA, 2011a; STATISTICS FINLAND, 2011). The resulting Austrian sample comes from 27 municipalities of which nine are urban, nine semi-urban and nine rural; while the Finnish sample encompasses 38 municipalities of which 14 are urban, 12 semi-urban and 12 rural. Figs 2 and 3 present the sample regions on country maps. Further details of the regional sampling logic are available from the authors upon request.

The postal survey produced 2263 responses in Finland and 1024 responses in Austria. Thus, the respective response rates were 23% and 7%, respectively. The difference in response rates is partly explained by cultural factors (the research team's prior experience suggests that response rates in Austria are much lower than in Finland) and partly by differences in the sampling approach. The Finnish research team could derive an exactly specified sample with up-to-date addresses from the Population Register Centre; while the Austrian team had to apply a heuristic approach based on names and addresses derived from an online phone book. While applying regional weighting, ensuring a gender balance and maintaining the random sampling logic were unproblematic in both countries; the Austrian task was less efficient because of outdated address information that resulted in 1519 undeliverable mailings and a lack of *ex-ante* information on people's ages. As a result, many of the responses received were from people outside the specified age range. Therefore, the actual usable sample of 766 Austrian individuals between 20 and 64 years of age is considerably smaller than the initial sample of 1024 individuals.

Since this article concerns entrepreneurial intentions and their subsequent translation into start-up behaviour, individuals who were already self-employed in 2011 (18% of the total sample) were excluded from the analysis, leaving 2446 eligible observations (23% Austrian). Furthermore, 421 cases had to be deleted because of an excessive number of missing responses, which would have compromised the validity of the multi-item indices. A comparison of the demographic characteristics of the final sample of 2025 cases with the sample of 2446 eligible cases suggests that the exclusions on the grounds of missing responses have not introduced a notable demographic bias to the data.

The second wave of data collection included all eligible respondents in the final first-wave Austrian sample and those Finnish respondents who were included in the final first-wave sample and who had given their permission to be contacted in a follow-up study. Consequently, researchers distributed 1002

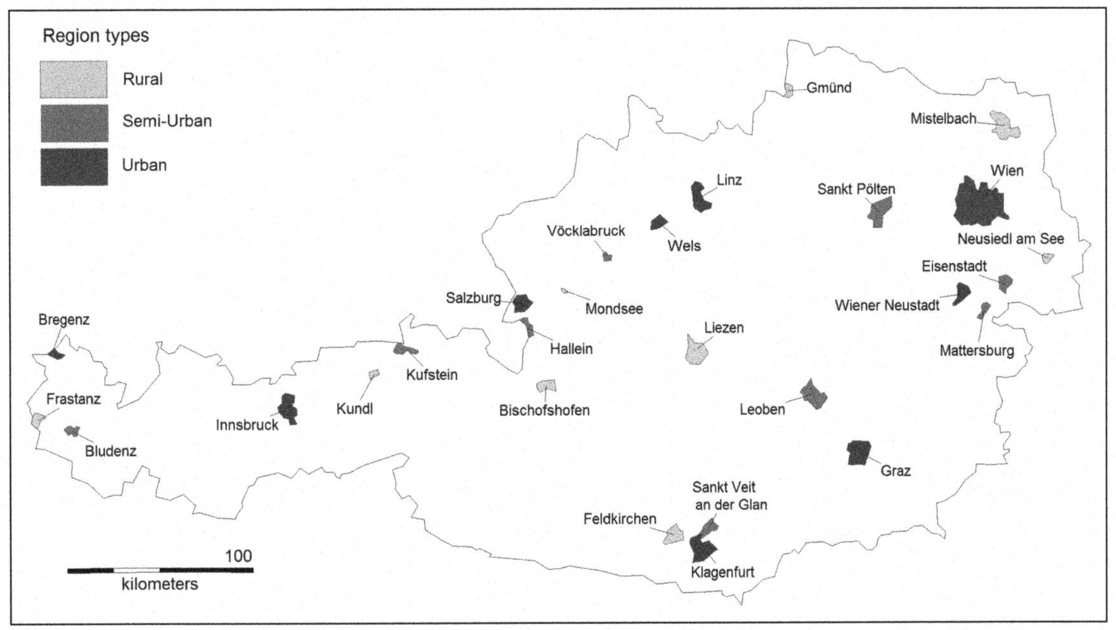

Fig. 2. Austrian regions in the sample

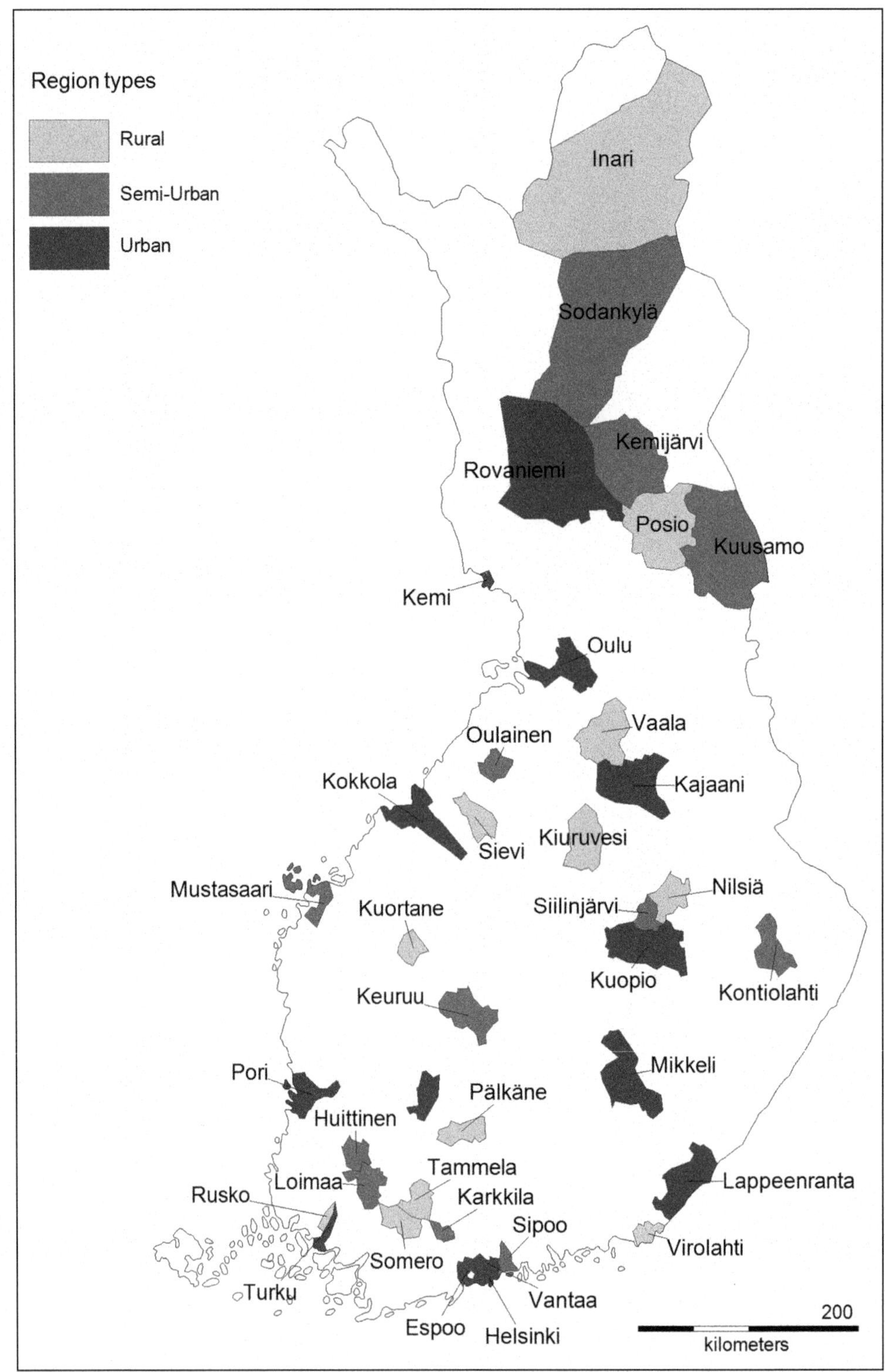

Fig. 3. Finnish regions in the sample

questionnaires in Finland and 455 in Austria by post. Subjects from Finland who had not responded within three weeks were sent a reminder by post. In Austria, prior experience indicated that telephone calls would be the more effective follow-up method. This process resulted in 732 responses in Finland (a response rate of 73%) and 252 in Austria (a response rate of 55%).

Non-response bias

The current research adopts an archival analysis approach to examining non-response bias (ROGELBERG and STANTON, 2007). Accordingly, the Finnish first-wave sample of 1570 respondents was compared with the original list of 10 000 randomly selected individuals received from the Population Register Centre; similarly, the

Austrian first-wave sample of 455 respondents was compared with an officially available list of the age and gender distribution supplied by STATISTICS AUSTRIA (2011b). The comparison shows that the average ages of the respondents in the sample are the same as the national averages in the age group 20–64 years (44 in Finland and 42 in Austria). Finnish women have a higher comparative participation rate than Finnish men, since 60% of the respondents in the Finnish sample are women compared with 49% in the original list. The Austrian sample, on the other hand, has an almost even gender distribution with 51% of respondents being women. Within the municipality types of urban, semi-urban and rural, the response rates range from 22% to 24% in Finland and from 6% to 8% in Austria. Thus, there is no notable regional type bias in the sample.

In the second-wave sample, the average age was 44 years in both countries; and the proportion of women in the sample was 62% in Finland and 55% in Austria. The distribution of the respondents across the three region types is nearly identical in the first and second survey waves. Hence, the most notable bias appears to be the over-representation of women in both waves of the Finnish sample. However, since the purpose of this research is to test theoretical relationships rather than to provide representative descriptive statistics, minor differences between the sample and the population are not expected to exert a major influence on the analysis.

Variables

Theory of planned behaviour (TPB). Intention, behaviour, attitude, subjective norms and PBC were operationalized by referring to AJZEN's (2011) instructions and previous empirical work applying the TPB in the entrepreneurial context (KAUTONEN *et al.*, 2015; KOLVEREID, 1996; SOUITARIS *et al.*, 2007). Each construct was measured with multiple items using six-point rating scales (see Table A1 in Appendix A). Following AJZEN (2011), all items refer to the same behaviour (engaging in activities to start a business) and the same time frame (within the coming 12 months). After factor-analysing the multi-item scales (see below), composite indices were computed for all constructs by averaging the relevant items. The Cronbach's alpha scores for the five indices ranged from 0.81 to 0.94.

Regional social legitimacy of entrepreneurship. The regional social legitimacy of entrepreneurship is operationalized in line with SUCHMANN's (1995) conceptualization and includes three subscales of legitimacy – *practical, moral* and *cognitive* – with each scale comprising two underlying foci – *actions* and *essences* (see Table A1 in Appendix A). The practical legitimacy subscale measures whether an individual perceives the activity of entrepreneurs in their region to be beneficial for themselves (action) and the values held by local entrepreneurs to be similar to their own (essence). The cognitive legitimacy subscale reflects taken-for-granted assumptions, measuring the degree to which an individual views the activity of local entrepreneurs as necessary (action) and the absence of entrepreneurs in their region as inconceivable (essence). The moral legitimacy subscale indicates whether an individual perceives local entrepreneurs as trustworthy and operating according to the common norms in their region (essence) as well as contributing to the local economy (action) and social well-being of all local people (action). Thus, the final index capturing the regional social legitimacy of entrepreneurship consists of seven items (Cronbach's alpha = 0.85).

Regional socio-economic characteristics. In line with the theoretical reasoning, eight regional socio-economic sets of data were selected from the databases of STATISTICS FINLAND (2013) and STATISTICS AUSTRIA (2013). While the required data were fully accessible through the publicly available databases of Statistics Finland, specific access and assistance was required from STATISTICS AUSTRIA (2013) to guarantee an accurate secondary regional data-collection process in both countries. The description of the regional socio-economic variables is depicted in Table 1.

Table 1. Regional socio-economic characteristics

Variable	Description	Mean	SD
Population density	Number of inhabitants per km^2 (2011); log transformed for regression analysis	479.9	873.7
Educational level	Proportion of people (%) aged 25–64 years with a tertiary education degree (levels 5 or 6 in the International Standard Classification of Education (ISCED) classification, 2010)	0.14	0.04
Age structure	Proportion of people (%) aged 25–44 years in the population aged between 20 and 64 years (2011)	0.42	0.07
Service sector employment	Proportion of the labour force (%) employed in the service sector (2010)	0.70	0.13
Unemployment rate	Number of unemployed individuals divided by the number of individuals in the labour force (2011)	0.08	0.03
Entry rate	Number of business start-ups in the period 2005–2010 divided by the stock of firms	0.08	0.02
GRP	Gross regional product (€ per capita) (2010); log transformed for regression analysis	30 047	7806
GRP growth	Growth of GRP, 2005–10 (%)	0.13	0.08

Note: Means and standard deviations (SD) across the 65 regions in the sample.

Covariates. The regression models include several covariates at the individual and regional levels. The first one of the four individual-level covariates is a dummy indicating whether the individual is *female* or *male*, which controls the potential effect of the common and consistent finding of a lower entrepreneurial propensity among women (XAVIER *et al.*, 2013). The second one is the respondent's *age* in years in a quadratic specification, which adjusts the models for the well-known inverse 'U'-shaped effect of age on entrepreneurial activity (LÉVESQUE and MINNITI, 2006). Third, a dummy variable, measuring whether the respondent has (never) started a business in the past controls for the influence of previous *entrepreneurial experience*, which has been found to be an important influence in the TPB context (CONNER and ARMITAGE, 1998). The fourth individual-level covariate is the respondent's perception of the *local acceptance of business failure* (LAFUENTE *et al.*, 2007; VAILLANT and LAFUENTE, 2007). This variable is measured with a six-point rating scale inquiring the extent to which the respondent thinks that entrepreneurs who fail in their business are frowned upon by local people. At the regional level, the analysis controls for the impact of the *type of region* (urban, semi-urban and rural) (BOSMA *et al.*, 2008; STAM, 2010), as well as the *country* the region is in.

Factor analysis

Before index scores were computed, the multi-item measurement scales (see Table A1 in Appendix A) were factor analysed. Since the exploratory principal components analysis (PCA) did not indicate a need to remove items, a confirmatory factor analysis (CFA) was performed in order to subject the factor structure to a stringent test. The CFA was estimated separately for the first- and second-wave Finnish and Austrian subsamples. All indicators loaded on their intended constructs with the 0.1% significance level. The conventional fit indices suggested an acceptable fit between the model and the data according to the criteria proposed by HU and BENTLER (1999) for maximum

Table 2. Descriptive statistics for the survey data

	Range		(1) First wave (all, N = 2025)		(2) First wave (not in second wave, N = 1041)		(3) Second wave (N = 984)		Difference between (2) and (3)
	Minimum	Maximum	Mean	SD	Mean	SD	Mean	SD	t/χ^2
Behaviour	1	5.67					1.23	0.63	
Intention	1	6	1.67	1.14	1.64	1.10	1.70	1.18	t = 1.23
Attitude	1	6	2.74	1.29	2.72	1.26	2.77	1.32	t = 0.82
Subjective norm	1	24	4.52	3.75	4.47	3.71	4.56	3.79	t = 0.54
Perceived behavioural control (PBC)	1	6	3.19	1.31	3.15	1.30	3.23	1.32	t = 1.26
Regional social legitimacy	1	6	4.65	0.77	4.59	0.80	4.72	0.73	t = 3.92**
Acceptance of failure	1	6	3.82	1.05	3.78	1.08	3.85	1.02	t = 1.37
Age	20	64	43.68	12.65	43.12	12.85	44.27	12.40	t = 2.05*
Female	0	1	0.58		0.56		0.60		$\chi^2_{1d.f.}$ = 3.78
Entrepreneurial experience	0	1	0.14		0.14		0.14		$\chi^2_{1d.f.}$ = 0.01
Education									$\chi^2_{3d.f.}$ = 6.75
Primary	0	0	0.08		0.09		0.06		
Vocational	0	1	0.22		0.23		0.21		
Secondary	0	1	0.33		0.32		0.34		
Tertiary	0	1	0.37		0.36		0.38		
Occupational status									$\chi^2_{3d.f.}$ = 2.10
Employed	0	0	0.71		0.70		0.72		
Job seeker	0	1	0.06		0.06		0.05		
Retired/incapacity	0	1	0.10		0.10		0.10		
Other not in labour force	0	1	0.13		0.14		0.13		
Austria	0	1	0.22		0.20		0.26		$\chi^2_{1d.f.}$ = 10.84**
Region type[a]									$\chi^2_{2d.f.}$ = 0.40
Rural	0	1	0.16/0.31		0.15		0.16		
Semi-urban	0	1	0.22/0.32		0.23		0.22		
Urban	0	0	0.62/0.37		0.62		0.62		

Notes: [a]Column (1) presents the percentages of observations and regions, e.g. 16% of respondents live in rural regions while 31% of the included regions are classified as rural.

The difference column displays the t-statistic (2023 d.f.) for continuous and the Chi-squared statistic for indicator variables, $*p < 0.05$ and $**p < 0.01$ (two-tailed t-test).

likelihood estimation: the comparative fit index (CFI) ≥ 0.95 (Austria: first wave = 0.96/second wave = 0.95; Finland: 0.96/0.96), the root mean square error (RMSEA) < 0.06 (Austria: 0.054/0.058; Finland: 0.055/0.050) and the standardized root mean squared residual (SRMR) < 0.08 (Austria: 0.043/0.051; Finland: 0.037/0.042). Models using the full sample including respondents from both countries result in similarly satisfactory fit indices in both waves (CFI = 0.96/0.97, RMSEA = 0.051/0.046 and SRMR = 0.033/0.038). Therefore, the analysts concluded it was safe to compute indices for each construct by averaging the item scores.

Descriptive statistics

Table 2 presents the descriptive statistics for the survey data including a comparison of the first and second survey waves. Table 3 displays the correlation matrix for the continuous and binary variables in the survey data. Some of the intercorrelations are relatively high. However, the variance inflation factor (VIF) scores are moderate (with a mean of 2.9) and thus do not suggest the presence of serious multicollinearity.

ANALYSIS

Model specification

The data used in this analysis contain two levels: individual and regional. In addition to the data containing independent variables at both levels (the dependent variables are both measured at the individual level), the individual responses are not independent because they are clustered in the 65 municipalities included in the analysis. The hierarchical structure of the data has two important consequences for econometric strategy. First, the clustering of individual responses in the 65 municipalities means that residual errors may not be independently distributed. As a result, the analysis had to address the Moulton problem arising from the clustered nature of the data, as it could affect the reliability of the standard error estimates (ANGRIST and PISCHKE, 2009). Second, in order to examine the extent to which the effect of social legitimacy varies regionally, the analysis required information on its variance across the 65 municipalities.

These requirements dictated that the econometric technique of choice would be multilevel regression. This technique not only solves the Moulton problem of clustered data by distinguishing between the individual- and regional-level error components, it also provides information on the variance of the effect of social legitimacy across regions by allowing the effect to vary at the regional level (HOX, 2010).

The research design includes two dependent variables: intention to engage in activities aimed at starting a business and subsequent behaviour. A series of model specifications pertaining to each will be estimated. The principal econometric model is given by:

$$y_{ij} = \alpha_j + \beta_1 x_{1ij} + \cdots + \beta_k x_{kij} + \gamma_1 z_{1j} + \cdots + \gamma_q z_{qj} + u_j + v_j x_{\mathrm{SL}ij} + \varepsilon_{ij} \qquad (1)$$

where the variable y_{ij} represents the level of intention or behaviour for an individual $i(i = 1, \ldots, n)$ who lives in region $j(j = 1, \ldots, 65)$. The symbols $x_{1ij}, \ldots, x_{kij}$ denote individual-level variables; $z_{1j}, \ldots, z_{qj}$ are the regional-level variables; and $\beta_1, \ldots, \beta_k$ and $\gamma_1, \ldots, \gamma_q$ are the respective coefficients. The residual error terms for the intercept (u_j) and the coefficient of social legitimacy $(v_j x_{\mathrm{SL}ij})$ measure region-specific effects that are not included in the model and thus control for unobserved heterogeneity across regions. The symbol ε_{ij} denotes the individual-level residual error.

Estimations of unconditional effects

The first stage of analysis estimated a series of model specifications containing the unconditional effects of the explanatory variables and covariates on both dependent variables to provide a foundation for subsequent testing of the conditional hypotheses involving

Table 3. Correlations for the survey data

	1	2	3	4	5	6	7	8	9	10
1. Behaviour	1									
2. Intention	0.57*	1								
3. Attitude	0.42*	0.62*	1							
4. Subjective norm	0.41*	0.61*	0.57*	1						
5. Perceived behavioural control (PBC)	0.31*	0.39*	0.41*	0.29*	1					
6. Regional social legitimacy	0.04	0.07*	0.12*	0.10*	0.10*	1				
7. Age	−0.05	−0.04	−0.09*	−0.07*	0.02	0.07*	1			
8. Acceptance of failure	−0.04	−0.04	−0.00	−0.02	0.03	0.27*	0.01	1		
9. Entrepreneurial experience	0.15*	0.19*	0.15*	0.14*	0.21*	0.02	0.19*	−0.01	1	
10. Female	−0.05	−0.14*	−0.14*	−0.08*	−0.17*	0.04	−0.07*	0.07*	−0.07*	1
11. Austria	−0.02	−0.02	−0.09*	−0.10*	0.03	−0.08*	−0.08*	−0.02	−0.03	−0.07*

Note: Values are Pearson correlations. All correlations are based on the full first-wave sample ($N = 2025$) except for column 1 which is based on the second-wave sample ($N = 984$). *Significance at the 5% level.

Table 4. Random-intercept regression estimates of the unconditional effects

	Dependent variable: intention		Dependent variable: behaviour	
	β	SE	*β*	SE
Individual level				
Intention			0.28**	0.02
Regional social legitimacy	–0.01	0.02	–0.00	0.02
Attitude	0.32**	0.02		
Subjective norm	0.11**	0.01		
Perceived behavioural control (PBC)	0.10**	0.02	0.05**	0.01
Age	0.03*	0.01	–0.00	0.01
Age-squared	–0.00*	0.00	0.00	0.00
Female	–0.08*	0.04	0.06	0.03
Entrepreneurial experience	0.19**	0.05	0.09	0.05
Acceptance of failure	–0.03	0.02	–0.02	0.02
Education				
Vocational	0.03	0.08	–0.03	0.08
Secondary	0.05	0.08	–0.04	0.07
Tertiary	0.04	0.08	–0.03	0.08
Occupational status				
Job seeker	0.10	0.08	0.04	0.07
Retired	0.08	0.07	–0.04	0.06
Other	0.13*	0.06	0.02	0.06
Regional level				
Austria	0.18	0.14	0.13	0.13
Region type				
Rural	–0.07	0.09	0.05	0.08
Semi-urban	–0.10	0.07	0.06	0.07
Population density (log)	0.00	0.02	0.01	0.02
Entry rate	0.02	0.04	–0.03	0.03
Educational level	–0.02	0.62	–0.41	0.56
Unemployment rate	–10.05	10.07	–10.26	0.97
Gross regional product (GRP) (log)	–0.31*	0.15	0.08	0.14
Growth of GRP	–0.09	0.29	–0.12	0.27
Age structure	0.19	0.56	–0.25	0.53
Service sector employment	0.06	0.28	0.08	0.26
Intercept	2.56	1.53	0.52	1.44
Number of observations	2025		984	
Overall R^2	0.30		0.19	
Log-likelihood	–2417.94		–729.49	

Note: Values are maximum likelihood estimates. Random-intercept variances in all models are negligibly small and not significant, and thus not reported. * and **Statistical significance at the 5% and 1% levels (two-tailed), respectively. Overall R^2 is computed as the residual variance of the focal model subtracted from the residual variance of the null model (without predictors) and then divided by the residual variance of the null model.

Table 5. Marginal effects of attitude, subjective norms, perceived behavioural control (PBC) and intention at different levels of regional social legitimacy of entrepreneurship

	Dependent variable: intention			Dependent variable: behaviour	
	Attitude	Subjective norms	PBC	Intention	PBC
Social legitimacy –2 SD	0.27** (0.03)	0.10** (0.01)	0.09** (0.03)	0.23** (0.04)	0.12** (0.03)
Social legitimacy –1 SD	0.30** (0.02)	0.11** (0.01)	0.09** (0.02)	0.25** (0.03)	0.08** (0.02)
Social legitimacy +1 SD	0.34** (0.02)	0.11** (0.01)	0.10** (0.02)	0.29** (0.02)	0.02 (0.02)
Social legitimacy +2 SD	0.36** (0.04)	0.11** (0.01)	0.11** (0.03)	0.31** (0.03)	–0.01 (0.03)

Note: Values are maximum likelihood estimates of coefficients and standard errors. * and **Statistical significance at the 5% and 1% levels (two-tailed), respectively. In addition to the multiplicative interaction terms, each model estimate contains the full set of covariates in the respective models in Table 4.

Table 6. Marginal effects of attitude, subjective norms, perceived behavioural control (PBC), and intention at different levels of regional social legitimacy and socio-economic characteristics

	Dependent variable: intention						Dependent variable: behaviour			
	Attitude		Subjective norms		PBC		Intention		PBC	
Social legitimacy	−1 SD	+1 SD	−1 SD	+1 SD	−1 SD	+1 SD	−1 SD	+1 SD	−1 SD	+1 SD
Population density										
−1 SD	0.27**	0.35**	0.09**	0.11**	0.11**	0.15**	0.27**	0.27**	0.09**	0.01
+1 SD	0.31**	0.33**	0.12**	0.12**	0.06*	0.08**	0.28**	0.29**	0.06*	0.04
Entry rate										
−1 SD	0.30**	0.35**	0.12**	0.13**	0.06*	0.07*	0.30**	0.25**	0.09**	0.03
+1 SD	0.28**	0.35**	0.08**	0.11**	0.12**	0.16**	0.24**	0.32**	0.06*	0.01
Educational level										
−1 SD	0.29**	0.35**	0.10**	0.11**	0.08**	0.14**	0.29**	0.28**	0.08**	−0.00
+1 SD	0.28**	0.34**	0.11**	0.12**	0.09**	0.08**	0.26**	0.28**	0.07**	0.04*
Unemployment rate										
−1 SD	0.30**	0.37**	0.11**	0.13**	0.06*	0.12**	0.39**	0.32**	0.13**	0.02
+1 SD	0.29**	0.31**	0.09**	0.10**	0.11**	0.10**	0.15**	0.22**	−0.01	0.02
Gross regional product (GRP)										
−1 SD	0.29**	0.36**	0.10**	0.12**	0.10**	0.14**	0.24**	0.29**	0.10**	0.02
+1 SD	0.29**	0.33**	0.11**	0.11**	0.07*	0.08**	0.31**	0.27**	0.04	0.03
Growth of GRP										
−1 SD	0.30*	0.32**	0.10**	0.10**	0.08**	0.08**	0.21**	0.32**	0.08**	0.05*
+1 SD	0.28**	0.37**	0.10**	0.13**	0.09**	0.15**	0.34**	0.25**	0.08**	−0.00
Age structure										
−1 SD	0.29**	0.32**	0.09**	0.11**	0.10**	0.13**	0.22**	0.26**	0.10**	0.03
+1 SD	0.29**	0.37**	0.11**	0.12**	0.07**	0.09**	0.33**	0.29**	0.06*	0.02
Service sector employment										
−1 SD	0.30**	0.36**	0.10**	0.11**	0.10**	0.15**	0.29**	0.30**	0.09**	0.02
+1 SD	0.28**	0.33**	0.10**	0.12**	0.07*	0.07**	0.25**	0.27**	0.04	0.03

Notes: Values are maximum likelihood estimates. * and **Statistical significance at the 5% and 1% levels (two-tailed), respectively. In addition to the multiplicative interaction terms, each model estimate contains the full set of covariates in the respective models in Table 4.

Table 7. Summary of the main findings

Unconditional effect	Conditional on regional social legitimacy	Conditional on regional social legitimacy and socio-economic characteristics
Attitude has a positive effect on intention	Attitude has a stronger effect when regional social legitimacy is high	Not affected by socio-economic characteristics of the region
Subjective norms have a positive effect on intention	Effect of subjective norms is not conditional on regional social legitimacy	Not affected by socio-economic characteristics of the region
Perceived behavioural control (PBC) has a positive effect on intention	Effect of PBC is conditional on regional social legitimacy only in certain regional contexts	PBC has a stronger effect on intention when regional social legitimacy is high and … : … population density is low … entry rate is high … education level is low … unemployment rate is low … gross regional product (GRP) is low … service sector employment is low
Intention has a positive effect on behaviour	Effect of intention is stronger when regional social legitimacy is high; however, the effect varies notably when socio-economic features of the region are accounted for	Effect of intention is stronger when regional social legitimacy is high and … : … entry rate is high … unemployment rate is high … GRP or its growth is low … proportion of people aged 25–44 years is low Effect of intention is weaker when regional social legitimacy is high and … : … entry rate is low … unemployment rate is low … GRP or its growth is high … proportion of people aged 25–44 years is high
PBC has a positive impact on behaviour	PBC has a stronger effect when regional social legitimacy is low; there is minor variation in the effect when the socio-economic features of the region are accounted for	Effect of PBC is non-significant at either level of regional social legitimacy when … : … unemployment rate is high … GRP is high … service sector employment is high

interaction effects. Initially, intercept-only models were estimated for intention and behaviour using random-intercept regression with maximum likelihood estimation. Those estimations show non-significant variance components for both dependent variables, implying that the variability in the levels of intention and behaviour does not depend on the regional clustering of the data.

The next model specification included the individual's perception of the regional social legitimacy of entrepreneurship as the sole predictor. Its effect on intention was positive and significant at the 1% level (coefficient = 0.11, z-statistic = 3.22), while the effect on behaviour was not significant (coefficient = 0.04, z-statistic = 1.29). Adding a random slope to the equation did not improve the fit of the model in either case (intention: $\chi^2_{2\text{d.f.}} = 0.40$; behaviour: $\chi^2_{2\text{d.f.}} = 1.31$). As a result, the remaining model specifications do not include a random coefficient for social legitimacy. However, despite the lack of significant regional variability in intention and behaviour suggesting that a multilevel design is not necessary for these data, the analysis retains the random-intercept modelling logic owing to the model including variables at the regional level (equation 1).

The full unconditional model estimations for intention and behaviour are displayed in Table 4. The results support the relevance of the TPB in the entrepreneurial context: attitude, subjective norms, and PBC are positive and significant predictors of intention, while intention and PBC predict subsequent behaviour.

Hypothesis tests

The hypotheses H1 (a–c) and H2 (a, b) propose that the relationships in the TPB are conditional on the perceived level of regional social legitimacy of entrepreneurship. Testing these hypotheses requires the estimation of multiplicative interaction effects. Hence, interaction terms were formed by multiplying attitude, subjective norms, PBC and intention with social legitimacy. The relevant interaction terms were added to the model specifications presented in Table 4. After estimating each model, the marginal effects of the TPB predictors were computed when social legitimacy is set to 1 and 2 SDs (standard deviation) units below and above its mean. This article omits the full results tables, since the standard regression output provides little information useful for understanding conditional marginal effects when the interaction involves continuous variables (BRAMBOR *et al.*, 2006). While graphing the interaction effects is customary, this analysis tabulates the results, which permits the efficient presentation of multiple interactions.

The estimations in Table 5 show that the effect of attitude on intention and, the effect of intention on behaviour, become stronger when the level of social legitimacy increases. While the effects of subjective norms and PBC on intention are unaffected by the level of social legitimacy, PBC exerts a positive and significant impact on behaviour only when social legitimacy is below its sample mean. In short, these findings support H1a, but not H1b and H1c. The results further support H2a and do find a significant, but opposite effect of PBC on entrepreneurial action as proposed in H2b.

Sensitivity analysis: interactions with regional characteristics

In order to assess the influence of regional socio-economic features on the relationships estimated thus far, the analysis proceeded with the estimation of a series of models where each relationship in Table 5 is further interacted with the eight regional variables depicted in Table 1 (e.g. attitude*social_legitimacy*population_density). Each interaction was estimated separately in order to facilitate interpretation and each model estimated includes the full list of variables displayed in Table 4. The marginal effects of the TPB predictors were computed with social legitimacy and the regional variable in question, each set 1 SD unit below and above their means, resulting in four marginal effects estimated for each relationship in the TPB (Table 6). A verbal summary of the main results based on Tables 4–6 is presented in Table 7. The interpretation of the three-way interactions between the TPB predictors, regional social legitimacy of entrepreneurship and socio-economic features of the region, depicted in the third column of Table 7, focuses on how the regional variables influence the effect of social legitimacy on the relationships in the TPB, rather than on how the regional variables modify the effects of the TPB predictors on intention and behaviour.

DISCUSSION AND CONCLUSION

This study is an initial attempt to examine the conditioning effect of the *regional social legitimacy of entrepreneurship* on the relationships laid out in the TPB (AJZEN, 1991), which lead to the formation of entrepreneurial intentions and their subsequent translation into start-up behaviour. Complementing the TPB with institutional approaches to sociology (SCOTT, 1995), economic geography (GERTLER, 2010) and regional entrepreneurship (LAFUENTE *et al.*, 2007), the regional social legitimacy of entrepreneurship was defined as a convergence of beliefs in a region that entrepreneurial activity is 'desirable, proper or appropriate' (SUCHMANN, 1995, p. 574). It was argued that the regional social legitimacy of entrepreneurship influences the degree to which a region provides a beneficial environment for the emergence of enterprising behaviour (ETZIONI, 1987).

Based on two waves of survey data on working-age individuals (wave 1 = 2025; wave 2 = 984) from 65 regions of Austria and Finland, the econometric analysis provides strong evidence that the emergence of an entrepreneurial intention and its impact on subsequent start-up behaviour depends on the perceived regional social legitimacy of entrepreneurship. A regional sensitivity analysis utilizing regional-level variables derived from the official national statistics in Austria and Finland further demonstrates that certain effects of social legitimacy on intention formation and action initiation are conditioned by demographic, economic and labour market features of, and past entrepreneurial activity levels in, the region. The sensitivity analysis thus complements the understanding of the role of the perceived social legitimacy of entrepreneurship in a region by accounting for the conditioning effects of socio-economic regional characteristics suggested in the previous literature.

In particular, the study's findings suggest that the more entrepreneurship is considered a socially legitimate activity in a region, the stronger will be an individual's entrepreneurial attitudes that form their intention to become an entrepreneur. Thus, following the regional interaction logic applied here (KIBLER, 2013), an individual's certainty that entrepreneurship is a beneficial career path (attitude) increases when they are embedded in a region where entrepreneurial activity is morally accepted or taken for granted, and this certainty in turn strengthens their entrepreneurial intentions. The results further show that the social legitimacy effect on the attitude–intention relationship is unaffected by the regional socio-economic factors included in the sensitivity analysis. Accordingly, the study extends the work of BOSMA and SCHUTJENS (2011), which emphasizes that certain local norms and socio-economic factors enhance the emergence of entrepreneurial attitudes by suggesting that the strength with which these attitudes support the formation of intentions is conditioned by the regional social legitimacy of entrepreneurship and independent from regional socio-economic factors.

Counter to the assumption, the findings illustrate that the regional social legitimacy of entrepreneurship does not affect how perceived social support from family and friends (subjective norms) influences an individual's intentions to start a business. The non-effect of social legitimacy on the relationship between subjective norms and intentions is robust in the face of regional socio-economic factors. It seems that when they derive approval and support for enterprising activity from their close social environment, individuals consider it less necessary to seek approval from the residual local environment when developing entrepreneurial intentions. Thus, in this context, the influence of regional social legitimacy is negligible.

The findings further suggest that the impact of perceived entrepreneurial ability (PBC) on entrepreneurial intentions becomes stronger when entrepreneurship enjoys a higher degree of regional social legitimacy. However, this is only the case in regions with higher business entry rates in the past, and lower levels of population density, education, unemployment, gross regional product (GRP) and service sector employment, which arguably reflect the conditions often present in peripheral, rural areas. This implies that a local cultural environment supporting entrepreneurship becomes particularly relevant for strengthening an individual's perception that they are able to run a successful business in rural regions with a limited local stock of financial and human capital (ORGANISATION FOR ECONOMIC CO-OPERATION AND DEVELOPMENT (OECD), 2006). In addition, the identified positive influence of high business entry rates on social legitimacy provides new empirical evidence of how prior entrepreneurial activity can strengthen an entrepreneurship-friendly culture (AUDRETSCH and KEILBACH, 2004), particularly in rural areas (LAFUENTE *et al.*, 2007). Accordingly, it is concluded that individuals embedded in rural areas are particularly reliant on approval from the regional cultural environment, supported by accounts of successful firm formation (VAILLANT and LAFUENTE, 2007), when developing their entrepreneurial intentions, because such a climate fosters their confidence in having control over their successful start-up behaviour (LANG *et al.*, 2013).

Moreover, the empirical analysis provides prima facie evidence that high levels of regional social legitimacy enhance the impact of intentions on the likelihood of an individual subsequently engaging in start-up behaviour. This finding emphasizes that an individual's perception of high regional social legitimacy strengthens their expectation of receiving social capital (LIAO and WELSCH, 2005) and positive social feedback from the regional community when turning intentions into entrepreneurial action. The analysis further suggests that this is of particular relevance for aspiring entrepreneurs needing to overcome potential entrepreneurial obstacles in economically 'disadvantaged' regions. In other words, the local community's support and supply of resources for aspiring entrepreneurs is likely to be greater if entrepreneurship is highly socially legitimate (ETZIONI, 1987). This in turn can compensate for economic restrictions in the local environment and can give those with entrepreneurial intentions the final impulse needed to turn their intentions into actual start-up behaviour.

However, high levels of regional social legitimacy for entrepreneurship do not always foster the transformation of intentions into action. The study also uncovers regional configurations where the likelihood of an individual moving from entrepreneurial intention to actual start-up behaviour decreases with a higher degree of regional social legitimacy of entrepreneurship. More specifically, when regions show high GRP levels, high prior GRP growth rates, a high proportion of people aged 25–44 years and low prior entrepreneurial activity levels, the positive impact of entrepreneurial intention on entrepreneurial behaviour becomes weaker with high levels of regional social legitimacy. It is argued that relatively wealthy regions with a large proportion of younger individuals in their populations might establish entrepreneurship-friendly cultures, but at the same time high salaries imply high opportunity costs for employees in becoming entrepreneurs (ASHCROFT *et al.*, 1991). The high opportunity costs of entrepreneurship seem to undermine the positive effects of high regional social legitimacy, with the result that entrepreneurial intentions are less likely to be translated into action.

The results further emphasize that the role of an individual's perceived entrepreneurial ability in the taking of entrepreneurial action is more important in regions where entrepreneurship is less socially legitimate. If potential entrepreneurs perceive entrepreneurship as possessing low social legitimacy in their region, they might anticipate having only limited access to local social capital, meaning that the final step from intention to actual establishment of a firm will require a strong belief in their own entrepreneurial capabilities.

Implications

Overall, this study supports the proposition that the regional social normative context influences entrepreneurial cognitions and the emergence of individual entrepreneurial activity. The empirical findings further suggest that the implications of regional cultural norms for entrepreneurship (partly) relate to different stages of the entrepreneurial process at the individual level and to different socio-economic contexts at the regional level. This underlines the importance of longitudinal and multilevel designs in regional entrepreneurship research. The large body of previous regional studies provides useful insights into the effects of the demographic, economic, regulative and industry features of a region. However, this research suggests that the development of a location-sensitive institutional understanding (LANG *et al.*, 2013) of the social norms that facilitate individual entrepreneurial activity can complement and enrich the body of knowledge on regional influences on entrepreneurship. Moreover, the conceptualization and operationalization of the regional social legitimacy of entrepreneurship developed and tested in this study provide a novel and valid conceptual and empirical instrument for measuring a major determinant of a regional entrepreneurship culture (FRITSCH and WYRWICH, 2014) and its impact on entrepreneurial cognitive processes and start-up behaviour.

The main policy implication of this study is that the perceived regional social legitimacy of entrepreneurship clearly matters in the early stages of an individual's firm formation process. As such, the regional understanding of social legitimacy developed in this paper can serve as one important measure by which policy-makers and the enterprise support community can improve regional entrepreneurship levels. It is suggested that, independent of the regional socio-economic context, an increased regional social legitimacy of entrepreneurship could help policy-makers to mobilize the formation of entrepreneurial intentions in a region by influencing individuals' entrepreneurial attitudes. The findings further imply that (institutional) actors involved in rural entrepreneurship support need, above all, to create an environment that socially approves entrepreneurial activity in order to strengthen individuals' confidence and the perceived ability to run a business in a rural area; this, in turn, will facilitate higher entrepreneurial intention levels. Moreover, fostering the regional social legitimacy of entrepreneurship should play a crucial role in helping with the design of effective entrepreneurship support initiatives in economically 'disadvantaged' regions, by increasing the likelihood that individuals will not only hold entrepreneurial intentions, but also turn them into actual start-up behaviour. The study further suggests that, independent of a region's socio-economic composition, policy-makers need to focus particularly on supporting individuals' perceived entrepreneurial ability in order to enhance the critical translation of entrepreneurial potential into entrepreneurial activity in regions with – temporarily – lower levels of social legitimacy of entrepreneurship.

Since establishing new grounds for social legitimacy is challenging and often only possible when a group of established organizations and institutions actively apply pressure on the moral order (SUCHMANN, 1995), potential entrepreneurs are seldom able to influence and change their own socio-cultural environments. Thus, creating a regional culture where entrepreneurial activity enjoys a high level of social legitimacy, and which is optimally adjusted to the socio-economic characteristics of the region, requires collective (policy) action by different institutional and organizational actors. Promotional measures aiming to facilitate social legitimacy should aspire to establish a common awareness of the economic and social benefits of entrepreneurship among the individuals living in the region and the regional economy as a whole. Entrepreneurship policies should also not neglect the potential of the likes of social and sports clubs or cultural events to act as catalysts for institutionalized social interaction at the local level (FINK *et al.*, 2012). Such events and venues stimulate social interaction, and may thus serve as vehicles for the transmission of information that can help to establish regional social legitimacy of entrepreneurship.

Acknowledgements – The authors thank the Editors and the three anonymous reviewers for invaluable comments and suggestions.

Funding – This research received support from the Academy of Finland [grant numbers 135696 and 140973].

APPENDIX A

Table A1. *Measurement scale items*

Variable (all measured on a six-point Likert-style scale)	CFA Wave 1	CFA Wave 2
Intention		
('How well do the following statements describe you?')		
I plan to take steps to start a business in the next 12 months	0.89	0.90
I intend to take steps to start a business in the next 12 months	0.93	0.93
I will try to take steps to start a business in the next 12 months	0.94	0.94
Behaviour		
('Please assess:')		
How much effort have you applied to activities aimed at starting a business in the last 12 months?		0.95
How much time have you spent on activities aimed at starting a business in the last 12 months?		0.96
How much money have you invested in activities aimed at starting a business in the last 12 months?		0.71
Attitude		
('Please rate the following statement based on the word pairs provided: "For me, taking steps to start a business in the next 12 months would be ... "')		
... unpleasant – attractive	0.84	0.85
... useless – useful	0.88	0.87
... foolish – wise	0.87	0.88
... negative – positive	0.89	0.89
... insignificant – important	0.87	0.87
... tiresome – inspiring	0.80	0.80
Subjective norm		
The subjective norm items have been computed by multiplying the following attitude items ('How well do the following statements describe your situation?') with their respective motivation-to-comply items ('And how much do you care about what these people think, if you want to take steps to start a business in the next 12 months?')		
My closest family members think that I should take steps to start a business in the next 12 months	0.84	0.84
My best friends think that I should take steps to start a business in the next 12 months	0.84	0.82
Perceived behavioural control		
('Please indicate your opinion to the following statements.')		
If I wanted to, I could take steps to start a business in the next 12 months	0.74	0.75
If I took steps to start a business in the next 12 months, I would be able to control the progress of the process to a great degree myself	0.77	0.79
It would be easy for me to take steps to start a business in the next 12 months	0.75	0.78
If I wanted to take steps to start a business in the next 12 months, no external factor, independent of myself, would hinder me in taking such action	0.64	0.64
Regional social legitimacy of entrepreneurship		
('How well do the following statements describe your current place of residence?') NB: In the German and Finnish questionnaires, the words used for place of residence refer unambiguously to the city, town or municipality where the person lives (German: '*Wohnort*'; Finnish: '*asuinkunta*')		
Pragmatic legitimacy		
The activity of entrepreneurs in my place of residence improves the quality of my own life	0.75	0.74
The values and beliefs of entrepreneurs in my municipality are similar to my own	0.63	0.57
Moral legitimacy		
Entrepreneurs in my place of residence contribute to the well-being of local people	0.68	0.65
Local entrepreneurs operate according to the commonly accepted norms in my place of residence	0.66	0.62
The activity of the entrepreneurs in my place of residence supports the local economy	0.73	0.74
Cognitive legitimacy		
The activity of entrepreneurs in my place of residence is necessary	0.66	0.65
The absence of entrepreneurs in my place of residence is inconceivable	0.61	0.63

Note: The confirmatory factor analysis (CFA) column reports the standardized loading of the item on the respective factor in the CFA for the first-wave (N = 2025) and the second-wave (N = 984) data.

REFERENCES

AJZEN I. (1991) The theory of planned behaviour, *Organizational Behaviour and Human Decision Processes* **50**, 179–211.

AJZEN I. (2011) *Constructing a Theory of Planned Behavior Questionnaire* (available at: http://people.umass.edu/aizen/tpb.diag.html) (accessed on 18 March 2011).

ALDRICH H. E. and FIOL C. M. (1994) Fools rush in? The institutional context of industry creation, *Academy of Management Review* **19**, 645–670.

ANDERSON M. and KOSTER S. (2011) Sources of persistence in regional start-up rates – evidence from Sweden, *Journal of Economic Geography* **11**, 179–201.

ANGRIST J. A. and PISCHKE J.-S. (2009) *Mostly Harmless Econometrics: An Empiricist's Companion*. Princeton University Press, Princeton, NJ.

AOYAMA Y. (2009) Entrepreneurship and regional Culture: the case of Hamamatsu and Kyoto, Japan, *Regional Studies* **43**, 495–512.

ARMINGTON C. and ACS Z. J. (2002) The determinants of regional variation in new firm formation, *Regional Studies* **36**, 33–45.

ARMITAGE C. J. and CONNER M. (2001) Efficacy of the theory of planned behaviour: a meta-analytic review, *British Journal of Social Psychology* **40**, 471–499.

ASHCROFT B., LOVE J. H. and MALLOY E. (1991) New firm formation in the British counties with special reference to Scotland, *Regional Studies* **25**, 395–409.

AUDRETSCH D. B. and FRITSCH M. (1994) The geography of firm births in Germany, *Regional Studies* **28**, 359–365.

AUDRETSCH D. B. and KEILBACH M. (2004) Entrepreneurship capital and economic performance, *Regional Studies* **38**, 949–959.

BITEKTINE A. (2011) Towards a theory of social judgments of organizations: the case of legitimacy, reputation, and status, *Academy of Management Review* **36**, 151–179.

BOSMA N. and SCHUTJENS V. (2011) Understanding regional variation in entrepreneurial activity and entrepreneurial attitude in Europe, *Annals of Regional Science* **47**, 711–742.

BOSMA N., STEL A. and SUDDLE K. (2008) The geography of new firm formation: evidence from independent start-ups and new subsidiaries in the Netherlands, *International Entrepreneurship and Management Journal* **4**, 129–146.

BRAMBOR T., CLARK W. R. and GOLDER M. (2006) Understanding interaction models: improving empirical analyses, *Political Analysis* **14**, 63–82.

BRIXY U. and GROTZ R. (2007) Regional patterns and determinants of birth and survival of new firms in Western Germany, *Entrepreneurship and Regional Development* **19**, 293–312.

CONNER M. and ARMITAGE C. J. (1998) Extending the theory of planned behavior: a review and avenues for further research, *Journal of Applied Social Psychology* **28**, 1429–1464.

DAVIDSSON P. and WIKLUND J. (1997) Values, beliefs and regional variations in new firm formation rates, *Journal of Economic Psychology* **18**, 179–199.

DEEPHOUSE D. L. and SUCHMANN M. C. (2008) Legitimacy in organizational institutionalism, in GREENWOOD R., OLIVER C., SAHLIN K. and SUDDABY R. (Eds) *The SAGE Handbook of Organizational Institutionalism*, pp. 49–77. Sage, Thousand Oaks, CA.

DIMAGGIO P. and POWELL W. W. (1983) The iron cage revisited: Institutional isomorphism and collective rationality in organizational fields, *American Sociological Review* **48**, 147–160.

ETZIONI A. (1987) Entrepreneurship, adaptation and legitimation, *Journal of Economic Behavior and Organization* **8**, 175–189.

FINK M., LOIDL S. and LANG R. (2012) *Community Based Entrepreneurship and Rural Development*. Routledge: London.

FORNAHL D. (2003) Entrepreneurial activities in a regional context, in FORNAHL D. and BRENNER T. (Eds) *Cooperation, Networks, and Institutions in Regional Innovation Systems*, pp. 38–57. Edward Elgar, Cheltenham.

FRITSCH M. (1997) New firms and regional employment change, *Small Business Economics* **9**, 437–448.

FRITSCH M. and FALCK O. (2007) New business formation by industry over space and time: a multidimensional analysis, *Regional Studies* **41**, 157–172.

FRITSCH M. and MUELLER P. (2004) Effects of new business formation on regional development over time, *Regional Studies* **38**, 961–975.

FRITSCH M. and MUELLER P. (2007) The persistence of regional new business formation-activity over time – assessing the potential of policy promotion programs, *Journal of Evolutionary Economics* **17**, 299–315.

FRITSCH M. and WYRWICH M. (2014) The long persistence of regional levels of entrepreneurship: Germany 1925 to 2005, *Regional Studies* (in this issue).

GERTLER M. (2010) Rules of the game: the place of institutions in regional economic change, *Regional Studies* **44**, 1–15.

GIDDENS A. (1984) *The Constitution of Society*. University of California Press, Berkeley, CA.

GONZÁLEZ S. and HEALEY P. (2005) A Sociological institutionalist approach to the study of innovation in governance capacity, *Urban Studies* **42**, 2055–2069.

GREENWOOD R., RAYNARD M., KODEIH F., MICELOTTA E. R. and LOUNSBURY M. (2011) Institutional complexity and organizational responses, *Academy of Management Annals* **5**, 317–371.

HAYTER R. (2004) Economic geography as dissenting institutionalism: the embeddedness, evolution and differentiation of regions, *Geografiska Annaler B* **86**, 95–115.

HODGSON G. M. (2006) What are institutions?, *Journal of Economic Issues* **40**, 1–25.

HOLMÉN H. (1995) What's new and what's regional in the 'new regional geography'?, *Geografiska Annaler B* **77**, 47–63.

HOX J. J. (2010) *Multilevel Analysis: Techniques and Applications*. Routledge, New York, NY.

HU L. and BENTLER P. M. (1999) Cutoff criteria for fit indexes in covariance structure analysis: conventional criteria versus new alternatives, *Structural Equation Modeling* **6**, 1–55.

KAUTONEN T., VAN GELDEREN M. and FINK M. (2015) Robustness of the theory of planned behaviour in predicting entrepreneurial intentions and actions, *Entrepreneurship Theory and Practice* **39(3)**, DOI:10.1111/etap.12056.

KAUTONEN T., VAN GELDEREN M. and TORNIKOSKI E. T. (2013) Predicting entrepreneurial behaviour: a test of the theory of planned behaviour, *Applied Economics* **45**, 697–707.

KEEBLE D. and WALKER S. (1994) New firms, small firms and dead firms: spatial patterns and determinants in the United Kingdom, *Regional Studies* **28**, 411–427.

KIBLER E. (2013) The formation of entrepreneurial intentions in a regional context, *Entrepreneurship and Regional Development* **25**, 293–323.

KOLVEREID L. (1996) Prediction of employment status choice intentions, *Entrepreneurship Theory and Practice* **21**, 47–57.

LAFUENTE E., VAILLANT Y. and RIALP J. (2007) Regional differences in the influence of role models: comparing the entrepreneurial process of rural Catalonia, *Regional Studies* **41**, 779–795.

LANG R., FINK M. and KIBLER E. (2013) Understanding place-based entrepreneurship in rural Central Europe: a comparative institutional analysis, *International Journal of Small Business* DOI:10.1177/0266242613488614.

LANG R. and ROESSL D. (2011) Contextualizing the governance of community co-operatives: evidence from Austria and Germany, *Voluntas* **22**, 706–730.

LEE S. Y., FLORIDA R. and ACS Z. J. (2004) Creativity and entrepreneurship: a regional analysis of new firm formation, *Regional Studies* **38**, 879–891.

LÉVESQUE M. and MINNITI M. (2006) The effect of aging on entrepreneurial behavior, *Journal of Business Venturing* **21**, 177–194.

LIAO J. and WELSCH H. (2005) Roles of social capital in venture creation: key dimensions and research implications, *Journal of Small Business Management* **43**, 345–362.

LIÑÁN F., URBANO D. and GUERRERO M. (2011) Regional variations in entrepreneurial cognitions: start-up intentions of university students in Spain, *Entrepreneurship and Regional Development* **23**, 187–215.

MAILLAT D. (1995) Territorial dynamic, innovative milieus and regional policy, *Entrepreneurship and Regional Development* **7**, 157–165.

MARQUIS C. and BATTILANA J. (2009) Acting globally but thinking locally? The enduring influence of local communities on organizations, *Research in Organizational Behavior* **29**, 283–302.

MARTIN R. (2000) Institutional approaches in economic geography, in SHEPPARD E. and BARNES T. J. (Eds) *A Companion to Economic Geography*, pp. 77–94. Blackwell, Oxford.

MINNITI M. (2005) Entrepreneurship and network externalities, *Journal of Economic Behavior and Organization* **57**, 1–27.

MUELLER P., VAN STEL A. J. and STOREY D. J. (2008) The effects of new firm formation on regional development over time: the case of Great Britain, *Small Business Economics* **30**, 59–71.

NORTH D. C. (1990) *Institutions, Institutional Change and Economic Performance*. Cambridge University Press, Cambridge.

ORGANISATION FOR ECONOMIC CO-OPERATION AND DEVELOPMENT (OECD) (2006) *The New Rural Paradigm: Policy and Governance*. Working Paper on Territorial Policy in Rural Areas. OECD, Paris.

OSTROM E. (2005) Doing institutional analysis: digging deeper than markets and hierarchies, in MÉNARD C. and SHIRLEY M. (Eds) *Handbook of New Institutional Economics*, pp. 819–848. Springer, Dordrecht.

PARKER S. C. (2009) *The Economics of Entrepreneurship*. Cambridge University Press, Cambridge.

RAFIQUI P. S. (2009) Evolving economic landscapes: why new institutional economics matters for economic geography, *Journal of Economic Geography* **9**, 329–353.

REYNOLDS P. D. (1997) Who starts new firms? Preliminary explorations of firms-in-gestation, *Small Business Economics* **5**, 449–462.

REYNOLDS P. D., STOREY D. J. and WESTHEAD P. (1994) Cross-national comparisons of the variation in new firm formation rates, *Regional Studies* **28**, 443–456.

RODRIQUEZ-POSE A. (2013) Do institutions matter for regional development?, *Regional Studies* **47**, 1034–1047.

ROGELBERG S. G. and STANTON J. M. (2007) Understanding and dealing with organizational survey nonresponse, *Organizational Research Methods* **10**, 195–209.

SCOTT W. R. (1995) *Institutions and Organizations*. Sage, Thousand Oaks, CA.

SCOTT W. R. (2010) Reflections: the past and future of research on institutions and institutional change, *Journal of Change Management* **10**, 5–21.

SHEERAN P. (2002) Intention–behaviour relations: a conceptual and empirical overview, *European Review of Social Psychology* **12**, 1–36.

SORENSON O. and AUDIA P. G. (2000) The social structure of entrepreneurial activity: geographic concentration of footwear production in the United States, 1940–1989, *American Journal of Sociology* **106**, 424–462.

SOUITARIS V., ZERBINATI S. and AL-LAHAM A. (2007) Do entrepreneurship programmes raise entrepreneurial intention of science and engineering students? The effect of learning, inspiration and resources, *Journal of Business Venturing* **22**, 566–591.

STAM E. (2010) Entrepreneurship, evolution and geography, in BOSCHMA R. and MARTIN R. L. (Eds) *The Handbook of Evolutionary Economic Geography*, pp. 307–348. Edward Elgar, Cheltenham.

STATISTICS AUSTRIA (2011a) *Statistical Classifications of Regions* (available at: http://www.statistik.at/web_en/classifications/regional_breakdown/index.html) (accessed June 2011).

STATISTICS AUSTRIA (2011b) *Population by Demographic Characteristics* (available at: http://www.statistik.at/web_de/statistiken/bevoelkerung/bevoelkerungsstruktur/bevoelkerung_nach_alter_geschlecht/index.html) (accessed June 2011).

STATISTICS AUSTRIA (2013) *Regional Statistical Database – StatCube Service* (available at: http://www.statistik.at/web_en/publications_services/superstar_database/index.html) (accessed March 2013).

STATISTICS FINLAND (2011) *Statistical Grouping of Regions* (available at: http://www.stat.fi/meta/luokitukset/kuntaryhmitys/001-2011/index_en.html) (accessed June 2011).

STATISTICS FINLAND (2013) *Regional Statistical Database – StatFin Service* (available at: http://pxweb2.stat.fi/database/StatFin/databasetree_en.asp) (accessed February 2013).

STERNBERG R. (2009) Regional dimensions of entrepreneurship, *Foundations and Trends in Entrepreneurship* **5**, 211–340.

SUCHMANN M. C. (1995) Managing legitimacy: strategic and institutional approaches, *Academy of Management Review* **20**, 571–611.

THORNTON P. H. and FLYNN K. H. (2003) Entrepreneurship, networks, and geographies, in ACS Z. J. and AUDRETSCH D. B. (Eds) *Handbook of Entrepreneurship Research*, pp. 401–433. Kluwer, New York, NY.

TÖDTLING F. and WANZENBÖCK H. (2003) Regional differences in structural characteristics of start-ups, *Entrepreneurship and Regional Development* **15**, 351–370.

TRETTIN L. and WELTER F. (2011) Challenges for spatially oriented entrepreneurship research, *Entrepreneurship and Regional Development* **23**, 575–602.

VAILLANT Y. and LAFUENTE E. (2007) Do different institutional frameworks condition the influence of local fear of failure and entrepreneurial examples over entrepreneurial activity?, *Entrepreneurship and Regional Development* **19**, 313–337.

VAN STEL A. J. and STOREY D. J. (2004) The link between firm births and job creation: is there a upas tree effect?, *Regional Studies* **38**, 893–910.

WELTER F. (2011) Conceptual challenges and ways forward, *Entrepreneurship Theory and Practice* **35**, 165–184.

XAVIER S. R., KELLEY D., KEW J., HERRINGTON M. and VORDERWÜLBECKE A. (2013) *Global Entrepreneurship Monitor, 2012 – Global Report*. Babson College, Babson Park, MA; Universidad del Desarrollo, Santiago; Universiti Tun Abdul Razak, Kuala Lumpur; and Global Entrepreneurship Research Association, London.

Entrepreneurship as an Urban Event? Empirical Evidence from European Cities

NIELS BOSMA*† and ROLF STERNBERG‡
*Utrecht University School of Economics, Utrecht, the Netherlands.
†Vlerick Business School, Gent, Belgium
‡Institute of Economic and Cultural Geography, University of Hannover, Hannover, Germany.

BOSMA N. and STERNBERG R. Entrepreneurship as an urban event? Empirical evidence from European cities, *Regional Studies*. This paper investigates whether urban areas are more entrepreneurial than other parts of countries and to what extent the observed differences between cities are caused by individual characteristics and context effects. Using Global Entrepreneurship Monitor (GEM) data from 47 urban areas in 22 European Union member states, it is found that in particular opportunity-motivated (instead of necessity-motivated) entrepreneurship tends to be higher in urban areas. Adopting a multilevel framework focusing on 23 urban areas in 12 European Union countries, it is found that urban regions with high levels of economic growth and diversity of economic activities exhibit higher levels of opportunity-motivated entrepreneurial activity than their counterparts.

Entrepreneurship Global Entrepreneurship Monitor (GEM) Multilevel analysis Cities Urban areas

BOSMA N. and STERNBERG R. 创业作为城市活动？来自欧洲城市的经验证据，*区域研究*。本文探讨一国的城市区域是否较国内其他地区更具有创业精神，以及城市之间观察到的差异，在什麽程度上是由各别特徵与脉络效应所导致。本研究运用全球创业观察 (GEM) 中，来自二十二个欧盟会员国的四十七座城市区域的数据，特别发现在城市区域中，由机会所驱动的（而非由需求驱动的）创业倾向较高。本文运用多重层级架构，聚焦欧盟十二国中的二十三座城市区域，发现拥有较高度经济成长和经济活动多样化的城市区域，较其他地区展现出较高程度的由机会所驱动的创业。

创业 全球创业观察 (GEM) 多重层级分析 城市 城市区域

BOSMA N. et STERNBERG R. L'esprit d'entreprise comme un événement urbain? Des résultats empiriques provenant des grandes villes européennes, *Regional Studies*. Cet article examine si, oui ou non, les zones urbaines s'avèrent plus entrepreneuriales que ne le sont d'autres parties des pays et jusqu'à quel point les différences observées des grandes villes s'expliquent par des caractéristiques individuelles et par le contexte. Employant des données provenant de l'observatoire mondial de l'entrepreneuriat (Global Entrepreneurship Monitor; GEM) auprès de 47 zones urbaines dans 22 pays-membres de l'Union européenne, il s'avère que notamment l'esprit d'entreprise axé sur les possibilités (au lieu d'être axé sur la nécessité) a tendance à être plus élevé dans les zones urbaines. En employant un cadre multi-niveaux qui porte sur 23 zones urbaines dans 12 pays-membres de l'Union européenne, il s'avère que les régions urbaines dont les niveaux de croissance et la diversité des activités économiques sont élevés font preuve des niveaux plus élevés de l'activité entrepreneuriale axée sur les possibilités que ne le font leurs homologues.

Esprit d'entreprise Global Entrepreneurship Monitor (GEM) Analyse multi-niveaux Grandes villes Zones urbaines

BOSMA N. und STERNBERG R. Firmengründungen als urbanes Phänomen? Empirische Belege aus europäischen Städten, *Regional Studies*. Dieser Artikel untersucht, ob städtische Gebiete gründungsstärker sind als andere Teile desselben Landes und in welchem Maße die diesbezüglichen Unterschiede zwischen Städten durch personenbezogene Merkmale der Bewohner und durch Kontexteffekte erklärt werden. Unter Verwendung von Daten des Global Entrepreneurship Monitor für 47 Städte aus 22 EU-Ländern können wir zeigen, dass insbesondere Opportunity-getriebene Gründer (anders als Gründer aus der ökonomischen Not heraus) häufiger in Städten zu finden sind. Mittels einer Mehrebenenanalyse von 23 Städten aus 12 EU-Ländern können wir zudem zeigen, dass wachstumsstarke und ökonomisch diversifizierte Städte einen höheren Anteil an Opportunity-getriebenen Gründern aufweisen als Städte ohne diese Eigenschaften.

Unternehmertum Global Entrepreneurship Monitor (GEM) Mehrebenenanalyse Städte Städtische Gebiete

BOSMA N. y STERNBERG R. ¿Es el espíritu empresarial un efecto urbano? Evidencia empírica de ciudades europeas, *Regional Studies*. En este artículo investigamos si las zonas urbanas tienen más cultura empresarial que otras áreas de los países y en qué medida las diferencias observadas entre las ciudades se deben a características individuales y efectos de contexto. A partir de datos del estudio Global Entrepreneurship Monitor (GEM) para 47 zonas urbanas en 22 Estados miembros de la Unión Europea, observamos que el empresariado motivado principalmente por oportunidades (y no por necesidades) tiende a ser más alto en zonas urbanas. Mediante un esquema de varios niveles en 23 zonas urbanas de 12 países de la Unión Europea, se desprende que las regiones urbanas con altos niveles de crecimiento económico y diversidad de actividades económicas muestran niveles más altos de actividades empresariales motivadas por oportunidades que las ciudades sin estas características.

Espíritu empresarial Global Entrepreneurship Monitor (GEM) Análisis de varios niveles Ciudades Zonas urbanas

INTRODUCTION

Entrepreneurship research only recently began to build evidence that entrepreneurial activities are not evenly distributed across space and between places (FELDMAN, 2001; ARMINGTON and ACS, 2002; PARKER, 2005, STERNBERG, 2009). Furthermore, entrepreneurship processes are, to a degree, region-specific, i.e. different types of regions may be affected by different types of start-up processes (GUESNIER, 1994). The implications for places, especially for bigger urban areas, are manifold since in most of the urban areas in Europe – which are the focus in this study – more or less place-specific public entrepreneurship support programmes were developed in recent years, the impact and effects of which are almost unknown. Two assumptions underlie this research. First, in most European countries urban areas serve as the drivers of national economic growth and many policy-makers in national governments try to create knowledge-intensive clusters in and around some of these areas. In some cases entrepreneurship clusters play a prominent role within these strategies. Second, the regional economic impact of entrepreneurship seems to be positive and significant, while differences exist according to the type of regions, the duration of these effects and the type of entrepreneurial activity (e.g., FRITSCH and SCHROETER, 2011; FRITSCH, 2013; VAN OORT and BOSMA, 2013). Large urban areas seem to profit more than rural areas, for example. However, there seems to be an independent relationship between entrepreneurial activities and the urban economy as some of the latter's characteristics also generate an impact on entrepreneurship.

This paper has a dual focus. First, it develops theoretical arguments for a varying relevance of different types of entrepreneurship in (large) urban areas compared with the rest of the respective country. The related section considers two concepts: urbanization economies and localization economies and their specific implication for opportunity-driven entrepreneurship and for necessity-driven entrepreneurship. Second, the empirical core of this paper uses individual-level data of the Global Entrepreneurship Monitor (GEM) representing 47 urban areas in 23 European countries (see REYNOLDS *et al.*, 2005, for the methodological background; and BOSMA *et al.*, 2012, for relevant updates). This unique new dataset is combined with aggregated regional data to respond to hitherto unanswered questions of empirical entrepreneurship research. This paper first analyses to what extent differences in entrepreneurship levels between urban areas, in comparison with other areas within countries, can be ascribed to different motivations to start a company. Furthermore, focusing on inhabitants of 23 urban areas in Europe, it provides individual- and regional-level explanations for individuals' active participation in opportunity- and necessity-driven entrepreneurship. Finally, this multilevel framework allows it to be assessed to what extent *individuals'* involvement in entrepreneurial activity can be explained by *regional* characteristics in terms of geography, economic performance, culture and institutions.

The findings point at the relevance of entrepreneurship as an urban event, but also demonstrate that the topic deserves a nuanced approach. Rather clear positive effects are found of regional economic growth for opportunity-motivated entrepreneurship that is higher in identified urban areas. A reduction in regional employment growth, however, increases involvement in necessity-motivated entrepreneurship in urban areas. Thus, as a range of GEM-based research shows, it matters what kind of entrepreneurial activities are being studied (e.g., WONG *et al.*, 2005; MINNITI, 2011). The results of this multilevel analysis suggest that urban areas characterized by observed economic growth (rather than regional measures of opportunity recognition for start-ups) and diversity of economic activities (rather than specialization) have more opportunity-motivated early-stage entrepreneurs.

The remainder of the paper is structured as follows. The next section provides a brief overview of the theoretical concepts mentioned above. It analyses whether these concepts are able to support the arguments of higher entrepreneurial activities in and around urban areas compared with rest of a country, different levels of entrepreneurial activities among European urban areas, and different impacts of individual and regional characteristics. Six theory-led hypotheses are developed. The third section describes the methodological approach and the data used. The fourth section focuses on the results of the descriptive and multivariate analyses to answer the four empirical research questions described above. The final section presents some preliminary interpretations of the empirical results in light of the existing entrepreneurship literature followed by cautious policy conclusions and an outlook on further research.

THEORETICAL FOUNDATION: HOW DOES ONE EXPLAIN AN ENTREPRENEURIAL ADVANTAGE OF URBAN AREAS TAKING INTO CONSIDERATION DIFFERENT TYPES OF ENTREPRENEURSHIP?

Interregional disparities in terms of entrepreneurial activities

In recent years entrepreneurship research has significantly increased the attention given to the spatial (or geographical) dimension of entrepreneurial activities and their (regional economic) causes and effects (e.g., BOSMA, 2009) – see also the special issues of *Regional Studies* in 1984 (STOREY, 1984), 1994 (REYNOLDS *et al.*, 1994) and 2004 (ACS and STOREY, 2004). The majority of the related work has been focused on empirical attempts to assess the regional economic *effects* of entrepreneurial activities (e.g., FRITSCH, 2011, for an overview). Empirical work on the *regional causes* (as part of context causes in general) for regional entrepreneurship activities has gained in importance, too, but is less common (e.g., HINDLE, 2010; or for an overview, STERNBERG, 2009).

There is consensus meanwhile in empirical regional entrepreneurship research that space matters, i.e. there are significant spatial differences in entrepreneurial activities and entrepreneurial attitudes across sub-national regions within the same country (for the United States, see REYNOLDS, 2007, or ARMINGTON and ACS, 2002; for Germany, see FRITSCH and MUELLER, 2004; for the UK, see KEEBLE and WALKER, 1994). Only a very limited number of empirical studies, however, consider differences in entrepreneurship activities for sub-national spatial entities (i.e., comparing regions or local areas) of *different* countries (see BOSMA and SCHUTJENS, 2007; ACS *et al.*, 2011, for exceptions; see also BELITZKI and KOROSTELEVA, 2010, who, however, define entrepreneurship as self-employment). The majority of empirical studies on regional entrepreneurship do not explicitly differ between urban areas and other region types but urbanity is, at best, covered by population density as a proxy for the urban–rural dichotomy. Exceptions include FRITSCH *et al.* (2006) who show that new firm survival rates differ between 'agglomerations', 'moderately congested regions' and 'rural regions' in Germany, and BARRENECHE-GARCÍA (2012) who focus on the determinant of entrepreneurship as a creative act in 209 European cities. A limited set of studies argues that rurality has a positive effect on firm formation. For example, PETTERSSON *et al.* (2010) show that if the relative growth of the number of firms (with respect to population change) is used, rural areas in Sweden perform better than urban areas.

Considering spatial or geographical aspects in entrepreneurship means distinguishing between four spatial levels: supra-national (e.g., European Union), national (country), regional (e.g., urban area), and local (e.g., neighbourhood). Many studies do not accurately distinguish between these levels, although they may be important when assessing spatial (i.e., not individual) causes or effects. As the present paper is restricted to European urban areas and no differentiation between quarters *within* a city is made, it only considers two spatial levels (emphasizing the regional level, but also considering the national level in the descriptive analysis) and, as a third level, the micro-level of the individual entrepreneur.

Spatial entrepreneurship research has developed dramatically during the last two decades. However, it was dominated by empirical research. This is understandable given the enormous empirical research gap in this field two decades ago when the spatial dimension of entrepreneurship was largely ignored. This is true for all potentially relevant disciplines including, e.g. urban economics (e.g., GLAESER *et al.*, 2010b), economic geography (MALECKI, 1997; DELGADO *et al.*, 2010), and regional science (e.g., BATABYAL and NIJKAMP, 2010). This improvement in empirical findings, however, is still not backed by an appropriate theoretical foundation (SHANE and VENKATARAMAN, 2000). This is especially true for regional entrepreneurship theories that intend to explain entrepreneurship processes at the regional (sub-national) level and with explicit consideration of this spatial level. Most theoretical work on entrepreneurship simply ignores the spatial level, i.e. it is unknown whether the theory or concept works on the national, regional, local or individual level.

There is still a long way to go to generate an adequate theory (or at least a concept) to explain regional entrepreneurship processes, causes and effects. There are, however, a number of partial theories that were not created for entrepreneurship research, but which were later adapted for this purpose (DAVIDSSON, 2006). To mention just a few: innovation-based regional growth theory, network theory, innovation system approaches, 'creative class' concept, cluster theory, agglomeration theory (urbanization and localization economies), the incubator hypothesis or the growth regime concept. Given the lack of a grand theory on both regional as well as urban entrepreneurship literature, the hypotheses are developed here by employing two partial concepts. The following sections deal with the theoretical implications of these concepts for entrepreneurship in (large) European urban areas.

Opportunity entrepreneurship: urbanization economies and urban economic growth

A current of entrepreneurship research that was very influential for a long time stresses the role of opportunities for entrepreneurial activities (e.g., SHANE and

VENKATARAMAN, 2000). Consequently, it might be helpful to define at least one (probably important) type of entrepreneurship as opportunity-driven. Following GEM terminology, opportunity entrepreneurs are defined as those who are pulled into entrepreneurship by the prospect of opportunity (e.g., because they see market demand for their products). Most such entrepreneurs desire greater independence in their work and seek to improve their income. As GEM data show, in 2013 entrepreneurs in the European Union were an average of 2.1 times more likely to be improvement-driven opportunity entrepreneurs than what are known as necessity-driven entrepreneurs (AMORÓS and BOSMA, 2014). From a contextual perspective of regional entrepreneurship, an individual's propensity to start a firm due to the opportunity motivation defined above is dependent, among other determinants, on characteristics of the regional economy in which he/she lives and works.

Potential agglomeration effects are an important characteristic of this regional/urban environment. In regional economics these agglomeration effects are usually differentiated either into localization and urbanization economies (see BEAUDRY and SCHIFFAUEROVA, 2009, for an overview) or in three types of micro-foundations, based upon sharing, matching and learning mechanisms (DURANTON and THISSE, 2004). The localization versus urbanization dichotomy is preferable as there are several theoretical and empirical studies on regional entrepreneurial activities that use them a theoretical basis (e.g. STAM, 2007; GLAESER, 2007). While localization effects are dealt with in the second section, urbanization economies are defined as those that derive from the spatial concentration of firms of *different* industries and *different* sectors. They generate manifold inter-industrial linkages and diversified labour markets of substantial size (ROSENTHAL and STRANGE, 2004; CAPELLO, 2002). Such urbanization economies produce positive impulses for new firm formation. In general the scale of urbanization effects is size dependent, i.e. the bigger is the urban agglomeration, the greater are these effects. In particular, the size of the urban area or agglomeration is positively correlated with the quantitative and qualitative potential of entrepreneurial opportunities.

Empirical studies show that entrepreneurial activities are supported by urbanization economies by at least four processes (ROSENTHAL and STRANGE, 2004; STAM, 2007). First, large heterogeneous and diversified urban economies provide start-up opportunities for potential entrepreneurs. The latter may benefit from information spillover ('buzz') that occurs in large urban areas, but definitely not in smaller urban areas or rural regions in the same country. Second, while entry cost might have a negative influence in some large urban areas with a high cost of living, the potential large (local) market size serves as a substantial comparative advantage of large urban areas over rural areas in the same country. Third, founders may profit from the availability of a heterogeneous labour market offering all sorts of skills for a variety of costs. While *specific* skills might be rather costly in an expensive large urban environment (start-ups cannot afford, incumbent firms do), the great variety of labour is a real advantage of large urban agglomeration compared with the remaining regions in any given country. Fourth, as Jacobs' externalities are predominant in early stages of an industry's life cycle (different from localization economies), they coincide with the emergence of new firms that are also relatively important during the genesis of an industry (NEFFKE *et al.*, 2011).

Additionally there are other supporting mechanisms of urbanization economies (especially in large functional urban regions, the objects of this paper) like the close proximity to concentrations of (potential) customers (purchasing power), lower transaction costs (in particular costs for the acquisition of customers, suppliers, services and knowledge), and substantial economies of information flows on both the demand and the supply side due to the existence of various interaction arenas (KARLSSON *et al.*, 2008). HELSLEY and STRANGE (2009) stress another reason why urbanization economies favour entrepreneurship. Since, according to LAZEAR (2005), founders carry out so many different tasks, a balance of skills, as available in large urban areas, may be beneficial to them. Complex projects that are not feasible in small urban areas may be feasible in large urban areas, where adaptation costs are lower. It may be possible for less balanced entrepreneurs to manage successfully in large urban areas by substituting local market thickness for a balance of skills. HELSLEY and STRANGE (2009) also show that LAZEAR's (2005) result on the balance of entrepreneurs is related to JACOBS' (1969) argument of urban diversity. Recently GLAESER *et al.* (2010a) found some empirical support for the hypothesis that the level of entrepreneurship is higher when fixed costs are lower and when there are more entrepreneurial people. Both aspects are related to urban agglomerations and their agglomeration economies – and they are more related to opportunity entrepreneurship than to other types of entrepreneurship.

A more recent aspect of the relationship between an urban environment and entrepreneurship is the complex relationship between super-diversity, immigration and (related to both phenomena) entrepreneurial activities by new arrivals in some very large European urban areas (SEPULVEDA *et al.*, 2011). London, Paris, Berlin and Stockholm are important receiving urban areas for immigrants not just from their traditional partner countries, but also from an increasing number of diverse places and with more and more different ethnicities. These immigrants very often perceive and exploit specific business opportunities. Consequently, it is not surprising that such urban areas have experienced strong absolute and relative growth in migrant enterprise and entrepreneurship that contributes to an overall opportunity entrepreneurship rate above the average of other urban areas and/or the national average. Based on the previous arguments the first hypothesis to be tested in the empirical part can be defined as follows:

> *Hypothesis 1: Urban areas owe higher entrepreneurship rates (compared with the rest of the country) to higher opportunity-motivated early-stage entrepreneurship rates.*

In parts of the literature (e.g., ANTONIETTI and CAINELLI, 2011) urbanization economies are separated into Jacobs' externalities and urbanization economies in the narrower sense. Jacobs' externalities (JACOBS, 1969) are based on the relevance of diversity and the assumption that the more intensive intra-regional competition is among firms, the higher is the level of regional economic growth. Consequently, an increasing number of firms, resulting from more start-ups, would increase competition and thus regional economic growth. Jacobs' externalities have a dynamic perspective in their focus upon *inter*-industry agglomeration. Entry of new firms, exit of incumbent ones and firm turnover have stronger effects on regional innovativeness and productivity than competition among incumbent firms (FALCK, 2007). Jacobs' externalities are spurred on by the variety and diversity of geographically proximate industries, and capture knowledge spillovers from the cross-fertilization of ideas by firms operating in related or unrelated sectors (FRENKEN *et al.*, 2007; BOSCHMA and IAMMARINO, 2009).

While it is widely acknowledged that such diversity-driven spillover effects are distance-sensitive, some argue that they do not occur automatically. Not every large firm is willing or able to exploit the entrepreneurial opportunities generated by its own research and development (R&D). Entrepreneurship in the form of new ventures may act as a knowledge filter, in this case meaning that such entrepreneurs are able (and motivated) to distinguish between new knowledge with and without commercial potential (AUDRETSCH and ALDRIDGE, 2009). This kind of knowledge spillover generates entrepreneurial opportunities that are exploited by new firm founders via spinoffs from their parent company (AUDRETSCH, 2005). Many of the firm founders rely heavily on the resources provided by their former employer, especially in the early stage of their spinoff firm. For this reason, and possibly also because of private networks, they tend to locate in the same region (also LEJPRAS and STEPHAN, 2011).

Consequently the related region, normally a large urban area, increases its number of new firms due to this urbanization-led knowledge filter process. Consequently one may call this type of entrepreneurship opportunity-driven as the new firm founders exploit an opportunity they had perceived beforehand. Thus the second hypothesis is as follows:

> *Hypothesis 2: Diversity of economic activities is associated with higher involvement in total early-stage entrepreneurship.*

Regional economic growth may not only be an important effect of entrepreneurial activities (e.g., FRITSCH, 2013), but also a cause, in particular when it comes to opportunity-driven entrepreneurship. A growing regional economy is characterized by growing opportunities for all kinds of existing or future firms, including those that qualify as opportunity entrepreneurs. It is also characterized by increasing demand for products, services and, very often, by an increasing population. As these entrepreneurial framework conditions create signals to latent and nascent entrepreneurs that a (growing) market for their future products and services may exist, potential entrepreneurs may more easily recognize such business opportunities (opportunity recognition). Consequently, it is plausible to assume that urban areas with such characteristics show higher entrepreneurial activity levels than others. Not surprisingly, therefore, some empirical studies confirm this and show how regional economic growth in the recent past has had positive impact on entrepreneurial activities in the near future (e.g., ARMINGTON and ACS, 2002; REYNOLDS, 2007). The specific impact on *opportunity* entrepreneurship has, however, not been empirically covered yet. In addition, MEESTER and PELLENBARG (2006) point out that subjective assessments, such as opportunity recognition, may provide for better explanations than objective ones. This proposition resonates with the body of literature from the management perspective, emphasizing opportunity recognition as the first of the three key phases of entrepreneurship, i.e. before evaluating and exploiting the opportunity (SHANE and VENKATARAMAN, 2000; SHORT *et al.*, 2010). Thus, two more hypothesises can be created:

> *Hypothesis 3: Growth in regional economic output is associated with higher involvement in opportunity-driven early-stage entrepreneurship across urban areas.*

> *Hypothesis 4: Higher levels of opportunity recognition for start-ups are associated with higher involvement in opportunity-driven early-stage entrepreneurship across urban areas.*

To sum up, the urbanization economies concept may help find answers to two of the empirical research questions. First, urban areas gain from urbanization economies since the latter emerge only in urban agglomerations. The bigger is this urban agglomeration, the larger are urbanization economies. Consequently, urban areas are expected to have higher levels of entrepreneurial activities than rural areas. Opportunity-driven entrepreneurship (start-ups) is supported by access to business opportunities, absolute market size and the supply of a variety of labour (various skills and cost levels). Hence, the entrepreneurial advantages of urban areas are expected to manifest particularly in terms of opportunity-driven entrepreneurship as well as entrepreneurship aimed at the creation of (new) jobs. While urbanization effects provide plausible explanations why the *regional* context effect is influential, they do not offer a solution for the relevance of possible composition effects.

Necessity entrepreneurship: localization economies versus urbanization economies and urban employment patterns

While opportunity entrepreneurship is the most frequent motivation-related type of entrepreneurship, another motivation is highly relevant for several other individuals and regions. It is called here necessity entrepreneurship and necessity entrepreneurs are defined as people pushed into starting a business because they have no other opportunities for work and need a source of income (following the GEM terminology again; AMORÓS and BOSMA, 2014). Unemployment is a possible reason for such push-driven entrepreneurship, but others are also possible. In principle, necessity entrepreneurship is influenced by the same characteristics of the regional environment as opportunity entrepreneurship – and urbanization and localization economies should play a role here as well. Localization economies, often synonymously named Marshall–Arrow–Romer (MAR) externalities, are the result of the spatial concentration of firms belonging to the same or similar industries. According to CAPELLO (2002), in the case of localization economies, the advantages of scale relate primarily to increases in the scale of activity in a particular industry, with all benefits accruing primarily to that industry. Typically MAR externalities include labour market pooling, specialist supplier availability and technological knowledge spillovers – all related to a specific industry at a given place (e.g., an urban area). These externalities provide local economic benefits for firms in the same industry or in similar industries and underpin geographical agglomeration (PIKE *et al.*, 2006).

There are four specific positive impacts of localization economies on new entrepreneurial firms. First, entrepreneurs attain, at least potentially, access to specialized inputs they need for their new product (e.g., workforce; GLAESER, 2007). Second, strong competition in a cluster with several firms in the same industry may result in higher quality of products and firms (but also in lower survival rates of start-ups). Third, entrepreneurs may gain from role models provided by other entrepreneurs in the very same industry (and location) and the related learning effects. Fourth, localization economies may help create demand for the (very specific) new product of the entrepreneur who often does not really know the market for his new product. Empirical studies find mixed results concerning the impact of clusters or sectorial specialization on entrepreneurship (ROCHA and STERNBERG, 2005) or no impact at all (BAPTISTA and SWANN, 1999). The distinction between necessity and opportunity entrepreneurship, however, does not play any role in the literature on localization effects on entrepreneurship to date.

PORTER's (1990) argument in favour of local-regional clusters also considers localization economies in specific, geographically concentrated industries. However, while supporters of MAR externalities consider local specialization to be the crucial mechanism that links localization economies to innovation and local economic growth, Porter instead attributes this to local competition. Both kinds of localization effects are maximized in large urban areas with one or several geographically specialized industries. Empirical evidence supports this positive causal relationship between sectoral-regional clusters and both entrepreneurial activities and entrepreneurial attitudes (e.g., STERNBERG and LITZENBERGER, 2004; ROCHA, 2004). FELDMAN *et al.* (2005, p. 131) provide convincing empirical evidence for the ability of entrepreneurs to create a cluster (and – consequently – localization economies) as they build their firms, and build resources and community. Hence, there is an interdependent relationship between firms (including start-ups) and the surrounding cluster (i.e., a group of firms in the same industry or in similar industries that profit from localization economies). Consequently localization economies (by definition occurring between firms of the same industry) are potentially highest in sectoral-regional clusters since the latter consist of firms of the same industry (see also DELGADO *et al.*, 2010).

What does this mean for urban areas and their impact on necessity entrepreneurship? One has to consider, first, that localization effects – in contrast to urbanization effects – are not necessarily limited to urban areas. In principle, they may also occur in rural or in urban places outside urban areas where a cluster of firms of the same industry is located. Some large-scale steel or shipbuilding locations (heavily dependent on 'first-nature geography' location factors according to OVERMAN *et al.*, 2001, like proximity to transport infrastructure or to raw materials) fall into this category. However, they are the exceptions to the rule. The majority of localization economies can be found in urban agglomerations. There are two main reasons for this assessment. First, localization effects, to a degree, depend on urbanization effects – and the latter are, as described above, restricted to urban areas. Second, the higher the number of firms in the sectoral-regional cluster, the higher, in absolute terms, the localization effects (although the relationship is not a linear one). However, when it comes to the *relative* importance of localization economies (compared with urbanization economies) in large urban areas and in other regions of the same countries, it seems plausible that it is lower in large agglomerations. While localization economies can occur both in large urban areas *and* in small cities or even in rural areas (sectoral specialization is not a question of population size), urbanization economies are clearly size dependent: the larger the urban area/region is, the greater the probability of urbanization economies.

With respect to the types of entrepreneurship, it was stated that urbanization economies are relatively more relevant in large urban areas and that they favour opportunity entrepreneurship. This means, on the other hand, that the relative importance of necessity-entrepreneurship is higher in areas where the relative importance of localization economies is higher, i.e. outside large urban areas. This is particularly true for smaller urban areas or even rural areas with a strong industry specialization and very often with a dominance of a small number of large firms. Such an environment may hamper new firm formation and new firm growth, e.g. due to lock-in effects in formerly dynamic, but now shrinking clusters suffering from a lack of innovativeness and characterized by high unemployment. New firm formation may nevertheless take place in such an environment, but primarily as necessity entrepreneurship.

It may consequently be argued that regional unemployment serves as a relevant determinant of necessity entrepreneurship. First, a high rate of unemployment often coincides with low regional demand (also for products of the new firms), so that there is no motivation for opportunity entrepreneurship. Second, for several of the unemployed, starting a business may be a real option to get income, but this, of course, should be called necessity entrepreneurship as it happens because these people do not see (or have) any alternative. Thus, urban areas with high rates of unemployment may have higher rates of necessity entrepreneurship. This argumentation is similar to that for the relationship between per capita gross domestic product (GDP) (often associated with rates of unemployment) and necessity-driven entrepreneurship at the national level: most of the GEM countries with very low GDP per capita show very high levels of necessity-based entrepreneurship (AMORÓS and BOSMA, 2014). Consequently the fifth hypothesis is as follows:

Hypothesis 5: Higher rates of unemployment are associated with greater involvement in necessity-driven early-stage entrepreneurship across urban areas.

It seems plausible that regional employment growth is associated with lower involvement in necessity-driven entrepreneurship. As regional employment growth is positively associated with regional economic growth (see the second section and hypothesis 3) one might think at first glance that opportunity (and not necessity) entrepreneurship has a positive association with regional employment growth. However, this argumentation would ignore the fact that during a phase of employment growth many jobs are also created for low-skilled workers and the unemployed, meaning necessity-driven entrepreneurship will be reduced if some of the new jobs are given to formerly unemployed and/or poorly paid people. In that sense, an increase in the number of jobs in a region may lead to a decrease in necessity-driven entrepreneurship. Consequently, the final hypothesis is as follows:

Hypothesis 6: Employment growth is associated with lower involvement in necessity-driven early-stage entrepreneurship across urban areas.

Finally, it should be considered that urbanization economies and localization economies are, to a degree, interdependent. Localization economies are favourable to entrepreneurial activities (i.e., start-ups) due to role model processes, access to specialized labour, information and material, and to specific demand. Regarding to the causes of inter-urban area differences in start-up rates, this concept may explain why the regional context effect is influential. Given the potential and long-run impact of entrepreneurs on their regional environment (e.g., role models, networks, employment effects, regional structural change) and the well-known reverse impact of the regional environment on local entrepreneurs (e.g., 'entrepreneurial culture' (e.g., BEUGELSDIJK, 2007), localization and urbanization effects), it seems more than plausible that interaction effects between the levels described exist.

DATA AND METHODOLOGY

Data

Data on entrepreneurial activity was obtained by pooling annual Global Entrepreneurship Monitor (GEM) data between 2001 and 2008 using a very similar approach as in ACS *et al.* (2011) identifying entrepreneurial activity rates in world cities.[1] The GEM indicators are based on telephone surveys among the adult population. A key GEM indicator is the total early-stage entrepreneurial activity (TEA) rate. This measure is defined as the prevalence rate (in the 18–64-year-old population) of individuals who are involved in either nascent entrepreneurship or as an owner-manager in a new firm in existence for up to 42 months.

Nascent entrepreneurs are identified as individuals who are, at the moment of the GEM survey, setting up a business. Moreover they have indicated (1) that they have 'done something to help start a new business, such as looking for equipment or a location, organizing a start-up team, working on a business plan, beginning to save money, or any other activity that would help launch a business'; and (2) that they will be the single owner or a co-owner of the firm in gestation. Also, they have not paid any salaries, wages or payments in kind (including to themselves) for longer than three months; if they have, they are considered to be an owner-manager of a (new) firm. BOSMA *et al.* (2012) show that even though GEM's point of departure in measuring entrepreneurship differs entirely from initiatives focusing on business registrations, the pattern of start-up rates that emerges for GEM data (by adopting definitions so that a maximum fit with registration data is achieved) matches that of Eurostat Business Demography data fairly well.

While the TEA rate is an overall measure of early-stage entrepreneurial activity, identifying different types of TEA is also possible. In particular, a separate analysis is applied to necessity-motivated TEA, where the individual is involved in entrepreneurial activity merely because he or she sees no better option for earning a living. The remainder of the early-stage entrepreneurs were, at least partly, motivated because they recognized an opportunity. The three types of early-stage entrepreneurship included as dependent variables in the paper are thus as follows:

- Total early-stage entrepreneurial activity: TEA.
- Necessity motivated early-stage entrepreneurial activity: TEA_NEC.
- Opportunity motivated early-stage entrepreneurial activity: TEA_OPP.

Individuals in the GEM dataset were assigned to the region – possibly a major urban area – in which they lived at the time of the survey. It should be noted that for the years of observations used in this study, the information on the location of the respondent does not follow a uniform classification that can be applied across the countries included. Also, since the approach taken by the GEM project does not focus on urban regions as such, some of the larger cities in highly populated countries may be covered with a limited sample size while rather modestly sized urban areas in 'smaller' countries may be covered with a high sample size. In effect, the dataset is determined by both data availability and theoretical considerations: a minimum sample size per urban area of 1000 cases is required, while the area itself needs to have at least 500 000 inhabitants or be the first or second largest main urban region of the country. A sample size of 1000 is lower than the GEM standard requirements for national samples but equal to the sample size for many countries in the Eurobarometer survey data on entrepreneurship (e.g., GRILO and THURIK, 2008, for an analysis on this data). In sum, a sample of 517 549 individuals from 22 European countries is used, including information on the sub-national location of the respondents. The 47 main urban areas identified are represented by 104 746 individuals in this dataset. This sample of urban areas covers major urban areas in terms of population size. This does not mean, however, that *every* European urban area with a population above a certain threshold is included. In some countries the total sample size is still simply too small (even when pooled for several years) to include all urban areas with more than 500 000 inhabitants. On the other hand, the data-driven urban area selection process ensures that smaller or medium-sized urban areas are not designated 'major'. As data from different European countries (small as well as large ones) are used, there is an implicit bias towards urban areas from low-populated countries when applying the same population limit to all urban areas in all countries. Details of the urban areas included in the analysis are provided in Table 1. Regions have been defined in congruence with labour market or urban areas as far as the data allowed to do this. In some cases the definitions run parallel to the often-used European NUTS-2 classification, in other cases a deliberate deviation was sought, for instance using the German planning regions ('Raumordnungsregionen') and the UK's metropolitan areas. The definition of an urban area comes rather close to what is named 'functional urban regions' (FUR) (developed by COOMBES *et al.*, 1986) or, more recently, 'functional urban areas' (FUA) (PETERS, 2011). These spatial entities cover larger areas than just the cities (or even the inner cities) and are well introduced in the urban studies literature by scholars established in the urban studies field (e.g., PARR, 2007). The European Functional Urban Areas (EFUA) concept includes a core urban area defined morphologically on the basis of population density, plus the surrounding labour pool defined on the basis of commuting. While the functional urban area are conceptually very similar to the urban areas, due to data limitations, however, the urban areas analysed in this paper do not exactly match the official EFUAs. The average area size of the urban areas equals 4200 km^2.

In order to capture the potential causes of entrepreneurial activity at the urban area level (hypotheses 2–6), several data sources are used. The index of sectoral specialization/diversity is a key variable in the models as it allows one to identify nuances on agglomeration effects in the urban empirical setting. The degree of regional specialization is determined by the Theil index over the location quotients of 59 products including agriculture, manufacturing and services (see THISSEN *et al.*, 2011; and DOGARU *et al.*, 2011, for a more detailed assessment of this measure – also in a European setting). This unique underlying dataset was collected by the Netherlands Environmental Assessment Agency (PBL) and is based on regionalized production and trade data for 256 European NUTS-2 regions, 14 sectors and 59 product categories (COMBES and OVERMAN, 2004). The Theil coefficient represents deviations from the European average distribution of production specializations in all sectors. A high score represents a large degree of sectoral specialization in a region, and a low score represents sectoral diversity.

Other variables included at the urban area level relate to the gross regional product (in purchasing power parity (PPP)), growth in GDP between 2001 and 2006 and the rate of unemployment in 2001, all taken from the Cambridge Econometrics database. Employment growth between 2001 and 2006 was also taken from the PBL. Perceived opportunities to start a business in the urban area were derived from GEM by aggregating the individual answers to this question. By taking this to the urban area level rather than the individual level, some potential selection biases are prevented as the GEM Adult Population Surveys are cross-sectional in nature. As such, the data show almost perfect explanations between individual perceptions (such as the opportunity to start a business)

Table 1. Urban areas included: definitions and size

Country	City	Urban area definition	Population (×1000)	Area (km^2 ×1000)
Belgium	Brussels[a]	NUTS-1	1100	0.2
	Antwerp	NUTS-2	1800	2.9
	Ghent	NUTS-2	1400	3.0
Croatia	Zagreb	Metro	1100	3.7
Denmark	Copenhagen	NUTS-2	1900	3.7
	Aarhus	NUTS-3	1200	1.0
Finland	Helsinki	Metro	1400	6.4
France	Paris[a]	NUTS-1	11300	12.0
Germany	Berlin[a]	NUTS-1	3400	0.9
	Duisburg-Essen	Planning	5200	4.4
	Düsseldorf[a]	Planning	5200	5.3
	Cologne[a]	Planning	4400	7.4
	Frankfurt[a]; Rhein-Main	Planning	5800	13.0
	Stuttgart[a]	Planning	2700	3.6
	Munich[a]	Planning	2600	5.5
Greece	Athens[a]	NUTS-1	3800	3.8
Hungary	Budapest[a]	NUTS-2	2800	6.9
Ireland	Dublin[a]	NUTS-3	1200	1.0
Italy	Milan (Lombardia)[a]	NUTS-2	9300	23.9
Latvia	Riga	NUTS-3	700	0.3
Netherlands	Utrecht	NUTS-3	1200	1.4
	Amsterdam[a]	NUTS-3	1200	0.9
	The Hague	NUTS-3	1200	0.6
	Rotterdam[a]	NUTS-3	1400	1.2
Norway	Oslo-Akerhüs	Metro	1000	5.4
Portugal	Lisbon[a]	NUTS-2	2800	3.0
Romania	Bucharest	NUTS-2	2300	1.8
Serbia	Belgrade	District	1700	3.2
Slovenia	Ljubljana	NUTS-3	500	2.5
	Maribor	NUTS-3	300	2.2
Spain	Madrid[a]	NUTS-1	5600	8.0
	Barcelona[a]	NUTS-3	5400	4.3
	Valencia[a]	NUTS-3	2500	10.8
	Sevilla	NUTS-3	1800	14.0
	Malaga	NUTS-3	1500	7.3
Sweden	Stockholm[a]	Metro	1900	6.5
Switzerland	Zurich	NUTS-3	1400	1.7
Turkey	Istanbul	Metro	13800	5.3
UK	London[a]	NUTS-1	7600	1.6
	Birmingham[a]	NUTS-3	3700	0.9
	Manchester[a]	NUTS-2	2600	1.3
	Leeds-Bradford[a]	Metro	2300	0.9
	Liverpool-Birkenhead	Metro	2200	0.9
	Newcastle-Sunderland	Metro	1600	0.5
	Sheffield	Metro	1600	1.6
	Nottingham-Derby	Metro	1500	4.3
	Glasgow	Metro	1400	2.0

Note: [a]Included in regression Tables 5 and 6.

and entrepreneurial activity (cf. BOSMA, 2013). The final urban area-level variable included is a dummy variable that is equal to 1 if the urban area hosts a university that is represented in the top 75 of the Shanghai university ranking list. This indicates a potential spillover effect (ACS and ARMINGTON, 2004) and is expected to influence in particular the aspiration types of entrepreneurial activity as urban areas that host basic research are more conducive to entrepreneurial activity (AUDRETSCH *et al.*, 2011). Unfortunately, the independent variables included in the models explaining individuals' entrepreneurial behaviour are only available for 23 urban areas out of the 47 main European urban areas. We were initially able to abstract from the GEM dataset and that met the requirements mentioned above. The correlations of the variables at the urban area level are provided in Table 2. There is a positive correlation between employment growth and GDP growth; however, test statistics showed no indication of multicollinearity issues: the variance inflation factor adopting a regional-level regression equals 2.09.

Table 2. Descriptive statistics and correlations of urban area measures included in the regression (N = 23)

		Mean	SD	Minimum	Maximum	Correlations 1	2	3	4	5	6	7
1	GDP per capita (ln)	3.38	0.43	2.21	3.97							
2	GDP growth	0.20	0.06	0.06	0.33	−0.43 *						
2	Employment growth	0.11	0.09	0.03	0.30	−0.29	0.58 **					
3	Unemployment rate	6.04	3.17	2.44	15.10	−0.37	0.05	0.16				
4	Specialization-diversity	0.06	0.04	0.02	0.20	0.16	0.39	0.40	−0.09			
5	University: top 75	0.61	0.50	0	1	0.44 *	−0.18	−0.18	0.13	0.00		
6	Perceived opportunities	0.32	0.09	0.16	0.51	0.46 *	−0.05	0.29	−0.49 *	0.28	0.37	
7	Know recent start-up entrepreneurs	0.34	0.06	0.23	0.47	0.31	0.17	0.05	−0.02	0.28	0.23	0.07

Note: $*p < 0.05$; and $**p < 0.01$.

Methodology

The empirical analysis consists of two parts. The first part is aimed at demonstrating any difference in entrepreneurship levels between 'main urban areas' and the remainder of the country. To test the first hypothesis, i.e. the claim that the level of opportunity-motivated entrepreneurial activities among urban areas is generally higher than in the remaining parts of the country, 'within-and-between' country effects are explored in the database. Hence, on the urban area level, the three entrepreneurship rates described above are regressed on a dummy variable, assigning 1 to the event that the observation concerns a urban area and 0 otherwise (i.e., the observation represents the area outside the identified urban areas in the country). National effects are accounted for by applying fixed effects and random effects.

In the second part, a multilevel logit model is used to establish urban area-level determinants for several types of entrepreneurship, next to individual level explanations. Consequently, in the model individuals are hierarchically nested in their urban environment. As in the classic example in educational studies where pupils are nested within schools, and will therefore differ from pupils in other schools (VAN DUIJN *et al.*, 1999; GOLDSTEIN, 2007), it can be argued that people in entrepreneurial regions will resemble each other with respect to entrepreneurial attitudes and behaviour, and as such demonstrate different entrepreneurial behaviour to that of individuals in other regions, even if they have the same characteristics. In effect, the assumption of independent observations would then be violated if standard multivariate models were to be used. Multilevel models control for the assumption of the independence of observations in grouped data. In terms of the specific analysis, this means that it can be acknowledged that urban characteristics may shape individual entrepreneurial behaviour, and that this context may not be independent for individuals because of such influences as regional role models and knowledge spillovers. The co-variation between individuals' behaviour sharing the same regional externalities can be expressed by the intra-class correlation (HOX, 2002). With this, the variance between regions contributes to individual behaviour in addition to the variance between individuals. If standard-significance tests are used, treating the individual as the single unit of analysis and regional level variables are included for each individual, the important assumption of the independence of residual error terms would be violated, potentially leading to large errors and too liberal significance levels (e.g., RABE-HESKETH and SKRONDAL, 2005). Processes that in fact play a role at different (individual or spatial) level should not be analysed at only one level, since conclusions would be damaged by ecological fallacies (aggregated correlations and individual correlations are not the same, either in magnitude or in sign). Multilevel analysis has been developed for this reason; it resolves these kinds of problem. Applications to explain entrepreneurial activities by individuals have only emerged recently; examples covering various topics include BOSMA (2009), AUTIO and ACS (2010), ELAM and TERJESEN (2010) and DE CLERCQ *et al.* (2011).

EMPIRICAL RESULTS: ENTREPRENEURIAL ACTIVITIES IN EUROPEAN URBAN AREAS

The first aim is to establish whether, and if so to what extent, European urban areas indeed have an 'entrepreneurial advantage' over the remaining parts of the country. As a first indication, Table 3 presents TEA rates for the 47 urban areas included in the initial analysis. Striking examples of high (opportunity-motivated) TEA rates, relative to the remaining parts of the country, are German urban area such as Cologne, the Rhine-Main area (hosting Frankfurt/Main, Wiesbaden and Mainz), Munich and Berlin. However, for the UK the urban area of Inner London is only observed as standing out from other (urban) areas in the UK. Thus, while for some urban areas there seems to be an entrepreneurship 'premium', the pattern is quite mixed.

Table 3. Main total early-stage entrepreneurial activity (TEA) indicators by urban area (N = 47)

Country	Urban area	TEA	SE	Necessity TEA	SE	Opportunity TEA	SE
Belgium	Brussels	4.3	(0.46)	0.2	(0.11)	3.6	(0.43)
	Antwerp	3.7	(0.36)	0.1	(0.07)	3.2	(0.33)
	Ghent	2.7	(0.36)	0.1	(0.07)	2.5	(0.35)
	Rest of the country	3.3	(0.17)	0.4	(0.06)	2.6	(0.16)
Croatia	Zagreb	6.8	(0.88)	1.6	(0.44)	4.9	(0.76)
	Rest of the country	7.7	(0.54)	2.8	(0.34)	4.8	(0.43)
Denmark	Copenhagen	5.9	(0.35)	0.3	(0.08)	5.3	(0.33)
	Aarhus	5.5	(0.48)	0.3	(0.12)	4.9	(0.45)
	Rest of the country	5.2	(0.20)	0.2	(0.04)	4.8	(0.19)
Finland	Helsinki	5.2	(0.37)	0.3	(0.09)	4.5	(0.35)
	Rest of the country	4.2	(0.23)	0.5	(0.08)	3.3	(0.20)
France	Paris	5.1	(0.50)	1.0	(0.22)	3.9	(0.44)
	Rest of the country	3.8	(0.23)	0.9	(0.11)	2.6	(0.19)
Germany	Cologne	6.9	(0.78)	1.7	(0.39)	4.7	(0.65)
	Frankfurt; Rhein-Main	6.8	(0.71)	1.7	(0.37)	4.6	(0.60)
	Munich	6.7	(0.75)	1.5	(0.37)	4.6	(0.63)
	Berlin	6.7	(0.62)	2.0	(0.35)	4.0	(0.49)
	Duisburg-Essen	5.6	(0.74)	1.5	(0.40)	3.3	(0.58)
	Düsseldorf	5.4	(0.62)	1.8	(0.36)	3.6	(0.51)
	Stuttgart	4.8	(0.62)	1.5	(0.36)	2.8	(0.48)
	Rest of the country	4.7	(0.12)	1.1	(0.06)	3.4	(0.11)
Greece	Athens	6.7	(0.51)	1.3	(0.23)	5.1	(0.45)
	Rest of the country	6.8	(0.33)	1.8	(0.18)	4.4	(0.27)
Hungary	Budapest	7.7	(0.64)	1.8	(0.32)	5.3	(0.54)
	Rest of the country	4.6	(0.21)	1.4	(0.11)	3.0	(0.17)
Ireland	Dublin	8.6	(0.53)	0.9	(0.18)	7.5	(0.50)
	Rest of the country	8.6	(0.27)	1.3	(0.11)	6.6	(0.24)
Italy	Milan	3.2	(0.46)	0.1	(0.10)	2.6	(0.41)
	Rest of the country	4.8	(0.22)	0.7	(0.08)	3.5	(0.19)
Latvia	Riga	7.1	(0.71)	1.1	(0.29)	5.6	(0.64)
	Rest of the country	4.8	(0.22)	0.7	(0.08)	3.5	(0.19)
Netherlands	Utrecht	6.6	(0.78)	0.4	(0.19)	5.4	(0.71)
	Amsterdam	5.7	(0.60)	0.8	(0.23)	4.3	(0.52)
	The Hague	4.8	(0.70)	0.4	(0.20)	3.9	(0.63)
	Rotterdam	3.9	(0.54)	0.5	(0.19)	3.1	(0.48)
	Rest of the country	4.4	(0.20)	0.4	(0.06)	3.4	(0.17)
Norway	Oslo	8.2	(0.47)	0.5	(0.13)	7.0	(0.44)
	Rest of the country	7.4	(0.30)	0.5	(0.08)	6.4	(0.28)
Portugal	Lisbon	4.2	(0.64)	1.0	(0.31)	2.9	(0.53)
	Rest of the country	5.0	(0.49)	1.0	(0.22)	3.6	(0.42)
Romania	Bucharest	4.6	(0.70)	0.5	(0.24)	3.1	(0.58)
	Rest of the country	3.8	(0.38)	1.1	(0.21)	2.1	(0.29)
Serbia	Belgrade	8.2	(1.00)	2.2	(0.54)	5.1	(0.80)
	Rest of the country	8.0	(0.51)	3.5	(0.35)	4.2	(0.38)
Slovenia	Ljubljana	5.9	(0.59)	1.0	(0.25)	4.9	(0.55)
	Maribor	6.4	(0.79)	0.8	(0.28)	5.5	(0.73)
	Rest of the country	5.3	(0.38)	0.4	(0.11)	4.8	(0.36)
Spain	Madrid	7.3	(0.33)	0.9	(0.12)	6.3	(0.31)
	Barcelona	7.1	(0.46)	0.9	(0.16)	6.0	(0.42)
	Valencia	6.3	(0.42)	0.8	(0.15)	5.2	(0.39)
	Malaga	5.8	(0.56)	1.1	(0.25)	4.5	(0.50)
	Sevilla	5.0	(0.54)	0.9	(0.24)	4.1	(0.49)
	Rest of the country	6.1	(0.10)	0.8	(0.04)	5.1	(0.09)
Sweden	Stockholm	5.2	(0.49)	0.4	(0.13)	4.6	(0.46)
	Rest of the country	3.4	(0.10)	0.4	(0.03)	2.9	(0.10)
Switzerland	Zurich	6.7	(0.84)	0.8	(0.30)	5.6	(0.77)
	Rest of the country	6.0	(0.29)	0.9	(0.11)	4.9	(0.26)
Turkey	Istanbul	3.9	(0.47)	1.4	(0.28)	2.2	(0.36)
	Rest of the country	6.5	(0.33)	2.2	(0.20)	3.7	(0.25)
UK	London	7.5	(0.39)	0.8	(0.13)	6.0	(0.36)
	Manchester	5.8	(0.47)	0.8	(0.18)	4.6	(0.42)
	Birmingham	5.6	(0.43)	0.9	(0.18)	4.4	(0.38)
	Nottingham-Derby	5.6	(0.60)	0.7	(0.21)	4.3	(0.53)

(*Continued*)

Table 3. Continued

Country	Urban area	TEA	SE	Necessity TEA	SE	Opportunity TEA	SE
	Leeds-Bradford	5.1	(0.42)	0.6	(0.15)	4.1	(0.38)
	Glasgow	4.7	(0.44)	0.5	(0.14)	4.0	(0.42)
	Liverpool-Birkenhead	4.5	(0.40)	0.5	(0.14)	3.9	(0.37)
	Newcastle-Sunderland	3.8	(0.43)	0.4	(0.14)	3.1	(0.39)
	Sheffield	3.8	(0.37)	0.5	(0.14)	3.0	(0.33)
	Rest of the country	5.8	(0.07)	0.8	(0.03)	4.6	(0.06)

Table 4 shows the results of regressing entrepreneurship rates on a dummy that has the value of 1 if the subject of observation is a major urban area (rather than a 'rest of the country' region). Overall, the results confirm that in general opportunity-driven early-stage entrepreneurial activity is higher in urban areas, also when controlling for country effects. While a positive effect is found for opportunity-motivated TEA, the effect is weakly negative for necessity-motivated TEA. In effect the results indicate that on average there is a 'main urban area premium' adding 0.5 percentage points (13%) to the average of 4.0% of involvement in opportunity-motivated TEA in the other regions. At the same time there would be an estimated 'main urban area discount' of 12% for necessity-motivated entrepreneurship – bearing in mind that this coefficient is only weakly significant. Additional analysis showed that whereas the highest opportunity-motivated TEA rates were observed in regions in the UK and Scandinavia, the positive 'main urban area' effect was mainly driven by urban areas in Eastern and Central Europe. Necessity-motivated TEA rates are highest in Southern and Eastern European areas. The 'main urban area' effect for necessity-driven TEA tends to be most negative in areas in Southern Europe and most positive in urban areas in Central Europe – where necessity-motivated TEA tends to be low – and the results indicate that this is particularly the case for non-urban areas. It should be noted that all the relevant main urban areas in every country have not been identified. For instance, in the case of France only Paris was identified, not Lyon, Marseille or Lille. This may have an effect on the results. As a check for robustness, the same regressions were conducted, while leaving out the observations in the UK (the country with most urban areas in the dataset). This did not affect the overall pattern of the results, nor did it when excluding the German cases. Also when excluding the observations from the two countries with arguably the poorest coverage in the dataset, France and Italy, the general results from Table 4 were not affected, except for the coefficients on necessity entrepreneurship to turn insignificant.

As the results in Table 4 showed that distinguishing between opportunity and necessity entrepreneurship is relevant in an urban setting, the paper moves on to explaining individual participation in different types of early-stage entrepreneurial activity by (1) individual characteristics and (2) urban area-level characteristics. Unfortunately, data collection at the urban area-level is – although increasing – still in an infant and ad-hoc stage in Europe. Effectively this means that one is left with a sample of 23 urban areas for which urban area-level explanations can be provided, given the data availability of the relevant variables. One essentially arrives at the same conclusion when also using these 23 urban areas and adopting the same methodology in Table 5: there appears to be a 'premium' for opportunity-motivated early-stage entrepreneurial activity in urban areas. For this reduced sample a significant 'main urban area' effect for necessity-motivated entrepreneurship was not found. As the 23 main urban areas included in Table 5 are mainly larger urban areas that generally face challenges hosting many inhabitants with limited options for work, this finding is not a surprising one.

Table 4. Regression results: 'urban area effects' for entrepreneurial activity, by motivation: total sample

	Country fixed effects		Country random effects	
Dependent variable	Urban area effect	Constant	Urban area effect	Constant
Total early-stage entrepreneurial activity (TEA)	0.43	5.3***	0.40	5.5***
	(0.26)	(0.21)	(0.26)	(0.33)
Necessity early-stage entrepreneurial activity	−0.13*	1.0***	−0.14*	1.1***
	(0.07)	(0.06)	(0.08)	(0.15)
Opportunity early-stage entrepreneurial activity	0.51**	3.9***	0.49**	4.0***
	(0.21)	(0.17)	(0.20)	(0.28)

Notes: $N = 69$ in all regressions (47 urban areas in 22 countries). Standard errors are reported in parentheses. Hausman tests provide support for using random effects in all three models.

$*p < 0.1$; $**p < 0.05$; and $***p < 0.01$.

Table 5. Regression results: 'urban area effects' for entrepreneurial activity, by motivation: regression sample

	Country fixed effects		Country random effects	
Dependent variable	Urban area effect	Constant	Urban area effect	Constant
Total early-stage entrepreneurial activity (TEA)	0.65**	5.2***	0.67**	5.1***
	(0.34)	(0.27)	(0.34)	(0.46)
Necessity early-stage entrepreneurial activity	0.04	1.0***	0.04	0.9***
	(0.08)	(0.06)	(0.08)	(0.15)
Opportunity early-stage entrepreneurial activity	0.61**	3.9***	0.62**	3.8***
	(0.27)	(0.22)	(0.27)	(0.38)

Notes: $N = 35$ in all regressions (23 urban areas in 12 countries). Standard errors are reported in parentheses. Hausman tests provide support for using random effects in all three models.

$*p < 0.1$; $**p < 0.05$; and $***p < 0.01$.

To explain the involvement in TEA as reported by the inhabitants of urban areas a multilevel framework was developed to explain the occurrence of opportunity-motivated entrepreneurship among inhabitants of urban areas. The regression results for explaining TEA and its two components by motivation of the individual are shown in Table 6. The multilevel perspective first calls for empirically assessing the multilevel aspects at play in the dependent variables and – according to standard procedures – to determine the *intra-class correlation* (SNIJDERS, 1999) to see which part of the variation in individuals' entrepreneurial behaviour can be attributed to the regional level. To this end, the three measures of TEA were regressed on an intercept only, while allowing the intercept to exhibit a statistical distribution. From this analysis an intra-class correlation coefficient of 1.9% for TEA is derived. The finding that only 2% of the observed overall variation in individuals' involvement in opportunity-motivated entrepreneurial activity can be attributed to the urban area level certainly puts the role of cities into perspective. Still, given the low prevalence rates of entrepreneurial activity as presented in Table 3, if the characteristics of the urban area make up 2% of the variation of all individuals in their decision to start a business (or not), it could very well be a decisive aspect for a considerable group of inhabitants. Put differently, for some groups of people with similar individual characteristics the urban context could matter in making such decisions. In one urban area the regional features could prevent an individual back from becoming entrepreneurially active, while those of other areas could be supportive. Interestingly, the intra-class correlation for necessity-driven entrepreneurship is substantially higher than opportunity-driven entrepreneurship: 6.2% versus 2.0%. Thus, urban characteristics can be expected to explain the variance in necessity-driven TEA better than opportunity-driven TEA.

The pattern of individual level effects that emerges from Table 6 confirms the existing empirical evidence in the literature. The age distribution linked to early-stage entrepreneurial activity is hill-shaped, a significant gender effect and higher education are found as well as the fact that higher levels of household income tend to be associated with opportunity-motivated entrepreneurial activity. The paper now turns to the discussion of the urban area effects that relate to the hypotheses. As argued in the theoretical section, diversity (rather than specialization) is linked to more early-stage entrepreneurial activity. The second and third models show that this holds true for both necessity and opportunity-motivated entrepreneurial activity. Therefore, confirmation for hypothesis 2 is found. Examining the effects of regional characteristics on necessity motivated entrepreneurship a statistically significant relationship with rates of unemployment is not observed. However a negative relationship with employment growth is observed, suggesting that decreases in employment are a better indicator for push effects into self-employment than rates of unemployment. Hence, no support is found for hypothesis 5, whereas hypothesis 6 is supported. The positive effect of regional GDP growth on necessity-motivated entrepreneurial activity may be explained by an influx of people moving to promising urban areas, including those with few options to make a living and hence possibly resorting to necessity-motivated entrepreneurship.

Even though no link was found in the sample between GDP per capita levels of the urban area and the probability to be involved in early-stage entrepreneurial activity, this effect was found to vary across groups of individuals. This was achieved by testing for random slopes with the urban area-level determinants and found positive and significant standard deviation with opportunity-motivated and total early-stage entrepreneurial activity. Growth in economic wealth, as measured by regional GDP growth, is also linked to opportunity-motivated entrepreneurship. This may be due to the same reason as mentioned above – people moving into the region may actually have alternative options for work and simply see good opportunities for starting a firm – but also due to growing demand. Interestingly, in the presence of observed regional growth in economic output, the 'softer' variable that captures opportunity recognitions for start-ups becomes insignificant. Hence, and unlike for instance

Table 6. Regression results: probability being involved in (necessity/opportunity motivated) early-stage entrepreneurial activity (base: 18–64 population)

	Type of early-stage entrepreneurial activity								
	Total early-stage entrepreneurial activity			Necessity early-stage entrepreneurial activity			Opportunity early-stage entrepreneurial activity		
	Estimated	SE	*p*	Estimated	SE	*p*	Estimated	SE	*p*
Individual level determinants									
Age	0.15	(0.01)	***	0.19	(0.03)	***	0.13	(0.01)	***
Age squared	−0.02	(0.00)	***	−0.02	(0.00)	***	−0.02	(0.00)	***
Gender (female)	−0.74	(0.04)	***	−0.51	(0.10)	***	−0.79	(0.05)	***
Education									
Some secondary	0.04	(0.06)		0.05	(0.14)		0.06	(0.07)	
Secondary degree	0.29	(0.06)	***	−0.17	(0.14)		0.40	(0.07)	***
Post-secondary	0.39	(0.06)	***	0.13	(0.14)		0.46	(0.07)	***
Household income									
Medium	0.13	(0.07)	*	−0.12	(0.16)		0.19	(0.08)	**
High	0.38	(0.07)	***	−0.36	(0.17)	**	0.51	(0.08)	***
Unknown	0.25	(0.08)	***	−0.16	(0.18)		0.35	(0.09)	***
Year (Reference 2001)									
2002	0.08	(0.12)		0.22	(0.26)		0.27	(0.14)	*
2003	0.07	(0.12)		0.55	(0.26)	**	0.23	(0.14)	*
2004	−0.16	(0.11)		0.15	(0.26)		0.04	(0.13)	
2005	0.10	(0.11)		0.33	(0.25)		0.26	(0.13)	*
2006	0.17	(0.11)	*	0.26	(0.24)		0.39	(0.13)	***
2007	0.20	(0.13)		−0.35	(0.36)		0.36	(0.15)	**
2008	0.09	(0.14)		0.07	(0.33)		0.22	(0.16)	
Urban area level determinants									
GDP per capita (ln)	0.09	(0.13)		0.12	(0.21)		0.07	(0.13)	
GDP growth 2001–06	3.73	(0.88)	***	5.38	(1.51)	***	3.25	(0.84)	***
Employment growth	−0.59	(0.58)		−2.35	(0.99)	**	0.03	(0.54)	
Unemployment rate	0.02	(0.01)	*	0.03	(0.02)		0.02	(0.01)	*
Diversity – Specialization	−3.26	(1.03)	***	−7.99	(1.92)	***	−2.39	(0.97)	**
University: top 75	0.09	(0.09)		−0.02	(0.19)		0.12	(0.08)	
Perceived opportunities	0.52	(0.59)		−1.30	(1.01)		0.82	(0.56)	
Know recent start-up entrepreneurs	0.92	(0.67)		2.42	(1.19)	**	0.34	(0.66)	
Constant	−6.86	(0.56)	***	−9.09	(1.05)	***	−6.83	(0.56)	***
SD (GDP per capita effect)	0.03	(0.01)	**				0.03	(0.01)	**
SD (constant)	0.00	(0.15)		0.00	(0.09)		0.00	(0.21)	
Number of observations		44209			44209			44209	
Number of urban areas		23			23			23	
−log*L*		9639			2252			8091	
Intra-class correlation		1.9%			6.2%			2.0%	

Note: Stata command xtmlelogit was used. $*p < 0.10$; $**p < 0.05$; $***p < 0.01$.

proposed by MEESTER and PELLENBARG (2006), 'harder' economic indicators seem to predict opportunity-motivated entrepreneurial activities better than 'softer' indicators. Thus, support is found for hypothesis 3, but not for hypothesis 4.

CONCLUSIONS

This paper has investigated whether urban areas are more entrepreneurial than the other parts of the countries and to what extent the observed regional differences in urban entrepreneurship are caused by differences in individual characteristics and context effects. Hypotheses based on the relevant literature were derived and these were tested by using a new, unique dataset that captures entrepreneurial activity by over 400000 individuals across 23 urban areas in 12 European countries. It should be pointed out that while the analysis was focused on urban entrepreneurship, this does not imply that other areas are deemed irrelevant. While urban regions are distinguished to some extent from 'the rest of the country', it is acknowledged that the importance of rural entrepreneurship should not be neglected (STATHOPOULOU *et al.*, 2004).

The contributions of the paper are diverse. First, it elaborated on the debate on urbanization economies and localization economies by discussing the role of entrepreneurial activity in (major) urban settings. Second, it tested the propositions with unique, harmonized data on entrepreneurship that allows comparisons along various types of entrepreneurship and is thus not restricted to the static measure of self-employment that has been used in similar studies to date. Third, an appropriate multilevel analysis was conducted to disentangle individual-level and regional-level effects.

The results partially confirmed the expectations. While the literature led to a hypothesis that larger urban areas have an 'entrepreneurial advantage', the results indicate that urban rates of entrepreneurship do not unequivocally exceed those of the rest of the country. However, focusing on opportunity-motivated entrepreneurship, stronger support for such an 'entrepreneurial advantage' was found. The multilevel analysis confirms the notion that both individual effects and regional contexts are important for the occurrence of particular types of entrepreneurial activity. Specialization and diversity, both relevant measures in the debate on localization economies and urbanization economies, matter for different types of entrepreneurial activity. Diversity in economic activity affects TEA as expected. GDP growth and the presence of start-up examples are also predictors of TEA. Whereas GDP growth particularly impacts opportunity-motivated entrepreneurship, a reduction in employment growth increases involvement in necessity-motivated entrepreneurship in urban areas. Furthermore, and notwithstanding the importance of opportunity recognition in the process of entrepreneurship, no support was found for the regional measure of opportunity recognition for start-ups to affect (opportunity motivated) early-stage entrepreneurial activity. Finally, the analysis suggests that a decrease in employment may serve as a better explanation of the 'entrepreneurship-push' hypothesis than a high level of rates of unemployment. It was found that urban areas characterized by decreases in employment exhibit more necessity-motivated early-stage entrepreneurs. This suggests that the bulk of necessity-motivated entrepreneurs in urban areas stems from the pool of employees (losing their jobs or fearing they may do so) rather than from the pool of unemployed and perhaps that transitions from employee to entrepreneur tend to be made rather swiftly.

Overall, the results demonstrate that the spatial environment matters for entrepreneurial activities and, as such, they confirm recent empirical analysis on regional determinants on new firm formation. It should be noted that although in the empirical set-up addressing all economic activities more evidence was found for urbanization effects (when linked to measures of diversity) than for localization effects (proxied with specialization in economic activities), this does not rule out that localization effects are present. For example, LASCH *et al.* (2013) reveal for a supposedly footloose industry like the (French) communication and information technology sector that geographical proximity to other large firms of the same industry, local market opportunities and client-customer interactions are the predominant regional factors in new firm formation.

The analysis confirms that context matters for entrepreneurship, however further elaboration is certainly required. MUSTERD and GRITSAI (2010) provide some relevant contextual evidence that may be linked to the analysis in future research. They point out that large urban areas in Europe are quite heterogeneous, also in their role as vanguards of innovation, entrepreneurship and change. In strongly centralized countries like France and the UK these are mostly the national capitals, with their unique and diverse urban environment they remain particularly attractive for talented individuals, including those working in creative and knowledge-intensive industries (with above-average start-up rates among members of the 'creative class', see also BOSCHMA and FRITSCH, 2009). They normally present quite a contrast to other urban areas lower down the urban hierarchy. This is particularly the case in countries with relatively small populations such as Bulgaria, Latvia, Finland, Hungary, Ireland, Greece and Slovenia. In more decentralized countries like Germany, Poland or Spain, the situation is quite different. Here, following MUSTERD and GRITSAI (2010), regional capitals have important political functions and therefore often produce stronger impulses for dynamic development and show higher entrepreneurial dynamics than national capitals. Other research designs such as case studies and longitudinal set-ups may be used to get a better grip on the causality of the relations studied in this paper.

Finally, the results may help to answer the question a Kauffman report in 2008 rightly asked: What kinds of entrepreneurship support policies are useful for urban areas and why (ACS *et al.*, 2008)? The regional aspect of entrepreneurship has until recently been mostly ignored both by entrepreneurship support policies and by regional economic policies (the German 'Exist' programme is one of the few, rare exceptions, see KULICKE and SCHLEINKOFER, 2008). Policymakers are now increasingly considering the specific opportunities of entrepreneurship policies dedicated to (large) urban areas and the location-specific needs of such policies, for example through the establishment of location-based growth accelerators (BOSMA and STAM, 2012) and adopting frameworks of entrepreneurial ecosystems (PITELIS, 2012). The results and potential follow-up research, e.g. explaining growth- or innovation-oriented types of entrepreneurship, may help to probe further urban area-specific entrepreneurship policies that appreciate the particular country- and region-specific characteristics in terms of entrepreneurship activities and entrepreneurship attitudes.

Acknowledgments – The authors would like to thank the guest editors and two anonymous reviewers for helpful comments and suggestions. They also thank the Global Entrepreneurship Monitor (GEM) consortium (http://www.gemconsortium.org) and its members for their dedicated involvement in creating a large international comparative dataset on entrepreneurship. Both authors contributed equally to the writing of this paper.

NOTE

1. See Reynolds *et al.* (2005) for a detailed overview of the GEM methodology; Bosma (2013) for an overview of the GEM-based empirical papers; and Bosma *et al.* (2012) for a GEM manual.

REFERENCES

Acs Z. and Armington C. (2004) Employment growth and entrepreneurial activity in cities, *Regional Studies* **38**, 911–927.

Acz Z. and Storey D. (2004) Introduction: Entrepreneurship and economic development, *Regional Studies* **38**, 871–877.

Acs Z., Glaeser E., Litan R., Fleming L., Goetz S., Kerr W., Klepper S., Rosenthal S., Sorenson O. and Strang W. (2008) *Entrepreneurship and Urban Success: Toward a Policy Consensus*. Kauffman Foundation (available at: http://papers.ssrn.com/sol3/papers.cfm?abstract_id=1092493) (accessed April 2014).

Acs Z. J., Bosma N. and Sternberg R. (2011) Entrepreneurship in world cities, in Minniti M. (Ed.) *The Dynamics of Entrepreneurial Activity*, pp. 125–152. Oxford University Press, Oxford.

Amorós J. E. and Bosma N. S. (2014) *Global Entrepreneurship Monitor 2013 Global Report*. Global Entrepreneurship Research Association (GERA), London.

Antonietti R. and Cainelli G. (2011) The role of spatial agglomeration in a structural model of innovation, productivity and export: a firm-level analysis, *Annals of Regional Science* **46**, 577–600.

Armington C. and Acs Z. J. (2002) The determinants of regional variation in new firm formation, *Regional Studies* **36**, 33–45.

Audretsch D. (2005) The knowledge spillover theory of entrepreneurship and economic growth, in Vinig G. T. and van der Voort R. C. W. (Eds) *The Emergence of Entrepreneurial Economics*, pp. 37–54. Elsevier, New York, NY.

Audretsch D. and Aldridge T. (2009) Knowledge spillovers, entrepreneurship and regional development, in Capello R. and Nijkamp P. (Eds) *Handbook of Regional Growth and Development Theories*, pp. 201–210. Elgar, Cheltenham.

Audretsch D., Falck O. and Heblich M. (2011) Who's got the aces up his sleeve? Functional specialization of cities and entrepreneurship, *Annuals of Regional Science* **46**, 621–636.

Autio E. and Acs Z. J. (2010) Intellectual property protection and the formation of entrepreneurial growth aspirations, *Strategic Entrepreneurship Journal* **4**, 234–251.

Baptista R. and Peter Swann G. M. (1999) A comparison of clustering dynamics in the US and UK computer industries, *Journal of Evolutionary Economics* **9**, 373–399.

Barreneche-García A. (2012) Analysing the determinants of entrepreneurship in European cities. Paper presented at the Danish Research Unit for Industrial Dynamics (DRUID) Academy 2012, University of Cambridge, Cambridge, UK, 2012.

Batabyal A. A. and Nijkamp P. (2010) Asymmetric information, entrepreneurial activity, and the scope of fiscal policy in an open regional economy, *International Regional Science Review* **33**, 421–436.

Beaudry C. and Schiffauerova A. (2009) Who's right, Marshall or Jacobs? The localization versus urbanization debate, *Research Policy* **38**, 318–337.

Belitzki M. and Korosteleva J. (2010) Entrepreneurial activity across European cities. Paper presented at the 50th European Regional Science Association (ERSA) Conference, Jönköping, Sweden, 20–23 August 2010.

Beugelsdijk S. (2007) Entrepreneurial culture, regional innovativeness and economic growth, *Journal of Evolutionary Economics* **17**, 187–210.

Boschma R. A. and Fritsch M. (2009) Creative class and regional growth: empirical evidence from seven European countries, *Economic Geography* **85**, 391–423.

Boschma R. and Iammarino S. (2009) Related variety, trade linkages and regional growth in Italy, *Economic Geography* **85**, 289–311.

Bosma N. (2009) The geography of entrepreneurial activity and regional economic development. PhD dissertation, University of Utrecht, Utrecht.

Bosma N. (2013) The global entrepreneurship monitor (GEM) and its impact on entrepreneurship research, *Foundations and Trends in Entrepreneurship* **9**, 143–248.

Bosma N. and Schutjens V. (2007) Patterns of promising entrepreneurial activity in European regions, *Tijdschrift voor ecconomische en sociale Geografie* **98**, 675–686.

Bosma N. and Stam E. (2012) *Local Policies for High Employment Growth Enterprises*. Organisation for Economic Co-operation and Development (OECD) Report (available at: http://www.oecd.org/cfe/leed/Bosma-Stam_high-growth%20policies.pdf).

Bosma N., Coduras A., Litovsky Y. and Seaman J. (2012) *GEM Manual: A Report on the Design, Data and Quality Control of the Global Entrepreneurship Monitor* (available at: http://www.gemconsortium.org).

Capello R. (2002) Entrepreneurship and spatial externalities: theory and measurement, *Annals of Regional Science* **36**, 386–402.

Combes, P. P. and Overman H. (2004) The spatial distribution of economic activities in the European union, in Henderson J. V. and Thisse J. (Eds) *Handbook of Regional and Urban Economics*, pp. 2120–2167. Elsevier, Amsterdam.

Coombes M. G., Green A. E. and Openshaw S. (1986) An efficient algorithm to generate official statistical reporting areas: the case of the 1984 travel-to-work areas revision in Britain, *Journal of Operational Research Society* **37**, 943–953.

Davidsson P. (2006) Nascent entrepreneurship: empirical studies and developments, *Foundations and Trends in Entrepreneurship* **2**, 1–76.

De Clercq D., Lim D. S. and Oh C. H. (2011) Individual-level resources and new business activity: the contingent role of institutional context, *Entrepreneurship: Theory and Practice* DOI:10.1111/j.1540–6520.2011.00470.x

Delgado M., Porter M. and Stern S. (2010) Clusters and entrepreneurship, *Journal of Economic Geography* **10**, 495–518.

Dogaru T., van Oort F. and Thissen M. (2011) Agglomeration economies in European regions: perspectives for objective-1 regions, *Tijdschrift voor Economische and Sociale Geografie* **102**, 486–494.

Duranton G. and Puga D. (2004) Micro-foundations of urban agglomeration economies, in Henderson J. V. and Thisse J. (Eds) *Handbook of Regional and Urban Economics*, pp. 2063–2117. Elsevier, Amsterdam.

ELAM and Terjesen S. (2010) Gendered institutions and cross-national patterns of business creation for men and women, *European Journal of Development Research* **22**, 331–348.

Falck O. (2007) *Emergence and Survival of New Businesses*. Physica, Heidelberg.

Feldman M. P. (2001) The entrepreneurial event revisited: firm formation in a regional context, *Industrial and Corporate Change* **10**, 861–891.

Feldman M. P., Francis J. and Bercovitz J. (2005) Creating a cluster while building a firm: entrepreneurs and the formation of industrial clusters, *Regional Studies* **39**, 129–141.

Frenken K., van Oort F. and Verburg T. (2007) Related variety, unrelated variety and regional economic growth, *Regional Studies* **41**, 685–697.

Fritsch M. (Ed.) (2011) *Elgar Handbook of Research on Entrepreneurship and Regional Development – National and Regional Perspectives*. Edward Elgar, Cheltenham.

Fritsch M. (2013) New business formation and regional development: a survey and assessment of the evidence, *Foundations and Trends in Entrepreneurship* **9**, 249–364.

Fritsch M. and Mueller P. (2004) Effects of new business formation on regional development over time, *Regional Studies* **38**, 961–975.

Fritsch M. and Schroeter A. (2011) Why does the effect of new business formation differ across regions?, *Small Business Economics* **36**, 383–400.

Fritsch M., Brixy U. and Falck O. (2006) The effect of industry, region and time on new business survival – a multi-dimensional analysis, *Review of Industrial Organization* **28**, 285–306.

Glaeser E. (2007) *Entrepreneurship and the City*. NBER Working Paper No. 13551. National Bureau of Economic Research (NBER), Cambridge, MA.

Glaeser E. L., Kerr W. R. and Ponzetto G. A. M. (2010a) Clusters of entrepreneurship, *Journal of Urban Economics* **67**, 150–168.

Glaeser E. L., Rosenthal S. S. and Strange W. C. (2010b) Urban economics and entrepreneurship, *Journal of Urban Economics* **67**, 1–14.

Goldstein, H. (2007). Becoming familiar with multilevel modeling, *Significance* **4**, 133–135.

Grilo I. and Thurik A. R. (2008) Determinants of entrepreneurial engagement levels in Europe and the US, *Industrial and Corporate Change* **17**, 1113–1145.

Guesnier B. (1994) Regional variations in new firm formation in France, *Regional Studies* **28**, 347–358.

Helsley R. W. and Strange W. C. (2009) Entrepreneurs and cities: complexity, thickness and balance, *Regional Science and Urban Economics* **41**, 550–559.

Hindle K. (2010) How community context affects entrepreneurial process: a diagnostic framework, *Entrepreneurship and Regional Development* **9**, 599–647.

Hox J. J. (2002) *Multilevel Analysis: Techniques and Applications*. Erlbaum, Mahwah, NJ.

Jacobs J. (1969) *The Economy of Cities*. Random House, New York, NY.

Karlsson C., Johansson B. and Stough R. (2008) *Entrepreneurship and Innovations in Functional Regions*. CESIS Electronic Working Paper Series No. 144. Royal Institute of Technology Centre of Excellence for Science and Innovation Studies (CESIS) (available at: http://www.cesis.se).

Keeble D. and Walker S. (1994) New firms, small firms and dead firms: spatial patterns and determinants in the United Kingdom, *Regional Studies* **28**, 411–427.

Kulicke M. and Schleinkofer M. (2008) *Wirkungen von EXIST-SEED aus Sicht von Geförderten – Ergebnisse einer Befragung im Rahmen der wissenschaftlichen Begleitung von EXIST – Existenzgründungen aus der Wissenschaft im Auftrag des Bundesministeriums für Wirtschaft und Technologie (BMWi)*. Fraunhofer IRB, Stuttgart.

Lasch F., Robert F. and Le Roy F. (2013) Regional determinants of ICT new firm formation, *Small Business Economics* **40**, 671–686.

Lazear E. P. (2005) Entrepreneurship, *Journal of Labor Economics* **23**, 649–680.

Lejpras A. and Stephan A. (2011) Locational conditions, cooperation, and innovativeness: evidence from research and company spin-offs, *Annals of Regional Science* **46**, 543–575.

Malecki E. (1997) Entrepreneurs, networks, and economic development: a review of recent research, in Katz J. A. (Ed.) *Advances in Entrepreneurship, Firm Emergence and Growth*, pp. 57–118. JAI Press, Greenwich, CT.

Meester W. J. and Pellenbarg P. H. (2006) The spatial preference map of Dutch entrepreneurs; subjective ratings of locations, 1983–1993–2003, *Journal of Economic and Social Geography* **97**, 364–376.

Minniti M. (Ed.) (2011) *The Dynamics of Entrepreneurial Activity*. Oxford University Press, Oxford.

Musterd S. and Gritsai O. (2010) *Conditions for 'Creative Knowledge Cities'. Findings from a Comparison between 13 European Metropolises.* ACRE Report No. 9. Amsterdam Institute for Social Science Research (AISSR), University of Amsterdam, Amsterdam.

Neffke F. H., Henning M., Boschma R., Lundquist K. J. and Olander L. O. (2011) The dynamics of agglomeration externalities along the life cycle of industries, *Regional Studies* **45**, 49–65.

Overman H. G., Redding S. and Venables A. J. (2001) *The Economic Geography of Trade, Production, and Income: A Survey of the Empirics.* CEPR Discussion Paper No. 2978. Centre for Economic Policy Research (CEPR), London.

Parker S. C. (2005) Explaining regional variations in entrepreneurship as multiple equilibriums, *Journal of Regional Science* **45**, 829–850.

Parr J. B. (2007) Spatial definitions of the city: four perspectives, *Urban Studies* **44**, 381–392.

Peters D. (2011) *The Functional Urban Areas Database.* Technical Report; ESPON Project. IGEAT, Free University of Brussels, Brussels.

Pettersson L., Sjölander P. and Widell L. M. (2010) Firm formation in rural and urban regions explained by demographical structure. Paper presented at the 50th European Regional Science Association (ERSA) Conference, Jönköping, Sweden, 20–23 August 2010.

Pike A., Rodriguez-Pose A. and Tomaney J. (2006) *Local and Regional Development.* Routledge, London.

Pitelis C. (2012) Clusters, entrepreneurial ecosystem co-creation, and appropriability: a conceptual framework, *Industrial and Corporate Change* **21**, 1359–1388.

Porter M. E. (1990) *The Competitive Advantage of Nations.* Free Press, New York, NY.

Rabe-Hesketh S. and Skrondal A. (2005). *Multilevel and Longitudinal Modeling Using Stata.* Stata Press, College Station, TX.

Reynolds P. D. (2007) *Entrepreneurship in the United States.* Springer, New York, NY.

Reynolds P., Storey D. J. and Westhead P. (1994) Cross-national comparisons of the variation in new firm formation rates: an editorial overview, *Regional Studies* **28**, 343–346.

Reynolds P. D., Bosma N., Autio E., Hunt S., De Bono N., Servais I., Lopez-Garcia P. and Chin N. (2005) Global Entrepreneurship Monitor: data collection and implementation 1998–2003, *Small Business Economics* **24**, 205–231.

Rocha H. O. (2004) Entrepreneurship and development: the role of clusters. A literature review, *Small Business Economics* **23**, 363–400.

Rocha H. O. and Sternberg R. (2005) Entrepreneurship: the role of clusters. Theoretical perspectives and empirical evidence from Germany, *Small Business Economics* **24**, 267–292.

Rosenthal S. S. and Strange W. C. (2004) Evidence on the nature and sources of agglomeration economies, in Henderson J. V. and Thisse J. F. (Eds) *Handbook of Urban and Regional Economics*, Vol. 4, pp. 2119–2172. Elsevier, Amsterdam.

Sepulveda L., Syrett S. and Lyon F. (2011) Population superdiversity and new migrant enterprise: the case of London, *Entrepreneurship and Regional Development* **23**, 469–497.

Shane S. and Venkataraman S. (2000) The promise of entrepreneurship as a field of research, *Academy of Management Review* **25**, 217–226.

Short J. C., Ketchen D. J., Shook C. L. and Ireland R. D. (2010) The concept of 'opportunity' in entrepreneurship research: past accomplishments and future challenges, *Journal of Management* **36**, 40–65.

Snijders T. and Bosker R. (1999) *Multilevel Analysis: An Introduction to Basic and Advanced Multilevel Modelling.* Sage, Thousand Oaks, CA.

Stam E. (2007) Why butterflies don't leave. Locational behavior of entrepreneurial firms, *Economic Geography* **83**, 27–50.

Stathopoulou S., Psaltopoulos D. and Skuras D. (2004) Rural entrepreneurship in Europe: a research framework and agenda, *International Journal of Entrepreneurial Behaviour and Research* **10**, 404–425.

Sternberg R. (2009) *Regional Dimensions of Entrepreneurship.* Foundations and Trends in Entrepreneurship, Vol. 5, Issue 4. Now, Boston, MA.

Sternberg R. and Litzenberger T. (2004) Regional clusters in Germany – their geography and their relevance for entrepreneurial activities, *European Planning Studies* **12**, 767–791.

Storey D. J. (1984) Editorial, *Regional Studies* **18**, 187–188.

Thissen M. J. P. M., Ruijs A., van Oort F. and Diodato D. (2011) *De concurrentiepositie van Nederlandse regio's. Regionaal-economicsche samenhang in Europa.* Netherlands Environmental Assessment Agency (PBL), The Hague.

Van Duijn M. A. J., van Busschbach J. T. and Snijders T. A. B. (1999) Multilevel analysis of personal networks as dependent variables, *Social Networks* **21**, 187–209.

Van Oort F. and Bosma N. (2013) Agglomeration economies, inventors and entrepreneurs as engines of European regional economic development, *Annals of Regional Science* **51**, 213–244.

Wong P. K., Ho Y. P. and Autio E. (2005) Entrepreneurship, innovation and economic growth: evidence from GEM data, *Small Business Economics* **24**, 335–350.

Population Change and New Firm Formation in Urban and Rural Regions

HEIKE DELFMANN, SIERDJAN KOSTER, PHILIP MCCANN and JOUKE VAN DIJK
Department of Economic Geography, Faculty of Spatial Sciences, University of Groningen, Groningen, theNetherlands

DELFMANN H., KOSTER S., MCCANN P. and VAN DIJK J. Population change and new firm formation in urban and rural regions, *Regional Studies*. Many regions across the European Union, including regions in the Netherlands, face population decline, entailing changing demographics and related social and economic implications. This paper looks into the connection between population change and structure, and rates of new firm formation. Although it is clear that fewer people will eventually lead to fewer firms, as well as fewer new firms, it is assessed whether this negative relationship differs with the intensity of population change and across regional contexts. In order to establish the impact of population change on new firm formation, this paper examines data on population density, size, growth and decline, together with firm dynamics for the period 2003–09. The results show that the relationship between new firm formation and population change depends heavily on the regional context. The results indicate that new firm formation in urban regions tends to be negatively influenced by population change, while the impact in rural regions remains positive. In conclusion, clear differences are found in the intensity of the impact of population change on new firm formation according to the type of region. The regional context and the intensity of decline must be taken into account when determining the kind of coping mechanism needed to deal with the consequences of decline.

Population decline New firm formation Urban and rural regions

DELFMANN H., KOSTER S., MCCANN P. and VAN DIJK J. 城市与乡村区域中，人口变迁与新企业的形成，*区域研究*。欧盟中的诸多区域，包含荷兰境内的区域，正在面临人口减少的问题，并造成了人口的改变及相关的社会与经济意涵。本文探讨人口变迁与结构之间的连结，以及新企业的形成率。儘管较少的人口终将导致较少的企业与新兴企业是个显而易见的事实，但本文评估这种负面关係是否会随着人口改变的程度以及不同的区域脉络而有所不同。为了建立人口变迁对于新企业形成的影响，本文将检视自 2003 年至 2009 年期间，人口密度、规模、成长与减少的数据及企业的动态。研究结果显示，新企业的形成与人口变迁的关係，大幅取决于区域的脉络。研究结果指出，城市区域中新企业的形成，倾向受到人口变迁的负面影响，而其对乡村地区的影响则仍维持正面。结论中，我们发现了人口变迁依据区域的类型，对新企业形成的影响程度的清楚差异。当决定处理人口减少造成的后果所需的处理机制时，必须将区域脉络与减少的程度纳入考量。

人口减少 新企业形成 城市与乡村区域

DELFMANN H., KOSTER S., MCCANN P. et VAN DIJK J. La variation de la population et la création de nouvelles entreprises dans les zones urbaines et rurales, *Regional Studies*. Nombreuses sont les régions à travers l'Union européenne, y compris les régions néerlandaises, qui font face au déclin de la population, ce qui amène la variation de la population et les conséquences économiques et sociales que cela implique. Cet article examine le lien entre la variation de la population et sa structure, et les taux de création de nouvelles entreprises. Bien qu'il soit tout à fait évident que de moins en moins de gens entraînera de moins en moins d'entreprises, ainsi que de moins en moins de nouvelles entreprises, on évalue si, oui ou non, ce rapport négatif varie selon l'ampleur de la variation de la population et selon les régions. Pour établir l'impact de la variation de la population sur la création de nouvelles entreprises, cet article examine des données auprès de la densité, de la taille, de la croissance et du déclin de la population, conjointement avec la dynamique des entreprises pour la période qui va de 2003 jusqu'à 2009. Les résultats laissent voir que le rapport entre la création de nouvelles entreprises et la variation de la population dépend fortement du contexte régional. Les résultats indiquent que la création de nouvelles entreprises dans les zones urbaines a tendance à être négativement influencée par la variation de la population, tandis que l'impact dans les zones rurales reste positif. En conclusion, il s'avère des différences très évidentes dans l'intensité de l'impact de la variation de la population sur la création de nouvelles entreprises suivant la catégorie de zone. Pour déterminer le genre de mécanisme d'adaptation nécessaire pour répondre aux conséquences du déclin, il faut tenir compte du contexte régional et de l'intensité du déclin.

Déclin de la population Création de nouvelles entreprises Régions urbaines et rurales

DELFMANN H., KOSTER S., MCCANN P. und VAN DIJK J. Demografischer Wandel und Firmengründungen in städtischen und ländlichen Regionen, *Regional Studies*. Viele Regionen überall in der Europäischen Union, darunter auch Regionen in den Niederlanden, stehen vor einem Bevölkerungsrückgang, der demografischen Wandel und die damit verbundenen sozialen und wirtschaftlichen Auswirkungen mit sich bringt. In diesem Beitrag wird der Zusammenhang zwischen den Veränderungen und der Struktur der Bevölkerung und den Anteilen der Firmengründungen untersucht. Obwohl auf der Hand liegt, dass niedrigere Bevölkerungszahlen letztendlich zu weniger Firmen und auch zu weniger neuen Firmen führen, wird untersucht, ob diese negative Beziehung je nach der Intensität des demografischen Wandels und je nach regionalem Kontext unterschiedlich ausfällt. Zur Ermittlung der Auswirkungen des demografischen Wandels auf die Firmengründungen untersuchen wir Daten über die Dichte, die Größe, das Wachstum und den Rückgang der Bevölkerung sowie über die Firmendynamik im Zeitraum von 2003 bis 2009. Aus den Ergebnissen geht hervor, dass die Beziehung zwischen den Firmengründungen und dem demografischen Wandel stark vom regionalen Kontext abhängt. Die Ergebnisse lassen darauf schließen, dass Firmengründungen in Stadtregionen vom demografischen Wandel tendenziell negativ beeinflusst werden, während die Auswirkung in ländlichen Regionen weiterhin positiv ausfällt. Die Schlussfolgerung lautet, dass die Intensität der Auswirkung des demografischen Wandels auf die Firmengründungen je nach Art der Region deutlich unterschiedlich ausfällt. Bei der Ermittlung des zur Bewältigung der Konsequenzen des Bevölkerungsrückgangs erforderlichen Mechanismus müssen der regionale Kontext und die Intensität des Rückgangs berücksichtigt werden.

Bevölkerungsrückgang   Firmengründung   Städtische und ländliche Regionen

DELFMANN H., KOSTER S., MCCANN P. y VAN DIJK J. Cambios demográficos y creación de nuevas empresas en regiones urbanas y rurales, *Regional Studies*. Muchas regiones de la Unión Europea, incluyendo las regiones de los Países Bajos, están afectadas por un descenso de la población, lo que acarrea cambios demográficos y repercusiones sociales y económicas relacionadas. En este artículo examinamos la relación entre el cambio y la estructura de la población y las tasas de la creación de nuevas empresas. Aunque es evidente que al reducirse la población también disminuyen las empresas, y la creación de nuevas empresas, analizamos si esta relación negativa es diferente en función de la intensidad del cambio demográfico y de los diferentes contextos regionales. A fin de determinar el efecto del cambio demográfico en la creación de nuevas empresas, examinamos los datos sobre la densidad, el tamaño, el crecimiento y el descenso de la población, así como datos de empresas para el periodo entre 2003 y 2009. Los resultados indican que la relación entre la creación de nuevas empresas y el cambio demográfico depende en gran medida del contexto regional. Los resultados también muestran que la creación de nuevas empresas en regiones urbanas tiende a estar negativamente influenciada por el cambio demográfico, mientras que el efecto en regiones rurales sigue siendo positivo. Llegamos a la conclusión de que existen claras diferencias en la intensidad del impacto del cambio demográfico en la creación de nuevas empresas según el tipo de región. Al determinar qué tipo de mecanismo es necesario para tratar con las consecuencias de este descenso, hay que tener en cuenta el contexto regional y la intensidad del descenso de población.

Descenso de la población   Creación de nuevas empresas   Regiones urbanas y rurales

INTRODUCTION

Regional population decline increasingly takes place in developed countries (FÉSÜS *et al.*, 2008; POLÈSE and SHEARMUR, 2006; VAN WISSEN, 2010). Population decline is often associated with decline in employment and amenities. It is a complex issue with many social and economic implications: with primarily young people leaving for mainly educational purposes, fewer children are born and the ageing population is left with fewer employment opportunities, and fewer retail and care facilities (HAARTSEN and VENHORST, 2010; VAN WISSEN, 2010). Social expenditure is put under strain because of a shrinking labour force, a direct consequence of young people migrating out. This process makes it difficult for small communities to maintain adequate infrastructure, educational and medical facilities, and other public services, which in turn can make it difficult to attract new immigrants or prevent current residents from relocating, creating a negative spiral (FÉSÜS *et al.*, 2008; HAARTSEN and VENHORST, 2010; MAI and BUCHER, 2005; POLÈSE and SHEARMUR, 2006; SIMMIE and MARTIN, 2010). Further, social ties are disrupted by continuous out-migration, causing a decrease in support systems and social capital, which can have detrimental effects on liveability. Population decline can thus constitute a deeply rooted problem.

The number of studies addressing population decline and its consequences has increased substantially in the past decade. Though research on depopulation is far from novel – in 1890, Arsene Dumont had already addressed the issue of the declining population in France – the effects of population decline are still unclear (SER, 2011). Entrepreneurship can play an important part in maintaining quality of life in declining regions. The economic impact of entrepreneurship has been firmly established (e.g., ACS and ARMINGTON, 2004; STAM, 2009). It drives competition and innovation, and consequently gross domestic product (GDP) and employment growth. Entrepreneurship can also contribute to other aspects of quality of life, such as the level of social capital, in that it creates trust, maintains social relations and provides meeting places (MORRIS and LEWIS, 1991; WESTLUND, 2003). However, private businesses, including grocery stores, restaurants and other commercial establishments, are less likely to start in declining regions. The businesses are more spread out and more likely to be smaller in areas with a relatively small number of residents, as they require a minimum number of customers to remain viable (McGranahan and Beale, 2002). It is clear that fewer people (less demand) leads to fewer new firms (reduced supply). It is examined here whether this inherently negative relationship varies with the rate of population change and across regional contexts. Traditionally, entrepreneurship has been seen as a mechanism of economic growth. Research regarding the characteristics of entrepreneurship in a context of economic stagnation seems lacking, however, and this study aims at contributing to this issue.

This study focuses on two aspects of the regional context that are expected to impact start-up rates – our operationalization of entrepreneurship. The first aspect is the actual change in population. A growing population is positively related to new firm formation in a country or region (Armington and Acs, 2002; Audretsch and Fritsch, 1994; Bosma *et al.*, 2008; Verheul *et al.*, 2001). This positive impact of growth will be lacking in declining regions, possibly leading to an additional loss of (small) businesses and fewer start-ups. In contrast, despite declining population/circumstances, it can be assumed that a minimum number of firms are needed in a region to fulfil demand, pushing the start-up rate upwards and thus smoothing the negative trend. The aim of this study is to determine the relationship between population change, in particular decline, and new firm formation. Therefore, population growth must also be incorporated, since consideration of diminishing regions entails an implicit comparison with growing regions. The term 'population change' is therefore used from this point onwards. The first research question addresses the impact of population change on the level of entrepreneurship. Specifically, how does this impact change depending on the intensity of population decline or growth? The second focus of this paper is on the context in which population change takes place. Population change occurs in different regional settings, possibly leading to different outcomes; urban areas offer important advantages to entrepreneurs such as a closer proximity to the consumer market, but the periphery could attract cottage industry with, for example, internet-based service firms operating from home. This paper therefore distinguishes between urban and rural areas. The second research question is whether the relationship between new firm formation and population change is mediated by the urban or rural regional contexts?

The paper first elaborates on the impact of population change on entrepreneurship, and then describes the data and methodology used. Next the key findings are presented and discussed. The final section presents the conclusions.

POPULATION CHANGE AND NEW FIRM FORMATION

Entrepreneurship is a broad and often fuzzy concept, given the many definitions used in both the theoretical and empirical literature.[1] In this study entrepreneurship is defined as new firm formation; these terms are used interchangeably. More precisely, new firm formation is defined as the number of newly founded firms per 1000 of the labour market population in a particular region, also referred to as the start-up rate. A well-recognized way to explain the regional distribution of start-up rates is the eclectic framework employed by Verheul *et al.* (2001). It integrates the supply side, the demand side and the institutional environment of entrepreneurship (Verheul *et al.*, 2001; Wennekers *et al.*, 2005). Demand-side variables concern entrepreneurial opportunities, while supply-side variables concern the resources and abilities of individuals and their attitudes towards entrepreneurship, including demographics, wage rates and employment status (Bosma *et al.*, 2008; Verheul *et al.*, 2001; Wennekers *et al.*, 2005). The institutional environment shapes the context in which supply and demand assessments are made. The supply side is determined by a combination of push and pull factors, often translated as opportunity- or necessity-driven entrepreneurship. The institutional context is often related to culture (Wennekers *et al.*, 2010). Examples of institutional issues are the fiscal environment, labour market regulations and intellectual property rights (Wennekers *et al.*, 2010) as well as 'background' institutions such as trust and the education system (Verheul *et al.*, 2001). This framework is applied to assess the potential impact of population change on new firm formation across distinct regional contexts.

Population change

Population change can create more demand as new and bigger consumer markets emerge because of the growing population (Armington and Acs, 2002; Wennekers *et al.*, 2005), stimulating new firm formation by providing opportunities for new economic activity. Goods and services sought by individuals, in particular, should create new prospects for new firms and lead to start-ups (Reynolds *et al.*, 1995). Population growth may also be a pull factor for new entrepreneurship as an expanding population places additional strain on salaries and thereby lowers the opportunity costs for entrepreneurship (Verheul *et al.*, 2001). While several studies have shown that population growth is positively related to start-up rates (e.g., Armington and Acs, 2002; Bosma *et al.*, 2008; Reynolds *et al.*, 1995; Wennekers *et al.*, 2005), other studies have not found a significant effect (Audretsch and Fritsch, 1994; Garofoli, 1994). As population growth reflects an increase in both demand and supply, it is expected that its effect on the rate of new firm formation will be positive.

Population change, however, can occur in two directions – growth and decline – and the effect on new firm formation may well not be stationary across the whole distribution of levels of population change. Building on the theory of branching and self-feeding growth hypothesized by FRENKEN and BOSCHMA (2007), population change could potentially have an additional effect on new firm formation when the change is more intense. According to this evolutionary perspective, growth is self-feeding. Frenken and Boschma argue that the probability of innovation increases more than proportional with the number of routines available for recombination. The idea of endogenous growth also holds for cities: the more variety already present, the higher the probability that new varieties can be created through recombining old routines. In other words, the creation of opportunities is self-reinforcing: more people means more possible combinations and more opportunities. It also implies that that a given number of newcomers lead to more recombinations. This results in an exponential relationship between population and opportunities through recombination, reflected in new firm formation. Frenken and Boschma also indicate that the relation is not endlessly exponential: a 'ceiling' will be reached when the positive feedback process is offset by negative effects including congestion and high wage levels.

Population change lies at the root of societal change. Population decline and ageing often go hand in hand (MAI and BUCHER, 2005). Given the likely declining labour market, population decline is strongly associated with economic decline, though this is not always the case. A study by GÁKOVÁ and DIJKSTRA (2010) demonstrated that population decline rarely leads to economic decline per capita at the same time in developed countries. As an example Parkstad Limburg in the Netherlands is taken where a declining population occurs simultaneously with a growing employment rate (PARKSTAD LIMBURG, 2011). This paper therefore does not focus on economic decline, but rather on how entrepreneurship is shaped in these changing regions. An ageing society changes demand as the need for care facilities increases. It may also impact on the number of people starting a business, as people of a certain age are considered more likely to start a business. Several publications show that the probability of a person starting his/her own business first increases with age and later declines, an inverted 'U'-shape between the regional age structure and new firm formation (BÖNTE *et al.*, 2009).

Population decline may also have a self-reinforcing effect. Start-up risk will be higher in a declining region given the uncertainties that accompany decline. Therefore, population decline is likely to have an adverse impact on the level of new firm formation because it increases the risk of starting up a new business. In addition, the likely reduction in support systems caused by out-migration might also have an impact. Starting a new firm is a highly social process, as information, new ideas and resources are predominantly acquired via personal networks (ALDRICH *et al.*, 1998; DAVIDSSON and HONIG, 2003). Population decline affects the level of support – financial, emotional and other kinds of support (FÉSÜS *et al.*, 2008). In contrast, decline can lead to restructuring by anticipating or responding to the changing demographics; declining regions could also experience more self-employment due to necessity-driven entrepreneurship. Necessity-driven entrepreneurship refers to the trigger or initial motivation of starting a business. That is, necessity-driven entrepreneurs are those who view entrepreneurship as the best, but not necessarily preferred, option. Their counterparts are opportunity-driven entrepreneurs: entrepreneurs who start out of choice (ACS, 2006; BOSMA *et al.*, 2008; WILLIAMS and WILLIAMS, 2012).

Population change in urban and rural regions

The impact of population change also depends on the specific regional context. Several studies show that agglomeration, controlled for other determinants, has a positive impact on the rate of new firm formation (ARMINGTON and ACS, 2002; AUDRETSCH and FRITSCH, 1994; BOSMA *et al.*, 2008). Urban areas – given their larger existing stock of both people and firms – can potentially generate many new recombinations with every new connection, until they reach their ceiling and the effect stabilizes. Urban areas are often characterized by a more diverse population, leading to more variety in demand. Higher diversity also stimulates new firm start-ups; cities that are more diversified have a higher chance of fostering innovation than those that are less diversified (BOSMA *et al.*, 2008; FRENKEN and BOSCHMA, 2007). Conditions for entering a market are thought to be more favourable in more densely populated regions (AUDRETSCH and FRITSCH, 1994; STERNBERG, 2011) because of closer proximity to the consumer market and the more developed business infrastructure (BRÜDERL and PREISENDÖRFER, 1998; FRITSCH and MUELLER, 2008). In addition, agglomeration effects can positively affect new firm formation through increased local market opportunities relating to the consumer market and necessary inputs (REYNOLDS *et al.*, 1995). Urbanization also increases the likelihood of the presence of a more skilled workforce and facilitates a freer flow and exchange of ideas and knowledge. Moreover, the risk of starting a business in urban areas is considered relatively low due to the rich employment opportunities that function as a safety net in case the new firm fails (STAM, 2009).

The influence of urbanization on new firm formation is, however, not univocally agreed upon. A higher degree of urbanization can lead to the pursuit of economies of scale, which enables firms to serve their clients more efficiently and leaves fewer opportunities for small firms (VERHEUL *et al.*, 2001). Other negative effects of agglomeration include excessive competition, possibly resulting in increased wages and elevated input prices, thus discouraging entry (NYSTRÖM, 2007; VAN STEL and SUDDLE, 2008). VAN STEL and SUDDLE (2008) found a negative effect for start-ups in the Netherlands as reflected by the number of service start-ups, as they are less dependent on the agglomeration benefits mentioned. Overall, however, empirical results appear to confirm the importance of urbanization for entrepreneurship (STERNBERG, 2011).

In a sense, urban and rural regions represent two opposites; the first denotes positive impacts and the latter negative. When interacting with population change, these differences will most likely lead to different outcomes: urbanization could have a mediating effect on population decline, causing urban areas to experience less severe consequences of population decline (HAARTSEN and VENHORST, 2010). Furthermore, regions will continue to need a minimum supply of facilities in retail trade, repair and personal services (WENNEKERS, 2006), regardless of their size and population decline or growth. This would imply that there is a lower limit of supply and demand. Another potential mediating effect, especially in green and attractive rural regions, is a region's ability to attract nascent entrepreneurs that are looking to start up a business from home to facilitate a specific lifestyle. Such cottage industry does not depend on a close physical proximity to the market as it is mainly internet-based.

Both urban and rural contexts have potential for generating both opportunity-driven entrepreneurship and necessity-driven entrepreneurship. It is often assumed that entrepreneurs in disadvantaged populations are more likely to be necessity driven, because of limited employment opportunities (WILLIAMS and WILLIAMS, 2012). This provides an interesting way to explain firm formation in both prosperous and deprived regions. In the case of the Netherlands it could be less extremely divided; a strong welfare state, as is present in the Netherlands, may reduce the incentives for necessity entrepreneurs. Even for opportunity entrepreneurs, however, a strong welfare state has a negative impact (AIDIS *et al.*, 2012). Rural entrepreneurship in particular is typically seen as necessity-driven entrepreneurship, but entrepreneurs who choose a specific lifestyle and even the 'Schumpeterian entrepreneurs' can be found in the periphery (MISHRA, 2005).

From the above, two hypotheses are derived. The first and most basic hypothesis is: population change is positively related to new firm formation. Second: the impact of population change on new firm formation depends on the regional context. The exact direction of the hypothesis is unclear a priori, however. Scale economies in urban areas may depress the impact of population change in urban areas, while population change and decline in particular may be offset by the emergence of cottage industries in rural areas. Also, rural areas remain to need a minimum level of facilities which likely influences the impact of population change in rural areas.

DATA, METHODOLOGY AND EMPIRICAL STRATEGY

To determine the spatial distribution of new firm formation in the context of population change, this study examined data on population density, size, growth and decline, retrieved from Statistics Netherlands (CBS). To assess the current and past state of entrepreneurial activities and firm dynamics, the LISA database (Landelijk Informatiesysteem van Arbeidsplaatsen en vestigingen) was used. To avoid effects of coincidental occurrences in a particular year, the average start-up rates from 2003 to 2009 were used. The LISA database provides yearly information at the establishment level, thereby uncovering start-ups, establishment closures, sector changes and the total number of jobs for all establishments with paid employees in the Netherlands. The start-up data include new establishments and new firm, excluding relocations. Every establishment is traceable through time and space by a unique identification number. The dataset consists of over 6.4 million cases between 2003 and 2009, which were aggregated by municipality for the analyses. A total of 8900 cases were excluded from the analyses, as these establishments showed a total of zero jobs including the entrepreneur in a particular year. As the data are truncated, information on new start-ups in 2003 is unavailable. The analyses were performed on all municipalities, which were aggregated to match the number of municipalities in 2009 (441) in order to facilitate comparisons between several years.

A low level of aggregation, such as the municipality, is needed in order to understand specific local issues in the Netherlands, such as identifying urban and rural regions (ORGANISATION FOR ECONOMIC CO-OPERATION AND DEVELOPMENT (OECD), 2008). Also, new firm formation is a local phenomenon (STERNBERG, 2011). One consequence of using a relatively low aggregation level is the probability that municipalities are spatially dependent. After running diagnostics, we corrected for spatial autocorrelation by using a spatial Durbin model (SDM), with a spatial weight matrix based on first-order contiguous neighbours. The merits of the SDM have been discussed by LESAGE and PACE (2009) and further refined by ELHORST (2010). One of the strengths of the SDM is that it does not enforce prior restrictions on the scale of potential spatial spillover of both direct and indirect effects. Contrary to other spatial regressions, these spillover effects can be different for different explanatory variables (ELHORST, 2010); this allows one to estimate direct, indirect and total impacts on the start-up rates by changing each explanatory variable in the model.

The dependent variable is the rate of new firm formation, calculated using the labour market approach, illustrated in Fig. 1a. The labour market approach uses the potential workforce in a region as the denominator for standardizing the number of entrants (AUDRETSCH and FRITSCH, 1994; KOSTER, 2006). The alternative, the ecological approach, standardizes the number of new firms relative to the stock of firms in the given market at the beginning of the period, implying new firms emerge from existing firms (VAN STEL and SUDDLE, 2008). The labour market approach was chosen as it is based on the theory of entrepreneurial choice; each new firm is started by an individual person (AUDRETSCH and FRITSCH, 1994). Most new

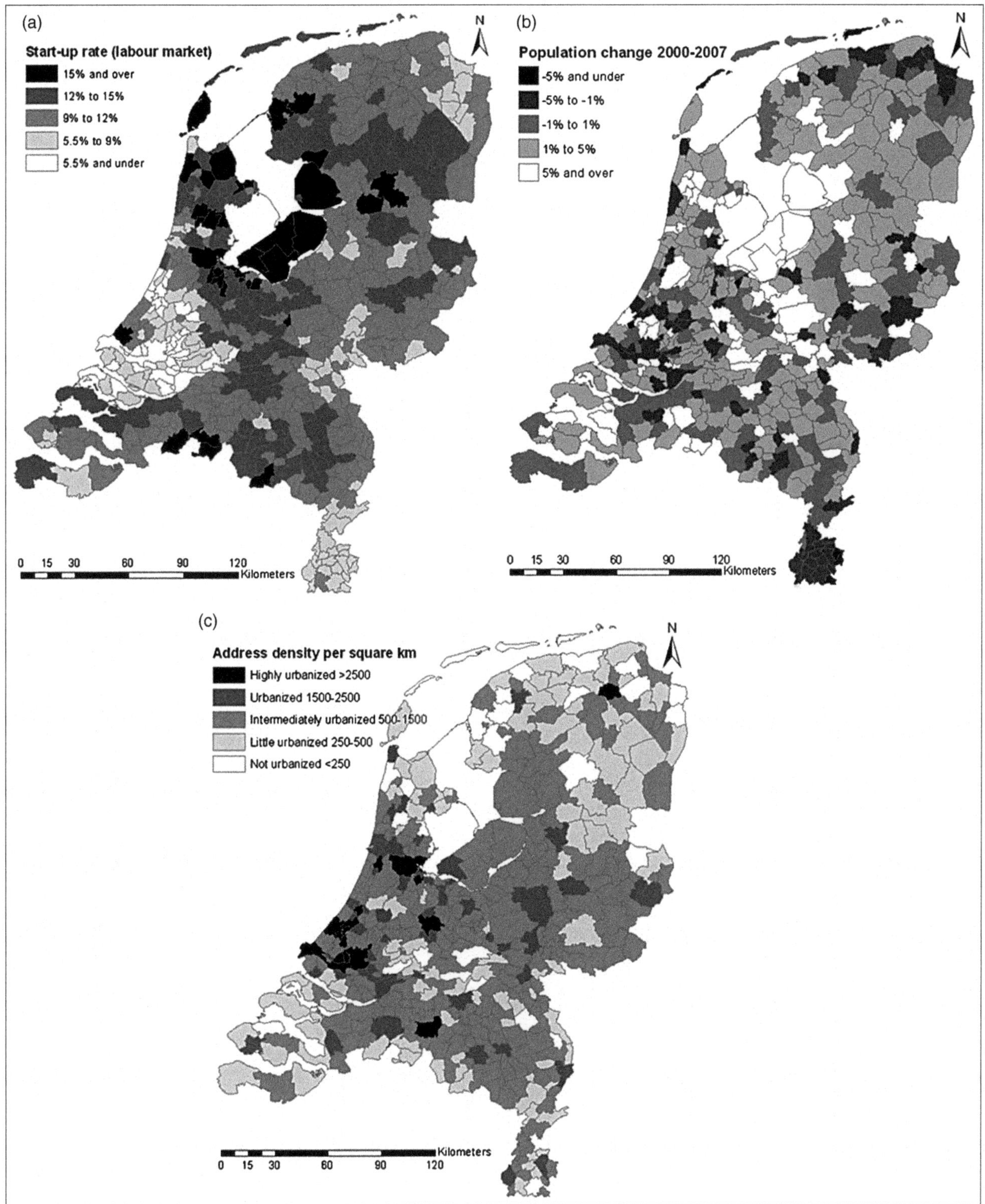

Fig. 1. (a) Average start-up rate, 2004–09, labour market approach; (b) population change 2000–07; and (c) degree of urbanization in 2009 based on address density

firms are initially established at home or in close proximity to it (STAM, 2007, 2009). This is important, as an implicit assumption made by the labour market approach is that the entrepreneur is in the same labour market within which his/her new firm operates. In the case of the Netherlands, SCHUTJENS and STAM (2003) show that 87% of new firms are home-based and nearly two-thirds of surviving firms remain home-based after five years. Empirically we corrected for the small geographical unit by applying spatial regressions and including commuting behaviour as a control variable.

Identifying declining regions

Although the overall Dutch population is not expected to decrease until 2040 (HAARTSEN and VENHORST, 2010), rural and peripheral regions such as the north-east of Groningen, Zeeuwsch-Vlaanderen and de Achterhoek are already undergoing population decline. An urbanized region that is already experiencing decline is the south of Limburg. The state of population change is shown in Fig. 1b. The changing population was examined over the period 2000–07 in order to allow some response time for the dependent variable. In total, 78 municipalities have seen more than a 1% decline; of these declining regions only nine experienced more than a 5% decline. It is evident that population change has not yet taken dramatic proportions as it has elsewhere in Europe (BARCA, 2009; EUROPEAN COMMISSION, 2010). However, the change is structural and incremental; population change is quite a prominent issue in regional policy developments and current affairs. Particularly for sparsely populated regions, even stagnation or moderate decline will potentially have a big impact on the decision-making process of new firms.

Urban and rural regions in the Netherlands

The relationship between urban and rural regions in the Netherlands is a special case within Europe; the Netherlands is highly urbanized and densely populated. Rural regions in the Netherlands are relatively close to an urban centre in geographical terms, while at the same time compared with other European countries they are fairly autonomous in terms of locally oriented economies. However, rural regions are also becoming more connected to urban areas, for instance by increasing commuting between both regions (OECD, 2008).

The OECD defines rural areas as those having a population density below 150 inhabitants/km^2 (OECD, 2008). If the standard OECD definition at the NUTS-3 level is applied to rural areas in the Netherlands, it would appear that there are no predominantly rural areas in the country. The same applies to Belgium and, to a lesser extent, to the UK (OECD, 2008). However, according to common perception among the Dutch, rural areas do exist. For example, the northern part of the country is considered a typically rural area (HAARTSEN, 2002; OECD, 2005, 2008). Therefore, a different approach is adopted here based on address density, which is frequently used in Dutch policy but also in scientific papers such as by VAN STEL and SUDDLE (2008). This measure uses the average number of addresses/km^2 within a radius of 1 km from each individual address. Address density uses the concentration of human activities such as living, working and utilizing amenities as indicators of urbanization – the lower the concentration of these activities, the lower the level of urbanization (HAARTSEN, 2002). Rural areas are then defined as areas with fewer than 500 addresses/km^2. A low level of aggregation is used to be able to identify the predominantly rural areas. In line with the general perception, the three northern provinces of Friesland, Drenthe and Groningen are the most rural, together with Zeeland (Fig. 1c).

Control variables

In addition to changes in population size and regional contexts, many other economic, technological, demographic, cultural and institutional variables determine the level of new firm formation. The study groups these variables into three broad categories: demand factors, supply factors and institutions (BOSMA *et al.*, 2008; VERHEUL *et al.*, 2001). Supply and demand factors have already been mentioned and these will be discussed simultaneously. A summary of the expected signs for the control variables is given in Table 1; data sources and descriptives of all variables can be found in Table 2.

Table 1. Summary of expected signs for control variables

Supply and demand	
Age distribution	
Share of youngsters	Negative
15–25	Negative
25–35	Negative
35–50	Reference
50–65	Negative
Share of elderly	Negative
Level of education	Positive
Immigration	Positive
Income	Positive
Unemployment	Ambiguous
Sector structure	
Service industry	Positive
Herfindahl index	Negative
Institutional environment	
Share of the public sector	Negative
Voter turnout	Positive
Commuting	Positive

Table 2. Overview of variables including data sources

		Mean (SD)
New firm formation – dependent variable		
Start-up rates except agriculture, labour market approach (dividing the number of start-ups by the potential labour market (age 15–65) per region. Mean over 2004–09, LISA dataset		10.43 (3.32)
Explanatory variables		
POP_CHANGE: changes in population size between 2000 and 2007, from Statistics Netherlands on a municipality level. For analysis, five categories are used: strong growth (> 5%), growth (> 1–5% growth), stable (–1% > < 1%), decline (1–5% decline) and strong decline (> 5% decline). Stable regions are used as a reference category	*STRONG DECLINE*	0.02 (0.15)
	DECLINE	0.16 (0.36)
	STABLE	0.24 (0.43)
	GROWTH	0.42 (0.49)
	STRONG GROWTH	0.17 (0.37)
URBANIZATION: population density – based on address density per square kilometre, from Statistics Netherlands at municipality and neighbourhood levels. For analysis, three categories are used: urban, intermediately urban and rural. Urban denotes municipalities with address density > 1500 and rural denotes municipalities with an address density of < 500. Intermediately urban regions are used as the reference category	*RURAL*	0.29 (0.45)
	INTERMEDIATE	0.53 (0.49)
	URBAN	0.17 (0.38)
Control variables		
Age distribution – measured by changes in age structure per municipality between 2003 and 2009, in six categories. The age group 35–50 is used as the reference category. Data from Statistics Netherlands	*UNDER_15*	–1.07 (0.74)
	15–25	2.37 (8.36)
	25–35	–19.83 (7.97)
	35–50	–0.22 (6.33)
	50–65	11.18 (6.97)
	OVER_65	1.99 (0.95)
HIGH_EDU: share of higher educated inhabitants relative to the active workforce, mean over 2000–07 due to data availability. Sixty-one small municipalities were excluded from the source dataset for privacy reasons. These municipalities are estimated based on the share of higher educated in the NUTS-3 region. Data from the Enquete Beroepsbevolking (EBB) executed by Statistics Netherlands		22.93 (7.10)
IMMIGRANTS: average number of internal and international migrants between 2003 and 2009 per inhabitant per municipality. Statistics Netherlands, municipality level		3.98 (1.19)
INCOME: the development in average income between 2003 and 2007 (mean income after taxes of those aged 15–65 during 52 weeks that year). Due to changes in the definitions used by Statistics Netherlands, 2008 and 2009 are excluded from the analysis		0.05 (0.02)
UNEMPL: unemployment rates – over the years 2003–08, data from Statistics Netherlands, computations by A. Edzes		5.03 (1.75)
HERF_INDEX: the sum of the squares of the market share(s) of firms in all municipalities (*i*) in 2003 ($\mathbf{H} = \sum_{i=1}^{N} \mathbf{S}_i^2$). Measured by firm size in the number of jobs, based on the LISA dataset		0.02 (0.03)
SERVICE_SEC: share of the service sector per municipality, measured in share of jobs per municipality, based on the LISA dataset		63.62 (9.32)
PUBLIC_SEC: share of the public sector (sbi two digit: 84, 85, 91; roughly public administration, education and libraries, archives, museum and nature preservation), measured in share of jobs per municipality, based on the LISA dataset		10.42 (4.91)
VOTING: voter turnout for the elections for the Lower House (Tweede Kamer) in 2006. Data from Statistics Netherlands		82.81 (3.81)
COMMUTE: commuting behaviour between municipalities, measured by the number of incoming commuters in 2005. Data from Statistics Netherlands		7.56 (18.7)

Supply and demand

Age distribution is an important determinant for the formation of new firms on both the supply and demand side. The largest group of new entrepreneurs belong to the 35–39-year age group (KAMER VAN KOOPHANDEL NEDERLAND (KvK), 2013). At the same time, 45 is the average age of those who are self-employed without personnel (in Dutch: ZZP-er), a group that has been growing rapidly in the last decade. They often continue their business beyond the age of 65 (KÖSTERS, 2009). Ageing is expected to have an inverted 'U'-shape relation with the rate of new firm formation: in particular, for the variable measuring the *changing share of elderly*, with respect to the reference category '*35–50*', a negative sign is expected. Next, the *share of young people*, that is under 15 years old, is an indicator of the presence of young families. Although research regarding family dynamics is quite rare (ALDRICH and CLIFF, 2003), it can be argued that potential entrepreneurs with young families might be more reluctant to take on the risk of starting a new firm, influencing start-up rates negatively. Also, a growing proportion of children live in single-parent families (ALDRICH and CLIFF, 2003), for whom the perceived risks will be even greater. Therefore, it can be argued that an increase in the number of young people in a region will have an adverse effect on the start-up rates in that region. On the supply side, the *level of education* is positively associated with entry rates. Highly skilled labour and the proportion of college graduates are found to be positively related to start-up rates (ARMINGTON and ACS, 2002; AUDRETSCH and FRITSCH, 1994).

Immigration can have an indirect effect via population growth, creating more demand (VERHEUL *et al.*, 2001). However, the impact of the total immigration, not the net amount, was assessed. Immigration is therefore interpreted as a supply factor, with an expected positive relation to start-up rates. Immigrants are on average less risk-averse; moving to another country (international) or region (intra-national) carries a certain risk, as does starting a business (WENNEKERS *et al.*, 2005).

Income can be seen as both a demand and a supply factor. Income growth increases demand but also facilitates access to capital for aspirant entrepreneurs. VERHEUL *et al.* (2001) discussed conflicting hypotheses explaining the impact of one particular form of income, wages, on start-up rates. The first hypothesis argues that high wages lead to high opportunity costs of starting a firm, and therefore relate to a lower level of new firm formation. The second hypothesis argues that high wages are positively correlated to start-up rates, as higher income is a sign of a prosperous economy with above-average survival rates of firms. In addition, BOSMA *et al.* (2008) mention the potential negative influence on entrepreneurship due to the high costs of hiring employees. *Unemployment rates* generate similar hypotheses as described for wages. On the one hand, high unemployment may indicate a push factor, causing necessity-driven entrepreneurship, thus increasing start-ups. On the other hand, high unemployment rates can indicate a lack of entrepreneurial opportunity, thus the association with low new firm formation (AUDRETSCH and THURIK, 2000; VERHEUL *et al.*, 2001).

Other control variables influencing demand in a region, and thereby the rate of new firm formation, are technologies, consumer demand and the industrial structure of the economy (VERHEUL *et al.*, 2001). These factors influence the *sectoral structure* and the diversity in market demand leading to opportunities for entrepreneurship. Variety in a region's sector structure represents more opportunities for new firm formation (BOSMA *et al.*, 2008). A high degree of services in a certain municipality may also positively affect entry rates because of lower average start-up costs (e.g. FRITSCH, 1997). BOSMA *et al.* (2008) also include the size of the local industry as a demand factor, since greater competition can contribute to new start-ups. The Herfindahl index for 2003 was used to measure the degree of concentration in the market, as an indicator for competition. The closer to zero this index is, the more intense the competition in the region. Therefore, a negative relationship is expected with new firm formation.

Institutional environment

The institutional environment influences the supply side of entrepreneurship and is often related to culture (WENNEKERS *et al.*, 2010). Given that this study focuses on the Netherlands only, many institutional aspects such as property rights and bankruptcy laws are the same for all regions because they are set at the national level. We focused therefore on so-called background institutions: the entrepreneurship culture of the region and the level of social capital. Entrepreneurial culture is often measured at the country level by including a region-specific fixed effect (BEUGELSDIJK, 2007). Institutions are difficult to measure in practice (AIDIS *et al.*, 2012). Instead of fixed effects, the share of the public sector in the region is used as a proxy for an entrepreneurial culture. Several studies have found that a large government sector has a negative impact on new firm formation (AIDIS *et al.*, 2012; NYSTRÖM, 2008). Similar results were found in the UK (FAGGIO and OVERMAN, 2012). The size of the public sector is therefore hypothesized to have a negative impact on the dependent variable. The level of social capital is measured via the proxy *voter turnout* for the elections for the House of Representatives (Tweede Kamer in Dutch) in 2006. Voter turnout is a simple measure, but it is associated with the level of social capital and reflects participation and involvement (COX, 2003; GUISO *et al.*, 2004). The final control variable concerns commuting behaviour between municipalities. As explained above in the methodology section, there is a need to account for people working and living in different municipalities. By including the number of incoming commuters, we also control for the size of the city and its role in the region.[2]

RESULTS

This section first presents descriptive results illustrating the link between population change and the rate of new firm formation in different regional contexts. Second, it shows multivariate regression models that explain the rate of new firm formation across different intensities of population change and depending on the degree of urbanization.

Population change and start-ups

Three steps were taken towards answering the first research question. The first step relates population size and the number of start-ups: a positive relationship was expected between the absolute number of new establishments and the size of the population. At first glance the general picture shown in the scatterplot diagram in Fig. 2a appears more or less linear, with larger populations experiencing more start-ups. The relationship between population size and start-up *rate*, shown in Fig. 2b, does not appear to vary systematically with the size of the local economy. The perforated reference lines show the average population size and average start-up rates for each municipality; start-up rates do not appear to diverge systematically from the average according to the size of the local economy. The number of municipalities in each category that are above or below the national average in terms of start-up rates and population size, or population change, are denoted in each of the four quadrants – I, II, III and IV – in Figs 2b and 2c. On this basis, more (180/150) smaller regions appear to out-perform the national average than do large regions (48/63). It does appear to be the case, however, that the dispersion of start-up rates is much higher for small populations and more sparsely populated municipalities than for larger municipalities. Fig. 2c shows that that there is no clear and systematic relationship between start-up rates and population change. Fewer declining municipalities appear to out-perform the national average start-up rates

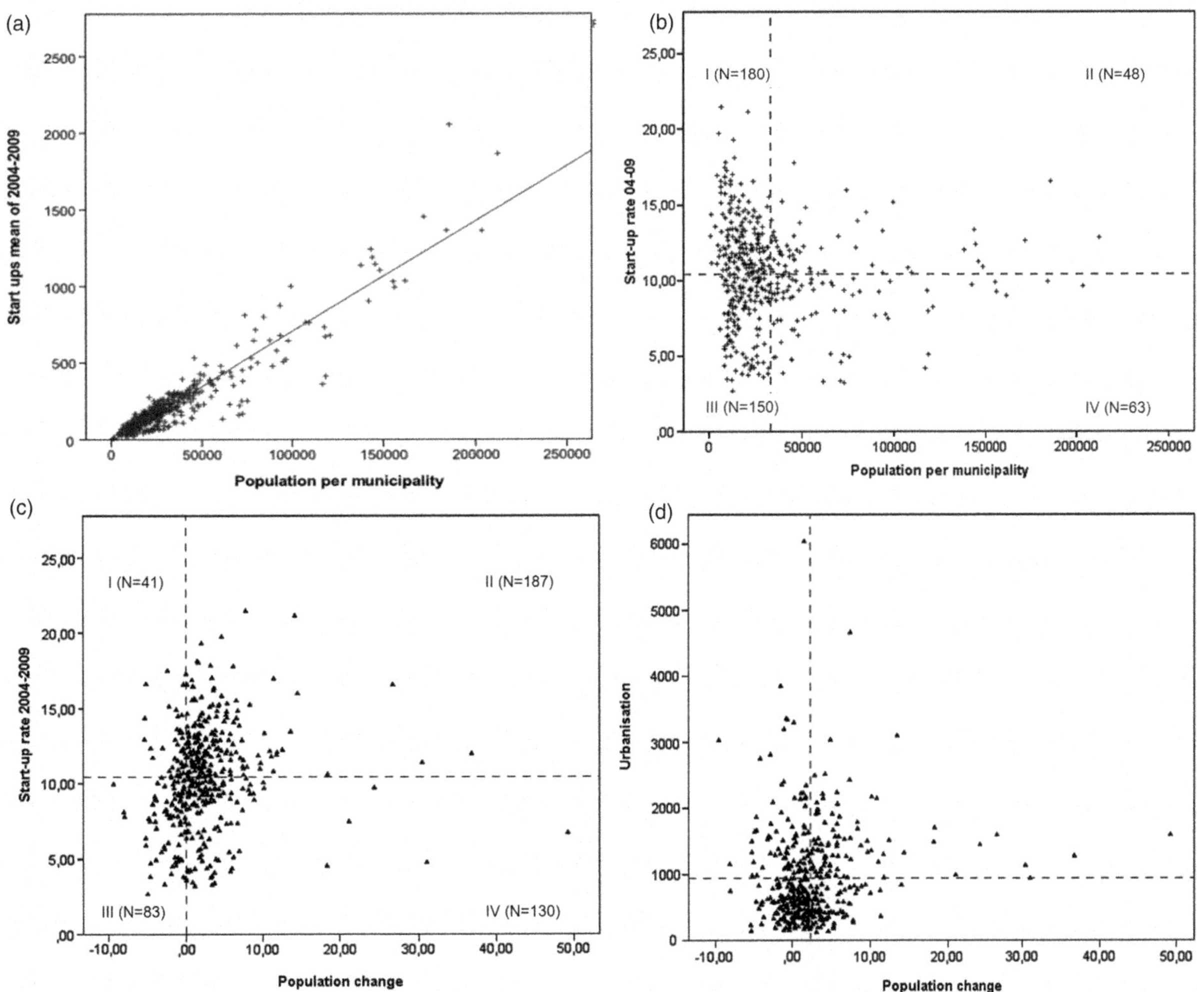

Fig. 2. (a) Number of start-ups and population size; (b) start-up rate and population size; (c) start-up rate and population change; and (d) population change and degree of urbanization

than do larger regions (41/83) compared with growing municipalities (187/130). These inferences need to be treated with caution, however, because of what is called the modifiable areal unit problem (MAUP). MAUP refers to the challenge of using aggregated data in spatial analysis when changing the scale of observation while using the same data, potentially resulting in different outcomes (ARBIA and PETRARCA, 2011).

Urbanization, population change and start-ups

The lack of any clear-cut picture regarding the relationship between entrepreneurship and regional population changes (see also Fig. 2d), along with theoretical arguments that point in different directions (SER, 2011; WENNEKERS, 2006), calls for a more detailed decomposition of the regional context. Fig. 3 shows the correlation between population change in five categories and the start-up rate, with localities split into urban and rural regions (see also Table A1 in Appendix A).

From Fig. 3, it follows that that the relationship between new firm formation, population change and regional context is more complex than many existing studies suggest. The effects of declining and stable populations, particularly, appear more marked for urban regions, suggesting that cumulative effects may be more prevalent in this context (FRENKEN and BOSCHMA, 2007), while rural regions appear to be less affected by population growth. In terms of new firm formation, it can be seen that a moderate decline of –1% to –5% is most strongly related to start-up rates, along with rapid population growth rates of over 5%, whereas strong decline shows small but positive coefficients.

Regression analysis

Table 3 presents three models of start-up rates as a function of a series of explanatory variables: two ordinary least squares (OLS) regressions and a SDM with direct, indirect and total effects. To decide on the best possible model, the decision rules suggested by ELHORST (2010) were followed. Initially, the OLS model was estimated and the robust Lagrange multiplier was used to test whether a spatial lag (LM^{r}_{ρ}) or spatial error model (LM^{r}_{λ}) was more appropriate to describe the data (ANSELIN, 1996). The results of both LM lag and LM error tests rejected the null hypothesis of no spatial correlation in the model's residuals. Subsequently, it was evaluated whether the SDM was indeed the best model for the data. The SDM was estimated and the hypothesis of whether the SDM could be simplified to the spatial lag model or the spatial error model was tested by performing a Wald or likelihood ratio (LR) test. The results of both tests, reported in Table 3, indicate that the model cannot be simplified and that the SDM is the best model to describe the data. The fit of the model improved from R^2 0.31 in Model 1 to 0.50 in the SDM, further confirming it to be a good fit. The variance inflation factor (VIF) remained well under 5, indicating that multicollinearity is not a problem (HAAN, 2002).

This section discusses the estimation results in general before returning to the main variables of interest. It first focuses the discussion on the direct effects of the SDM. The direct effects can be interpreted as being rather similar as the coefficients of an OLS or spatial lag, that is a change in one observation (municipality) related with any given explanatory variable will affect the municipality itself (LESAGE and PACE, 2009). The significant outcomes of the indirect effects, the spillover effects, are discussed below.

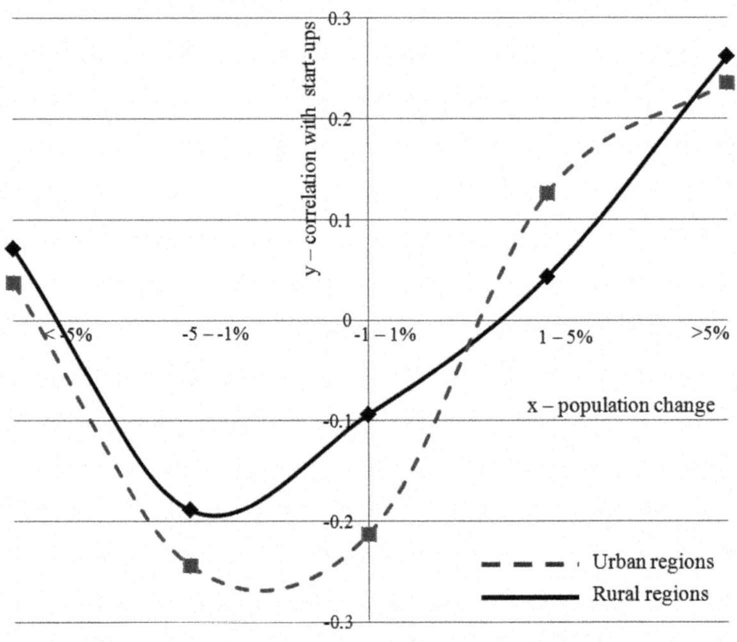

Fig. 3. Pearson's correlations population change and start-up rates

Table 3. Regression results: OLS and SDM direct, indirect and total impact estimates

	Model 1	Model 2	SDM		
Dependent: New firms per 1000 potential workers	OLS 1	OLS 2	Direct	Indirect	Total
	B (SE)	B (SE)	B	B	B
Levels of population change					
STRONG_DECLINE	−0.85 (3.78)	−1.99 (1.25)	−0.93	7.91	6.98
DECLINE	−1.17 (1.06)**	−1.49 (0.63)**	−1.10**	−5.23	−6.34*
Stable	Reference	Reference	Reference	Reference	Reference
GROWTH	0.55 (0.36)	0.16 (0.47)	0.04	1.97	−1.93
STRONG_GROWTH	1.16 (0.54)**	0.23 (0.67)	0.177	−0.32	−0.14
Degree of urbanization					
RURAL	1.64 (0.33)***	0.97 (0.62)	1.14**	−2.51	−1.37
Intermediately urban	Reference	Reference	Reference	Reference	Reference
URBAN	−1.55 (0.48)***	−3.33 (1.05)***	−3.05***	−5.77	−8.82
Interaction variables					
*Strong_Decline**Intermediate		Reference	Reference	Reference	Reference
*STRONG DECLINE*RURAL*		2.71 (2.51)	1.59	1.02	2.60
*STRONG DECLINE*URBAN*		5.30 (3.27)	7.29**	50.78**	58.08**
*Decline*Intermediate*		Reference	Reference	Reference	Reference
*DECLINE*RURAL*		0.41 (1.04)	0.94	6.69	7.64
*DECLINE*URBAN*		1.89 (1.33)	1.89*	3.48	5.37
*Growth*Intermediate*		Reference	Reference	Reference	Reference
*GROWTH*RURAL*		0.55 (0.77)	0.22	0.47	0.69
*GROWTH*URBAN*		2.11 (1.21)*	2.09**	4.28	6.37
*Strong Growth*Intermediate*		Reference	Reference	Reference	Reference
*STRONG GROWTH*RURAL*		2.80 (1.14)**	2.18**	14.92**	17.10**
*STRONG GROWTH*URBAN*		2.10 (1.27)*	2.31**	10.68	12.99
Control variables					
UNDER_15	0.20 (0.30)	0.21 (0.29)	0.09	0.09	0.18
AGE15–25	−0.02 (0.02)	−0.01 (0.02)	0.007	−0.11	−0.11
AGE25–35	−0.05 (0.02)*	−0.04 (0.02)*	−0.07***	−0.4	−0.10
Age35–50	Reference	Reference	Reference	Reference	Reference
AGE50–65	0.07 (0.03)**	0.07 (0.03)***	0.03	0.14	0.17
OVER_65	0.34 (0.25)	0.36 (0.26)	−0.006	1.50	1.49
HIGH_EDU	0.07 (0.03)**	0.07 (0.03)**	0.04*	0.08	0.12
IMMIGRANTS	0.26 (0.19)	0.24 (0.19)	0.32**	−0.63	−0.31
INCOME	33.02 (6.48)***	34.02 (6.49)***	19.42***	69.68**	89.09**
UNEMPL	0.004 (0.09)	0.04 (0.10)	−0.002	0.25	0.25
SERVICE	−0.002 (0.02)	−0.001 (0.02)	0.008	−0.02	−0.008
HERF_INDEX	−14.16 (5.66)**	−15.28(5.73)***	−5.59	29.64	24.05
COMMUTE	0.03 (0.009)***	0.02 (0.01)**	0.02***	0.06	0.08*
Institutional context					
PUBLIC_SEC	0.03 (0.04)	0.04 (0.04)	−0.002	0.13	0.12
VOTING	−0.04 (0.04)	−0.03 (0.04)	0.005	−0.17	−0.16
N	441	441	441	441	441
R^2	0.31	0.33			0.55
LM_ρ	366.63***	363.00***	Wald test spatial lag		77.63***
LM^r_ρ	36.52***	42.73***	LR test spatial lag		72.83***
LM_λ	346.15***	333.62***	Wald test spatial error		48.95***
LM^r_λ	16.05***	13.34***	LR test spatial error		64.25***

Note: *Statistically significant at the 10% level; **statistically significant at the 5% level; and ***statistically significant at the 1% level.

No evidence was found that an aging society would affect new firm formation negatively, as compared with the reference category *AGE35–50*; only change in the share of 25–35-year-olds shows a significant negative sign. Given that the age group *35–50* is expected to generate most new entrepreneurs, a negative sign was expected for all other categories. The share of highly educated people in the local population is, as expected, positively related to new firm formation. The proportion of migration is also positively related to start-up rate, and municipality income levels are strongly positive, while unemployment rates did not seem to have any significant influence on start-up rates. The service sector and the intensity of competition measured by the Herfindahl index had no significant impact, and neither the public sector nor the voting turnout – used as proxies for the institutional context – was statistically significant. The volume of incoming commuters does show the expected positive impact. Municipalities that are attractive to work in are also attractive to start a business in.

Main effects of population change and urbanization

The results show that the effects of population change on new firm formation differ markedly and systematically depending on the context they occur in and the intensity of the population change. Regions facing declining populations exhibit lower start-up rates but, rather surprisingly, the role of population growth in new firm formation appears limited, with the only significant results found in Model 1. This implies that the relationship between population change and new firm formation is primarily determined by the depressing effect of decline and not by the positive effects of growth: entrepreneurship driven by necessity rather than opportunity. In addition, there is no indirect effect of the different levels of population change, implying the effects are localized and that MAUP is not an issue.

Both rural and urban regions only show a direct impact on new firm formation, positive and negative respectively, when compared with the baseline intermediate region. Focusing on the direct impacts, rural regions systematically exhibit higher start-up rates, while urban regions systematically exhibit lower start-up rates. Having said that, in terms of start-up rates, urban regions do show particularly positive additional effects of the interaction terms, as compared with the baseline of intermediate regions: strongly and moderately declining urban regions show a clear positive direct impact on start-up rates.

Additional effects of interaction

A more nuanced picture is obtained when the interaction effect of population change and degree of urbanization are included, as illustrated in Fig. 4. The interaction terms are additional to the main variables. Fig. 4 shows the cumulated significant coefficients of the degree of population change, the regional context and the interaction effect of both (the reference categories are *INTERMEDIATE* and *STABLE*). The horizontal axis represents the reference categories; both lines are set out to this reference category. Even though a growing population alone does not generate a significant effect, the interaction term shows that in urban and rural municipalities, population growth has a positive impact on start-up rates in comparison with intermediate regions. It shows that population decline is not negative by definition and nor does growth have a positive effect in all cases. The picture is very mixed.

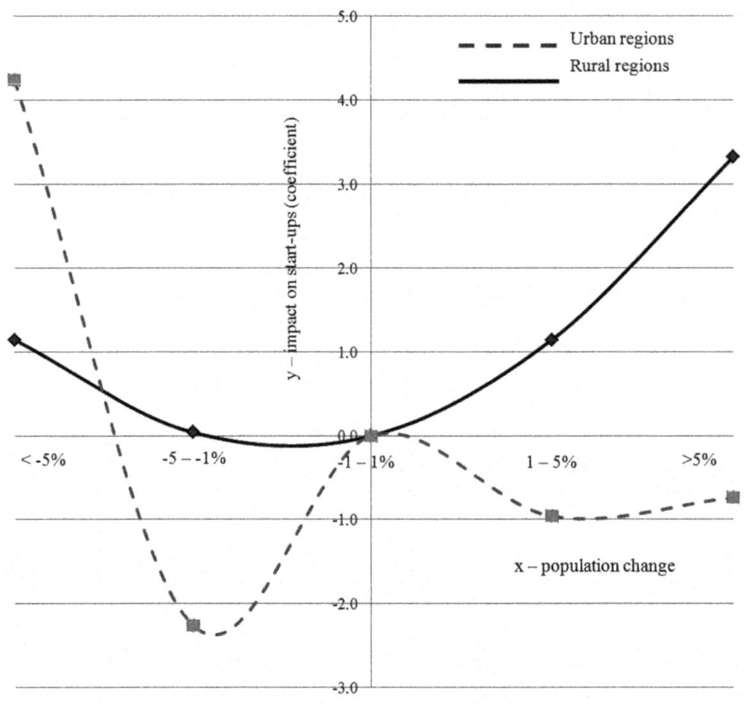

Fig. 4. Significant outcomes of the spatial Durbin model (SDM) direct impacts tallied up coefficients with regard to the reference category intermediate and stable regions

Fig. 4 shows a gap between urban and rural regions. The positive effect of rurality is strong enough to eliminate the negative impact of decline. Relatively speaking, as compared with intermediate regions facing decline, rural regions do better than urban areas; the impact of population change is the largest in rural regions. This can be partially explained by a denominator effect, but for the declining regions a strong development of necessity-driven self-employment is also likely. The start-up rates do not take firm growth potential into account and the survival rate is not incorporated in this measurement. It is possible that the formation of new firms in declining rural regions is strongly influenced by serial small scale entrepreneurship. Population growth in rural regions has a positive effect in terms of new firm formation, which may be related to selective migration. The cottage industry is a good illustration of this phenomenon: nascent entrepreneurs relocate their home to the urban periphery and start an – often part-time – business from their home. Cottage industries are less dependent on agglomeration benefits. Also, in a remote village with a growing population it is more common to start a small business or shop from home. These types of businesses are likely to be motivated by lifestyle choice, rather than necessity.

Urban municipalities show an overall negative effect of population change, despite the positive impacts of the interaction terms. The negative impact of urbanization on new firm formation corresponds with the findings of VAN STEL and SUDDLE (2008) for the Netherlands, but is rather different to findings in many other countries (STERNBERG, 2011). It appears that urban regions in the Netherlands have already achieved the maximum benefit from agglomeration effects. Another potential explanation may lie in the presence of a service sector that is less reliant on agglomeration benefits. However, a clear positive outcome for urban areas that face strong decline is also found, indicative of stronger resilience than intermediate or rural regions. Both interaction terms with a declining population are positively significant, indicating that urban municipalities are more capable of absorbing the changes in population. These results are confirmed when testing for a 'U'-shape relationship, indicating a monotonic or inverse 'U'-shape relation for declining rural regions but a 'U'-shape for the urban declining regions (see also Table 4) (LIND and MEHLUM, 2010).

It is important to note that the results must be interpreted with regard to the reference categories, the intermediately urban regions. In the Dutch context, this means that urban areas lose a significant number of start-ups to the intermediate urban regions, which may largely explain the negative effect. The surrounding intermediate regions of the Randstad area are highly competitive in housing prices and availability, provide similar facilities as the urban areas and appear to offer more entrepreneurial opportunities.

Table 4. 'U'-shape test results

Population change	Decline	Growth
Urban	'U'-shape (trivial)	Inverse 'U'-shape ($p < 0.05$)
Rural	Monotomic or inverse 'U'-shape	'U'-shape (trivial)

Spillover effects

The indirect effects resulting from the SDM can be considered spillovers. A change in the explanatory variable of a region will affect the region itself – the direct impact – but this change may also affect all other municipalities, which constitutes the indirect impact (LESAGE and PACE, 2009; PIJNENBURG and KHOLODILIN, 2011). There are only three significant indirect impacts on start-up rates: two interaction terms and the control variable *INCOME*. Statistically significant indirect effects are often difficult to find, as one needs many observations over time (ELHORST, 2012). FISCHER *et al.* (2009) discuss how to interpret the indirect effects. Indirect impacts may be a measure of the cumulative impact of a change in a specific region's initial level, averaged over all other regions. In other words, change in one region's initial level of population and urbanization has a small impact on each of the other regions' start-up rates, but cumulatively the impact is significantly positive (50.78). Obviously, the impact on regions in close proximity to that specific region would be greater than the impact on more distant regions. The same applies to the interaction of strong growth and rural regions. In both cases the indirect effect is larger than the direct effect. It is therefore concluded that the impact of greater levels of population change on a particular region is larger on its neighbours' start-up rates than on its own start-up capacity. Strongly declining urban regions show that this type of region can benefit from its surrounding regions, in the same way that rapidly growing rural regions can benefit from spillover effects.

CONCLUSION

The main goal of this paper was to analyse the empirical relationship between new firm formation and population change in different regional contexts. Data from the LISA database and Statistics Netherlands for the period 2003–09 were used to test the relationship. It was found that population change is, unsurprisingly, positively related to the rate of new firm formation, but that the effect of population change differs markedly depending on the regional context and the intensity of the population changes. Population growth is not positive per se for start-up rates, nor is population decline necessarily negative for new firm formation. It is the regional context that determines the relationship.

Population decline did show the expected negative impact on new firm formation, but only for mild, not strong, decline. As for decline in rural regions, a moderate positive effect was observed, suggesting that these start-up rates are a response to the minimum levels of supply of services and activities that are needed regardless of a declining population; it is likely that the impact of necessity-driven entrepreneurship is being measured.

The relationship between new firm formation and population change is fairly different in urban regions. It is argued that many economic benefits are associated with an urban context, and the availability of entrepreneurial opportunities is often seen as a key urban advantage. However, the results paint quite a different picture. Dutch urban areas show systematically lower start-up rates than rural and intermediate areas. Urban areas have a largely negative impact on start-ups, but in the specific context of an urban region, strong decline actually showed a solid positive impact on new firm formation. This suggests that even though urban areas appear less favourable for new firm formation than intermediate areas, they seem more resilient and able to absorb the effects of decline better than both intermediate and rural regions. In terms of entrepreneurial activities, they do appear to be responsive to population change. However, this does not compensate for the negative impact of urbanity. The baseline of intermediate regions plays an important role in explaining this outcome. Intermediately urban municipalities are very competitive and still have the opportunity to grow and benefit from agglomeration effects, whereas urban areas appear close to their maximum level (ceiling).

The results also suggest that mild population decline is actually less inductive for new firm formation than stronger decline exceeding 5%. Urban regions especially showed a great difference between the two types of decline. Rural municipalities show less extreme results, with the steady positive impacts of both growth and stability followed by recovery after decline. In terms of demographic transitions, this suggests that when a region first experiences population decline, negative aspects capture the attention, but when the decline continues many rural regions appear to adjust to the adverse shocks by increasing entrepreneurship: something of a classic Schumpeterian story.

In conclusion, a clear distinction is found between regional contexts in the impact of population change on new firm formation. In light of this conclusion, the regional context and the intensity of decline should be taken into account when determining the kind of coping mechanism that is needed for dealing with the consequences of decline. Important questions beyond the scope of this current paper also arise. Can entrepreneurship contribute to building or maintaining a resilient region? In the Netherlands this is not yet a pressing matter, but given the forecasts of future population decline it will become increasingly relevant. Having found a positive impact of declining rural regions on start-ups, it would be interesting to know whether these new firms grow beyond the initial small scale with perhaps one or two employees, and whether they serve the local market or export their products or services. Also, with the data available for this paper, it is not possible to determine who are the new entrepreneurs and what are their motivations for start-up. It is likely that motivations in a declining region differ from those in a growing region. Are there indeed more necessity-driven entrepreneurs in declining regions, and opportunity-driven entrepreneurs in growing regions? Future research is required in order to answer the question: to what extent does new firm formation enhance the resilience of regions and the well-being of its inhabitants and how this can be influenced by appropriate policy measures?

Acknowledgements – The authors would like to thank Paul Elhorst for help with the econometric methodology. They also thank the three anonymous reviewers for valuable and constructive feedback.

APPENDIX A

Table A1. Detailed correlations and count

	NFF all regions	NFF in rural regions	NFF in intermediate regions	NFF in urban regions	*N*
Strong decline	−0.044	0.071	−0.119*	0.037	9
Decline	−0.207***	−0.189**	−0.183***	−0.244**	69
Stable	−0.042	−0.094	−0.029	−0.213*	104
Growth	0.113**	0.043	0.101	0.126	185
Strong growth	0.116**	0.262***	0.122*	0.236*	74
N	441	128	238	75	

Notes: NFF, new firm formation.

*Statistically significant at the 10% level; **statistically significant at the 5% level; and ***statistically significant at the 1% level.

NOTES

1. For a comprehensive overview of the concept, see AUDRETSCH *et al.* (2011) and CASSON *et al.* (2006).
2. The city's role in the region is of importance when interpreting the results. The Randstad area is a particularly important region. Several variables were experimented with, but the results were never significant and other coefficients barely changed. It was therefore concluded that the SDM and other control variables – particularly incoming commuters – already take the city's role into account.

REFERENCES

ACS Z. (2006) How is entrepreneurship good for economic growth?, *Innovations* **1(1)**, 97–107.

ACS Z. J. and ARMINGTON C. (2004) Employment growth and entrepreneurial activity in cities, *Regional Studies* **38(8)**, 911–927.

AIDIS R., ESTRIN S. and MICKIEWICZ T. (2012) Size matters: entrepreneurial entry and government, *Small Business Economics* **39(1)**, 119–139.

ALDRICH H. E. and CLIFF J. E. (2003) The pervasive effects of family on entrepreneurship: toward a family embeddedness perspective, *Journal of Business Venturing* **18(5)**, 573–596.

ALDRICH H. E., RENZULLI L. A. and LANGTON N. (1998) Passing on privilege: resources provided by self-employed parents to their self-employed, *Research in Stratification and Mobility* **16**, 291–317.

ANSELIN L. (1996) Simple diagnostic tests for spatial dependence, *Regional Science and Urban Economics* **26(1)**, 77–104.

ARBIA G. and PETRARCA F. (2011) Effects of MAUP on spatial econometric models, *Letters in Spatial and Resource Sciences* **4(3)**, 173–185.

ARMINGTON C. and ACS Z. J. (2002) The determinants of regional variation in new firm formation, *Regional Studies* **36(1)**, 33–45.

AUDRETSCH D. B., FALCK O., HEBLICH S. and LEDERER A. (2011) *Handbook of Research on Innovation and Entrepreneurship*. Edward Elgar, Cheltenham.

AUDRETSCH D. B. and FRITSCH M. (1994) The geography of firm births in Germany, *Regional Studies* **28(4)**, 359–365.

AUDRETSCH D. B. and THURIK A. R. (2000) Capitalism and democracy in the 21st century: from the managed to the entrepreneurial economy, *Journal of Evolutionary Economics* **10(1)**, 17–34.

BARCA F. (2009) *An Agenda for a Reformed Cohesion Policy: A Place-Based Approach to Meeting European Union Challenges and Expectations*. European Commission, Brussels.

BEUGELSDIJK S. (2007) Entrepreneurial culture, regional innovativeness and economic growth, *Journal of Evolutionary Economics* **17**, 187–210.

BÖNTE W., FALCK O. and HEBLICH S. (2009) The impact of regional age structure on entrepreneurship, *Economic Geography* **85**, 269–287.

BOSMA N., VAN STEL A. and SUDDLE K. (2008) The geography of new firm formation: evidence from independent start-ups and new subsidiaries in the Netherlands, *International Entrepreneurship and Management Journal* **4(2)**, 129–146.

BRÜDERL J. and PREISENDÖRFER P. (1998) Network support and the success of newly founded businesses, *Small Business Economics* **10(3)**, 213–225.

CASSON M., YEUNG B., BASU A. and WADESON N. (2006) *The Oxford Handbook of Entrepreneurship*. Oxford University Press, Oxford.

COX M. (2003) When trust matters: explaining differences in voter turnout, *Journal of Common Market Studies* **41(4)**, 757–770.

DAVIDSSON P. and HONIG B. (2003) The role of social and human capital among nascent entrepreneurs, *Journal of Business Venturing* **18(3)**, 301–331.

ELHORST J. P. (2010) Applied spatial econometrics: raising the bar, *Spatial Economic Analysis* **5(1)**, 9–28.

ELHORST J. P. (2012) Matlab software for spatial panels, *International Regional Science Review* DOI: 10.1177/0160017612452429.

EUROPEAN COMMISSION (2010) *Investing in Europe's Future: Fifth Report on Economic, Social and Territorial Cohesion*. European Commission, Brussels.

FAGGIO G. and OVERMAN H. G. (2012) *The Effect of Public Sector Employment on Local Labour Markets*. SERC Working Paper. Spatial Economics Research Centre (SERC), London.

FÉSÜS G., RILLAERS A., POELMAN H. and GÁKOVÁ Z. (2008) *Regions 2020. Demographic Challenges for European Regions*. Background document to Commission Staff Working Document Sec (2008), 2868 Final Regions 2020, An Assessment of Future Challenges for EU Regions. European Commission, Brussels.

FISCHER M. M., BARTKOWSKA M., RIEDL A., SARDADVAR S. and KUNNERT A. (2009) The impact of human capital on regional labor productivity in Europe, *Letters in Spatial and Resource Sciences* **2(2)**, 97–108.

FRENKEN K. and BOSCHMA R. A. (2007) A theoretical framework for evolutionary economic geography: industrial dynamics and urban growth as a branching process, *Journal of Economic Geography* **7(5)**, 635–649.

FRITSCH M. (1997) New firms and regional employment change, *Small Business Economics* **9(5)**, 437–448.

FRITSCH M. and MUELLER P. (2008) The effect of new business formation on regional development over time: the case of Germany, *Small Business Economics* **30(1)**, 15–29.

GÁKOVÁ Z. and DIJKSTRA L. (2010) Does population decline lead to economic decline in EU rural regions?, *Regional Focus* No. 01/2010. European Union, Regional Policy, Brussels.

GAROFOLI G. (1994) New firm formation and regional development: the Italian case, *Regional Studies* **28(4)**, 381–393.

GUISO L., SAPIENZA P. and ZINGALES L. (2004) The role of social capital in financial development, *American Economic Review* **94(3)**, 526–556.

HAAN C. T. (2002) *Statistical Methods in Hydrology*, 2nd Edn. Iowa State University Press, Ames, IA.

HAARTSEN T. (2002) *Platteland: boerenland, natuurterrein of beleidsveld? Een onderzoek naar veranderingen in functies, eigendom en representaties van het Nederlandse platteland*. Nederlandse Geografische Studies, Utrecht, 309.

HAARTSEN T. and VENHORST V. (2010) Planning for decline: anticipating on population decline in the Netherlands, *Tijdschrift voor Sociale en Economische Geografie* **101(2)**, 218–228.

KOSTER S. (2006) *Whose Child? How Existing Firms Foster New Firm Formation: Individual Start-ups, Spin-outs and Spin-offs*. University of Groningen, Groningen.

KÖSTERS L. (2009) *Sterke groei zelfstandigen zonder personeel, Sociaaleconomische trends, 3e kwartaal 2009*. Statistics Netherlands (CBS), The Hague.

KAMER VAN KOOPHANDEL NEDERLAND (KVK) (2013) *Rapport Startersprofiel 2012, Startende ondernemers in beeld*. KvK.

LESAGE J. P. and PACE R. K. (2009) *Introduction to Spatial Econometrics*. Chapman & Hall/CRC, Boca Raton, FL.

LIND J. T. and MEHLUM H. (2010) With or without U? The appropriate test for a U-shaped relationship, *Oxford Bulletin of Economics and Statistics* **72(1)**, 109–118.

MAI R. and BUCHER H. (2005) *Depopulation and its Consequences in the Regions of Europe*. DG III – Social cohesion. European Commission, Brussels.

MCGRANAHAN D. and BEALE C. L. (2002) Understanding rural population loss, *Rural America* **17**, 2–11.

MISHRA A. (2005) Entrepreneurial motivations in start-up and survival of micro- and small enterprises in the rural non-farm economy, *Journal of Small Business and Entrepreneurship* **18(3)**, 289–326.

MORRIS M. H. and LEWIS P. S. (1991) Entrepreneurship as a significant factor in societal quality of life, *Journal of Business Research* **23(1)**, 21–36.

NYSTRÖM K. (2007) An industry disaggregated analysis of the determinants of regional entry and exit, *Annals of Regional Science* **41(4)**, 877–896.

NYSTRÖM K. (2008) The institutions of economic freedom and entrepreneurship: evidence from panel data, *Public Choice* **136(3–4)**, 269–282.

ORGANISATION FOR ECONOMIC CO-OPERATION AND DEVELOPMENT (OECD) (2005) *New Approaches to Rural Policy: Lessons from Around the World*. OECD, Paris and Washington, DC.

ORGANISATION FOR ECONOMIC CO-OPERATION AND DEVELOPMENT (OECD) (2008) *OECD Rural Policy Reviews: Netherlands*. OECD, Paris and Washington, DC.

PARKSTAD LIMBURG (2011) *Krimp en economische groei gaan prima samen*. Nieuwsbrief Parkstad Limburg, Speciale editie voor Kamerleden: Krimp. 22 June.

PIJNENBURG K. and KHOLODILIN K. A. (2011) *Do Regions with Entrepreneurial Neighbors Perform Better? A Spatial Econometric Approach for German Regions*. Discussion Papers Number 1103. German Institute for Economic Research, Berlin.

POLÈSE M. and SHEARMUR R. (2006) Why some regions will decline: a Canadian case study with thoughts on local development strategies, *Papers in Regional Science* **85(1)**, 23–46.

REYNOLDS P. D., MILLER B. and MAKI W. R. (1995) Explaining regional variation in business births and deaths: U.S. 1976–88, *Small Business Economics* **7(5)**, 389–407.

SCHUTJENS V. and STAM E. (2003) Entrepreneurship, regional differences and locational trajectories in the Netherlands, in WEVER E. (Ed.) *Recent Urban and Regional Developments in Poland and the Netherlands*, pp. 51–66. KNAP/FRW Universiteit Utrecht, Utrecht.

SER (2011) *Bevolkingskrimp benoemen en benutten*. Commissie Ruimtelijke Inrichting en Bereikbaarheid No. 3, The Hague.

SIMMIE J. and MARTIN R. (2010) The economic resilience of regions: towards an evolutionary approach, *Cambridge Journal of Regions, Economy and Society* **3(1)**, 27–43.

STAM E. (2007) Why butterflies don't leave: locational behavior of entrepreneurial firms, *Economic Geography* **83**, 27–50.

STAM E. (2009) Entrepreneurship, evolution and geography, *Papers in Evolutionary Economic Geography* **9(13)**, 1–23.

STERNBERG R. (2011) Regional determinants of entrepreneurial activities – theories and empirical evidence, in FRITSCH M. (Ed.) *Handbook of Research on Entrepreneurship and Regional Development. National and Regional Perspectives*, pp. 33–57. Edward Elgar, Cheltenham.

VAN STEL A. and SUDDLE K. (2008) The impact of new firm formation on regional development in the Netherlands, *Small Business Economics* **30(1)**, 31–47.

VAN WISSEN L. (2010) *Population Decline is Not a Threat* (available at: http://www.rug.nl/corporate/nieuws/opinie/2010/Opnie08_2010?lang=en) (accessed on 5 October 2010).

VERHEUL I., WENNEKERS A. R. M., AUDRETSCH D. B. and THURIK A. R. (2001) *An Eclectic Theory of Entrepreneurship: Policies, Institutions and Culture*. Tinbergen Institute Discussion Paper Number TI 2001-030 (available at: http://hdl.handle.net/1765/6873).

WENNEKERS S. (2006) *Entrepreneurship at Country Level: Economic and Non-Economic Determinants*. ERIM, Rotterdam.

WENNEKERS S., VAN STEL A., CARREE M. and THURIK R. (2010) The relationship between entrepreneurship and economic development: is it U-shaped?, *Foundations and Trends in Entrepreneurship* **6(3)**, 167–237.

WENNEKERS S., VAN STEL A., THURIK R. and REYNOLDS P. (2005) Nascent entrepreneurship and the level of economic development, *Small Business Economics* **24(3)**, 293–309.

WESTLUND H. (2003) Local social capital and entrepreneurship, *Small Business Economics* **21(2)**, 77–113.

WILLIAMS N. and WILLIAMS C.C. (2012) Beyond necessity versus opportunity entrepreneurship: some lessons from English deprived urban neighbourhoods, *International Entrepreneurship and Management Journal*, 1–18.

The Significance of Entry and Exit for Regional Productivity Growth

UDO BRIXY*†
*Institute for Employment Research, Nuremberg, Germany.
†Department for Geography, Ludwigs-Maximilians-University, Munich, Germany

BRIXY U. The significance of entry and exit for regional productivity growth, *Regional Studies*. This study addresses the debate about whether start-ups increase regional productivity growth through such effects as the fostering of competition. A new longitudinal dataset at the establishment level for eastern and western Germany is used to analyse the impact of the number of start-ups and their survival on the growth of total factor productivity and employment. It is demonstrated that start-ups do affect regional productivity growth. But the impact is not proved continually: it varies between the manufacturing and the service sector and between the two parts of Germany.

Start-ups Total factor productivity (TFP) growth Employment growth Creative destruction Revolving doors New-firm survival

BRIXY U. 进入与退出之于区域生产力成长的显着性，*区域研究*。本研究处理有关新创企业是否透过诸如促进竞争之影响，增进了区域生产力成长的辩论。本研究运用在东德与西德中，创立层级企业的崭新纵向数据集，分析新创企业的数量及其生存对于全要素生产率及就业成长的影响。研究証实，新创企业确实会影响区域生产力的成长，但该影响却无法証实具有连贯性，并在製造业与服务部门之间，以及东德与西德之间产生差异。

新创企业 全要素生产率（TFP）成长 就业成长 创造性破坏 旋转门 新企业的生存

BRIXY U. L'importance de l'entrée et de la sortie des entreprises pour la croissance de la productivité régionale, *Regional Studies*. Cette étude aborde la question suivante: la création d'entreprise, est-ce qu'elle augmente la croissance de la productivité régionale au moyen des effets tels la stimulation de la concurrence. On emploie un nouvel ensemble de données longitudinales auprès de l'est et de l'ouest de l'Allemagne recueilli au niveau de l'établissement pour analyser l'impact du nombre de créations d'entreprise et de leur survie sur la croissance de la productivité totale des facteurs et l'emploi. On montre que la création d'entreprise influe sur la croissance de la productivité régionale. Toujours est-il que l'impact ne fournit pas de résultats définitifs: il varie entre le secteur manufacturier et le secteur des services et entre les deux parties de l'Allemagne.

Création d'entreprise Croissance de la productivité totale des facteurs Croissance de l'emploi Déstruction créatrice Portes tournantes Survie des nouvelles entreprises

BRIXY U. Die Bedeutung von Firmengründungen und -schließungen für das Wachstum der regionalen Produktivität, *Regional Studies*. Diese Studie ist ein Beitrag zu der Debatte, ob Neugründungen, durch Effekte wie z.B. die Stärkung des Wettbewerbs, das Produktivitätswachstum von Regionen erhöhen. Ein neuer Längsschnittdatensatz, der auf einzelbetrieblicher Ebene für West- und Ostdeutschland vorliegt, wird dazu genutzt, den Einfluss der Anzahl von Gründungen und der Überlebensdauer dieser Gründungen auf das Wachstum der regionalen Faktorproduktivität und der Beschäftigung zu analysieren. Es wird gezeigt, dass Gründungen tatsächlich das Produktivitätswachstum von Regionen beeinflussen. Dieser Einfluss ist aber nicht durchgängig nachweisbar: Er variiert sowohl zwischen Dienstleistungssektor und verarbeitendem Gewerbe als auch zwischen Ost- und Westdeutschland.

Firmengründungen Wachstum der Faktorproduktivität Beschäftigungswachstum Schöpferische Zerstörung Drehtüren Überleben neuer Firmen

BRIXY U. El significado de la creación y del cierre de empresas para el crecimiento de la productividad regional, *Regional Studies*. Este estudio contribuye al debate sobre si las empresas emergentes aumentan el crecimiento de la productividad regional a través de efectos como el estímulo a la competencia. Se utiliza un nuevo grupo de datos longitudinales sobre establecimientos del este y el oeste de Alemania para analizar el efecto del número de empresas emergentes y su supervivencia en el crecimiento de la productividad total de los factores y el empleo. Se demuestra que las empresas emergentes sí que influyen en el crecimiento de la productividad regional. Sin embargo, este efecto no se observa continuamente: varía entre el sector manufacturero y de servicios y entre las dos zonas de Alemania.

Empresas emergentes   Crecimiento de la productividad total de los factores   Crecimiento del empleo   Destrucción creativa   Puertas giratorias   Supervivencia de nuevas empresas

INTRODUCTION

Spatial differences in regional entrepreneurial activities are well documented (e.g., STERNBERG, 2009). Fundamentally distinct regional regimes that are more or less entrepreneurial underlie these differences (AUDRETSCH and FRITSCH, 2002; FRITSCH and MUELLER, 2006; AUDRETSCH *et al.*, 2012). The most popular concept for explaining the differences is Joseph Schumpeter's idea of 'creative destruction'. In Schumpeter's model, new firms compete with incumbent firms and force older firms to close down. AUDRETSCH and FRITSCH (2002) refer to industries or regions with many entrants that do not survive long as 'revolving door regimes' and claim that these regimes have only a limited impact on regional competitiveness. This is confirmed by FALCK (2007, p. 922) who shows that 'long-run start-ups have a significantly positive impact on industry growth', whereas short-run start-ups have no significant impact ('mayflies'). New firm survival also depends on the competiveness of incumbent firms and varies substantially with the characteristics of different regional environments, such as population density. In particular, densely populated regions are typically more competitive, which results in lower survival rates for new businesses in these regions (e.g., FRITSCH and MUELLER, 2006; FRITSCH *et al.*, 2006; RENSKI, 2011). The results concerning the impact of short-run start-ups on regional growth are therefore debatable, especially if growth is not just equated with regional employment growth but also with regional productivity growth. Whereas there are many studies available that show the impact of newly founded businesses on employment growth (for an overview, see, for example, FRITSCH, 2013), far fewer studies deal with their impact on productivity growth. One reason for this is that it is difficult to measure productivity on a regional scale, whereas data on employment growth are easily available for many countries at various regional levels. Although it is undisputed that in highly developed countries start-ups exert a positive impact on regional productivity (e.g., CARREE and THURIK, 2008; MINNITI and LÉVESQUES, 2010; FRITSCH, 2013), productivity growth can have different effects on employment growth (CINGANO and SCHIVARDI, 2004). With shrinking employment, labour productivity rises automatically, and rising employment can thus reduce regional productivity. The link between productivity growth and employment growth is the elasticity of demand. If start-ups face price-elastic demand for their services or products, productivity improvements lead to employment growth. However, if the opposite is the case, and new firms face inelastic demand, they must grow at the expense of incumbent firms; employment is therefore bound to stagnate or even decline.

Recently, BOSMA *et al.* (2011) attempted to measure the impact of creative destruction on regional productivity growth using a comprehensive dataset at the regional level. They measured the added impact of the number of newly founded firms and firm closures (firm dynamics or turbulence) on total factor productivity (TFP) growth. Because their data did not contain information about the ages of the exiting firms, however, BOSMA *et al.* were unable to distinguish between firms that close shortly after they are founded (revolving door) and those that are successful, stay in the market longer and become well established (creative destruction). In this paper, the approach used by BOSMA *et al.* is extended to create a model that considers the regional impact of creative destruction and revolving doors on TFP growth and regional employment growth separately. This paper therefore adds empirical evidence regarding the impact of creative destruction on the growth of regional productivity and employment for a large economy. Furthermore, in contrast to other papers that use German data, East Germany (the former German Democratic Republic (GDR)) is included. It can be demonstrated that with respect to both regional productivity growth and employment growth, it is not the number of start-ups alone but also their sustainability that is relevant. Moreover, it is shown that firms surviving a minimum of one year already have a strong positive impact on regional growth.

CREATIVE DESTRUCTION, REVOLVING DOORS AND REGIONAL GROWTH

Creative destruction, the ongoing renewal of the stock of firms, is a process that is vital for a competitive and innovative economy. New firms either replace (crowd out) existing firms or merely add to the pool of existing suppliers of goods and services, thereby increasing the variety of goods and services that are available.

In the field of entrepreneurship, the term 'creative destruction' was introduced by SCHUMPETER (1942/1994). In 1942, he focused on the role of large established firms in promoting technical progress in capitalistic systems; however, in an earlier book, published in 1912, he had already strongly advanced what he called the 'entrepreneurial principle'. This principle states that entrepreneurs enforce new re-combinations of the factors of production, thereby depriving the production factors of their 'static' usage by creating 'something new' (innovation). 'The result is economic development and progress' (p. 177; present author's own translation). The entrepreneur's role in this process is to force the re-combination of production factors while destroying existing combinations. The term 'Schumpeterian creative destruction' typically refers to these paired processes, which are widely recognized as indispensible to innovation. This process of creative destruction enhances productivity directly by replacing incumbent firms with new, more efficient ones (CAVES, 1998). According to the ORGANISATION FOR ECONOMIC CO-OPERATION AND DEVELOPMENT (OECD) (2003) and VIVARELLI (2013) entry and exit of firms play an important role in productivity growth. BALDWIN and GORECKI (1991) estimate that entry by replacement accounts for 24% of the productivity growth in the Canadian manufacturing sector. DISNEY *et al.* (2003) report that entry and exit of firms was even responsible 80–90% of establishment TFP growth in the British manufacturing sector during the period 1982–92.

Whereas many authors stress the importance of firm entry and exit for employment growth (for an overview, see FRITSCH, 2013), 'attempts directly linking firm birth and/or deaths to the regional aggregate product or aggregate value added remain exceptional' (DEJARDIN, 2011, p. 444). Recent exceptions are the studies of CARREE and THURIK (2008), DEJARDIN (2011), BOSMA *et al.* (2011), PIERGIOVANNI *et al.* (2012), and ANDERSSON *et al.* (2012).

The reasons discussed in the existing literature as to why creative destruction is important for the innovativeness of the economy can be summarized into three main categories: the prevention of structural inertia, the stimulation of competition and the exploitation of entrepreneurial opportunities.

Structural inertia is a typical phenomenon that hinders the advancement of new ideas in long-established organizations (HANNAN and FREEMAN, 1984; CARROLL and HANNAN, 2000). New ideas often struggle to find acceptance in established venues of society, and this struggle can affect both potential demand and potential supply. On a regional scale, structural inertia tends to produce regional 'lock-in', which refers to a diminished willingness to adopt new technologies which reduces regional economic growth (MARTIN and SUNLEY, 2006; SERI, 2010). In this context, start-ups provide a means of circumventing the structural obstacles that hamper the spread of new ideas.

The stimulating effect that new firm entry has on competition appears to be self-evident. Schumpeter notes that 'the very threat of entry might have a stimulating effect on the innovative performance of incumbent firms. The businessman feels himself to be in a competitive situation even if he is alone in his field' (SCHUMPETER, 1942/1994, p. 85). This concern raises the question of whether new firms do indeed compete with older, incumbent firms or whether they instead compete with other new (and typically small) firms that are attempting to occupy similar economic niches. If the latter phenomenon were the case, then the impact of new firms on economic competition and growth would be rather limited. MATA and PORTUGAL (1994) find that most of the firms that exit the market are recent entries. AUDRETSCH and FRITSCH (1994, 2002) and FRITSCH and MUELLER (2006) demonstrate that regions with strong turbulence, in other words regions with a large number of both firm entries and firm exits at any given point in time, do not demonstrate particularly high levels of innovativeness and exhibit relatively low growth levels ('revolving door regional growth regimes').

Regional variations in the degree of innovativeness of the market entries might therefore play a role in explaining firm survival rates. For productivity growth and technological progress, it is important to differentiate between imitative and innovative market entries (MINNITI and LÉVESQUES, 2010). Whereas imitative entries have to find their niches alongside existing firms and have to draw from the profit margins of those firms, typically by means of price competition, innovative entries attempt to create their own markets to serve if possible. So, incumbent firms compete in different ways with imitative and innovative market entries; in particular, imitative entries raise the efficiency of the regional economy, and innovative entries create new markets (MINNITI and LÉVESQUES, 2010). Most new firms are imitative in character, and their innovativeness is associated solely with their new combination of production factors (ALDRICH, 1999). However, in certain regions, e.g. those with a technical university, market entries are more frequently innovative in the sense that they offer a new product or service (BADE and NERLINGER, 2000; HUFFMAN and QUIGLEY, 2002; KIRCHHOFF *et al.*, 2007). These regions benefit not only from the technological advancements provided by innovative entries but also from the stimulating effects that these entries have on the innovativeness of the incumbent firms (AGHION *et al.*, 2009).

SHAVER (1995) wrote that 'Entrepreneurs may not be born, but they might be made'. Certain regions are obviously more successful than others at 'making entrepreneurs'. Although the existence of an 'entrepreneurial personality' is not supported by most scholars (GARTNER, 1988; STANWORTH *et al.*, 1989; SHAVER, 1995; DAVIDSSON, 2006), there are certain characteristics that influence an individual's probability of becoming an entrepreneur (for an overview, see PARKER, 2009; and recently OBSCHONKA *et al.*, 2013). These characteristics are not evenly spread across space, but instead tend to be clustered in certain types of regions such as agglomerations and regions with a large share of creative and well-educated people (FRITSCH and SCHROETER, 2011; REYNOLDS, 2011; AUDRETSCH and KEILBACH, 2004a, 2004b). Furthermore, many studies find that start-ups have stronger effects on employment growth in regions with higher levels of agglomeration (FRITSCH, 2013).

MINNITI and BYGRAVE (1999) and BYGRAVE and MINNITI (2000) present a theory that explains how the likelihood of becoming an entrepreneur is influenced by the regional context; in particular, they observe that this likelihood is affected by the level of entrepreneurial activity already present in a region. The current entrepreneurs in a region create network externalities that generate new entrepreneurial opportunities. These externalities are created mainly by peer-effects (FALCK *et al.*, 2012; BOSMA *et al.*, 2012). Hence, regions with an initial advantage cumulatively benefit from this advantage and are able to continue to enhance the favourability of their environments for entrepreneurs. However, empirical investigations also show that the marginal effect on regional employment growth decreases as the start-up rates increase. FRITSCH and SCHROETER (2011) even find that if the level of entrepreneurial activity reaches a certain threshold, it can have a negative impact on employment growth.

Many papers that address the topic of turbulence discuss the impact of turbulence on industry lifecycles (for an overview, see AUDRETSCH, 1995). AGARWAL and GORT (1996) demonstrate that the evolutionary stage of the product cycle dictates a pattern of market entries and exits. FOTOPOULOS and SPENCE (1998) conclude that 'turbulence might be characterizing more profitable industries in that they offer both the attractions and also the impediments leading to both higher entry and exit' (p. 261). However, the authors are unable to decide whether 'the 'forest' or the 'revolving door' metaphor applies' (p. 261).

Most of the studies mentioned above are cross-sectional and provide no information regarding the actual duration of firm survival; instead, they only analyse the combined impact of market entries and exits (turbulence). Longitudinal data are required in order to measure the validity of the antagonism between the creative destruction and the revolving door theses directly. In a recent paper, BAPTISTA and KARAÖZ (2011) use longitudinal data to analyse the dynamics of entry and exit during the industry life cycle. This approach is similar to that of AGARWAL and GORT (1996). The former authors distinguish between exits younger than three years old and those older and find that revolving door exits are more frequent in the large majority of industries that they analyse; however, during the life cycles of industries the significance of revolving door exits declines since both entries and exits decrease.

Only few studies address the topic of turbulence and regional growth. However, three such studies have been published recently (BOSMA *et al.*, 2011; FRITSCH and NOSELEIT, 2013a, 2013b; ANDERSSON *et al.*, 2012). FRITSCH and NOSELEIT (2013a) investigate the impact of regional market entry and exit on employment growth in western Germany between 1984 and 2002; and in FRITSCH and NOSELEIT (2013b) between 1976 and 2002. In contrast to the study by BOSMA *et al.* (2011), FRITSCH and NOSELEIT (2013a, 2013b) control for the age of the market exits in their investigation. Their results show that market entry does have a positive effect on the employment level of incumbent firms and that this effect is exclusively driven by market entries that are not of the revolving-door type. ANDERSSON *et al.* (2012) estimate production functions on the firm level in which the productivity of incumbents is a function of regional entrepreneurial activity. They find that the effect of entries on productivity growth varies over time. First, the effect of entries is negative and only after several years this effect turns to be positive. The authors call this a 'delayed entry effect'.

However, as stated above, regional productivity growth and regional employment growth are not clearly linked. Depending on the elasticity of demand, productivity growth can lead to employment growth or decline. To overcome this ambiguity, BOSMA *et al.* (2011) analyse the impact of market entry and exit from 1988 to 2002 on competitiveness in 40 Dutch regions. TFP is used as a measure of competitiveness. The study concludes that entry and exit activities have positive effects on TFP growth for service sectors, whereas no such relationship can be found in manufacturing.

This paper uses two measures of competitiveness: TFP growth and employment growth. The advantages of the TFP growth metric are that it measures directly the contributions of labour and capital to productivity growth and that, in contrast to the often-used metric of employment growth, TFP growth also accounts for growth that does not translate into greater employment. However, the disadvantage of this metric is that it does not measure all technological changes. Especially, changes that are not accompanied by costs, such as increases in publicly accessible knowledge, do not yield corresponding increases in TFP (OECD, 2001). A further disadvantage of the TFP growth metric is that the data necessary for TFP calculations are not directly available below the level of federal states. The available data therefore have to be converted to smaller scales for regional investigations (see the data section below).

This last issue poses no problem for employment growth, the second measure used in this study. Reliable data regarding this metric are available at many different regional levels, which is why they are used to measure economic growth in most regional studies. The most prominent disadvantage of the employment growth metric is that technological progress and the productivity growth resulting from this progress typically reduce the demand for labour; so employment growth is only observed if the demand for products and services grows sufficiently to overcompensate for this effect (DEW-BECKER and GORDON, 2008). In contrast to TFP growth, employment growth is an indicator of regional economic growth but is not a particularly appropriate measurement of regional competitiveness.

THE EMPIRICAL MODEL

Since AUDRETSCH and KEILBACH (2004b) and ÁCS and VARGA (2005) extended ROMER's (1990, 1994) endogenous growth model by including entrepreneurial capital, it has become standard practice when investigating the impact of entrepreneurship on regional output in settings of specified production functions. The model used in this study is broadly in accordance with the model of BOSMA *et al.* (2011), whose approach was, in turn, based on the work of GEROSKI (1989) and CALLEJÓN and SEGARRA (1999). However, the model utilized in the current study extends the model of Bosma *et al.* by explicitly including a measure of the proportion of firms that survive for a given duration. By changing the time interval over which a firm must survive, the levels of creative destruction and/or revolving-door business foundations are measured. The model is based on a Cobb–Douglas type of production function:

$$Y_{i,t} = A_{i,t} * K_{i,t}^{\alpha} * L_{i,t}^{\beta} \tag{1}$$

where A is an index of the level of productivity in region i and time t; and K and L are the quantities of physical capital and labour, respectively, that are needed to produce output Y. The factor-share of labour is given by α and can be calculated. Under the assumption of constant returns, the share of capital is given by $\beta = 1 - \alpha$.

Equation (1) may be expressed in terms of first derivatives to reflect growth rates if constant returns are assumed and can be rearranged into:

$$da_{i,t} = dy_{i,t} - \alpha dk_{i,t} - (1-\alpha)_{i,t} dl_{i,t} + \varepsilon_{i,t} \tag{2}$$

where d reflects growth rates expressed as first differences in logarithmic form, as indicated by small letters. Thus, for example, da_{it} represents the growth of TFP, which is also known as Solow's residual. This quantity describes the portion of output growth that is not explained by increased input of the production factors.

To evaluate the importance of creative destruction for productivity growth, the index reflecting productivity growth is decomposed into a component that is constant over time and region (da_i), a component representing the impact of newly founded firms on productivity changes (NF) and a term representing the impact of the creative destruction/revolving-door effect on productivity changes (CDR). This leads to equation (3), which expresses the Solow residual (da_{it}^s) as a combination of the regional impact of newly founded firms and the creative destruction and/or revolving-door effects:

$$\begin{aligned} da_{i,(t+1)}^s = da_i &+ \beta_1 \mathrm{NF}_{i,t} + \beta_2 \mathrm{CDR}_{i,t} + \beta_3 \mathrm{TU}_{i,t} \\ &+ \beta_4 \mathrm{KN}_{i,t} + \beta_5 \mathrm{DE}_{i,t} + \varepsilon_{i,t} \end{aligned} \tag{3}$$

$$\text{with } i \in (1, \ldots, n),\ t \in (T_0, \ldots, T)$$

In this equation, da_{it}^s refers to the Solow residual in region i and year t; da indicates technological progress in the strict sense that is assumed to be constant over time; NF represents the rate of newly founded firms; and CDR describes the proportion of start-ups that survive a given minimum time span (one, two or three years) and thus represent the share of creative destruction of NF. Firm dynamics are expressed by the turbulence rate (TU), and the numbers of start-ups and closures divided by the number of firms in each region and sector. Furthermore, the size of the regional knowledge base (KN) is represented by the share of employees with university degrees. DE represents population density as a measure associated with regional effects of the settlement structure. As an alternative measure of regional economic success, similar equations are estimated using employment growth as the dependent variable.

This model is estimated using ordinary least squares (OLS). The dependent variables, TFP and employment growth rates are the means over the period from 2001 to 2007. The independent variables are calculated as means over the period from 1994 to 2000. The regional levels are the 96 standard statistical regions known in German as planning regions ('*Raumordnungsregionen*' – ROR), each of which represents a large functional region comprising a regional centre and its market area. Because in many ways the differences between East and West Germany were very pronounced – especially in the years to which the independent variables refer – the estimates not only control for this by means of a dummy but also there are estimates based only on the 74 western German regions, which disregard the 22 eastern regions. Furthermore, to control for effects resulting from the 'top-down method' used to derive TFP growth data at the ROR level that is described in the following section, the estimates are clustered to the level of the 16 federal states and robust standard errors are calculated.

As a robustness check, 15 estimations are conducted that always omit a different federal state. The results of this robustness check are very similar to those obtained in the analysis.

DATA

Identification of market entries and exits

For the analysis described in this paper, a new and greatly improved version of a notably comprehensive longitudinal dataset that covers all newly founded firms with at least one employee who is covered by social security is used to measure market entry and new firm survival (the Institut für Arbeitsmarkt- und Berufsforschung (IAB) Establishment History Panel).[1] The dataset is created from the mandatory information on employees that employers have to submit to social security institutions. This information is transformed into a file that provides longitudinal information concerning the establishments and their employees on 30 June of every year. This file even includes marginal part-time workers who work only a few hours per week and earn a maximum of €400 per month. Only self-employed individuals with no employees and civil servants are excluded from the dataset. The comprehensive nature of the dataset used in this study ensures that the majority of the entrepreneurial activities in each region are relatively well represented.

To date, several papers have used this data source and have defined newly founded firms as entities with establishment identification numbers that had not previously been allocated (recently, FRITSCH and SCHROETER, 2011; SCHINDELE and WEYH, 2011). Because existing businesses may also be assigned new identification numbers for various reasons, such as changes in ownership, HETHEY and SCHMIEDER (2010) suggest using worker flows between establishments to identify genuine new establishments. Their reasoning is that the main issue confounding the identification of newly founded establishments can be addressed by analysing the worker flows between establishment IDs. If an existing firm is given a new ID number, all of that firm's employees may then be reported under this new ID number; alternatively, the new ID number may be used for only a portion of the personnel of an existing business, and both the old and the new ID numbers may be used by the business as a whole. To prevent such cases being counted incorrectly as new entries to the market, Hethey and Schmieder created a new supplementary dataset that tracks all worker flows between establishments. For each new establishment ID number, the maximum number of workers joining the new ID number who had the same previous establishment ID is calculated ('maximum clustered inflow' – MCI). Similarly, if an ID number can no longer be traced in the register, the 'maximum clustered outflow' (MCO) is calculated in order to identify firm closures more correctly. A number of criteria must be fulfilled to classify a firm as a newly founded entity. All new ID numbers that do not cover more than three reported employees for the first reporting year are generally considered to be newly founded, as it is unreasonable to analyse the MCI for these small firms. If a new ID number appears that covers four or more employees, it is considered to represent a newly founded entity if the MCI is less than 30%, i.e. if fewer than 30% of the employees that are reported under the new ID number previously worked at the same firm. In addition, this MCI should not exceed 30% of the employees of any relevant predecessor firm. The details of this procedure and its impact on the number of market entries and exits are given in HETHEY and SCHMIEDER (2010). The use of this information enhances the identification of market entries substantially.

This database provides excellent opportunities for measuring the creative destruction and revolving-door effects. By considering the age of exits at the regional level, it is possible to distinguish between creative destruction and revolving-door firms.[2]

Calculations of regional total factor productivity (TFP)

TFP growth was calculated using the data from the calculation of national accounts, which are published by the Federal Statistical Office and the Statistical Offices of the Länder (Statistische Ämter des Bundes und der Länder). The data obtained from this source include the annual averages of the employment volume[3] (hours worked), gross value added (GVA),[4] the gross stock of fixed assets[5] (the stock of capital), and the compensation of employees.[6] The latter three averages are price-adjusted. The number of self-employed individuals is also obtained from this source and used to calculate the hypothetical compensation of these self-employed individuals, as described in detail by WIEGMANN (2003) and AIYAR and DALGAARD (2005). This is necessary to calculate the factor shares of labour (α), which is done by dividing the compensation for employees and the self-employed the regional gross domestic product (GDP).

Most of the data necessary for calculating TFP are not available below the level of NUTS-1 (federal states), which is an overly broad definition for a meaningful regional analysis. To overcome this drawback, the NUTS-1 data were converted to the level of 96 standard statistical regions (ROR). The number of hours worked in the two sectors under analysis was used to split the state-level data into district-level figures. Thus, the data on capital stock etc. at the federal state level were distributed in proportion with the number of hours worked in each ROR and sector. This is a common conversion procedure in the context of regional data. In many countries employment data are typically gathered from individual employers, and the number of employees can therefore be calculated precisely by aggregating the data at the level needed (the 'bottom-up method'). Data on productivity – such as gross national product (GNP) and GVA – are far more complex, so the sophisticated data needed to calculate such measures are gathered at the national level by

Table 1. Definitions and sources of the data

Variables	Definition	Source
Dependent variables (average 2000–07)		
TFP growth	Growth of total factor productivity (%) (ln)	Author's own calculation based on data from Federal Statistical Offices
Employment growth	Increase in the number of employees subject to social security (%) (ln)	Statistics of Federal Employment Offices
Independent variables (average 1994–2000)		
Start-up rate	Rate of newly founded firms divided by the number of employees (%) (ln)	Establishment History Panel of the IAB and extension file entry & exit
Creative destruction (1–3)	Share of firms surviving the first 1–3 years (%) (ln)	Establishment History Panel of the IAB and extension file entry & exit
Turbulence	Sum of start-ups and firm closures by the number of employees (%) (ln)	Establishment History Panel of the IAB and extension file entry & exit
Population density	Population per km^2 (ln)	Inkar 2012: Indicators of regional development published by BBSR
Share of highly qualified	Share of employees with a university degree (ln)	Inkar 2012: Indicators of regional development published by BBSR
East–West dummy	1 = West	

Note: BBSR, Bundesinstitut für Bau-, Stadt- und Raumforschung; IAB, Institut für Arbeitsmarkt- und Berufsforschung.

official statistical offices using survey data. The regional results of these calculations are considerably less differentiated than the national-level data and are calculated via the 'top-down approach'. FREY and THALHEIMER (2010, p. 8) clarify this procedure using the example of regional GVA figures:

> national GVA is apportioned to the individual regions, without trying to classify it according to regionally based business units. Data are rather apportioned using indicators specific to the economic sectors, which should correlate with the calculated value of GVA as much as possible.

Following Frey and Thalheimer, 70% of the German regional GVA data were calculated using the 'top-down method'.

The federal states in Germany differ considerably in size; many of them are rather small (particularly the two major cities in Germany, Berlin and Hamburg, which constitute separate federal states of their own). The proportional conversion procedure is certainly stretched to its limits for larger federal states. Inaccuracies in the regional decomposition are thus to be expected. These could result in the residuals of RORs not being independent within a federal state, thereby leading to biased estimates of the standard errors. To control for this, a sandwich estimator is applied with clusters for the federal states. Because data at the federal state level are available from 2000 to 2007, this time frame was used for the analysis in this study. The dependent variables are calculated as average values from 2000 to 2007, whereas the independent variables refer to the period from 1994 to 2000 and are also calculated as averages over this seven-year period. In accordance with BOSMA *et al.* (2011), the analysis distinguishes between the manufacturing sector and the service sector. A more detailed analysis of other industries, such as business services, is not possible because the data regarding the capital stock are only available for these two sectors.

Table 1 shows the definitions and sources of the data used. Correlation matrices can be found in Appendix A.

RESULTS

Approximately one-quarter of all start-ups do not survive the first year. However, the proportion of failed start-ups decreases rapidly from year to year, reflecting the well-known diminishing function of the 'liability of newness' (Table 1). The differences between the manufacturing and service sectors are quite small.[7]

In order to determine the share of creative destruction it is necessary to assess when a firm ceases to be new and can be regarded as an incumbent firm. BRIXY *et al.* (2006) demonstrate that three years after the founding of a business no significant differences remain between start-ups and incumbent firms with respect to structural variables, such as labour turnover and wages. BOSMA *et al.* (2011) also conclude that a three-year time span is sufficient to regard firms as incumbents. The diminishing proportions of failed new firms illustrated in Table 2 also support this view. Accordingly, approximately 40% of all newly founded firms can be categorized as representative of revolving doors. However, the regional variation among the 96 regions examined is considerable and is more marked in the manufacturing sector than in the service sector, as is shown in Table 3.

Table 4 reveals the same distribution parameters for the dependent variables. TFP growth is shown separately for the two sectors examined. Mean TFP growth

Table 2. Share of creative destruction (%), 2001–07

	Year 1	Year 2	Year 3	Year 4	Year 5
Manufacturing	78.56	67.24	59.14	52.99	48.05
Services	78.43	67.19	59.16	52.86	47.75

Table 3. Distribution parameters of the independent variables, 1994–2000

	Minimum	Maximum	Mean	Median	CV
Manufacturing					
Start-up rate[a]	0.06	0.24	0.12	0.10	0.33
Creative destruction[b]	40.09	70.46	59.14	58.78	0.10
Turbulence[c]	0.11	0.43	0.21	0.18	0.33
Population density	15.68	1321.29	115.04	58.56	1.62
Share of highly qualified	2.89	15.08	6.76	6.18	0.40
Services					
Start-up rate[a]	0.33	0.82	0.50	0.46	0.24
Creative destruction[b]	52.24	63.12	59.16	59.61	0.04
Turbulence[c]	0.57	1.37	0.88	0.82	0.23
Population density	15.68	1321.29	115.04	58.56	1.62
Share of highly qualified	2.89	15.08	6.76	6.18	0.40

Notes: [a]Rate of newly founded firms (divided by the number of employees) (%).
[b]Share of firms surviving the first 3 years (%).
[c]Sum of start-ups and firm closures (by the number of employees) (%).
CV, coefficient of variation.

Table 4. Distribution parameters of the dependent variables, 2000–07

	Minimum	Maximum	Mean	Median	CV
Employment growth (both sectors)	−1.55	2.15	0.36	0.46	2.07
Manufacturing: TFP growth	3.81	7.61	5.15	4.84	0.18
Services: TFP growth	0.97	3.25	2.20	2.13	0.14

Note: CV, coefficient of variation; TFP, total factor productivity.

during this time interval is always positive and is substantially lower in the service sector than in manufacturing. As a measure of regional growth, employment growth is not measured for the individual sectors because the growth that is created in one sector produces employment in both sectors. One important feature of the data is that the relative variance is much higher for employment growth than it is for TFP growth.

One aspect that is of special interest for this analysis is the relationship between the number of start-ups on the one hand and the sustainability of these businesses on the other. The former is expressed by the start-up rate, the latter by the proportion of start-ups surviving a minimum of one to three years. The correlation between these two variables is especially pronounced in the service sector and is shown in Fig. 1. The correlation is negative (–0.7), confirming the expectation that in regions with high rates of newly founded firms, competition forces a large share of the newcomers to close down again soon. The shape of the dots indicates whether the region is located in eastern or western Germany, thus making it clear that the overall negative correlation is driven by the differences between the two parts of the country. In eastern Germany the start-up rates are high, but at the same time the proportion of those that survive is rather low. This underlines the importance of including an East/West dummy and justifies the regressions for the western German regions. However, it should not be overlooked that a negative correlation continues to exist (–0.3) even when western Germany is taken alone.

Results of the estimations

The estimations can be divided into four parts: the two dependent variables, the TFP growth rate and the employment growth rate, for each of the two sectors, manufacturing and services. Furthermore, estimates were conducted for Germany as a whole and for the 74 western German RORs. The number of eastern German RORs (22) is too small to obtain meaningful estimates. The results of the regressions are shown in Tables A1–A4 in Appendix A and a summary is given in Table 5. Separate estimations were conducted for

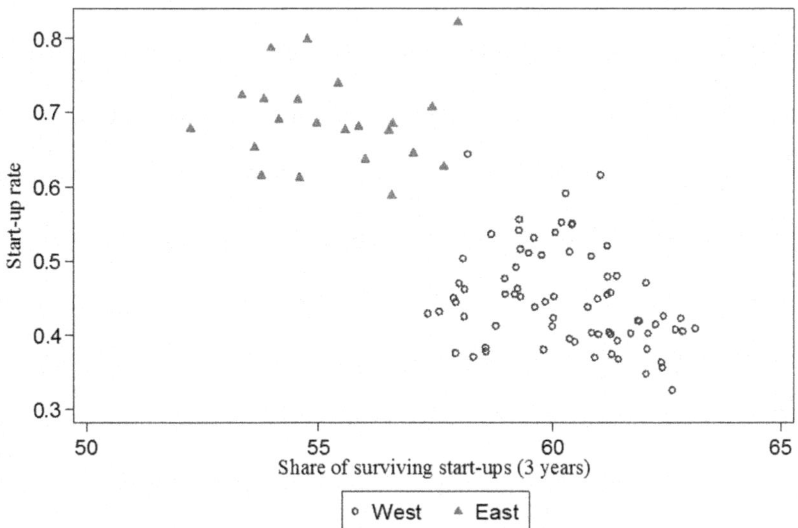

Fig. 1. Start-up rate and share of surviving start-ups – service sector, 1994–2000 (annual means of German regions)
Source: Institut für Arbeitsmarkt- und Berufsforschung (IAB) Establishment Panel (author's own calculations)

Table 5. Summary of the results of the ordinary least squares (OLS) estimations

	Manufacturing		Services	
	East and West	West only	East and West	West only
TFP growth				
Start-up rate	n.s.	+(**)	n.s.	n.s.
Turbulence rate	n.s.	+(**)	n.s.	n.s.
Surviving 1 year	+***	+***	n.s.	n.s.
Surviving 2 years	+***	+***	n.s.	−*
Surviving 3 years	+***	+***	n.s.	−*
Population density	+***	+***	n.s.	n.s.
Share of highly qualified	n.s.	n.s.	n.s.	n.s.
East–West dummy	+**	Not included	n.s.	Not included
Employment growth				
Start-up rate	+(**)	n.s.	+(**)	+(**)
Turbulence rate	+*	n.s.	+(**)	+(**)
Surviving 1 year	n.s.	+***	+*	+*
Surviving 2 years	n.s.	+***	+**	+**
Surviving 3 years	n.s.	+***	+***	+***
Population density	n.s.	n.s.	n.s.	n.s.
Share of highly qualified	n.s.	n.s.	n.s.	n.s.
East–West dummy	−**	Not included	−***	Not included

Note: ***Significant on the 99% level, **95% level and *90% level; n.s., not statistically significant; parentheses if not in all estimations.

each of these parts for three survival scenarios (year 1 to year 3). Furthermore, the high correlation between the start-up rate and the turbulence rate (see the correlations in Appendix A) made it necessary to consider them in separate models. They differ only very slightly from those including the start-up rate and are therefore shown in Appendix A (see Tables A4–A7 in Appendix A).

TFP growth

For the manufacturing sector the estimates using TFP growth as the dependent variable reveal a positive impact of start-ups that survive a minimum of one year (as well as two or three years). It is striking that the coefficients of the survival shares are declining from year to year (see Appendix A). The largest effects come from those start ups that survive a minimum of one year only.

The overall start-up rate can only be found to have an impact in western Germany. The insignificant results of the overall estimates show that the effects in eastern Germany offset those in western Germany. This is also supported by the changing sign for West and East in bivariate correlations (see Tables A1 and A2 in Appendix A). It can be assumed that the already very large number of start-ups in eastern Germany leads to decreasing marginal returns on TFP growth. Even higher rates of start-ups do not result in more growth.

Population density plays an important role for TFP growth in manufacturing; the regional productivity grows more rapidly in more densely populated areas and – as the dummy shows – productivity is growing faster in the East, which indicates that eastern Germany is catching up with western Germany. By contrast the human capital employed is seen to have no influence at all. This is remarkable since most studies find a high level of human capital to have a positive effect on economic growth (notably FRITSCH and NOSELEIT, 2013a, 2013b, for western Germany). The bivariate correlation is positive for the West, but negative for the East. The correlation is highest if the two parts of the country are taken together. This is driven by the large differences in the proportions of highly qualified manpower in eastern and western Germany (see Table A2 in Appendix A), and when a dummy for eastern Germany is introduced, human capital is no longer significant. If the regression is restricted only to western Germany, the rather weak impact of this variable disappears when population density is included. The same applies for this variable in the estimates for employment growth that are discussed below. Thus the differences between the results of the estimates conducted by FRITSCH and NOSELEIT (2013a, 2013b) and those obtained in this paper must be due to the different time frames and/or the enhanced database used in this analysis.

In the service sector the estimations yield hardly any significant results at all, apart from some weak evidence of a negative impact of the minimum survival rate – but only for western German start-ups surviving at least two years. This might be explained by the fact that in western Germany high rates of survival are mainly found in rural and peripheral regions which typically exhibit low levels of employment growth and low levels of entry (BRIXY and GROTZ, 2007). The negative coefficients therefore reflect the fact that TFP growth is low in these regions with low levels of competition and dynamics.

ANDERSSON *et al.* (2012) conclude that, in the long run, new firms have a positive impact on the productivity growth of incumbent firms, especially in the service sector. But, in contrast to the present study Andersson *et al.* do not estimate effects at regional level, but at firm level. Moreover, they do not control for the survival duration of the start-ups.

BOSMA *et al.* (2011) find a positive impact of net entry and of the regional turbulence rate on regional TFP growth in the service sector but not in manufacturing in their study of the Dutch economy. The same applies for the study conducted by DEJARDIN (2011) for Belgium for the 15-year period from 1982 to 1996. He also finds a positive impact of net entry on regional GDP growth only in the service industry, but none in manufacturing. One possible explanation for the differences between these results and those obtained in the present study could be the different structures of the two sectors in the two countries analysed. Germany traditionally has a large share of manufacturing, and especially in western Germany a substantial proportion of quite successful, small manufacturing firms, the so-called 'Mittelstand'. These firms, and the specific institutional environments they generate, might be rather helpful for creating new firms in this sector. The traditional strength of the Dutch and Belgian economies, on the other hand, can be seen more in services and sales, which might provide the right seedbed for corresponding start ups.

Employment growth

In contrast to TFP growth, start-up activities contribute to employment growth not only in the manufacturing sector but also in the service sector, where the contribution is even larger. The contribution of the start-up rate is significant in the service sector for both East and West, in manufacturing only for the West. Here, too, the coefficients of the survival shares show a clearly diminishing trend. The largest effects come from those start-ups that survive a minimum of one year (see the estimates in Appendix A). Thus, in the service sector, high rates of newly founded firms in combination with high rates of new firm survival are decisive for employment growth.

In the manufacturing sector the pattern is more complex. In western Germany it is not the number of start-ups but the sustainability of the newly founded firms that leads to employment growth. The estimates for Germany as a whole show the opposite pattern: not the survival of start-ups but the level of the start-up rates results in employment growth. Taking into account the negative correlation between the employment growth rates and the share of surviving start-ups in eastern Germany, this is no surprise, but again confirms the necessity to treat the two parts of Germany separately and is reflected in especially high values of the East–West dummy in the estimations. Nevertheless, this negative impact of start-up survival is striking, in particular because in eastern Germany survival rates are already lower and start-up rates higher.

Thus, first, in contrast to TFP growth in eastern German manufacturing, a positive impact of the start-up rates emerges and, accordingly, no diminishing marginal returns for start-up activities are found. Second, the insignificant impact of the survival rates and the even negative bivariate correlation with employment growth in eastern Germany could be interpreted in the same way as the negative survival rates for TFP growth in western German services: as an expression of a lack of competition in the eastern German regions. However, given the already short mean survival rates of start-ups in eastern Germany, this result points to a severe quality problem in the new manufacturing firms.

To sum up, the results of this study confirm the results of other studies in so far as start-up activities do affect growth. They also confirm that it is not always the mere volume of start-up activities as such that leads to growth, but that the survival of the new firms plays a role.

The differences between productivity growth and employment growth cannot be ignored. For TFP growth in the service sector, start-up activities are not decisive at all. But they are important in the manufacturing sector, where it is especially the survival of the new firms that is of importance. However, the survival period need not be long – one year is sufficient. This sheds a different light on the results obtained by FRITSCH and NOSELEIT (2013b), who distinguished between long-term and short-term survivors using a threshold of four years. In this setting, only the start-up rates of entries surviving more than four years show a significant positive impact on overall long-term employment growth. They also investigated whether start-up activities induced growth in the incumbent firm sector and concluded that the effect of newly founded firms on the growth of incumbent firms (the indirect effect) is more important than the growth of the start-ups themselves (direct effect). One result of the present study is that a much shorter period is already sufficient to induce regional TFP or employment growth. Thus, revolving door effects are restricted to those start-ups that survive less than one year.

The share of university graduates is not found to have any impact on either of the measures of regional growth. As the correlations (provided in Appendix A) show, there is only a very small correlation between the share of graduates and the two growth measures in the western part of the country. If East and West are combined, the coefficients of the correlations increase (though no significant impact is revealed in any of the estimates) but this only points to the striking differences in the shares of graduates in eastern and western Germany.

However, most studies that use similar variables in comparable settings (e.g., FRITSCH and NOSELEIT, 2013a, 2013b) do find a positive impact of the share of highly qualified. But those studies use a different time frame. A recently published study by PIERGIOVANNI *et al.* (2012) considers the same time period as this study and uses the number of university faculties as a proxy for regional knowledge. They even find a negative impact of the size of the regional knowledge base on regional value-added growth over the same time frame as that in this study.

However, the most important result is that the variables depicting the share of surviving start-ups do indeed have a positive impact. Moreover, it is shown that the share of the firms surviving a minimum of one year already has a strong positive impact.

CONCLUSIONS

The theoretical starting point of this study was to investigate whether start-up activities lead to regional productivity growth and whether there are differences between western and eastern Germany in this respect. The results show that start-ups do indeed exert a positive impact on regional productivity growth, but only in manufacturing and not in the service sector. It also emerges that start-up activities play a role in regional employment growth, not only in manufacturing, but also – and even more strongly – in the service sector.

However, more start-ups do not automatically generate more regional growth as the coefficients of the start-up rates are often insignificant. So simply calling for an increase in the number of start-ups is 'bad public policy' (SHANE, 2009). Instead, the focus should be on start-ups that survive and thereby truly make an impact on the market. The results of this study suggest that it is not necessary for start-ups to survive for a particularly long time, as they are found to have a positive impact even if they survive only one year. The impact of start-ups on regional productivity growth is therefore obviously largely indirect, meaning that the growth is created by incumbent firms that are responding to competitive pressure from the newly founded firms. The constant strain imposed by the start-ups on the incumbent firms therefore partly explains the existence of different levels of regional growth. This is in line with recent findings by FRITSCH and NOSELEIT (2013a, 2013b) and ANDERSSON *et al.* (2012), who investigated the impact of start-ups on employment growth.

Furthermore, the results suggest that there are substantial differences in the way that start-ups impact on regional growth in both parts of Germany, which underlines the need for different policies in East and West. In addition, the considerably higher start-up rates in eastern Germany combined with higher business failure rates suggest either that the start-ups there suffer from severe quality problems or that the institutional framework conditions in the East are less favourable than in the West.

Evidence can be found of both of the above-mentioned factors. There is still a lack of entrepreneurial role models, especially in some regions especially in the East (FRITSCH *et al.*, 2013; FRITSCH and WYRWICH, 2013), and for certain parts of the population this might cause an information or knowledge deficit that calls for enhanced consultancy schemes in eastern Germany. Moreover, given the constantly much higher unemployment rate in eastern Germany, the number of people who become entrepreneurs because they have no alternative can be expected to be rather large. This study covers a period during which an exceptionally large number of start-ups by unemployed persons were subsidized (CALIENDO and KRITIKOS, 2010).

In this situation, where people who would prefer to be employed decide to become entrepreneurs, professional advice should be paramount. This assumes that the quality of start-ups can be enhanced by such schemes. However, there is some doubt about that. The study by ROTGER *et al.* (2012) does find some evidence in favour of such schemes in Denmark, but the studies by FRANKISH *et al.* (2013) and COAD *et al.* (2013) contradict this view. These two studies come to the conclusion that chance plays a crucial role in new firm survival and other variables such as experience, human capital or gender play only minor roles. Furthermore, BRIXY *et al.* (2013) show that even though advice schemes are often free of charge or cost very little, only one in two nascent entrepreneurs takes advantage of such services. Especially young males with good qualifications do not consider seeking professional advice. They seem to be especially prone to cognitive biases that have been demonstrated to be typical characteristics of nascent entrepreneurs (SCHENKEL *et al.*, 2009; FORBES, 2005; SIMON *et al.*, 2000).

Besides these microeconomic reasons for the differences in the survival rates in eastern and western Germany, there are also macro-level factors. First of all, demand remains weak in eastern Germany. Not only are incomes still lower there than they are in western Germany but also the migration of the active and especially consumption-oriented younger and better qualified sections of the eastern German population to the western part of the country certainly poses a problem, not only for new firms. However, new firms tend to be very dependent on local demand in order to be successful.

Start-ups do have an impact on TFP growth. However, in particular the mostly lacking significance for the service sector indicates a need for more research in this area. In addition, longer time frames are required, as well as different strategies to determine TFP growth. ANDERSSON *et al.* (2012) and BERLEMANN and WESSELHÖFT (2012) calculate regional TFP growth by using data on the firm level. These bottom-up approaches appear to be a promising way to obtain more precise data on regional productivity growth.

Acknowledgements – The author is indebted to Tanja Hethey, Uwe Blien, Wolfgang Dauth, Stefan Brunow, Jürgen Wiemers, the anonymous referees, the Editors and the participants at a session of the 5th Summer Conference of the German-speaking section of the Regional Science Association, 'Modelling Spatial Structures and Processes', in Kiel, Germany, 28–30 June 2012, for helpful comments.

APPENDIX A

Table A1. *Correlations in the manufacturing sector*

	(1)	(2)	(3)	(4)	(5)	(6)	(7)	(8)
East and West								
(1) TFP growth	1.00							
(2) Employment growth	−0.42	1.00						
(3) Start-up rate	0.39	−0.57	1.00					
(4) Turbulence	0.39	−0.60	0.99	1.00				
(5) Share of start-ups surviving 1 year	−0.15	0.49	−0.47	−0.53	1.00			
(6) Share of start-ups surviving 2 years	−0.21	0.53	−0.51	−0.57	0.98	1.00		
(7) Share of start-ups surviving 3 years	−0.20	0.56	−0.53	−0.58	0.97	0.99	1.00	
(8) Population density	0.16	0.11	−0.44	−0.39	−0.21	−0.21	−0.19	1.00
(9) Share highly qualified	0.41	−0.48	0.30	0.35	−0.52	−0.56	−0.57	0.43
West only								
(1) TFP growth	1.00							
(2) Employment growth	0.00	1.00						
(3) Start-up rate	−0.02	0.24	1.00					
(4) Turbulence	−0.03	0.17	0.99	1.00				
(5) Share of start-ups surviving 1 year	0.20	0.30	−0.07	−0.17	1.00			
(6) Share of start-ups surviving 2 years	0.16	0.31	−0.05	−0.15	0.97	1.00		
(7) Share of start-ups surviving 3 years	0.19	0.34	−0.05	−0.15	0.96	0.99	1.00	
(8) Population density	0.39	−0.33	−0.48	−0.40	−0.36	−0.41	−0.40	1.00
(9) Share highly qualified	0.22	−0.17	−0.43	−0.36	−0.28	−0.32	−0.31	0.76
East only								
(1) TFP growth	1.00							
(2) Employment growth	−0.13	1.00						
(3) Start-up rate	−0.35	0.28	1.00					
(4) Turbulence	−0.34	0.36	0.98	1.00				
(5) Share of start-ups surviving 1 year	0.09	−0.34	0.21	0.05	1.00			
(6) Share of start-ups surviving 2 years	0.09	−0.38	0.18	0.02	0.98	1.00		
(7) Share of start-ups surviving 3 years	0.12	−0.36	0.23	0.06	0.98	0.99	1.00	
(8) Population density	0.18	0.25	−0.33	−0.22	−0.67	−0.66	−0.65	1.00
(9) Share highly qualified	−0.12	0.36	−0.04	0.01	−0.39	−0.35	−0.35	0.67

Note: TFP, total factor productivity.

Table A2. Correlations in the service sector

	(1)	(2)	(3)	(4)	(5)	(6)	(7)	(8)
East and West								
(1) TFP growth	1.00							
(2) Employment growth	–0.59	1.00						
(3) Start-up rate	0.56	–0.60	1.00					
(4) Turbulence	0.54	–0.59	0.99	1.00				
(5) Share of start-ups surviving 1 year	–0.62	0.77	–0.76	–0.75	1.00			
(6) Share of start-ups surviving 2 years	–0.60	0.75	–0.75	–0.76	0.97	1.00		
(7) Share of start-ups surviving 3 years	–0.59	0.75	–0.76	–0.76	0.95	0.99	1.00	
(8) Population density	–0.29	0.11	–0.32	–0.29	0.08	0.01	–0.02	1.00
(9) Share highly qualified	0.38	–0.48	0.43	0.42	–0.54	–0.54	–0.56	0.43
West only								
(1) TFP growth	1.00							
(2) Employment growth	–0.13	1.00						
(3) Start-up rate	–0.02	0.14	1.00					
(4) Turbulence	–0.01	0.09	0.99	1.00				
(5) Share of start-ups surviving 1 year	–0.11	0.33	–0.20	–0.27	1.00			
(6) Share of start-ups surviving 2 years	–0.15	0.40	–0.30	–0.37	0.90	1.00		
(7) Share of start-ups surviving 3 years	–0.15	0.44	–0.32	–0.38	0.82	0.97	1.00	
(8) Population density	–0.17	–0.33	–0.22	–0.17	–0.37	–0.39	–0.43	1.00
(9) Share highly qualified	–0.07	–0.17	–0.09	–0.06	–0.17	–0.21	–0.25	0.76
East only								
(1) TFP growth	1.00							
(2) Employment growth	0.04	1.00						
(3) Start-up rate	0.17	0.01	1.00					
(4) Turbulence	0.07	0.04	0.98	1.00				
(5) Share of start-ups surviving 1 year	0.09	0.24	–0.16	–0.30	1.00			
(6) Share of start-ups surviving 2 years	0.37	0.08	0.03	–0.15	0.89	1.00		
(7) Share of start-ups surviving 3 years	0.41	–0.03	–0.05	–0.24	0.85	0.96	1.00	
(8) Population density	–0.21	0.25	–0.21	–0.09	–0.05	–0.23	–0.27	1.00
(9) Share highly qualified	0.34	0.36	–0.10	–0.08	0.15	0.16	0.12	0.67

Note: TFP, total factor productivity.

Table A3. Descriptive statistics of the dependent and independent variables

	2001–07		1994–2000				
	Employment growth	TFP growth	Start-up rate[a]	Share of firms surviving[b]	Turbulence[c]	Population density	Share highly qualified
Manufacturing							
East only							
Minimum	−1.55	4.68	0.15	40.09	0.27	15.68	5.53
Maximum	0.41	7.55	0.24	58.82	0.43	1321.29	15.08
Mean	–0.68	6.02	0.18	52.21	0.32	105.18	9.66
Median	–0.76	5.98	0.18	51.73	0.32	42.87	9.44
CV	–0.70	0.15	0.13	0.08	0.12	2.60	0.22
West only							
Minimum	–0.44	3.81	0.06	51.59	0.11	21.48	2.89
Maximum	2.15	7.61	0.15	70.46	0.25	994.21	13.73
Mean	0.67	4.89	0.10	61.20	0.18	117.97	5.90
Median	0.66	4.77	0.10	60.74	0.18	65.52	5.36
CV	0.74	0.16	0.18	0.08	0.18	1.31	0.37
Services							
East only							
Minimum	−1.55	2.45	0.59	52.24	1.01	15.68	5.53
Maximum	0.41	3.36	0.82	57.99	1.37	1321.29	15.08
Mean	–0.68	2.98	0.69	55.30	1.18	105.18	9.66
Median	–0.76	3.03	0.68	55.20	1.17	42.87	9.44
CV	–0.70	0.08	0.09	0.03	0.08	2.60	0.22

(Continued)

Table A3. Continued

	2001–07		1994–2000				
	Employment growth	TFP growth	Start-up rate[a]	Share of firms surviving[b]	Turbulence[c]	Population density	Share highly qualified
West only							
Minimum	–0.44	0.97	0.33	57.35	0.57	21.48	2.89
Maximum	2.15	3.25	0.64	63.12	1.16	994.21	13.73
Mean	0.67	2.20	0.45	60.30	0.80	117.97	5.90
Median	0.66	2.13	0.44	60.38	0.78	65.52	5.36
CV	0.74	0.14	0.15	0.03	0.16	1.31	0.37

Note: CV, coefficient of variation.

Table A4. Ordinary least squares (OLS) estimates for total factor productivity (TFP) growth manufacturing

	(1)	(2)	(3)	(4)	(5)	(6)
West and East						
Start-up rate (ln)	0.188	0.191	0.194			
	(0.129)	(0.126)	(0.125)			
Turbulence rate (ln)				0.177	0.180	0.187
				(0.120)	(0.116)	(0.115)
Share of firms surviving a minimum of 1 year (ln)	1.731***			1.781***		
	(0.405)			(0.425)		
Share of firms surviving a minimum of 2 years (ln)		1.105***			1.138***	
		(0.292)			(0.301)	
Share of firms surviving a minimum of 3 years (ln)			0.906***			0.936***
			(0.213)			(0.220)
Population density (ln)	0.134***	0.139***	0.142***	0.131***	0.137***	0.140***
	(0.044)	(0.043)	(0.042)	(0.043)	(0.042)	(0.041)
Share of university graduates (ln)	–0.077	–0.079	–0.079	–0.078	–0.080	–0.081
	(0.073)	(0.072)	(0.071)	(0.073)	(0.071)	(0.070)
Dummy: Region in East Germany	0.312**	0.334**	0.352**	0.317**	0.339**	0.356**
	(0.134)	(0.140)	(0.136)	(0.128)	(0.134)	(0.131)
Constant	−6.016***	−3.131**	−2.183**	−6.350***	−3.385**	−2.417**
	(1.812)	(1.325)	(0.958)	(1.879)	(1.335)	(0.958)
Number of regions	96	96	96	96	96	96
R^2 (adjusted)	0.470	0.467	0.486	0.467	0.464	0.484
Mean VIF	3.58	3.71	3.74	3.63	3.76	3.78
Only West						
Start-up rate (ln)	0.308*	0.314*	0.321**			
	(0.147)	(0.142)	(0.139)			
Turbulence rate (ln)				0.280*	0.285*	0.296**
				(0.138)	(0.132)	(0.130)
Share of firms surviving a minimum of 1 year (ln)	1.831***			1.892***		
	(0.380)			(0.427)		
Share of firms surviving a minimum of 2 years (ln)		1.212***			1.250***	
		(0.265)			(0.294)	
Share of firms surviving a minimum of 3 years (ln)			0.981***			1.016***
			(0.196)			(0.218)
Population density (ln)	0.158***	0.163***	0.166***	0.151***	0.157***	0.160***
	(0.045)	(0.045)	(0.044)	(0.044)	(0.044)	(0.043)
Share of university graduates (ln)	–0.057	–0.055	–0.054	–0.060	–0.058	–0.057
	(0.061)	(0.059)	(0.059)	(0.061)	(0.060)	(0.060)
Constant	−6.313***	−3.441**	−2.342**	−6.772***	−3.800**	−2.683**
	(1.640)	(1.176)	(0.843)	(1.844)	(1.272)	(0.913)
Number of regions	74	74	74	74	74	74
R^2 (adjusted)	0.393	0.388	0.415	0.377	0.372	0.401
Mean VIF	1.97	2.02	2.01	1.95	2.00	2.00

Notes: $*p < 0.05$, $**p < 0.01$, $***p < 0.001$. Standard errors are given in parentheses.
VIF, variance inflation factor.

Table A5. Ordinary least squares (OLS) estimates for total factor productivity (TFP) growth services

	(1)	(2)	(3)	(4)	(5)	(6)
West and East						
Start-up rate (ln)	−0.104	−0.134	−0.154			
	(0.154)	(0.165)	(0.166)			
Turbulence rate (ln)				−0.092	−0.126	−0.146
				(0.144)	(0.157)	(0.156)
Share of firms surviving a minimum of 1 year (ln)	−1.893			−1.930		
	(1.469)			(1.500)		
Share of firms surviving a minimum of 2 years (ln)		−1.551			−1.611	
		(1.192)			(1.236)	
Share of firms surviving a minimum of 3 years (ln)			−1.307			−1.355
			(0.947)			(0.971)
Population density (ln)	−0.069	−0.078	−0.082	−0.068	−0.077	−0.081
	(0.053)	(0.057)	(0.059)	(0.052)	(0.057)	(0.058)
Share of University graduates (ln)	0.109	0.118	0.120	0.107	0.117	0.118
	(0.075)	(0.077)	(0.076)	(0.074)	(0.077)	(0.075)
Dummy: Region in East Germany	0.169	0.164	0.161	0.161	0.154	0.150
	(0.129)	(0.130)	(0.135)	(0.129)	(0.130)	(0.136)
Constant	9.084	7.354	6.163	9.306	7.683	6.445
	(6.431)	(5.071)	(3.940)	(6.601)	(5.304)	(4.085)
Number of regions	96	96	96	96	96	96
R^2 (adjusted)	0.516	0.521	0.524	0.515	0.520	0.524
Mean VIF	4.29	4.20	4.22	4.16	4.10	4.14
Only West						
Start-up rate (ln)	−0.174	−0.256	−0.291			
	(0.194)	(0.217)	(0.215)			
Turbulence rate (ln)				−0.154	−0.242	−0.272
				(0.180)	(0.206)	(0.201)
Share of firms surviving a minimum of 1 year (ln)	−3.824			−3.875		
	(2.690)			(2.764)		
Share of firms surviving a minimum of 2 years (ln)		−3.262*			−3.372*	
		(1.708)			(1.793)	
Share of firms surviving a minimum of 3 years (ln)			−2.673*			−2.741*
			(1.261)			(1.307)
Population density (ln)	−0.094	−0.110	−0.120	−0.092	−0.109	−0.118
	(0.091)	(0.089)	(0.091)	(0.090)	(0.089)	(0.091)
Share of university graduates (ln)	0.113	0.122	0.127	0.111	0.121	0.125
	(0.113)	(0.107)	(0.107)	(0.113)	(0.107)	(0.107)
Constant	17.576	14.612*	11.802*	17.899	15.220*	12.243*
	(11.821)	(7.260)	(5.241)	(12.210)	(7.707)	(5.516)
Number of regions	74	74	74	74	74	74
R^2 (adjusted)	0.104	0.147	0.162	0.100	0.144	0.159
Mean VIF	2.05	2.16	2.26	2.06	2.19	2.28

Notes: $*p < 0.05$, $**p < 0.01$, $***p < 0.001$ Standard errors are given in parentheses.
VIF, variance inflation factor.

Table A6. Ordinary least squares (OLS) estimates for employment growth manufacturing

	(1)	(2)	(3)	(4)	(5)	(6)
West and East						
Start-up rate (ln)	0.241**	0.234*	0.241*			
	(0.111)	(0.115)	(0.114)			
Turbulence rate (ln)				0.212*	0.202*	0.212*
				(0.102)	(0.105)	(0.105)
Share of firms surviving a minimum of 1 year (ln)	0.535			0.577		
	(0.338)			(0.337)		
Share of firms surviving a minimum of 2 years (ln)		0.259			0.281	
		(0.241)			(0.241)	
Share of firms surviving a minimum of 3 years (ln)			0.260			0.283
			(0.189)			(0.190)
Population density (ln)	–0.010	–0.012	–0.008	–0.015	–0.017	–0.013
	(0.047)	(0.048)	(0.047)	(0.046)	(0.047)	(0.047)
Share of university graduates (ln)	0.062	0.061	0.061	0.059	0.059	0.058
	(0.087)	(0.087)	(0.087)	(0.090)	(0.091)	(0.090)
Dummy: Region in East Germany	–0.619***	–0.618***	–0.609***	–0.604***	–0.602***	–0.594***
	(0.081)	(0.083)	(0.082)	(0.082)	(0.085)	(0.083)
Constant	–0.551	0.687	0.714	–0.898	0.430	0.458
	(1.439)	(0.955)	(0.720)	(1.431)	(0.957)	(0.720)
Number of regions	96	96	96	96	96	96
R^2 (adjusted)	0.654	0.652	0.654	0.650	0.647	0.650
Mean VIF	3.58	3.71	3.74	3.63	3.76	3.78
Only West						
Start-up rate (ln)	0.152	0.157	0.165			
	(0.115)	(0.121)	(0.122)			
Turbulence rate (ln)				0.116	0.121	0.132
				(0.104)	(0.110)	(0.112)
Share of firms surviving a minimum of 1 year (ln)	0.867***			0.862***		
	(0.199)			(0.212)		
Share of firms surviving a minimum of 2 years (ln)		0.592***			0.587***	
		(0.162)			(0.176)	
Share of firms surviving a minimum of 3 years (ln)			0.510***			0.512***
			(0.127)			(0.140)
Population density (ln)	–0.051	–0.048	–0.045	–0.057	–0.054	–0.051
	(0.035)	(0.037)	(0.036)	(0.034)	(0.036)	(0.034)
Share of university graduates (ln)	0.086	0.088	0.088	0.083	0.084	0.085
	(0.080)	(0.079)	(0.077)	(0.083)	(0.081)	(0.080)
Constant	−2.072**	–0.786	–0.375	−2.172**	–0.891	–0.507
	(0.854)	(0.613)	(0.447)	(0.889)	(0.677)	(0.499)
Number of regions	74	74	74	74	74	74
R^2 (adjusted)	0.192	0.194	0.211	0.180	0.181	0.198
Mean VIF	1.97	2.02	2.01	1.95	2.00	2.00

Notes: *$p < 0.05$, **$p < 0.01$, ***$p < 0.001$ Standard errors are given in parentheses.
VIF, variance inflation factor.

Table A7. Ordinary least squares (OLS) estimates for employment growth services

	(1)	(2)	(3)	(4)	(5)	(6)
West and East						
Start-up rate (ln)	0.189*	0.225**	0.250**			
	(0.092)	(0.102)	(0.103)			
Turbulence rate (ln)				0.166*	0.207**	0.229**
				(0.082)	(0.092)	(0.091)
Share of firms surviving a minimum of 1 year (ln)	3.945***			4.011***		
	(1.192)			(1.216)		
Share of firms surviving a minimum of 2 years (ln)		2.717***			2.801***	
		(0.821)			(0.829)	
Share of firms surviving a minimum of 3 years (ln)			2.148***			2.204***
			(0.651)			(0.648)
Population density (ln)	−0.005	0.005	0.010	−0.008	0.003	0.007
	(0.039)	(0.042)	(0.042)	(0.039)	(0.042)	(0.042)
Share of university graduates (ln)	0.006	−0.004	−0.004	0.009	−0.002	−0.001
	(0.081)	(0.085)	(0.086)	(0.081)	(0.086)	(0.086)
Dummy: Region in East Germany	−0.360***	−0.381***	−0.387***	−0.344***	−0.363***	−0.368***
	(0.108)	(0.099)	(0.099)	(0.111)	(0.103)	(0.103)
Constant	−15.798***	−10.012**	−7.346**	−16.191***	−10.495***	−7.719**
	(5.197)	(3.421)	(2.605)	(5.332)	(3.497)	(2.636)
Number of regions	96	96	96	96	96	96
R^2 (adjusted)	0.668	0.667	0.669	0.666	0.666	0.667
Mean VIF	4.29	4.20	4.22	4.16	4.10	4.14
Only West						
Start-up rate (ln)	0.143*	0.228**	0.278**			
	(0.077)	(0.091)	(0.089)			
Turbulence rate (ln)				0.104	0.194**	0.240**
				(0.065)	(0.080)	(0.078)
Share of firms surviving a minimum of 1 year (ln)	3.376*			3.298*		
	(1.573)			(1.607)		
Share of firms surviving a minimum of 2 years (ln)		3.120**			3.121**	
		(1.003)			(1.008)	
Share of firms surviving a minimum of 3 years (ln)			2.766***			2.759***
			(0.780)			(0.790)
Population density (ln)	−0.044	−0.026	−0.012	−0.048	−0.030	−0.016
	(0.041)	(0.039)	(0.037)	(0.041)	(0.038)	(0.037)
Share of university graduates (ln)	0.033	0.022	0.013	0.038	0.026	0.017
	(0.089)	(0.080)	(0.073)	(0.090)	(0.082)	(0.076)
Constant	−13.224*	−11.622**	−9.791**	−12.965*	−11.753**	−9.919**
	(6.905)	(4.232)	(3.184)	(7.063)	(4.280)	(3.258)
Number of regions	74	74	74	74	74	74
R^2 (adjusted)	0.188	0.247	0.288	0.180	0.237	0.275
Mean VIF	2.05	2.16	2.26	2.06	2.19	2.28

Notes: $*p < 0.05$, $**p < 0.01$, $***p < 0.001$ Standard errors are given in parentheses.
VIF, variance inflation factor.

NOTES

1. For a detailed description of this dataset and the conditions of its use, see http://fdz.iab.de/en/FDZ_Establishment_Data/Establishment_History_Panel.aspx/.
2. All data used in this study are available for use by other researchers.
3. Standard-Arbeitsvolumen in den kreisfreien Städten und Landkreisen der Bundesrepublik Deutschland 1999 bis 2009, Reihe 2, Band 2. Arbeitskreis 'Erwerbstätigenrechnung des Bundes und der Länder' (see http://www.statistik-portal.de and http://www.vgrdl.de).
4. Bruttoinlandsprodukt, Bruttowertschöpfung in den kreisfreien Städten und Landkreisen Deutschlands 1992 und 1994 bis 2009, Reihe 2, Band 1. Arbeitskreis 'Volkswirtschaftliche Gesamtrechnungen der Länder' im Auftrag der Statistischen Ämter der 16 Bundesländer, des Statistischen Bundesamtes und des Bürgeramtes, Statistik und Wahlen, Frankfurt a. M. (see http://www.vgrdl.de).
5. Anlagevermögen in den Ländern und Ost-West-Großraumregionen Deutschlands 1991 bis 2009 Reihe 1, Band 4, Arbeitskreis 'Volkswirtschaftliche Gesamtrechnungen der Länder' im Auftrag der Statistischen Ämter der 16 Bundesländer, des Statistischen Bundesamtes und des Bürgeramtes, Statistik und Wahlen, Frankfurt a. M. (see http://www.vgrdl.de).
6. Arbeitnehmerentgelt, Bruttolöhne und -gehälter in den Ländern und Ost-West-Großraumregionen Deutschlands 1991 bis 2010, Reihe 1, Band 2, Arbeitskreis 'Volkswirtschaftliche Gesamtrechnungen der Länder' im Auftrag der Statistischen Ämter der 16 Bundesländer, des

Statistischen Bundesamtes und des Bürgeramtes, Statistik und Wahlen, Frankfurt a. M. (see http://www.vgrdl.de).

7. However, as demonstrated by the literature (e.g., MANJÓN-ANTOLÍN and ARAUZO-CAROD, 2008, and by the literature referred to in that study), the heterogeneity of survival rates within the service sector is much greater than it is in the manufacturing sector.

REFERENCES

ÁCS Z. J. and VARGA A. (2005) Entrepreneurship, agglomeration and technological change, *Small Business Economies* **3**, 323–334.

AGARWAL R. and GORT M. (1996) The evolution of markets and entry, exit and survival of firms, *Review of Economics and Statistics* **78**, 489–498.

AGHION P., BLUNDELL R., GRIFFITH R., HOWITT P. and PRANTL S. (2009) The effects of entry on incumbent innovation and productivity, *Review of Economics and Statistics* **91**, 20–32.

AIYAR S. and DALGAARD C.-J. (2005) *Total Factor Productivity Revised: A Dual Approach to Development Accounting.* International Monetary Fund (IMF) Staff Papers 52, pp. 82–102.

ALDRICH H. (1999) *Organizations Evolving.* Sage, London.

ANDERSSON M., BRAUNERHJELM P. and THULIN P. (2012) Creative destruction and productivity: entrepreneurship by type, sector and sequence, *Journal of Entrepreneurship and Public Policy* **1**, 125–146.

AUDRETSCH D. (1995) *Innovation and Industry Evolution.* MIT Press, Cambridge, MA.

AUDRETSCH D. B. and FRITSCH M. (1994) Creative destruction: turbulence and economic growth, in HELMSTÄDTER E. and PERLMAN M. (Eds) *Behavioral Norms, Technological Progress, and Economic Dynamics: Studies in Schumpeterian Economics*, pp. 137–150. University of Michigan Press, Ann Arbor, MI.

AUDRETSCH D. B. and FRITSCH M. (2002) Growth regimes over time and space, *Regional Studies* **36**, 113–124.

AUDRETSCH D. and KEILBACH M. (2004a) Entrepreneurship and regional growth: an evolutionary interpretation, *Journal of Evolutionary Economics* **14**, 605–616.

AUDRETSCH D. and KEILBACH M. (2004b) Entrepreneurship capital and economic performance, *Regional Studies* **38**, 949–959.

AUDRETSCH D. B., FALCK O., FELDMAN M. P. and HEBLICH S. (2012) Local entrepreneurship in context, *Regional Studies* **46**, 379–389.

BADE F.-J. and NERLINGER E. A. (2000) The spatial distribution of new technology-based firms: empirical results for West Germany, *Papers in Regional Science* **79**, 155–176.

BALDWIN J. and GORECKI P. (1991) Entry, exit and productivity growth, in GEROSKI P. and SCHWALBACH J. (Eds) *Entry and Market Contestability: An International Comparison*, pp. 244–256. Basil Blackwell, Oxford.

BAPTISTA R. and KARAÖZ M. (2011) Turbulence in growing and declining industries, *Small Business Economics* **36**, 249–270.30

BERLEMANN M. and WESSELHÖFT J.-E. (2012) Total factor productivity in German regions, *CESifo-Forum* **13**, 58–65.

BOSMA N., STAM E. and SCHUTJENS V. (2011) Creative destruction and regional productivity growth: evidence from the Dutch manufacturing and services industries, *Small Business Economics* **36**, 401–418.

BOSMA N., HESSELS J., SCHUTJENS V., PRAAG M. V. and VERHEUL I. (2012) Entrepreneurship and role models, *Journal of Economic Psychology* **33**, 410–424.

BRIXY U. and GROTZ R. (2007) Regional patterns and determinants of the success of new firms in Western Germany, *Entrepreneurship and Regional Development* **19**, 293–312.

BRIXY U., KOHAUT S. and SCHNABEL C. (2006) How fast do newly founded firms mature? Empirical analyses on job quality in start-ups, in FRITSCH M. and SCHMUDE J. (Eds) *International Studies in Entrepreneurship*, pp. 95–112. Springer, Berlin.

BRIXY U., STERNBERG R. and STÜBER H. (2013) Why some nascent entrepreneurs do not seek professional assistance, *Applied Economic Letters* **20**, 157–161. Online first: http://dx.doi.org/10.1080/13504851.2012.684783

BYGRAVE W. and MINNITI M. (2000) The social dynamics of entrepreneurship, *Entrepreneurship Theory and Practice* **24**, 25–36.

CALIENDO M. and KRITIKOS A. (2010) Start-ups by the unemployed: characteristics, survival and direct employment effects, *Small Business Economics* **35**, 71–92.

CALLEJÓN M. and SEGARRA A. (1999) Business dynamics and efficiency in industries and regions: the case of Spain, *Small Business Economics* **13**, 253–271.

CARREE M. A. and THURIK A. R. (2008) The lag structure of the impact of business ownership on economic performance in OECD countries, *Small Business Economics* **30**, 101–110.

CARROLL G. R. and HANNAN M. T. (2000) *The Demography of Corporations and Industries.* Princeton University Press, Princeton, NJ.

CAVES R. E. (1998) Industrial organization and new findings on the turnover and mobility of firms, *Journal of Economic Literature* **36**, 1947–1982.

CINGANO F. and SCHIVARDI F. (2004) Identifying the sources of local productivity growth, *Journal of the European Economic Association* **2**, 720–744.

COAD A., FRANKISH J., ROBERTS R. G. and STOREY D. J. (2013) Growth paths and survival chances: an application of Gambler's Ruin theory, *Journal of Business Venturing* **28**, 615–632.

DAVIDSSON P. (2006) Nascent entrepreneurship: empirical studies and developments, *Foundations and Trends in Entrepreneurship* **2**, 1–76.

DEJARDIN M. (2011) Linking net entry to regional economic growth, *Small Business Economics* **36**, 443–460.

DEW-BECKER I. and GORDON R. J. (2008) *The Role of Labor Market Changes in the Slowdown of European Productivity Growth.* National Bureau of Economic Research (NBER) Working Paper Series No. 13840. NBER, Cambridge, MA.

DISNEY R., HASKEL J. and HEDEN Y. (2003) Restructuring and productivity growth in UK manufacturing, *Economic Journal* **113**, 666–694.

FALCK O. (2007) Mayflies and long-distance runners: the effects of new business formation on industry growth, *Applied Economics Letters* **14**, 919–922.

FALCK O., HEBLICH S. and LUEDEMANN E. (2012) Identity and entrepreneurship: do school peers shape entrepreneurial intentions?, *Small Business Economics* **39**, 39–59.

FORBES D. P. (2005) Are some entrepreneurs more overconfident than others?, *Journal of Business Venturing* **20**, 623–640.

FOTOPOULOS G. and SPENCE N. (1998) Entry and exit from manufacturing industries: symmetry, turbulence and simultaneity – some empirical evidence from Greek manufacturing industries, 1982–1988, *Applied Economics* **30**, 245–262.

FRANKISH J. S., ROBERTS R. G., COAD A., SPEARS T. C. and STOREY D. J. (2013) Do entrepreneurs really learn? Or do they just tell us that they do?, *Industrial and Corporate Change* **22**, 73–106.

FREY J. and THALHEIMER F. (2010) *Germany – Regional GVA Inventory. Stuttgart* (available at: http://www.vgrdl.de/Arbeitskreis_VGR/DE_GVA-NUTS2_Inventory_en-EN.pdf) (accessed on 5 April 2013).

FRITSCH M. (2013) New business formation and regional development: a survey and assessment of the evidence, *Foundations and Trends in Entrepreneurship* **9**, 249–364.

FRITSCH M. and MUELLER P. (2006) The evolution of regional entrepreneurship and growth regimes, in FRITSCH M. and SCHMUDE J. (Eds) *Entrepreneurship in the Region*, pp. 225–244. Springer, New York, NY.

FRITSCH M. and NOSELEIT F. (2013a) Investigating the anatomy of the employment effect of new business formation, *Cambridge Journal of Economics* **37**, 349–377.

FRITSCH M. and NOSELEIT F. (2013b) Start-ups, long- and short-term survivors, and their contribution to employment growth, *Journal of Evolutionary Economics* **23**, 719–733.

FRITSCH M. and SCHROETER A. (2011) Why does the effect of new business formation differ across regions?, *Small Business Economics* **36**, 383–400.

FRITSCH M. and WYRWICH M. (2013) The long persistence of regional levels of entrepreneurship: Germany, 1925–2005, *Regional Studies*. DOI: 10.1080/00343404.2013.816414.

FRITSCH M., BRIXY U. and FALCK O. (2006) The effect of industry, region, and time on new business survival – a multi-dimensional analysis, *Review of Industrial Organization* **28**, 285–306.

FRITSCH M., BUBLITZ E., SORGNER A. and WYRWICH M. (Forthcoming 2013) How much of a socialist legacy? The reemergence of entrepreneurship in the East German transformation to a market economy, *Small Business Economics*.

GARTNER W. B. (1988) 'Who is an entrepreneur?' Is the wrong question, *American Journal of Small Business* **12**, 11–32.

GEROSKI P. A. (1989) Entry, innovation and productivity growth, *Review of Economics and Statistics* **71**, 572–578.

HANNAN M. T. and FREEMAN J. (1984) Structural inertia and organizational change, *American Sociological Review* **49**, 149–164.

HETHEY T. and SCHMIEDER J. F. (2010) *Using Worker Flows in the Analysis of Establishment Turnover. Evidence from German Administrative Data*. FDZ Methodenreport, 06/2010 (en), Nuremberg, 43 S.

HUFFMAN D. and QUIGLEY J. M. (2002) The role of the university in attracting high tech entrepreneurship: a silicon valley tale, *Annals of Regional Science* **36**, 403–419.

KIRCHHOFF B. A., NEWBERT S. L., IFTEKHAR H. and AZRMINGTON C. (2007) The influence of university R&D expenditures on new business formations and employment growth, *Entrepreneurship Theory and Practice* **31**, 543–559.

MANJÓN-ANTOLÍN M. C. and ARAUZO-CAROD J.-M. (2008) Firm survival: methods and evidence, *Empirica* **35**, 1–24.

MARTIN R. and SUNLEY P. (2006) Path dependence and regional economic evolution, *Journal of Economic Geography* **6**, 395–437.

MATA J. and PORTUGAL P. (1994) Life duration of new firms, *Journal of Industrial Economics* **42**, 227–245.

MINNITI M. and BYGRAVE W. (1999) The microfoundations of entrepreneurship, *Entrepreneurship Theory and Practice* **23**, 41–52.

MINNITI M. and LÉVESQUES M. (2010) Entrepreneurial types and economic growth, *Journal of Business Venturing* **25**, 305–314.

OBSCHONKA M., SCHMITT-RODERMUND E., SILBEREISEN R. K., GOSLING S. and POTTER J. (2013) The regional distribution and correlates of an entrepreneurship-prone personality profile in the United States, Germany, and the United Kingdom: a socio-ecological perspective, *Journal of Personality and Social Psychology* **105**, 104–22.

ORGANISATION FOR ECONOMIC CO-OPERATION AND DEVELOPMENT (OECD) (2001) *Measuring Productivity Measurement of Aggregate and Industry-Level Productivity Growth* (available at: http://www.oecd.org/dataoecd/59/29/2352458.pdf). DOI: 10.1787/9789264194519-en

ORGANISATION FOR ECONOMIC CO-OPERATION AND DEVELOPMENT (OECD) (2003) *The Sources of Economic Growth in OECD Countries* (available at: http://www.oecd-ilibrary.org/economics/the-sources-of-economic-growth-in-oecd-countries_9789264199460-en). DOI: 10.1787/9789264199460-en

PARKER S. C. (2009) *The Economics of Entrepreneurship*. Cambridge University Press, Cambridge.

PIERGIOVANNI R., CARREE M. and SANTARELLI E. (2012) Creative industries, new business formation, and regional economic growth, *Small Business Economics* **39**, 539–560.

RENSKI H. (2011) External economies of localization, urbanization and industrial diversity and new firm survival, *Papers in Regional Science* **90**, 473–502.

REYNOLDS P. D. (2011) New firm creation: a global assessment of national, contextual, and individual factors, *Foundations and Trends in Entrepreneurship* **6**, 315–496.

ROMER P. M. (1990) Endogenous technological change, *Journal of Political Economy* **98**, 571–602.

ROMER P. M. (1994) The origins of endogenous growth, *Journal of Economic Perspectives* **8**, 3–23.

ROTGER G. P., GØRTZ M. and STOREY D. J. (2012) Assessing the effectiveness of guided preparation for new venture creation and performance: theory and practice, *Journal of Business Venturing* **27**, 506–521.

Schenkel M. T., Matthews C. H. and Ford M. W. (2009) Making rational use of 'irrationality'? Exploring the role of need for cognitive closure in nascent entrepreneurial activity, *Entrepreneurship and Regional Development* **21**, 51–76.

Schindele Y. and Weyh A. (2011) The direct employment effects of new businesses in Germany revisited: an empirical investigation for 1976–2004, *Small Business Economics* **36**, 353–363.

Schumpeter J. A. (1912) *Theorie der wirtschaftlichen Entwicklung*. Leipzig.

Schumpeter J. A. (1942/1994) *Capitalism, Socialism and Democracy*. Duncker & Humblodt; Routledge, New York, NY.

Seri P. (2010) Obstacles in regional renewing processes: the role of relational inertia in mature Italian industrial districts. Paper presented at the Danish Research Unit for Industrial Dynamics/Dynamics of Institutions & Markets in Europe (DRUID/DIME) Academy Winter 2010, 18. Aalborg, Denmark.

Shane S. (2009) Why encouraging more people to become entrepreneurs is bad public policy, *Small Business Economics* **33**, 141–149.

Shaver K. G. (1995) The entrepreneurial personality myth, *Business and Economic Review* **41**, 20–23.

Simon M., Houghton S. M. and Aquino K. (2000) Cognitive biases, risk perception, and venture formation: how individuals decide to start companies, *Journal of Business Venturing* **15**, 113–134.

Stanworth J., Stanworth C., Granger B. and Blyth S. (1989) Who becomes an entrepreneur?, *International Small Business Journal* **8**, 11–22.

Sternberg R. (2009) Regional dimensions of entrepreneurship, *Foundations and Trends in Entrepreneurship* **5**, 211–340.

Vivarelli M. (2013) Is entrepreneurship necessarily good? Microeconomic evidence from developed and developing countries, *Industrial and Corporate Change* **22**, 1453–1495.

Wiegmann J. (2003) *Entwicklung der totalen Faktorproduktivität (TFP) nach Wirtschaftszweigen in der Bundesrepublik Deutschland 1992–2000*. Deutsches Institut für Wirtschaftsforschung, Berlin.

Spatial Determinants of Entrepreneurship in India

EJAZ GHANI*, WILLIAM R. KERR† and STEPHEN O'CONNELL‡
*The World Bank, NW, Washington, DC, USA.
†Harvard University, Bank of Finland, and National Bureau of Economic Research (NBER), Rock Center 212, Harvard Business School, Boston, MA, USA.
‡The World Bank and City University of New York (CUNY) Graduate Center, New York, NY, USA

GHANI E., KERR W. R. and O'CONNELL S. Spatial determinants of entrepreneurship in India, *Regional Studies*. The spatial determinants of entrepreneurship in India in the manufacturing and services sectors are analysed. Among general district traits, the quality of the physical infrastructure and workforce education are the strongest predictors of entry, with labour laws and household banking access also playing important roles. Extensive evidence is also found of agglomeration economies among manufacturing industries. In particular, supportive incumbent industrial structures for input and output markets are strongly linked to higher establishment entry rates. In comparison with the United States, regional conditions in India play a stronger relative role for the spatial patterns of entrepreneurship compared with incumbent industry locations.

Entrepreneurship Agglomeration Development India South Asia

GHANI E., KERR W. R. and O'CONNELL S. 印度创业精神的空间决定因素，*区域研究*。本研究分析印度在製造业与服务业部门中，企业创业精神的空间决定因素。在一般的行政区特徵中，实质基础建设的质量与劳动力教育水平最能有效预测企业进入，而劳动法规与家户取得银行业务的渠道亦扮演了重要的角色。製造业中亦发现了聚集经济的大量证据。特别是投入与产出市场的当前支持性产业结构，与较高的创立进入率显着相关。与美国相较而言，印度的区域条件与目前的产业地点相较之下，在创业的空间模式上扮演了相对重要的角色。

创业精神 聚集 发展 印度 南亚

GHANI E., KERR W. R. et O'CONNELL S. Les déterminants spatiaux de l'esprit d'entreprise en Inde, *Regional Studies*. On analyse les déterminants spatiaux de l'esprit d'entreprise en Inde dans les secteurs de la fabrication et des services. Parmi les caractéristiques générales des districts, la qualité de l'infrastructure physique et de la formation professionnelle sont les meilleurs indicateurs de l'entrée, alors que le droit du travail et l'accès des ménages aux services bancaires jouent également un rôle important. Il s'avère aussi de nombreuses preuves des économies d'agglomération dans le secteur de la fabrication. En particulier, les structures d'appui industrielles établies pour les marchés amont et aval sont fortement liées à des taux d'entrée plus élevés des entreprises. Par rapport aux États-Unis, les conditions régionales en Inde jouent un rôle relatif plus fort pour ce qui est des structures spatiales de l'esprit d'entreprise par comparaison avec les emplacements industriels établis.

Esprit d'entreprise Agglomération Développement Inde Asie du Sud

GHANI E., KERR W. R. und O'CONNELL S. Räumliche Determinanten des Unternehmertums in Indien, *Regional Studies*. Wiranalysieren die räumlichen Determinanten des Unternehmertums im Produktions- und Dienstleistungssektor von Indien. Unter den generellen Merkmalen der Bezirke sind die Qualität der physischen Infrastruktur sowie der Bildungsgrad der Arbeitnehmer die stärksten Prädiktoren für Firmengründungen; die Arbeitsgesetze und die Verfügbarkeit von Haushaltsbanken spielen ebenfalls eine wichtige Rolle. Darüber hinaus finden wir unter den produzierenden Branchen umfangreiche Belege für Agglomerationsökonomien. Insbesondere besteht eine starke Verbindung zwischen den vorhandenen unterstützenden Branchenstrukturen für Input-und Outputmärkte und einem höheren Anteil an Unternehmensgründungen. Bei einem Vergleich mit den vorhandenen Branchenstandorten spielen die regionalen Bedingungen in Indien verglichen mit den USA eine größere relative Rolle für die räumlichen Muster des Unternehmertums.

Unternehmertum Agglomeration Entwicklung Indien Südasien

GHANI E., KERR W. R. y O'CONNELL S. Determinantes espaciales del empresariado en India, *Regional Studies*. En este artículo analizamos los determinantes espaciales del empresariado en los sectores de producción y servicios de India. Entre las características generales de las comarcas, la calidad de la infraestructura física y la educación de la mano de obra son los determinantes más importantes para predecir la creación de empresas, siendo las leyes laborales y la disponibilidad de servicios bancarios a hogares también factores muy importantes. Observamos asimismo pruebas extensas de economías de aglomeración entre las industrias de producción. En particular, las estructuras industriales establecidas y de apoyo para los mercados de insumos y productos están muy vinculadas a índices más altos en la creación de nuevas empresas. En comparación con los Estados Unidos, las condiciones regionales en India desempeñan un papel relativo más importante en los patrones espaciales del empresariado en comparación con las ubicaciones industriales establecidas.

Empresariado Aglomeración Desarrollo India Asia meridional

INTRODUCTION

Many policy-makers want to encourage entrepreneurship given its perceived role in economic growth and development.[1] The importance of this factor has led to extensive recent research on regional traits associated with entrepreneurship. Multiple studies consider advanced economies, but there is very little empirical evidence for developing countries. This lack of research hampers the effectiveness of policy: for example, the roles that education or infrastructure play in entry in the United States may be quite different from a setting where illiteracy and lack of roads and sanitation continue to hamper development.

AUDRETSCH *et al.* (2012) emphasize the local nature of entrepreneurship determinants. These questions are investigated for manufacturing and services in India in the present paper. Within these two industry groups, the organized and unorganized sectors are also compared. The traits of districts that systematically predict stronger entry levels are quantified. Several important themes emerge from the study. First, education levels and local infrastructure access are the most prominent local traits linked to entrepreneurship across all sectors. Second, local industrial conditions – the links that form across industries within a district – play an even stronger role in predicting entry within specific district–industries than the general district-level traits. Finally, in comparison with the United States, it is found that India's economic geography is still taking shape. At such an early point and with industrial structures not entrenched, there is room for policy to have substantial impact by shaping where industries plant their roots.

The study makes several contributions to the literature. It is among the first to quantify the spatial determinants of entrepreneurship in India. Moreover, it moves beyond manufacturing to consider services, and compares the organized and unorganized sectors. The latter analyses of the unorganized sector are among the most important contributions given the limited study of the informal economy previously and its substantial importance for India and other developing economies. More broadly, it is among the first studies to apply the incumbent industrial structures frameworks of GLAESER and KERR (2009) to a developing economy, providing insights into how agglomeration economies resemble and differ from each other. More research on agglomeration economies and entrepreneurship in developing countries is important for urban and development economics going forward.[2]

Identifying local conditions that encourage entrepreneurship and acting upon them is essential to foster economic growth. Fig. 1 shows that entrepreneurship rates are lower in South Asia than what its stage of development would suggest. Effective entrepreneurship will play a key role in job growth for India, the development of a strong manufacturing base (FERNANDES and PAKES, 2010), and the transition of people out of subsistence living and the informal sector. KHANNA (2008) emphasizes entrepreneurship for India's future, and reallocation can help close India's productivity gap (e.g., HSIEH and KLENOW, 2009).[3]

SPATIAL ENTREPRENEURSHIP RATES IN INDIA

Entrepreneurship is measured as the presence of young establishments. The primary measure, which can consistently be observed across all the datasets, is whether an establishment is less than three years old. For the organized manufacturing sector, establishments in their first year of existence can also be measured, and very similar results are found with this approach. Incumbent establishments, which are used to model existing activity in the district–industry, are firms that are three or more years old. Entry measures are principally defined through employment in young establishments, and counts of entering establishments are looked at in robustness checks.[4]

Establishment-level surveys of manufacturing and service enterprises carried out by the Government of India are employed. The manufacturing data are taken from surveys conducted in fiscal years 2005–06; services sector data come from 2001–02. While these surveys were conducted over two fiscal years, this paper refers to the initial year only. An unpublished appendix (which is available from the authors upon request) lists data sources and years employed, and additional information included in it is described below. NATARAJ (2009), KATHURIA *et al.* (2010), HASAN and JANDOC (2010), and DEHEJIA and PANAGARIYA (2010) provide detailed overviews of similar databases.

The distinction between organized and unorganized sectors relates to establishment size. In manufacturing, the organized sector is comprised of establishments with more than ten workers if the establishment uses

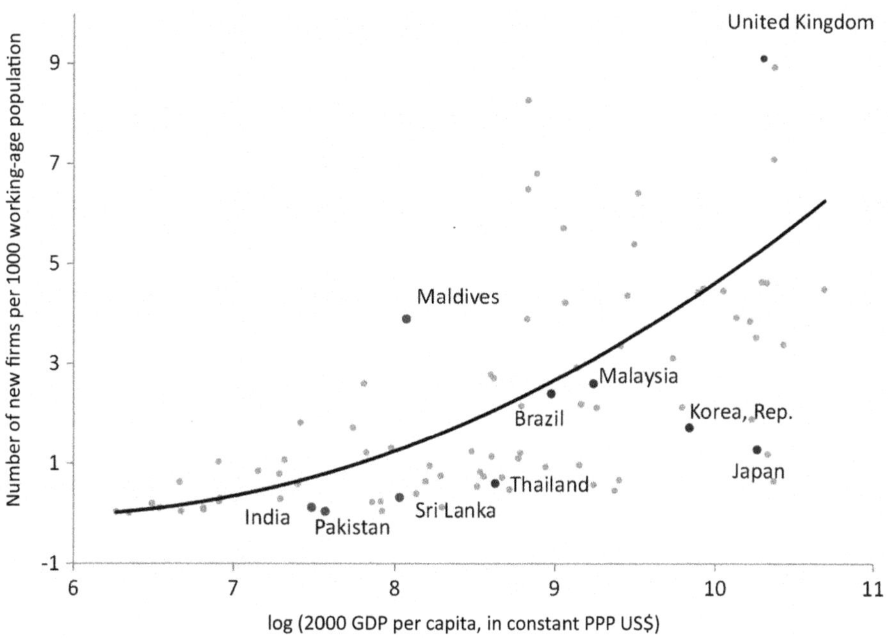

Fig. 1. Business registration density, 2008

Note: Countries designated as offshore tax shelters are excluded. Eighty-seven countries are shown

Sources: World Bank Group Entrepreneurship Survey, 2010; and World Development Indicators, 2010

electricity. If the establishment does not use electricity, the threshold is 20 workers or more. These establishments are required to register under the Factories Act of 1948. The unorganized manufacturing sector is, by default, comprised of establishments that fall outside the scope of the Factories Act.

Service establishments, regardless of size or other characteristics, are not required to register and thus are all officially unorganized. There are various approaches to differentiate comparably small-scale, autonomous establishments from the larger employers that constitute the organized sector, as generally defined. Services establishments with fewer than five workers and/or listed as an 'own-account enterprise' (OAE) are assigned to the unorganized sector. OAE enterprises are firms that do not employ any hired worker on a regular basis. The choice of five employees as the size cut-off recognizes that average establishment size in services is significantly smaller than in manufacturing. Using this demarcation, the organized sector makes up approximately 25% of employment in both manufacturing and services.

The organized manufacturing sector is surveyed by the Central Statistical Organisation (CSO) every year through the Annual Survey of Industries (ASI), while unorganized manufacturing and services establishments are separately surveyed by the National Sample Survey Organisation (NSSO) at approximately five-year intervals. Establishments are surveyed with state and four-digit National Industry Classification (NIC) stratification. For organized manufacturing, the business register described above forms the basis for the sampling frame. Establishments are notified if they fall into the sampled frame and are required by law to complete and return the survey questionnaire; the CSO investigates cases of non-response (typically closed plants). For the services and unorganized manufacturing sector, India's Economic Census comprises the basis for the sampling frame and stratification procedures. Establishments falling into the sample are then surveyed by government enumerators.[5]

The survey years used are the most recent data by sector for which the young establishment identifiers are recorded. The provided sample weights are used to construct population-level estimates of total establishments and employment by district and three-digit NIC industry. Employment is formally defined as 'persons engaged' and includes working owners, family and casual labour, and salaried employees.

Districts are administrative subdivisions of Indian states or territories. Currently there are approximately 630 districts spread across 35 states/union territories. Districts with a population less than 1 million (based on the 2001 Census) or with fewer than 50 establishments sampled are excluded. These small districts are excluded because limited sampling makes the data of limited value for the study (given that district–industry conditions that separate young and incumbent establishments need to be evaluated). States that experienced ongoing conflict and political turmoil during the period of study are also excluded. After these adjustments, the resulting sample retains districts in 20 major states that include more than 94% of Indian employment in both manufacturing and services.

Table 1 provides descriptive statistics; Figs 2 and 3 show spatial entry patterns; and the unpublished

Table 1. Local industrial conditions for Indian entrepreneurship

	Mean	SD	Median	Minimum	Maximum	Mean	SD	Median	Minimum	Maximum
District traits										
District population (n)	2 972 828	1 731 997	3 207 232	1 021 573	13 900 000					
District population density (persons/km^2)	810	2477	480	35	24 963					
Share of the population with a graduate education (%)	5.9	2.7	6.2	1.7	19.3					
Demographic dividend for a district (age profile)	1.32	0.26	1.41	0.92	2.12					
Index of infrastructure quality for a district	2.93	0.76	3.34	0.00	4.00					
Strength of household banking environment	0.35	0.13	0.38	0.09	0.73					
Stringency of labour laws: adjustments (state level)	0.69	0.84	0.00	0.00	3.00					
Stringency of labour laws: disputes (state level)	−0.41	1.24	0.00	−3.00	3.00					
Proximity to India's ten largest cities (minimum driving)	446	240	396	0	1020					
Consumption per capita (year 2005 US$ at purchasing power parity (PPP))	680	186	625	352	1397					
	Organized sector					Unorganized sector				
Industrial traits – manufacturing										
Total employment in district–industry	1383	5020	337	2	215 611	4517	15 389	831	1	422 193
Start-up employment in district–industry	151	788	0	0	28 576	553	2938	0	0	96 647
Labour market strength	0.09	0.13	0.05	0.00	0.97	0.09	0.11	0.04	0.00	0.97
Input/supplier strength	−1.64	0.25	−1.69	−2.00	−0.05	−1.71	0.24	−1.76	−2.00	−0.05
Chinitz index of small suppliers	0.48	1.33	0.25	0.00	45.52	n.a.	n.a.	n.a.	n.a.	n.a.
Output/customer strength (×10 for presentation)	0.01	0.02	0.03	0.00	7.64	0.01	0.02	0.00	0.00	0.97
Industrial traits – services										
Total employment in district–industry	1761	5892	400	3	173 293	2885	8145	376	1	195 863
Start-up employment in district–industry	268	1429	0	0	47 048	502	1581	46	0	50 243

Notes: Descriptive statistics are based on the Annual Survey of Industries and the National Sample Survey, various rounds.
n.a., Not applicable; SD, standard deviation.

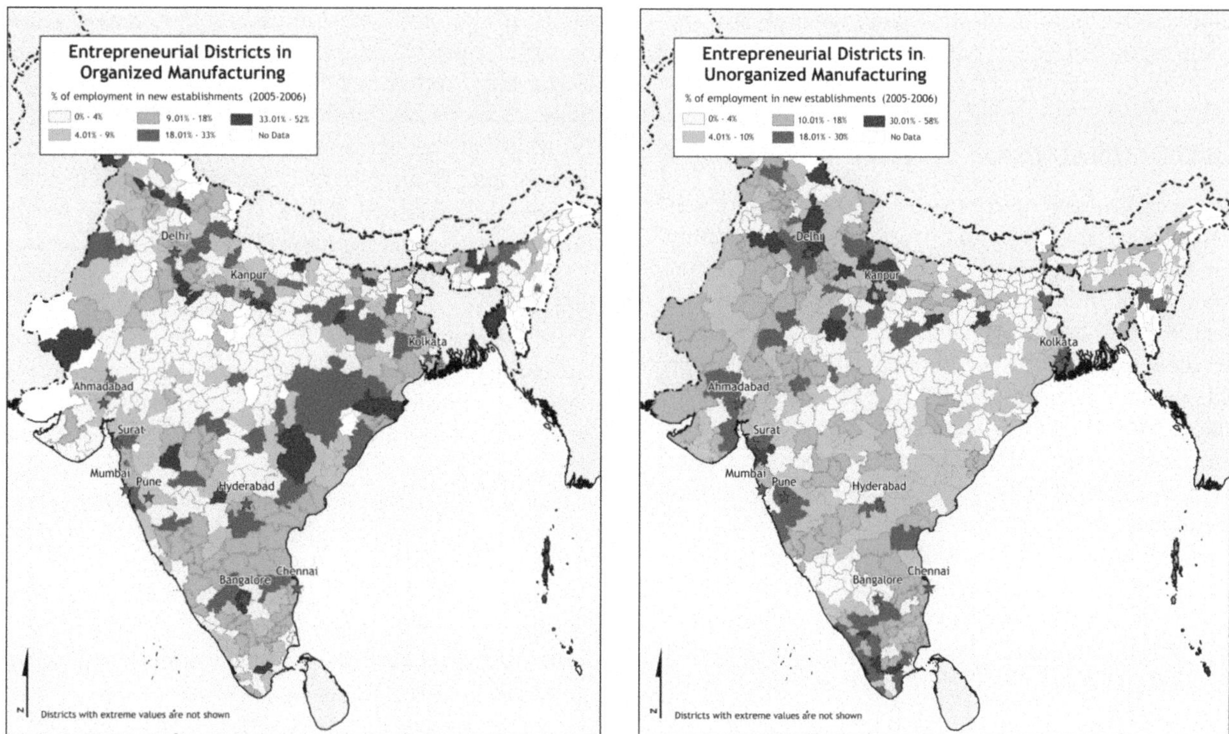

Fig. 2. Indian manufacturing entry rates, 2005–06

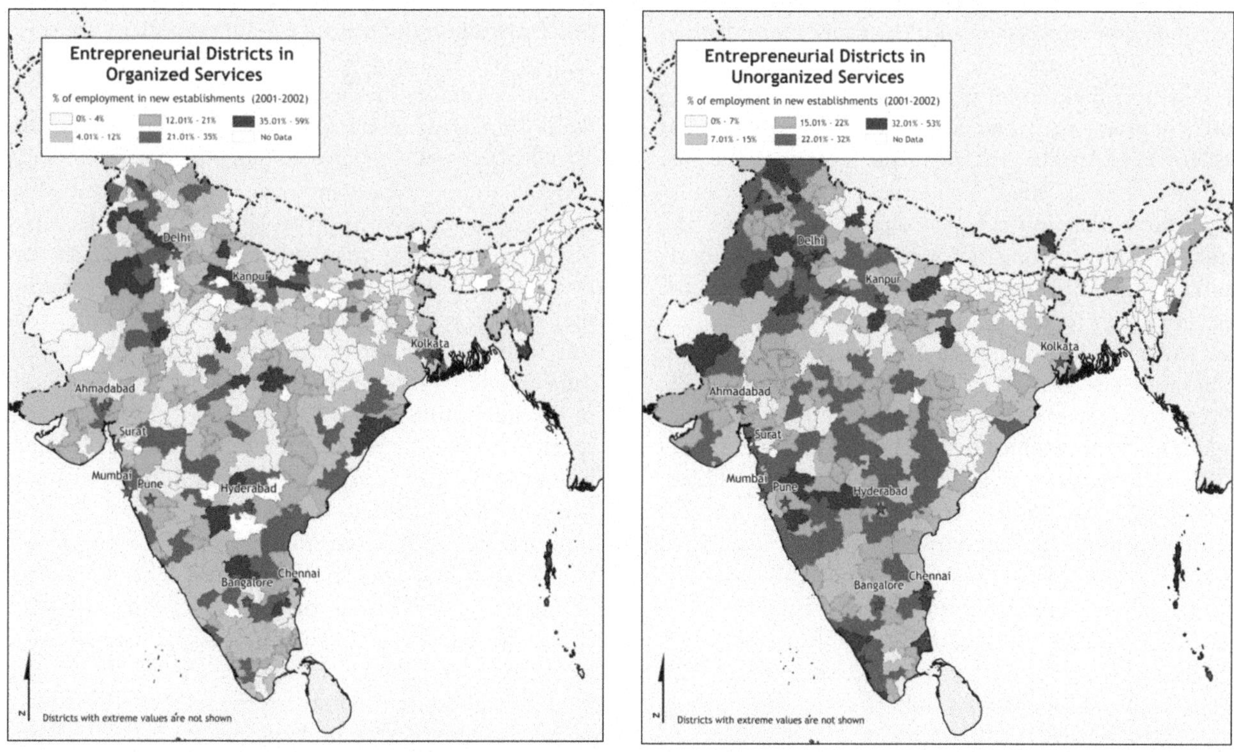

Fig. 3. Indian services entry rates, 2001–02

appendix offers additional tabulations by state. Entry rates, as a weighted average across all states, are 15% and 12% for organized and unorganized manufacturing, respectively. The entry rates are 20% for organized services and 17% for unorganized services. The spatial entry rates for organized and unorganized sectors have –0.2 and 0.3 correlations across states for manufacturing and services, respectively. VAN STEL *et al.* (2007)

emphasize the need to measure entry determinants separately across different types of entrepreneurs.

DETERMINANTS OF ENTREPRENEURSHIP

This section now describes the spatial and industrial factors that are used to predict entrepreneurship. General traits of the district that affect all entrepreneurs, regardless of industry, are first considered. These traits include both baseline features that are longstanding and slow to adjust, like the population distribution, and factors that are more directly influenced by policy-makers, such as education and infrastructure, recognizing that deep change in education and infrastructure also takes a long time to accomplish. Second, recent research stresses the central importance of heterogeneity across industries as well as regions for explaining start-up rates (e.g., FRITSCH and FALCK, 2007; GLAESER and KERR, 2009). The second category thus develops industry-specific conditions that yield this heterogeneity within regional experiences.

District-level conditions

The initial explanatory measures focus on the basic traits of districts. It is essential to understand the effect of local area traits on entrepreneurship, especially given the disproportionate degree to which entrepreneurs found businesses in their home areas (e.g., FIGUEIREDO *et al.*, 2002; MICHELACCI and SILVA, 2007). Population is first controlled for to provide a natural baseline of economic activity (e.g., consumer markets, general availability of workers). The district's age structure, measured as the ratio of the working-age population to the non-working-age population, is then considered given that the propensity to start new firms changes over the lifetimes of individuals, and the age structure of a region often connects to local entry rates (e.g., BÖNTE *et al.*, 2009; DELFMANN *et al.*, 2013). The age profile is often called the demographic dividend in the Indian context.

Third, a measure of population density is included. Unlike the clear positive predictions for the first two factors, the prediction for population density is ambiguous as it brings higher wages and land rents alongside greater market opportunities. Density has also been linked to stronger knowledge flows, and AUDRETSCH and FRITSCH (1994) use density as one source of convexity in local production that links to entry rates. Many studies link higher population density to reduced manufacturing entry rates, especially for larger plants that use established production techniques and seek to minimize costs. DURANTON and PUGA (2001) provide a formal theoretical model of this process. Ultimately, these multiple forces suggest an uncertain theoretical role for population density in explaining Indian entry rates.

Beyond these basic demographics, five primary traits of districts are considered: education of the local labour force, quality of the local physical infrastructure, access or travel time to major Indian cities, stringency of labour laws, and household banking conditions. These traits are motivated by theoretical models of entrepreneurship and their perceived importance to India's development, and other traits and their relationships to these variables are discussed below. Unless otherwise noted, these traits are taken from the 2001 Population Census.

Several studies link entrepreneurship to educated workforces in the United States (e.g., DOMS *et al.*, 2010; GLAESER *et al.*, 2010), often with the underlying conceptual model that entrepreneurship requires a degree of creativity and handling of many tasks and ambiguous circumstances that education prepares one for (e.g., the model of LAZEAR, 2005). Entrepreneurs may also benefit from the specific development of basic business skills. On the other hand, REYNOLDS *et al.* (1994) do not find this relationship holds within every country, and GLAESER and KERR (2009) find limited evidence for a link between education and US manufacturing entrepreneurship. Thus, the literature is again ambiguous. Clarifying education's role for India is very important, as many local policy-makers stress developing the human capital of their workforces, and India is no different (AMIN and MATTOO, 2008). The general education level of a district is measured by the percentage of adults with a graduate (post-secondary) degree. The results are robust to alternative definitions such as the percentage of adults with higher secondary education.

The second trait is the physical infrastructure level of the district. Basic services such as electricity are essential for all businesses, but new entrants can be particularly dependent upon local infrastructure (e.g., established firms are better able to provision their own electricity if need be, which is quite common in India). AGHION *et al.* (2012) provide a recent theoretical model. Entrepreneurship is likely to benefit from greater infrastructure so long as the tax burden imposed to provide the infrastructure is not too high. Many observers cite upgrading India's infrastructure as a critical step towards economic growth, and the Indian government has set aside substantial investment funds. The population census documents the number of villages in a district with telecommunications access, electricity access, paved roads and safe drinking water. The percentage of villages that have infrastructure access within a district is calculated and a sum is made across the four measures to create a continuous composite metric that ranges from zero (no infrastructure access) to four (full access).

India's economy is undergoing dramatic structural changes (DESMET *et al.*, 2011). From a starting point in the 1980s when the government used licensing to promote industrial location in regions that were developing slowly, the economic geography of India has been in flux as firms and new entrants shift spatially (e.g., FERNANDES and SHARMA, 2011). One feature that is important for a district in this transformation is its link to major cities. A measure from LALL *et al.*

(2011) of the driving time to the nearest of India's ten largest cities is thus included as a measure of physical connectivity and across-district infrastructure.

Local labour regulations are next modelled using state-level policy variation. Several studies link labour regulations in India to slower economic progress (e.g., BESLEY and BURGESS, 2004; AGHION *et al.*, 2008), and BOZKAYA and KERR (2013) provide a theory model where tighter labour laws suppress entry. This effect may occur through reduced likelihood of both wanting to start a new firm or opening new facilities from a desire to avoid regulations. There may also be reduced 'push' into entrepreneurship with more protected employment positions. A composite labour regulations index by state is created from the measures constructed by AHSAN and PAGES (2007).

The final measure is the strength of the household banking environment, reflecting the large literature on financial constraints and entrepreneurship, with EVANS and JOVANOVIC (1989) being a seminal model. The percentage of households that have banking services by district is measured. This measure is likely to be particularly reflective of financing environments for unorganized sector activity.

Local industrial traits

Recent research emphasizes how local entrepreneurship varies substantially across industries, and the second set of metrics quantifies how suitable the local industrial environment is for a particular industry. The first trait is the overall employment in a district–industry for incumbent firms. This is important given that entrepreneurs often leave incumbents to start their own companies (e.g., KLEPPER, 2010; FALCK *et al.*, 2008). From this baseline, metrics are further developed that unite the broad distribution of industry employments in districts with the extent to which industries interact through the traditional agglomeration rationales (e.g., MARSHALL, 1920; DURANTON and PUGA, 2004; ROSENTHAL and STRANGE, 2004). These forces are considered within the manufacturing sector, and these conditions are modelled through incumbent firms that predate the birth of the young businesses that are modelled in the outcome variables.[6]

The first agglomeration rationale is that proximity to customers and suppliers reduces transportation costs and thereby increases productivity. This reduction in shipping costs is the core agglomerative force of New Economic Geography theory (e.g., FUJITA *et al.*, 1999). Where customers and suppliers are geographically separate, firms trade-off distances. The extent to which districts contain potential customers and suppliers for a new entrepreneur is measured. This section begins with an input–output table for India developed by the CSO. $Input_{i\leftarrow k}$ is defined as the share of industry *i*'s inputs that come from industry *k*; and $Output_{i\rightarrow k}$ is defined as the share of industry *i*'s outputs that go to industry *k*. These measures run from zero (no input or output purchasing relationship exists) to one (full dependency on the paired industry).

The quality of a district *d* is summarized in terms of its input flows for an industry *i* as:

$$Input_{di} = -\sum_{k=1,\ldots,I} \mathrm{abs}\left(Input_{i\leftarrow k} - E_{dk}/E_d\right)$$

where *I* indexes industries. This measure aggregates absolute deviations between the proportions of industrial inputs required by industry *i* and district *d*'s actual industrial composition, with *E* representing employment. The measure is mostly orthogonal to district size, which is considered separately, and a negative value is taken so that the metric ranges between negative two (i.e., no inputs available) and zero (i.e., all inputs are available in the local market in precise proportions). This metric assumes that firms have limited ability to substitute across material inputs in their production processes.

To capture the relative strength of output relationships, a consolidated metric is also defined:

$$Output_{di} = \sum_{k=1,\ldots,I} E_{dk}/E_d \cdot Output_{i\rightarrow k}$$

This metric multiplies the national share of industry *i*'s output sales that go to industry *k* with the fraction of industry *k*'s employment in district *d*. By summing across industries, a weighted average of the strength of local industrial sales opportunities for industry *i* in the focal market *d* is taken. This $Output_{di}$ measure takes on higher values with greater sales opportunities. It allows greater substitution across customer industries than the design built into the input metric, and its robustness to several design variants was tested.

Moving from material inputs, entrepreneurship is quite likely to be driven by the availability of a suitable labour force (e.g., the model of COMBES and DURANTON, 2006). While education and demographics are informative about the suitability of the local labour force, these aggregate traits miss the very specialized nature of many occupations. The working paper summarizes theories as to why specialized workers and firms agglomerate together and provides extended references. Unlike studies of advanced economies, India lacks the data to model direct occupational flows between industries. GREENSTONE *et al.* (2010) calculate from the Current Population Survey the rate at which workers move between industries in the United States. Using their measure of labour similarity for two industries, the present paper defines:

$$Labor_{di} = \sum_{k=1,\ldots,I} E_{dk}/E_d \cdot Mobility_{i\leftarrow k}$$

This metric is a weighted average of the labour similarity of industries to the focal industry *i*, with the weights being each industry's share of employment in the local district. The metric is again by construction mostly orthogonal to district size.

These metrics condense large and diverse industrial structures for cities into manageable statistics of local industrial conditions. The advantages and limitations in their design are further discussed in the working paper. Perhaps the most important issue is that these district conditions do not capture interactions with neighbouring districts, but factor and product markets can be wider than a local area. The average size of an Indian district is about the same as two US counties at 5500 km^2.

The section finally turns to a special issue regarding local firm size distribution, building upon a literature that traces back to at least the work of JOHNSON and CATHCART (1979). FRITSCH and FALCK (2007) and PARKER (2009b) emphasize the strong degree to which an industrial base populated with small firms is associated with higher entrepreneurship rates. FRITSCH and FALCK (2007) note that the relationship could descend from a greater entrepreneurial culture (HOFSTEDE, 2001; BOSCHMA and FRITSCH, 2007; FALCK *et al.*, 2011),[7] better training for entrepreneurs due to them having worked in small businesses, or perhaps a reflection of the local industry's minimum efficient plant size. PARKER (2009b) emphasizes a self-selection role by entrepreneurs. For the organized manufacturing sector, the inclusion of a measure of the local small firm share (fewer than 40 employees) is tested in estimations. While there are many reasons to believe that this pattern in advanced countries will carry over to India, there are also reasons to be doubtful. For example, Indian labour laws and size regulations have long suppressed average firm size in India compared with its peers, perhaps weakening this robust relationship evident elsewhere.

A specific variant of this effect related to customer/supplier industries is also measured. CHINITZ (1961) observes that entrepreneurs often find it difficult to work with large, vertically integrated suppliers. The entrepreneur's order sizes are too small, and often the entrepreneur's needs are non-standard. Empirical studies for the United States find the Chinitz effect very important in local start-up conditions. The Chinitz effect – as distinct from the general conditions captured in $Input_{di}$ – is quantified through a metric that essentially calculates the average firm size in a district in industries that typically supply a given industry i:

$$Chinitz_{di} = \sum_{k=1,\ldots,I} Firms_{dk}/E_d \cdot Input_{i \leftarrow k}$$

Higher values of the $Chinitz_{di}$ metric indicate better supplier conditions for entrepreneurs.

ESTIMATION APPROACH

Factors related to entry are characterized through cross-sectional regressions at the district–industry level of India. This level of variation allows analysis of both district-level determinants and the underlying heterogeneity for entrants across industries due to incumbent industrial structures. Following the above literature and conceptual notes, these specifications take the form:

$$\ln(Entry_{di}) = \eta_i + \beta \cdot X_d + \gamma \cdot Z_{di} + \varepsilon_{di}$$

The dependent variable is the log measure of entry employment by district–industry. The sample includes the district–industry observations in which positive incumbent employment exists. The observation count thus differs across manufacturing and services and for organized and unorganized sectors. Many of the explanatory variables, such as incumbent district–industry employment, are also in log values so that the coefficients estimate proportionate responses. Non-log variables are transformed to have unit standard deviation for interpretation, estimations are weighted by an interaction of log industry size with log district population, and standard errors are clustered by district to reflect the multiple mappings of district-level variables across local industries.[8]

A vector of industry fixed effects η_i is included in the estimations. These fixed effects control for systematic differences across industries in their entrepreneurship rates, competition levels, average plant sizes, and similar. As FRITSCH and FALCK (2007) demonstrate, isolating spatial variations from these industry-level traits is very important. Also, the metrics of local industrial conditions utilize both fixed traits of industries (e.g., the input–output relationships, labour flows) and the distribution of industries within a district. The inclusion of industry fixed effects controls for these fixed industry-level traits except to the extent that they interact with the local industrial structure.

The vectors X_d and Z_{di} contain district and district–industry traits, respectively. The estimation approach balances several objectives. First, given that there has been so little work on India, the aim is to provide a sufficiently broad analysis to highlight where major correlations lie in the data. In doing so, one does not want to be too parsimonious in the specifications, but the analysis should not be overloaded. The set of metrics provides a good depiction of the Indian entrepreneurial landscape, motivated by theory, and the robustness section and the unpublished appendix discuss many additional factors considered when forming this baseline.

It must be emphasized that this work measures partial correlations in the data, rather than causal parameters, reflective of the initial enquiry. In all cases, local traits are predetermined for the entrepreneurship that was measured as the outcome variable. This provides some confidence against reverse causality, and including lagged entry rates as a control variable is further tested. A second concern is omitted factors that are highly correlated with the regressors, making interpretation difficult. For example, in the baseline model, education may capture the quality of the local workforce that entrepreneurs employ, the strength of the local pool of potential entrepreneurs and/or stronger local consumer demand. Some specific checks along these lines (e.g., controlling for consumption per capita) are provided, but there will be a natural limit against checking every feasible concern. These issues are further discussed below.

EMPIRICAL RESULTS

Table 2a considers organized manufacturing. Column (1) includes just district populations, district–industry employments and industry fixed effects. The existing district–industry employment strongly shapes the spatial location of entry: a 10% increase in incumbent employment raises entry employment by around 2%. In addition, a district's population increases entry rates with an elasticity of 0.5. Higher-order population terms are not found to be statistically significant or economically important. The adjusted R^2 value for this estimation is quite modest at 0.13.

It is useful to compare these results with those evident in the United States for two reasons. First, the United States' advanced economy – and policy environment which has relatively fewer distortions – provides a useful idea of what entrepreneurship and local conditions might look like at the frontier. This is not to say that India will necessarily look like the United States when it reaches current levels of US development, just as entrepreneurship rates differ across advanced economies today. Nevertheless, in terms of broad regularities, it is very helpful to compare the India statistics against a country like the United States to provide perspective. A very well-known example in this regard is the HSIEH and KLENOW (2009) comparison of the misallocation of production across plants in India and the United States. Second, and from an academic perspective, there is a growing body of evidence and intuition on how the US economy functions with respect to entrepreneurship. The extent to which the study can identify where the Indian experience resembles or differs from the US experience provides a reasonable starting point for ascertaining which lessons from the US studies can be applied to the Indian context. The conclusions section below describes some of these lessons that do or do not apply, and hopefully this paper provides a touchstone for identifying whether lessons from future studies made of the United States or other advanced economies should be taken into account when thinking about the Indian context.

GLAESER and KERR (2009) estimate a related specification for the United States that uses long-term employment for a city–industry as the key explanatory variable. If the estimation is adjusted to match their technique more closely, an elasticity of 0.8 is obtained that is very similar to their 0.7 elasticity. While this elasticity is comparable, the R^2 value for this estimation remains quite modest at 0.29, much lower than the R^2 value of 0.80 for GLAESER and KERR (2009). There are likely several factors behind this lower explanatory power for India, including data differences, estimations at the district versus city level, and similar. These natural differences between the Indian and US data limit perfect comparison, but the datasets are believed to be sufficiently similar to make some basic inference. Most important, it is clear that many industries within India's manufacturing sector are at a much earlier development stage than those in the United States, where the manufacturing sector is instead shrinking. Thus, while existing patterns of industrial activity explain the similarity of spatial distribution of entrepreneurship in India and the United States, India has much more variation in outcomes, which are characterized further below. FERNANDES and SHARMA (2011) also study these variations with respect to policy deregulations. KATHURIA (2011) provides a broader exploratory framework.

Column (2) includes the district-level traits. Three factors stand out as discouraging entrepreneurship in organized manufacturing: high population density, strict labour regulations and the greater distance to one of India's ten biggest cities. The first pattern has been observed in many settings and reflects large manufacturers seeking cheaper environments. The second pattern connects with earlier studies of India that argue that strict labour laws reduce economic growth. These policies are associated with reduced entry even after conditioning on district–industry size. The final factor highlights that while manufacturers avoid the high costs of urban areas, they also avoid the most remote areas of India in favour of settings that are relatively near to large population centres, are likely to access customers directly or connect to shipping routes. On the other hand, the education of a district's workforce is linked to higher entry rates. The elasticity that is estimated here is stronger than that found in comparable US estimations.

Column (3) introduces district–industry traits. The roles of input and output markets are exceptionally strong with elasticities of 0.4–0.5. Both the labour market and Chinitz measures have positive coefficients. The decline in the main effect of incumbent employment suggests that these four new metrics capture the positive effects of local clusters on entry.

Column (4) shows quite similar results if one further controls for consumption per capita, per the discussion in the above section. This control, along with the population metrics, suggests that demand-side factors are not solely responsible for the positive roles that are seen for metrics such as education.

Column (5) finds similar results when examining the log count of entering establishments, with the Chinitz metric being more prominent. The paper will return

Table 2a. District entrepreneurship estimations – organized manufacturing

	Base estimation (1)	District traits (2)	Full estimation (3)	Adding consumption (4)	Using log entry count (5)
Log of incumbent employment in district–industry	0.229+++	0.186+++	–0.028	–0.030	0.032+
	(0.043)	(0.040)	(0.048)	(0.047)	(0.018)
Log of district population	0.531+++	0.483+++	0.475+++	0.482+++	0.216+++
	(0.179)	(0.155)	(0.156)	(0.161)	(0.056)
District traits					
Log of district population density		–0.569+++	–0.563+++	–0.562+++	–0.197+++
		(0.088)	(0.080)	(0.079)	(0.029)
Share of the population with graduate education		0.211+	0.235++	0.230++	0.078+
		(0.110)	(0.107)	(0.111)	(0.042)
Demographic dividend for a district (age profiles)		0.605	0.567	0.535	0.271
		(0.458)	(0.446)	(0.468)	(0.177)
Index of infrastructure quality for a district		0.018	0.096	0.086	0.015
		(0.100)	(0.094)	(0.097)	(0.038)
Strength of household banking environment		0.143	0.095	0.085	0.027
		(0.104)	(0.100)	(0.106)	(0.036)
Stringency of labour laws in a district's state		–0.210+++	–0.161++	–0.157++	–0.095+++
		(0.070)	(0.064)	(0.065)	(0.023)
Log travel time to the closest large city		–0.275+++	–0.241+++	–0.237+++	–0.091+++
		(0.090)	(0.083)	(0.083)	(0.031)
Log per capita consumption				0.152	
				(0.505)	
Local industrial conditions by incumbent firms					
Labour market strength for district–industry			0.161	0.164	0.026
			(0.102)	(0.102)	(0.041)
Inputs/supplier strength for district–industry			0.485+++	0.485+++	0.154+++
			(0.098)	(0.098)	(0.043)
Outputs/customer strength for district–industry			0.388+++	0.387+++	0.167+++
			(0.140)	(0.140)	(0.057)
Chinitz small suppliers metric for district–industry			0.279	0.279	0.337+++
			(0.213)	(0.212)	(0.129)
Industry fixed effects	Yes	Yes	Yes	Yes	Yes
Number of observations	4843	4843	4843	4843	4843
Adjusted R^2	0.128	0.166	0.218	0.218	0.279

Notes: The dependent variable is log entry employment by district–industry,

Estimations quantify the relationship between district–industry employment in new establishments and local conditions. District-level traits are taken from the 2001 Census. Industrial conditions are calculated from 2005–06 using incumbent establishments in the district–industry. Labour regulations are a composite of adjustment and disputes laws. Estimations weight observations by an interaction of district size and industry size, include industry fixed effects and cluster standard errors by district. Non-logarithm variables are transformed to have unit standard deviation for interpretation.

+++, ++ and + indicate statistical significance at the 1%, 5% and 10% levels, respectively.

Table 2b. District entrepreneurship estimations – unorganized manufacturing

	Base estimation (1)	District traits (2)	Full estimation (3)	Adding consumption (4)	Using log entry count (5)
Log of incumbent employment in district–industry	0.163+++	0.123+++	–0.075++	–0.078+++	–0.040
	(0.031)	(0.029)	(0.029)	(0.029)	(0.026)
Log of district population	1.051+++	0.878+++	1.010+++	1.025+++	0.866+++
	(0.161)	(0.157)	(0.160)	(0.153)	(0.138)
District traits					
Log of district population density		–0.019	–0.044	–0.042	–0.044
		(0.070)	(0.068)	(0.073)	(0.057)
Share of the population with graduate education		–0.002	–0.026	–0.079	–0.046
		(0.080)	(0.084)	(0.087)	(0.074)
Demographic dividend for a district (age profiles)		0.954+++	1.053+++	0.770++	0.798+++
		(0.326)	(0.330)	(0.326)	(0.285)
Index of infrastructure quality for a district		0.386+++	0.365+++	0.259++	0.325+++
		(0.096)	(0.097)	(0.104)	(0.086)
Strength of household banking environment		0.222+++	0.211+++	0.152+	0.193+++
		(0.080)	(0.080)	(0.082)	(0.071)
Stringency of labour laws in a district's state		–0.007	0.000	0.020	0.030
		(0.069)	(0.069)	(0.066)	(0.062)
Log travel time to closest large city		–0.004	0.009	0.029	0.017
		(0.069)	(0.074)	(0.074)	(0.065)
Log per capita consumption				1.191+++	
				(0.365)	
Local industrial conditions by incumbent firms					
Labour market strength for district–industry			0.263+++	0.271+++	0.228+++
			(0.075)	(0.075)	(0.067)
Inputs/supplier strength for district–industry			0.553+++	0.542+++	0.504+++
			(0.107)	(0.108)	(0.096)
Outputs/customer strength for district–industry			0.291+++	0.292+++	0.246+++
			(0.050)	(0.051)	(0.044)
Industry fixed effects	Yes	Yes	Yes	Yes	Yes
Number of observations	6451	6451	6451	6451	6451
Adjusted R^2	0.195	0.233	0.264	0.267	0.294

Notes: The dependent variable is log entry employment by district–industry.
See also Table 2a.

to this difference below when analysing the entrant size distribution.

Across these columns of Table 2a, the R^2 value increases from 0.13 to almost 0.30. While still modest, this growth in explanatory power due to modelling regional conditions is more substantial than that evident in the work of GLAESER and KERR (2009) for the United States. This pattern highlights the greater relative importance of existing district conditions relative to incumbent positioning for explaining entrepreneurship in India, which will be returned to in the conclusions.

Table 2b considers unorganized manufacturing, and several differences exist when compared with Table 2a. First, the local population plays a much greater role, with approximately unit elasticity. Entrepreneurship in the unorganized sector is much more proportionate to local market sizes than in the organized sector. This theme is also evident in the independence of entry from local population density or travel time to a major city, the stronger relationship of entry to the age profile of the district, and the higher R^2 values in columns (1) and (2). Unorganized manufacturing clearly conforms much more closely to the overall contours of India's economic geography than does organized manufacturing.

The other two district traits that are associated with strong entry rates are the strength of local, within-district physical infrastructure and the strength of local household banking environments. This contrasts with organized manufacturing entry, where education stands out. An intuitive explanation, which will also be reflected in the services estimations, is that these patterns and their differences reflect the factors on which each sector depends most. Organized manufacturing establishments have broader resources that reduce dependency on local infrastructure and household finance. Likewise, it is reasonable to believe that the unorganized sector depends less on educated workers than the organized sector. While intuitive, these results should be viewed as partial correlations until they can be rigorously confirmed in future research.

Again evidence is found for agglomeration economies within the unorganized manufacturing sector. The framework is similar to Table 2a except that the Chinitz effect is not considered, since by definition the unorganized sector is comprised of small firms. Partly as a consequence of this, the inputs metric is relatively stronger in these estimations. The initial gap in explanatory power between the organized and unorganized sectors that was evident in columns (1) and (2) is diminished in the complete estimations in columns (3) to (5).

Table 3 considers organized and unorganized services entry. The contrast to organized manufacturing is again quite intriguing. First, overall district population is as important as it was for unorganized manufacturing, with elasticity greater than one. Similarly, the R^2 value grows to 0.20 and 0.47 with just the parsimonious set of explanatory factors in columns (1) and (5), respectively. The R^2 value using the GLAESER and KERR (2009) approach for organized services is 0.30. Also similar to unorganized manufacturing, population density and travel time to major cities are not important in the multivariate setting, while the district's age profile does contribute to higher entry levels.

To recap, education and infrastructure matter the most among district traits. Education is generally more important, with particular relevance to organized sectors. Physical infrastructure has particular relevance to the unorganized sectors of the economy. The strength of the household banking sector is again also very important in the unorganized sectors of the economy. These channels provide three of the main ways that policy-makers can influence the spatial distribution of entry.

The role of the existing incumbent employment by district–industry for services is weak in Table 3, likely suggesting that Marshallian economies are weaker in services. Unreported estimations further model Marshallian interactions in the services sector similar to manufacturing. These results are also weak, at most suggesting a small role for labour market interactions. However, the authors hesitate to interpret this difference strongly as the weak results may be due to the application of concepts and metrics originally designed for manufacturers to the service sector.

Table 4 provides some extensions for organized manufacturing. Following the discussion in the third section, column (1) first includes the small firm incumbent share control. Including this control sharpens the earlier results further, including making the Chinitz effect more robust. Evidence for the general small firm effects outlined by FRITSCH and FALCK (2007) and PARKER (2009b), as well as the Chinitz effect, are thus found.

Columns (2) to (5) break out entrants by their sizes; and Table 5 provides a broader depiction of the entrant size distribution. Starting with Table 5, panel (A) presents the full entrant distribution that includes the organized and unorganized sectors. The complete distribution across both sectors looks broadly similar to other environments. For example, 98% of entering establishments have fewer than ten employees, and only 0.09% of entering establishments have more than 100 workers. In terms of employment shares, 76% of employment in entering establishments is contained in establishments with fewer than ten employees, versus 9.5% in those entering with more than 100. Panel (B) isolates the organized sector, and within this group the largest entrant size category contains 5.5% of establishments and 53% of employment. The district-level variation is also consistent around these traits.

Thus, the unorganized sector accounts for most entrants and employments, and includes plants that are by definition very small. The larger plants included in

Table 3. District entrepreneurship estimations – services

	Organized services				Unorganized services			
	Base estimation (1)	District traits (2)	Adding consumption (3)	Using log entry count (4)	Base estimation (5)	District traits (6)	Adding consumption (7)	Using log entry count (8)
Log of incumbent employment in district–industry	–0.003	–0.104+++	–0.105+++	–0.054++	0.094+++	0.037+	0.037+	0.037+
	(0.038)	(0.033)	(0.033)	(0.023)	(0.024)	(0.021)	(0.021)	(0.021)
Log of district population	1.278+++	1.023+++	1.023+++	0.711+++	1.213+++	1.113+++	1.113+++	1.113+++
	(0.148)	(0.135)	(0.133)	(0.092)	(0.107)	(0.111)	(0.108)	(0.111)
Log of district population density		–0.014	–0.013	–0.028		–0.097+	–0.096+	–0.097+
		(0.086)	(0.087)	(0.056)		(0.057)	(0.058)	(0.057)
Share of the population with graduate education		0.348+++	0.333+++	0.230+++		0.179+++	0.160++	0.179+++
		(0.085)	(0.088)	(0.059)		(0.068)	(0.070)	(0.068)
Demographic dividend for a district (age profiles)		0.548+	0.469	0.329		0.574++	0.465++	0.574++
		(0.331)	(0.349)	(0.230)		(0.229)	(0.235)	(0.229)
Index of infrastructure quality for a district		0.339+++	0.315+++	0.242+++		0.420+++	0.378+++	0.420+++
		(0.096)	(0.106)	(0.067)		(0.068)	(0.074)	(0.068)
Strength of household banking environment		0.174++	0.159+	0.108+		0.323+++	0.302+++	0.323+++
		(0.087)	(0.088)	(0.060)		(0.068)	(0.069)	(0.068)
Stringency of labour laws in a district's state		–0.117+	–0.112+	–0.076+		–0.154+++	–0.146+++	–0.154+++
		(0.067)	(0.067)	(0.046)		(0.048)	(0.048)	(0.048)
Log travel time to closest large city		–0.011	–0.007	–0.021		0.048	0.056	0.048
		(0.054)	(0.054)	(0.037)		(0.051)	(0.050)	(0.051)
Log per capita consumption			0.295				0.454	
			(0.369)				(0.291)	
Industry fixed effects	Yes	Yes	Yes	Yes	Yes	Yes	Yes	Yes
Number of observations	3340	3340	3340	3340	6552	6552	6552	6552
Adjusted R^2	0.201	0.252	0.253	0.252	0.471	0.536	0.536	0.536

Notes: The dependent variable is log entry employment by district–industry.
See also Table 2a.

Table 4. Extended district entrepreneurship estimations – organized manufacturing

	Including small firm share	Entering establishment employment of:				One year entrants	Including lagged entry
		10–19	20–39	40–99	100+		
	(1)	(2)	(3)	(4)	(5)	(6)	(7)
Log of incumbent employment in district–industry	0.534+++	0.229+++	0.277+++	0.260+++	0.274+++	0.407+++	–0.082+
	(0.057)	(0.032)	(0.036)	(0.045)	(0.049)	(0.048)	(0.049)
Log of district population	0.358++	0.192++	0.266+++	0.178++	0.099	0.210	0.433+++
	(0.143)	(0.084)	(0.075)	(0.085)	(0.099)	(0.133)	(0.152)
District traits							
Log of district population density	–0.453+++	–0.169+++	–0.160+++	–0.249+++	–0.281+++	–0.343+++	–0.521+++
	(0.069)	(0.038)	(0.034)	(0.043)	(0.062)	(0.053)	(0.071)
Share of the population with graduate education	0.229++	0.107+	0.089	0.066	0.118++	0.184++	0.235++
	(0.099)	(0.060)	(0.055)	(0.051)	(0.054)	(0.086)	(0.106)
Demographic dividend for a district (age profiles)	0.392	0.185	0.340	0.388	0.049	0.196	0.503
	(0.410)	(0.255)	(0.240)	(0.244)	(0.309)	(0.335)	(0.449)
Index of infrastructure quality for a district	0.011	–0.017	–0.042	–0.095	–0.033	–0.104	0.082
	(0.085)	(0.061)	(0.047)	(0.058)	(0.063)	(0.070)	(0.086)
Strength of household banking environment	0.055	–0.002	0.017	0.058	0.090	0.187+++	0.061
	(0.085)	(0.049)	(0.045)	(0.060)	(0.061)	(0.070)	(0.098)
Stringency of labour laws in a district's state	–0.171+++	–0.094++	–0.145+++	–0.107+++	–0.036	–0.130++	–0.139++
	(0.060)	(0.037)	(0.037)	(0.038)	(0.047)	(0.059)	(0.060)
Log travel time to closest large city	–0.183+++	–0.067	–0.064+	–0.121+++	–0.113++	–0.139++	–0.202++
	(0.070)	(0.041)	(0.035)	(0.035)	(0.056)	(0.054)	(0.078)
Local industrial conditions by incumbent firms							
Labour market strength for district–industry	0.034	–0.151++	–0.004	0.048	0.195++	–0.036	0.186+
	(0.099)	(0.066)	(0.068)	(0.074)	(0.082)	(0.087)	(0.103)
Inputs/supplier strength for district–industry	0.204++	0.108+	0.064	0.049	0.059	0.050	0.429+++
	(0.086)	(0.056)	(0.069)	(0.068)	(0.072)	(0.076)	(0.100)
Outputs/customer strength for district–industry	0.230++	0.111++	0.159++	0.247+++	0.275+++	0.235+++	0.364+++
	(0.115)	(0.053)	(0.067)	(0.090)	(0.105)	(0.088)	(0.129)
Chinitz small suppliers metric for district–industry	0.429++	0.530+++	0.368++	0.150	–0.119	0.124	0.221
	(0.209)	(0.184)	(0.158)	(0.155)	(0.139)	(0.156)	(0.214)
Share of small incumbent firms in the district–industry	0.651+++	0.447+++	0.409+++	0.254+++	0.055	0.169+++	
	(0.115)	(0.060)	(0.068)	(0.072)	(0.085)	(0.034)	
Lagged organized manufacturing entry rate for district–industry							0.205+++
							(0.026)
Industry fixed effects	Yes	Yes	Yes	Yes	Yes	Yes	Yes
Number of observations	4843	4843	4843	4843	4843	4843	4843
Adjusted R^2	0.169	0.179	0.192	0.196	0.197	0.246	0.245

Notes: The dependent variable is log entry employment by district–industry indicated in the column header.
See also Table 2a. Column (7) includes an unreported dummy variable for zero entry in the lagged period.

Table 5. Distribution of entrant employments and plant counts across size categories

	Employment in entering establishments (%)			Counts of entering establishments (%)		
	India as a whole (1)	District-level mean (2)	District-level standard deviation (3)	India as a whole (4)	District-level mean (5)	District-level standard deviation (6)
(A) *Organized and unorganized sectors of manufacturing*						
0–4 employees	59.11	68.80	26.85	92.18	92.79	11.35
5–9 employees	16.57	10.46	15.00	5.83	4.76	9.67
10–19 employees	8.85	6.15	10.15	1.57	1.65	4.01
20–39 employees	2.11	2.34	4.33	0.18	0.31	0.78
40–99 employees	3.83	4.46	8.82	0.14	0.33	1.43
100+ employees	9.52	7.80	14.01	0.09	0.16	0.49
(B) *Organized sector only of manufacturing*						
10–19 employees	36.42	33.55	32.63	79.33	57.81	32.35
20–39 employees	8.69	14.39	21.04	9.18	18.28	22.00
40–99 employees	15.74	18.76	23.30	7.16	14.69	19.87
100+ employees	39.15	27.37	29.93	4.33	9.23	16.40

Note: The distribution of entrant employments and establishment counts across the establishment size distribution is documented. Columns (1) and (4) provide statistics for India as a whole. The district mean and standard deviation columns summarize the unweighted variation at the district level.

the organized sector are still skewed towards the smaller end of the size distribution (e.g., 79% have 10–19 employees) but the largest plants with more than 100 employees have 53% employment share. The definitions of entrants discussed in the second section highlight that the data include new firm formation, but also some elements of new establishments opening in a district. The former dominate the unorganized sector, given its small establishment sizes, while the latter become increasingly important in the larger size categories of the entrant size distribution for the organized sector. This makes a separation very useful, as household banking conditions, for example, may matter less for the organized sector than the labour laws present in India.

Returning to Table 4, the heterogeneity across the entrant size distribution is fascinating and confirms many underlying theories and intuitions advanced above. Small entrants in the organized sector follow existing populations much more, similar to the unorganized sector (shown in Table 2b), while larger entrants in the organized sector are less tied to local demand and avoid places with high population density. The small business and Chinitz effects are much more important for small entrants in the organized sector, while labour markets and industrial output conditions are more critical for large entrants. Column (6) shows fairly similar results when using one-year entrants, with the main differences being a greater emphasis on local banking conditions than local input markets. Column (7) likewise displays broadly similar results when instead controlling for lagged entry rates.

The unpublished appendix provides additional robustness checks on these results: excluding sample weights, including additional covariates such as the female population share and local religious affiliations (e.g., MACK *et al.*, 2013), and clustering standard errors by state. The authors have also tested controls for a district's caste population (IYER *et al.*, 2011), conflict, trade levels and general development levels (leading/lagging designations at the state and district level). These additional controls do not substantively affect the results presented, and the more parsimonious specification is maintained to mirror other work from outside of India. The main specifications are also robust to controlling for incumbent firm counts or value added rather than employment. The unpublished appendix also provides additional work regarding the local industrial traits. Similar results are obtained when district fixed effects are included in the estimations, or when changes in industrial conditions from 1989 to 2005 are used partially to address omitted variable bias concerns.

CONCLUSIONS

Entrepreneurship can be an important factor for economic growth, and India has historically had low entry rates for the formation of new businesses. This condition is starting to improve, and further growth in effective entrepreneurship is an important stepping stone in India's continued development. This paper explores the spatial determinants of local entrepreneurship for Indian manufacturing and services. Its analysis provides an important baseline for understanding what is important in India's developing economy, both as a first step for policy advice and as a guide to additional research efforts.[9] This foundation also serves a broader academic interest of comparing India's patterns with those of other economies like the United States.

At the district level, the strongest evidence points to the roles that local education levels and physical infrastructure quality play in promoting entry. Evidence is also found that strict labour regulations discourage entrepreneurship, and better household banking environments are associated with higher entry in the unorganized sector. Policy-makers wishing to encourage entrepreneurship in their local areas have several policy levers that can be exploited: investment in both people and places is an easy call for policy-makers, while reducing unnecessary regulations and restrictions is also warranted. This raises the importance of correct policy design for local areas, and it provides a nice testing ground for future work on agglomeration and urban economies. In particular, further research surrounding the time dimensions to entrepreneurship's role in the local economy (e.g., FRITSCH and MUELLER, 2004) for India might be particularly attractive given the rapid pace of the country's transformation.

Research in regional science has also stressed the heterogeneity in entry across industries within a local area. Extensive evidence is also found here that the incumbent compositions of local industries influence new entry rates at the district–industry level within manufacturing. This influence is through traditional Marshallian agglomeration economies, the small firm effect that has been observed in many countries, and the CHINITZ (1961) effect that emphasizes small suppliers. This evidence on localized agglomeration economies and entry is among the first in a developing economy for this growing literature.

Moving to comparative reflections, the similarities between the patterns observed for India and those in the United States are surprisingly large. For example, the strength of the small firm and Chinitz effects were a surprise given that many accounts of India describe how its firm size distribution has been artificially compressed. It could be imagined that the positive channels for entrepreneurship described for advanced economies are greatly diminished when the size distribution is being partially set by the government. Yet, these patterns are comparable. This general comparability is very important as it suggests a substantial degree of portability in the insights derived here in studying advanced economies (e.g., CHATTERJI *et al.*, 2013) to developing and emerging situations.[10]

The differences in the patterns between India and the United States are also instructive and provide important caveats and boundaries on this portability. First, the role and importance of education and physical infrastructure are higher in India than in comparable US studies. By contrast, other dimensions such as population density and regional age structures behave very similarly. The conjecture is that the spatial variation in the latter dimensions within India more closely resembles the variation in advanced economies, and so the same underlying economic forces operate comparably. On the other hand, many parts of India struggle with illiteracy and lack of paved roads, which are not issues on which regional comparisons from the United States can provide insights. Therefore, the important nuance to the broad comparability and portability noted above is that researchers and policy-makers need to contemplate carefully whether the variations utilized in earlier studies are reflective of the variations with which they are dealing.

A second point of comparison with the United States is very striking. While coefficient elasticities are often similar in magnitude, a very striking difference between the present work and that of GLAESER and KERR (2009) is that this paper can generally only account for about one-third of the spatial variation that the US-focused study could. It is posited that a large portion of this gap is due to India being at a much earlier stage of development, especially with the industrial landscape still adjusting to the deregulations of the 1980s and 1990s (e.g., FERNANDES and SHARMA, 2011). District traits and local conditions take on a much greater importance, vis-à-vis incumbent employment distributions, with the economy in transition. At such an early point and with industrial structures not entrenched, local policies and traits can have profound and lasting impacts by shaping where industries plant their roots. These key differences between developing and advanced economies are worthy subjects for further research.

Acknowledgments – The authors thank Ahmad Ahsan, Mehtabul Azam, Rajeev Dehejia, Gilles Duranton, Arti Grover, Michael Fritsch, Lakshmi Iyer, Henry Jewell, Arvind Panagariya, David Storey, Hyoung Gun Wang and three anonymous referees for helpful comments on this work. They thank The World Bank's South Asia Labor Flagship team for providing the primary datasets used in this paper. The authors are particularly indebted to Shanthi Nataraj for sharing her wisdom regarding the industrial survey data. The views expressed in this paper are those of the authors alone and not of any institution with which they may be associated.

Funding – Funding for this project was provided by The World Bank and Multi-Donor Trade Trust Fund.

NOTES

1. High rates of local entrepreneurship are linked to stronger subsequent job growth for regions in several countries (e.g., Fritsch, 2008; Ghani *et al.*, 2011; Glaeser *et al.*, 2012). Mueller *et al.* (2008) caution, however, about sweeping statements given the substantial heterogeneity in the British experience, where the job growth of regions depended strongly on the types of entrepreneurs entering and the initial conditions of the regions. Baumol (1990) also highlights how the positive or negative role of entrepreneurship depends upon the incentives in society.
2. In contemporaneous work, Mukim (2011) examines spatial entry patterns for India's unorganized sector. The working paper version of this article discusses similarities and differences between the studies. Other related work includes: Drucker and Feser (2007, 2012), Acs and Varga (2005), Ardagna and Lusardi (2008), Rosenthal and Strange (2010), Delgado *et al.* (2010), and Calá *et al.* (2013).
3. Parker (2009a) provides a complete review of the entrepreneurship literature. Storey (1994) and Storey and Greene (2010) give an overview of small businesses and their connections to entrepreneurship specifically. Deichmann *et al.* (2008) survey prior work on firm locations in developing economies.
4. The data combine single-unit start-ups with expansion facilities of multi-unit firms. One can, to some degree, separate the entry of multi-unit firms within organized manufacturing, although this distinction is not comprehensively available for all plants. With the splits available, very similar results are found when modelling single-unit entry rates. These splits are not possible for the unorganized sectors and services. A major development limitation for India is the growth and replication of successful initial businesses (e.g., Hsieh and Klenow, 2009). From this perspective, many policy-makers are equally concerned about encouraging entry of expansion establishments. The working paper version of this article provides an extended discussion about the measures of entrepreneurship and alternative approaches. The paper also returns to this discussion when considering the entrant size distribution.
5. The sampling frame for the organized sector depends on the business register, and a concern might exist that firms indirectly sample out if they select a size so as to avoid registration. As panel data are lacking, corrections like Disney *et al.* (2003) cannot be taken. Absent a correlation with one of the explanatory variables, this measurement error will primarily be for the outcome variables and thus it will not bias the estimates. With respect to the explanatory variables, the same covariates with the unorganized sector are also studied. No evidence of this type of gaming behaviour is observed when comparing results for the two sectors.
6. This approach is used by Glaeser and Kerr (2009), Jofre-Monseny *et al.* (2011), Dauth (2011), and Mukim (2011). It follows upon the co-agglomeration work of Ellison *et al.* (2010).
7. Culture and social capital aspects are taken up by Fritsch and Wyrwich (2013), Kibler *et al.* (2013), and Westlund *et al.* (2013).
8. A value of less than one entering employee on average is recoded as one entering employee. This maintains a consistent sample size, and the distinction between zero and one employee for a district–industry is not economically meaningful. These cells can be excluded without impacting the results.
9. For example, Ghani *et al.* (2012) extend the distance to major city work by considering the development of the Golden Quadrangle highway system in India and its impact on districts (e.g., Datta, 2011).
10. Rosenthal and Strange (2012) and Ghani *et al.* (2013) identify similar features between the United States and India in the spatial sorting patterns of female entrepreneurs.

REFERENCES

Acs Z. and Varga A. (2005) Entrepreneurship, agglomeration and technological change, *Small Business Economics* **24**, 323–334.

Aghion P., Akcigit U., Cage J. and Kerr W. (2012) *Taxation, Corruption, and Growth.* Mimeo. Harvard University.

Aghion P., Burgess R., Redding S. and Zilibotti F. (2008) The unequal effects of liberalization: evidence from dismantling the license *raj* in India, *American Economic Review* **98**, 1397–1412.

Ahsan A. and Pages C. (2007) *Are All Labor Regulations Equal? Assessing the Effects of Job Security, Labor Dispute and Contract Labor Laws In India.* World Bank Working Paper Number 4259. The World Bank, Washington, DC.

Amin M. and Mattoo A. (2008) *Human Capital and the Changing Structure of the Indian Economy.* World Bank Working Paper Number 4576. The World Bank, Washington, DC.

Ardagna S. and Lusardi A. (2008) *Explaining International Differences in Entrepreneurship: The Role of Individual Characteristics and Regulatory Constraints.* NBER Working Paper Number 14012. National Bureau of Economic Research, Cambridge, MA.

Audretsch D. and Fritsch M. (1994) The geography of firm births in Germany, *Regional Studies* **28**, 359–365.

Audretsch D., Feldman M., Heblich S. and Falck O. (2012) Local entrepreneurship in context, *Regional Studies* **46(3)**, 379–389.

Baumol W. (1990) Entrepreneurship: productive, unproductive, and destructive, *Journal of Political Economy* **98**, 893–921.

Besley T. and Burgess R. (2004) Can labor regulation hinder economic performance? Evidence from India, *Quarterly Journal of Economics* **119**, 91–134.

Bönte W., Falck O. and Heblich S. (2009) The impact of regional age structure on entrepreneurship, *Economic Geography* **85**, 269–287.

Boschma R. and Fritsch M. (2007) *Creative Class and Regional Growth – Empirical Evidence from Eight European Countries.* Jena Working Paper Number 2007-066.

Bozkaya A. and Kerr W. (Forthcoming 2013) Labor regulations and European venture capital, *Journal of Economics and Management Strategy.*

Calá C., Arauzo-Carod J. and Manjón Antolín M. (2013) *Regional Determinants of Firm Entry in a Developing Country*. Universitat Rovira i Virgili Working Paper Number 2072/203159.

Chatterji A., Glaeser E. and Kerr W. (2013) *Clusters of Entrepreneurship and Innovation*. NBER Working Paper Number 19013. National Bureau of Economic Research (NBER), Cambridge, MA.

Chinitz B. (1961) Contrasts in agglomeration: New York and Pittsburgh, *American Economic Review* **51**, 279–289.

Combes P. and Duranton G. (2006) Labour pooling, labour poaching, and spatial clustering, *Regional Science and Urban Economics* **36**, 1–28.

Datta S. (2011) The impact of improved highways on Indian firms, *Journal of Development Economics* **99**, 46–57.

Dauth W. (2011) *The Mysteries of the Trade: Interindustry Spillovers in Cities*. Institute for Employment Research Discussion Paper Number 201015.

Dehejia R. and Panagariya A. (2010) *Services Growth in India: A Look Inside the Black Box*. Columbia University School of International and Public Affairs Working Paper Number 4444.

Deichmann U., Lall S., Redding S. and Venables A. (2008) Industrial location in developing countries, *World Bank Observer* **23**, 219–246.

Delfmann H., Koster S., McCann P. and van Dijk J. (2013) *Population Change and New Firm Formation in Urban and Rural Regions*. Mimeo. University of Groningen.

Delgado M., Porter M. and Stern S. (2010) Clusters and entrepreneurship, *Journal of Economic Geography* **10**, 495–518.

Desmet K., Ghani E., O'Connell S. and Rossi-Hansberg E. (2011) *The Spatial Development of India*. World Bank Policy Research Working Paper Number 6060.

Disney R., Haskel J. and Heden Y. (2003) Entry, exit and establishment survival in UK manufacturing, *Journal of Industrial Economics* **51**, 91–112.

Doms M., Lewis E. and Robb A. (2010) Local labor force education, new business characteristics, and firm performance, *Journal of Urban Economics* **67**, 61–77.

Drucker J. and Feser E. (2007) *Regional Industrial Dominance, Agglomeration Economies, and Manufacturing Plant Productivity*. Center for Economic Studies (US Census Bureau) Working Paper Number 07-31.

Drucker J. and Feser E. (2012) Regional industrial structure and agglomeration economies: an analysis of productivity in three manufacturing industries, *Regional Science and Urban Economics* **42**, 1–14.

Duranton G. and Puga D. (2001) Nursery cities: urban diversity, process innovation, and the life cycle of products, *American Economic Review* **91**, 1454–1477.

Duranton G. and Puga D. (2004) Micro-foundations of urban agglomeration economies, in Henderson V. and François Thisse J. (Eds) *Handbook of Regional and Urban Economics*, Vol. 4, pp. 2063–2117. North-Holland, Amsterdam.

Ellison G., Glaeser E. and Kerr W. (2010) What causes industry agglomeration? Evidence from coagglomeration patterns, *American Economic Review* **100**, 1195–1213.

Evans D. and Jovanovic B. (1989) An estimated model of entrepreneurial choice under liquidity constraints, *Journal of Political Economy* **97**, 808–827.

Falck O., Fritsch M. and Heblich S. (2008) *The Apple Does Not Fall From the Tree: Location of Start-Ups Relative to Incumbents*. CESifo Working Paper Number 2486. Munich.

Falck O., Fritsch M. and Heblich S. (2011) The Phantom of the Opera: cultural amenities, human capital, and regional economic growth, *Labour Economics* **18**, 755–766.

Fernandes A. and Pakes A. (2010) *Factor Utilization in Indian Manufacturing: A Look at The World Bank Investment Climate Survey Data*. NBER Working Paper Number 14178. National Bureau of Economic Research (NBER), Cambridge, MA.

Fernandes A. and Sharma G. (2011) *Together We Stand? Agglomeration in Indian Manufacturing*. World Bank Policy Research Working Paper Number 6062.

Figueiredo O., Guimaraes P. and Woodward D. (2002) Home-field advantage: location decisions of Portuguese entrepreneurs, *Journal of Urban Economics* **52**, 341–361.

Fritsch M. (2008) How does new business formation affect regional development?, *Small Business Economics* **30**, 1–14.

Fritsch M. and Falck O. (2007) New industry formation by industry over space and time: a multidimensional analysis, *Regional Studies* **41**, 157–172.

Fritsch M. and Mueller P. (2004) Effects of new business formation on regional development over time, *Regional Studies* **38**, 961–975.

Fritsch M. and Wyrwich M. (2013) *The Long Persistence of Regional Entrepreneurship Culture: Germany 1925–2005*. Jena Economic Research Papers Number 2012-036.

Fujita M., Krugman P. and Venables A. (1999) *The Spatial Economy: Cities, Regions and International Trade*. MIT Press, Cambridge, MA.

Ghani E., Grover Goswami A. and Kerr W. (2012) *Highway to Success: The Impact of the Golden Quadrilateral Project for the Location and Performance of Indian Manufacturing*. Harvard Business School Working Paper Number 13-040.

Ghani E., Kerr W. and O'Connell S. (2011) Promoting entrepreneurship, growth, and job creation, in Ghani E. (Ed.) *Reshaping Tomorrow*, pp. 166–199. Oxford University Press, Oxford.

Ghani E., Kerr W. and O'Connell S. (2013) Local industrial structures and female entrepreneurship in India, *Journal of Economic Geography* **13(6)**, 929–964.

Glaeser E. and Kerr W. (2009) Local industrial conditions and entrepreneurship: how much of the spatial distribution can we explain?, *Journal of Economics and Management Strategy* **18**, 623–663.

Glaeser E., Kerr W. and Ponzetto G. (2010) Clusters of entrepreneurship, *Journal of Urban Economics* **67**, 150–168.

GLAESER E., PEKKALA KERR S. and KERR W. (2012) *Entrepreneurship and Urban Growth: An Empirical Assessment with Historical Mines.* NBER Working Paper Number 18333. National Bureau of Economic Research (NBER), Cambridge, MA.

GREENSTONE M., HORNBECK R. and MORETTI E. (2010) Identifying agglomeration spillovers: evidence from winners and losers of large plant openings, *Journal of Political Economy* **118**, 536–598.

HASAN R. and JANDOC K. (2010) *The Distribution of Firm Size in India: What Can Survey Data Tell Us?* Asian Development Bank (ADB) Economics Working Paper Number 213.

HOFSTEDE G. (2001) *Culture and Organizations.* HarperCollins, London.

HSIEH C. and KLENOW P. (2009) Misallocation and manufacturing TFP in China and India, *Quarterly Journal of Economics* **124**, 1403–1448.

IYER L., KHANNA T. and VARSHNEY A. (2011) *Caste and Entrepreneurship in India.* Harvard Business School Working Paper Number 12-028.

JOFRE-MONSENY J., MARÍN-LÓPEZ R. and VILADECANS-MARSAL E. (2011) The mechanisms of agglomeration: evidence from the effect of inter-industry relations on the location of new firms, *Journal of Urban Economics* **70(2–3)**, 61–74.

JOHNSON P. and CATHCART D. G. (1979) The founders of new manufacturing firms: a note on the size of their 'incubator's plants, *Journal of Industrial Economics* **28**, 219–224.

KATHURIA V. (2011) *What Causes Agglomeration? Policy or Infrastructure – A Study of Indian Manufacturing Industry.* eSocialSciences Working Paper Number 4473.

KATHURIA V., NATARAJAN S., RAJ R. and SEN K. (2010) *Organized Versus Unorganized Manufacturing Performance in India in the Post-Reform Period.* MPRA Working Paper Number 20317. Munich Personal RePEc Archive (MPRA), Munich.

KHANNA T. (2008) *Billions of Entrepreneurs: How China and India are Reshaping their Futures – And Yours.* Harvard University Press, Boston, MA.

KIBLER E., KAUTONEN T. and FINK M. (2013) *Regional Social Legitimacy of Entrepreneurship: Implications for Entrepreneurial Intention and Start-up Behaviour.* Mimeo. University of Turku.

KLEPPER S. (2010) The origin and growth of industry clusters: the making of Silicon Valley and Detroit, *Journal of Urban Economics* **67**, 15–32.

LALL S., WANG H. and DEICHMANN U. (2011) *Infrastructure and City Competitiveness in India.* World Institute for Development Economic Research Working Paper Number 2010/22.

LAZEAR E. (2005) Entrepreneurship, *Journal of Labor Economics* **23**, 649–680.

MACK E., FAGGIAN A. and STOLARICK K. (2013) *Does Religion Stifle Entrepreneurial Activity?* Mimeo. Arizona State University.

MARSHALL A. (1920) *Principles of Economics.* Macmillan, London.

MICHELACCI C. and SILVA O. (2007) Why so many local entrepreneurs?, *Review of Economics and Statistics* **89**, 615–633.

MUELLER P., VAN STEL A. and STOREY D. (2008) The effects of new firm formation on regional development over time: the case of Great Britain, *Small Business Economics* **30**, 59–71.

MUKIM M. (2011) *Industry and the Urge to Cluster: A Study of the Informal Sector in India.* Discussion Paper Number 0072. Spatial Economics Research Centre, London.

NATARAJ S. (2011) The impact of trade liberalization on productivity and firm size: evidence from India's formal and informal manufacturing sectors, *Journal of International Economics* **85(2)**, 292–301.

PARKER S. (2009a) *The Economics of Entrepreneurship.* Cambridge University Press, Cambridge.

PARKER S. (2009b) Why do small firms produce the entrepreneurs?, *Journal of Socio-Economics* **38**, 484–494.

REYNOLDS P., STOREY D. and WESTHEAD P. (1994) Regional characteristics affecting entrepreneurship: a cross-national comparison, in *Frontiers of Entrepreneurship Research*, pp. 550–564. Babson College, Babson Park, MA.

ROSENTHAL S. and STRANGE W. (2004) Evidence on the nature and sources of agglomeration economies, in HENDERSON V. and FRANÇOIS THISSE J. (Eds) *Handbook of Regional and Urban Economics*, Vol. 4, pp. 2119–2171. North-Holland, Amsterdam.

ROSENTHAL S. and STRANGE W. (2010) Small establishments/big effects: agglomeration, industrial organization and entrepreneurship, in GLAESER E. (Ed.) *Agglomeration Economics*, pp. 277–302. University of Chicago Press, Chicago, IL.

ROSENTHAL S. and STRANGE W. (2012) Female entrepreneurship, agglomeration, and a new spatial mismatch, *Review of Economics and Statistics* **94**, 764–788.

STOREY D. (1994) *Understanding the Small Business Sector.* Thomson Learning, London.

STOREY D. and GREENE F. (2010) *Small Business and Entrepreneurship.* Prentice Hall, Englewood Cliffs, NJ.

VAN STEL A., STOREY D. and THURIK R. (2007) The effect of business regulations on nascent and young business entrepreneurship, *Regional Studies* **28**, 171–186.

WESTLUND H., LARSSON J. and OLSSON A. (2013) *Startups and Local Social Capital in the Municipalities of Sweden.* European Regional Science Association Conference Papers Number ersa12p91.

Is Entrepreneurship a Route Out of Deprivation?

JULIAN S. FRANKISH*, RICHARD G. ROBERTS*, ALEX COAD†‡§ and DAVID J. STOREY¶

**Barclays Bank, Ground Floor GC, Barclays House, Poole, UK.*

†Science and Technology Policy Research (SPRU), University of Sussex, Jubilee Building, Falmer, Brighton, UK.

‡Department of Business and Management, Aalborg University, Aalborg, Denmark

§The Ratio Institute, Stockholm, Sweden

¶School of Business Management and Economics, University of Sussex, Falmer, Brighton, UK.

FRANKISH J. S., ROBERTS R. G., COAD A. and STOREY D. J. Is entrepreneurship a route out of deprivation?, *Regional Studies*. This paper investigates whether entrepreneurship constitutes a route out of deprivation for those living in deprived areas. The measure of income/wealth used is based on an analysis of improvements in an individual's residential address. The data consist of information on over 800 000 individuals, and come from the customer records of a major UK bank. Comparing business owners with non-owners, the results suggest that the benefits of business ownership are found across the wealth distribution. Hence, entrepreneurship can be a route out of deprivation.

Deprived areas Entrepreneurship Public policy Housing Deprivation

FRANKISH J. S., ROBERTS R. G., COAD A. and STOREY D. J. 创业精神是否为脱贫的途径，*区域研究*。本文探究创业精神是否为生活在贫困地区的人们提供了脱贫的途径。本研究所使用的收入 / 财富评量，是根据个人居住地址的提升所进行的分析。研究数据包含超过八十万人的信息，以及英国一个主要银行的顾客纪录。企业主与非企业主的比较结果显示，各阶层财富分佈皆可发现拥有企业的益处。因此，创业精神是一个脱贫的途径。

贫困地区 创业精神 公共政策 住房 贫困

FRANKISH J. S., ROBERTS R. G., COAD A. et STOREY D. J. L'entrepreneuriat, est-ce un moyen de sortir de la privation?, *Regional Studies*. Cet article examine si, oui ou non, l'entrepreneuriat constitue un moyen de sortir de la privation pour ceux qui habitent les zones défavorisées. La mesure du revenu/de la richesse employée est fondée sur une analyse des améliorations des lieux de résidence des individus. Les données comprennent des informations auprès de 800 000 individus et proviennent des dossiers-clients d'une grande banque au R-U. Lorsque l'on compare les chefs d'entreprises aux non-propriétaires, les résultats laissent supposer que les avantages d'être chef d'entreprise sont évidents à travers la distribution de la richesse. Par la suite, l'entrepreneuriat pourrait s'avérer un moyen de sortir de la privation.

Zones défavorisées Entrepreneuriat Politique publique Logement Privation

FRANKISH J. S., ROBERTS R. G., COAD A. und STOREY D. J. Bietet Unternehmertum einen Weg aus der Benachteiligung?, *Regional Studies*. In diesem Beitrag wird untersucht, ob das Unternehmertum für die Bewohner von benachteiligten Gegenden einen Weg aus der Benachteiligung bietet. Der Maßstab für das Einkommen bzw. Vermögen beruht auf einer Analyse der Verbesserungen hinsichtlich des Wohnsitzes einer Privatperson. Die Daten stammen von den Kundenakten einer britischen Großbank und beziehen sich auf mehr als 800.000 Privatpersonen. Aus den Ergebnissen eines Vergleichs zwischen Geschäftsinhabern und anderen Personen geht hervor, dass der Nutzen von Unternehmenseigentum im gesamten Spektrum der Vermögensverteilung zu finden ist. Unternehmertum kann also einen Weg aus der Benachteiligung bieten.

Benachteiligte Gegenden Unternehmertum Öffentliche Politik Wohnungswesen Benachteiligung

FRANKISH J. S., ROBERTS R. G., COAD A. y STOREY D. J. ¿Ofrece el espíritu empresarial una vía para salir de la marginalidad?, *Regional Studies*. En este artículo examinamos si el espíritu empresarial constituye una vía para que las personas que viven en zonas pobres puedan salir de la marginalidad. Hacemos una medición de los ingresos o la riqueza basándonos en un análisis sobre las mejoras en la dirección residencial de particulares. Los datos proceden de los registros de clientes de un importante banco británico y contienen información sobre más de 800.000 personas. Al comparar los datos de propietarios de negocios con los de otras personas, los resultados indican que ser propietario de un negocio confiere beneficios en todo el espectro de la distribución de la riqueza. Esto significa que el espíritu empresarial sí que puede ser una vía para salir de la marginalidad.

Zonas marginales Espíritu empresarial Política pública Vivienda Miseria

INTRODUCTION

This paper poses the beguilingly simple question of whether entrepreneurship constitutes a valid economic opportunity for those living in deprived areas. Is it a route out of deprivation? This is an important question since, if this link can be demonstrated and individuals living in those areas are made aware of the opportunities provided by entrepreneurship, they may be more willing to choose this option. This could benefit both themselves and perhaps society more widely. It is for this reason that governments, most notably in the UK, have developed a range of programmes to raise awareness of entrepreneurship and sought to target them at individuals living in areas of disadvantage.[1] The question therefore is of interest both to policy-makers, as well as to those seeking a better understanding of the contribution and processes of entrepreneurship.

The starting point for answering this question is to draw upon the simple economic model of entrepreneurship set out by BLANCHFLOWER and OSWALD (1998). This assumes individuals switch into entrepreneurship from another form of economic activity or inactivity when the returns to entrepreneurship exceed those from any other 'state'. The first step in operationalizing this model is to agree clear definitions of 'entrepreneurship' and 'returns'. In the literature the definitions of entrepreneurship vary from self-employment, through business creation to an exclusive focus on innovation-driven enterprises (PARKER, 2009). Similarly, defining the 'returns' to entrepreneurship is also fraught with difficulties. Even if these are restricted to monetary returns alone (TAYLOR, 1996), a central challenge is to decide whether these are best captured by changes in income or in wealth (QUADRINI, 1999).

A key contribution of this paper is to provide both novel and clear definitions of 'entrepreneurship' and of 'returns', and use these to address the central question of whether entrepreneurship is a 'route out of disadvantage'. Its definition of 'entrepreneurship' is that of being a business owner. Its definition of 'returns' is whether the business owner is more likely than an otherwise similar non-owner to move their residential location, over a five-year period, to a geographical area in which house prices are higher. It implies that, for reasons explain in detail below, moving their home from a neighbourhood classed as deprived to one classed as less-deprived reflects an improvement in the economic circumstances of the individual.

Data are examined on 473 094 individuals, aged 18–64 years, who were owners of active, non-agricultural, businesses in May 2006. These owners are compared with 386 174 individuals within the same age range who were *not* business owners in either 2006 or 2011. For both groups there are data on gender, age, region and the deprivation rank of their residential area. These variables are used as controls for 2006 and 2011.

By using this dataset three tests are undertaken:

- Whether, between 2006 and 2011, individuals who were business owners living in deprived locations were more likely to move their residential address than otherwise comparable non-owners.
- If they do move, whether business owners are more likely to move their residential address to a prosperous area than non-owners.
- Whether, amongst business owners, those with better performing businesses move to more prosperous areas.

It is shown that business owners in the most deprived areas of England are both more likely to move and, if they do move, significantly more likely to see an improvement in their residential address than otherwise similar non-owners in those areas. This suggests there may be merit in policies to promote enterprise amongst those living in areas of disadvantage. However, it is also found that business owners in the most prosperous areas of England were also significantly more likely to have made an improvement in the location of their residential housing by 2011 than otherwise similar non-owners. This implies that the benefits of enterprise are not limited to those living in deprived areas. The third test shows that business performance in the period 2006–11 is a powerful influence on whether the owner moves to a more prosperous area.

The paper concludes by both highlighting its own limitations and emphasizing the importance of drawing only valid inferences from the results.

THE THEORETICAL CONTEXT

Numerous studies of small firms have, as their starting point, reviewed the resources upon which an individual, or a group of individuals, is able to draw (JAYAWARNA *et al.*, 2011). Crucially for many small firm theorists, these resources are not simply financial; they also include human and social resources such as networks, prior experience, education and family ties.

Unfortunately, although the interdependency between all these forms of resources is occasionally acknowledged – since, for example, strong networks enhance the ability to obtain financial capital – the direction of any causation, and the overlaps between the networks, is often less than clearly specified. Nevertheless, what remains clear for such theorists is that improved access to resources – however defined – enhances firm performance.

This implies that individuals living in areas of deprivation are, almost by definition, likely to have access to fewer resources – particularly financial resources – than those living in more prosperous areas. So, if there is a minimum level of resources required to begin an enterprise, then individuals – or groups of individuals – living in deprived areas are more likely than those in more prosperous areas to lack access to such resources. They may therefore be prevented from starting businesses where initial capital requirements are high. Equally, if these resources were also required to ensure the survival and growth of a business, then businesses owned by individuals living in deprived areas would be expected to have lower survival, and lower growth rates, than businesses located in more prosperous areas.

But resources, as noted above, are not simply financial (LEE and COWLING, 2014). They also include human and social capital – such as educational skills and social networks. The role of non-financial resources in influencing enterprise creation is most clear when their absence is seen as a barrier. Take the case of education and qualifications as one measure of human capital. It is much more likely that an individual with high educational qualifications will start a technology-based business than an individual without qualifications (ROBERTS, 1991). Some businesses – such as those in professional services – require the business owner to have formal qualifications, so excluding the unqualified (JARVIS and RIGBY, 2012). This means that individuals without such qualifications are effectively barred from starting such enterprises. These enterprises would be expected to generate comparatively high returns for their owners – otherwise these individuals would, with their high human capital, become a high wage earner.

In short, deprived locations have a disproportionately large number of businesses in the 'easy to enter' sectors and, even those professional service businesses that are located in such areas, are likely to have owners who live elsewhere. Resources are theorized to influence not only the 'type' of businesses created but also the performance of the business once established. The inference is clear: more/better resources – social, human and financial – enhance the performance of the firm.

The evidence in support of such theories is, however, not always so clear-cut. In support of the entry barriers theory, GREENE *et al.* (2008) examined new firms in 'prosperous' Buckinghamshire, 'average' Shropshire and 'deprived' Teesside. They found that a considerably higher proportion of new businesses in Teesside than in Buckinghamshire were in the 'easy to enter' trades, such as vehicle repairers, hairdressers and window cleaners. In contrast, Buckinghamshire had a much higher proportion of new firms in business services. This is in line with seeing enterprises in high-value business services requiring more social, educational and financial capital in order to begin to trade.

What is less clear-cut is the evidence on new firm performance in the three locations. SARIDAKIS *et al.* (2013) found new enterprise survival rates in 'deprived' Teesside were lower than in either of the other English locations, but only at the 10% level of significance. There was no impact on growth. Perhaps more plausible is the distinction drawn by COAD *et al.* (2013) between financial capital – which clearly links to early period survival – and networking and other forms of social capital where the direct link with survival is less clear.

A radically different theory of enterprise in areas of disadvantage is proposed in the influential article by BLACKBURN and RAM (2006). These authors argue that it is the lack of capital, and the absence of alternative employment options, that forces many individuals living in deprived areas into starting their own enterprise. Nowhere is this better captured than the words of Lynne on Teesside: 'It was something I had to try. I was getting nowhere. I couldn't see any future in what I was doing. I'd levelled off and wanted to climb. I wanted self-esteem. Looking back it's been totally the opposite [...]' (MACDONALD and COFFIELD, 1991, p. 155). Enterprise creation in deprived areas, therefore, rather than promoting social inclusion, is merely a reflection of the existing distribution of wealth. For BLACKBURN and RAM (2006) policies seeking to promote entrepreneurship amongst those living in areas of social disadvantage may help limited numbers of individuals, but do not address the fundamental wealth distribution issue.

Underpinning all discussions of enterprise in areas of deprivation is the link with informality. WILLIAMS and NADIN (2012) claim that informality is rife, even in an advanced economy such as the UK. They helpfully distinguish between the permanently informal, the intermittently informal and those who see informality as the first step to becoming a formal business. Earlier work by WILLIAMS (2010, p. 897) claimed 'the vast bulk of entrepreneurs operate informally' but that such activities were five times more likely in a deprived than in a prosperous area.

To summarize: if human and financial resources are major influences on the scale and type of new firm creation and performance then new firm creation rates in deprived areas would be lower than those in more prosperous areas, the businesses would be more likely to be found in the 'easy to enter' sectors, their survival rate would be lower, as would their growth rates. The evidence, as noted above, is rather less clear-cut. Some is broadly supportive: firm formation rates in deprived areas are lower than in more prosperous areas – but even this is not the case when London is included (FRANKISH *et al.*, 2011). There is stronger evidence that the 'types' of new firms differ between prosperous and less prosperous locations. More open to question is the link with performance – where survival and growth are not clearly linked to the resources of the area – perhaps because, as BLACKBURN and RAM (2006) point out, the owners of such businesses may have no better economic option than to continue with their enterprise even if the returns are minimal – on the grounds that the alternatives are even worse.

THE POLICY CONTEXT

Since the late 1990s governments in the UK have been interested in the role that self-employment can play in reducing deprivation for both individuals and for local areas. An overview of the history and rationale for such policies is provided by FRANKISH *et al.* (2011). This policy area was first articulated in Enterprise and Social Exclusion (HMT, 1999). It stated: 'The goal of this report is to identify how to generate more enterprise in deprived areas' (p. 1). This policy interest continued with further reports by ODPM (2003), SMALL BUSINESS SERVICE (2004) and BERR (2008) which clearly saw a link between self-employment and lowering deprivation:

> Enterprise can be a route out of disadvantage and deprivation.
>
> (SMALL BUSINESS SERVICE, 2004, p. 59)

> The government will promote enterprise in more deprived areas and among the disadvantaged groups that are heavily represented there, to help raise enterprise levels in the UK as a whole. [...] Our understanding of success around enterprise in deprived areas is best informed by the self-employment rate.
>
> (BERR, 2008, p. 88)

> the problems of our high unemployment areas will not be solved by benefit cheques or by property subsidies but require more enterprises and the opportunity for enterprise open to all (BROWN, 2000).
>
> (HOC ALL PARTY URBAN DEVELOPMENT GROUP, 2007)

These documents constituted the evidence base for committing £280 million to support enterprise initiatives in deprived localities between 2008 and 2011. But inferring that if individuals living in areas of deprivation were to enter some form of entrepreneurship this would enable them to prosper seems to have depended heavily upon a simple correlation. This showed that, excluding London, the 20% most deprived local authority districts in England had 27 business start-ups per 10 000 residents, compared with 51 in the least deprived districts. From this it was inferred that 'there is a clear statistical relationship between deprivation and levels of enterprise activity' (SMALL BUSINESS SERVICE, 2004, p 56). Unfortunately, the limitations of inferring the direction of causation were not covered, neither was the potentially crucial exclusion of London. Nor was the evidence that it was the relatively low human and financial capital of those living in the most deprived areas that made entry into self-employment more difficult and that the provision of incentives to entrepreneurship to such individual could be counter-productive (MACDONALD and COFFIELD, 1991). Finally there was also no explicit recognition, as noted in the second section, that start-ups in these areas were disproportionately focused in those sectors with the lowest barriers to entry, resulting in high 'churn' rates in the business stock. The serious risk that the prime effect of more subsidized entries would lead primarily to more exits was not identified.

The evidence base presented in the public documents justifying the policy intervention therefore constituted a somewhat selective review of the wider evidence base. The central issue was to understand whether individuals living in areas of deprivation were likely to benefit from becoming entrepreneurs/business owners/self-employed. A second, more equity-based consideration was whether it was individuals in areas of disadvantage who benefitted most from becoming a business owner or whether the key beneficiaries were existing prosperous individuals. The third was whether the performance of a business was linked to this prosperity. Formally expressed, these questions are as follows:

Q1: Are business owners living in deprived areas more likely to improve their residential location over time than otherwise similar individuals living in the same area?

Q2: Do business owners living in deprived areas improve their residential location to the same extent as otherwise comparable business owners in other areas?

Q3: Do business owners living in deprived areas improve their residential location to the same extent as business owners in other areas, allowing for business performance?

KEY MEASURES

Addressing these questions require clear definitions and measurement of 'entrepreneurship', 'wealth' and 'deprivation'.

Measuring entrepreneurship

An all-encompassing definition of entrepreneurship might include the concepts of newness, innovation, risk and uncertainty (VAN PRAAG and VERSLOOT, 2007). It might also include self-employed individuals who may employ only themselves or those with employees. A further complication is how this links, or does not link, with the legal form of the enterprise they operate: sole traders, partnerships or limited companies.

In practice, however, several of these elements are either contradictory or impractical or both. An example of the contradictions is that the self-employed can legitimately choose a range of legal forms, and yet a requirement for innovation or novelty is required by none of them. Hence, imposing a requirement that a business or an individual has to be creative, innovative or novel has to be rejected simply on the grounds that making a decision on who qualifies and who does not is highly subjective (STOREY and GREENE, 2010).

The pragmatic view is the operational definition that gets closest to capturing the concept of entrepreneurship is that of the business owner. This is for two reasons. First, because the vast majority of these businesses are tiny and hence risky. Second, their owners have undertaken the ultimate entrepreneurial act of starting a business with its range of upside gains and downside losses.

Measuring wealth

To conduct the tests requires a metric that accurately captures the 'returns' to entrepreneurship in a way that makes them comparable with other forms of economic activity or inactivity. The choice is between using either income or wealth. Both have advantages and disadvantages.

MOORE *et al.* (2000) identify three problems to be overcome: non-response, interpretation and incorrect recall. The first is how to deal with non-responses, particularly when these can often be as high as 20–25%. At this magnitude it becomes difficult to draw robust conclusions. Interpretation covers both the clarity of the questions asked and any differences in the understanding of concepts by respondents, e.g. what is meant by the phrase 'household income'. Finally, the ability of those being asked to quantify values accurately is likely to vary between both individuals and the source of income. For example, recall of income from capital is much more problematic than that of either work or state benefits.

These potential sources of measurement error are likely to have an even more severe impact on assessments of wealth. At least with income there are periodic flows on which respondents have information; in contrast, the owners of assets may have no ready valuation available for them.

An alternative to using surveys to measure income and wealth is to make greater use of administrative data. Several Nordic countries lead in this respect by making such data available for research purposes (TIMMERMANS, 2010). MERZ (2000), for example, uses micro-data from tax records to examine the income distribution between employees and the self-employed. However, these sources also have their limitations. Tax records may exclude a substantial minority of the population where there are income thresholds below which tax is not paid.

Most importantly, tax-based data have notoriously imperfect coverage of the income and wealth of business owners because under-reporting is much more prevalent in this group. PISSARIDES and WEBER (1989), for example, estimate that the actual income of a typical self-employed individual in the UK is more than 50% higher than their declared income. WILLIAMS and NADIN (2012) reach broadly similar conclusions. Outside the UK, studies using similar methodologies (JOHANSSON, 2006, in Finland; ENGSTROM and HOLMLUND, 2009, in Sweden; HURST *et al.*, 2010, in the United States) indicate slightly lower, but still substantial differences between employees and the self-employed/business owners, with the self-employed being more likely to under-report than the owners of unincorporated businesses.

These constitute the challenges in validly estimating the 'returns' from business ownership in comparison with other forms of economic activity, emphasizing the point made by HURST *et al.* (2010) that 'Our results show that it is naïve for researchers to take it for granted that individuals will provide unbiased information to household surveys when they are simultaneously providing distorted information to other administrative sources' (p. i). The approach in this paper is to use more indirect measures or proxies. These have to be closely related to the financial position of individuals and ideally they have to be directly observable, so requiring no input from the individual. They also have to be widely available in order to permit robust analysis.

The case is that the residential address of an individual meets these requirements. Housing and housing change have been extensively used as explanatory variables in a range of prior studies such those on labour mobility (HENLEY, 2000) or entry into self-employment (COWLING and MITCHELL, 1997; ROBSON, 1998; TAYLOR, 2004). Such data have the key advantage of being both relatively straightforward to obtain and of having a high degree of accuracy, i.e. most individuals do provide their bank with their actual address. Furthermore, there is a close link between income and housing in the UK (Fig. 1). This sets out official survey data regarding household spending on mortgage repayments and rent in 2009 by income deciles. Clearly households with higher incomes spend more on housing. So, if a relative value can be placed on an address, there is a strong basis for linking residential property with inferences on the financial position of those living in the property. This is the case even when the property is rented because of the very close relationship between the rankings of capital values and rental costs.

Although there will always be a range of idiosyncratic factors behind residential addresses, the evidence from previous studies (CHESHIRE *et al.*, 2003; TUROK and GORDON, 2005) is that, over the medium-term, personal incomes strongly influence housing choices and location. Residential property is therefore viewed as the least problematic proxy for estimating the comparative financial returns from entrepreneurship and alternative labour market 'states'.

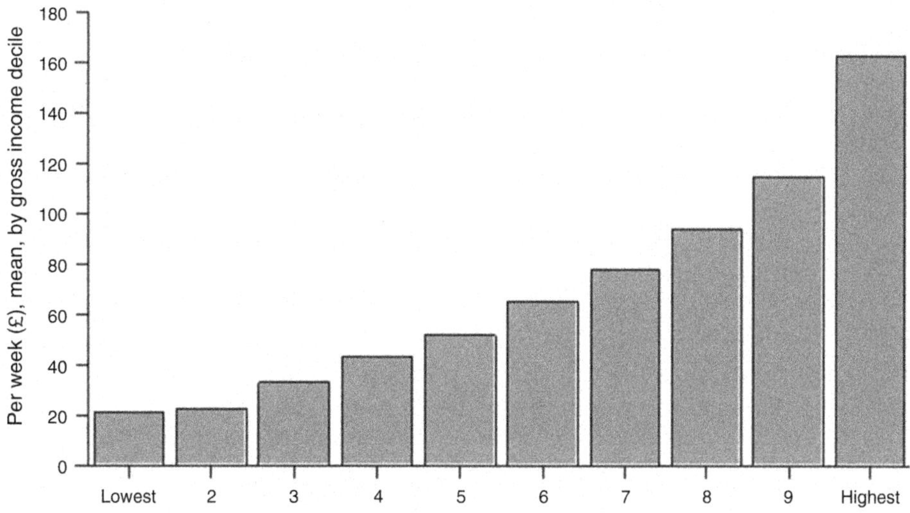

Fig. 1. Household spending on mortgage and net rent
Source: Office for National Statistics (ONS)

Measuring deprivation

The official measure of deprivation in England is the Index of Multiple Deprivation (IMD). The March 2011 version is an ordinal ranking of deprivation composed of seven 'domains' of deprivation: income, employment, health, education, housing, crime and environment.

To link the IMD to residential addresses each post sector in England – and thus each postcode – is assigned a deprivation rank expressed in percentiles from 1 (most deprived) to 100 (most prosperous) based on the mean deprivation rankings of the postcodes within them. As the IMD operates on a continuum, there is no definitive level where an area can be considered as 'deprived'. Therefore, for this paper, in addition to using the percentile ranking of post sectors, post sectors are also grouped into quintiles, taking the definition of deprived areas as those located in the lowest 20% of all areas.

Table 1. House prices and deprivation: ordinary least squares (OLS) regression results

Dependent variable	(log) house prices, March 2011
IMD rank	0.00323*** (0.000471)
London	1.132*** (0.0685)
South East	0.471*** (0.0544)
South West	0.360*** (0.0508)
East of England	0.260*** (0.0507)
West Midlands	0.157*** (0.0516)
East Midlands	0.0987* (0.0568)
Yorkshire	0.0312 (0.0472)
North West	0.0629* (0.0334)
Constant	11.38*** (0.0351)
Number of observations	150
R^2	0.812

Note: IMD rank is the Index of Multiple Deprivation (IMD) 2010 Rank of Local Authority: 1 = most deprived and 150 = least deprived. London, etc. are the dummy variables for the region of the local authority: 1 = Yes and 0 = No. $***p < 0.01$, $**p < 0.05$ and $*p < 0.1$. Robust standard errors are given in parentheses.

LINKING HOUSING TO WEALTH AND ENTREPRENEURSHIP

Table 1 shows the strong association between the deprivation of an area and its house prices. An ordinary least squares (OLS) regression of the log of house prices on the deprivation rank of 150 English local authorities and the regions in which they are located has an R^2 of 0.80. Each step up the ranking[2] results in house prices increasing by an average of 0.3%. This is in addition to the marked regional variations in price levels that see England divided into three broad regional groups: London, the 'South' (East of England, South East and South West) and the 'North' (the other five standard regions). So, when individuals move to a more prosperous area – with a higher IMD rank – they will typically be living in a more valuable property and have seen their income and/or wealth rise relative to other households.

It was noted above that while there is a close relationship between personal incomes and spending on housing costs, there will be changes in residential address driven by a range of factors other than increases in wealth. To ensure that such factors do not unduly impact on the analyses sufficiently large datasets that contain information on both business owners and other individuals at two points in time are required.

DATA DESCRIPTION

The three datasets used in this analysis are drawn from the customer records of Barclays Bank. The first two compare business with personal customers. The third examines only the business customers.

Barclays is one of the UK's main suppliers of banking services to small firms. It has more than 600 000 business customers, each with a turnover of less than £1 million, representing approximately 18% of all UK firms operating through a business current account. The data comprise an integrated source with the ability to track business entities and their owners over time, typically on a month-to-month basis. These accounts are the cornerstone of the day-to-day relationship between the bank and its customers, with both having a strong commercial incentive to ensure the data are accurate and timely.

In the context of this study two points are vital. The first is that having a business current account is *not* conditional on the provision of any other banking service (e.g., deposit account, overdraft, term loan). This is therefore *not* a dataset of a loans portfolio from which businesses may be excluded either by the bank or by being discouraged (KON and STOREY, 2003). The second is that although all businesses, other than those which are exclusively cash-based, require some form of bank account, this does not have to be a designated *business* current account. As a result there will be some small businesses within Barclays' customer base that are not identified. It is likely that the proportion of such businesses is higher in deprived areas.

The first dataset for May 2006 contains 470 136 individuals identified as owners of active, non-agricultural, businesses who were aged 18–64 years. The second comprises 406 207 individuals within the same age range who were in employment, but were not business owners either in 2006 or in 2011.[3]

Both datasets have four variables: gender, age, region, and residential location in 2006 and 2011. In addition, the business owner dataset also contains information on the firm as well as the owner at both dates. Table 2 sets out the variables and provides summary statistics.

Business owners and non-owners, on the basis of their location, are categorized according to an IMD rank at both reference dates. Using these, those who changed address between 2006 and 2011 can be identified, and if they did, whether they moved their residential address to a more deprived (lower ranked) or to more prosperous (higher ranked) location.

The left-hand side of Table 2 shows there are marked differences in the characteristics of business owners and non-owners in the full sample. For example, more than 73% of business owners are male, compared with only 52% of non-owners. Business owners are also generally older, less likely to live in London and less likely to live in the most deprived areas of England. They are also more likely to move address, and move into a higher IMD percentile. The right-hand side provides data on those living in the lowest quintile.

The final dataset – which comprises only business owners – is bank account information. It is the current account information from businesses that use Barclays for their banking services. The key parameters of these data are shown in Table 4 with information on the variables provided in Tables A1 and A2 in Appendix A.

Table 2. Datasets, owners and individuals: overview, percentage of sample; full sample and bottom quintile

	Full sample		Bottom IMD quintile	
	Owners	Non-owners	Owners	Non-owners
Variable	Mean	Mean	Mean	Mean
Proportion male	0.736	0.521	0.763	0.545
Age (years)				
Under 25	0.021	0.101	0.044	0.119
25–34	0.142	0.260	0.239	0.324
35–44	0.303	0.272	0.319	0.274
45–54	0.294	0.201	0.247	0.169
55–64	0.241	0.165	0.152	0.113
Region				
North	0.380	0.382	0.496	0.498
South	0.440	0.399	0.128	0.125
London	0.180	0.219	0.376	0.377
IMD quintile				
Lowest	0.109	0.188	1.000	1.000
Second	0.173	0.225	0.000	0.000
Third	0.209	0.207	0.000	0.000
Fourth	0.242	0.189	0.000	0.000
Highest	0.267	0.192	0.000	0.000
Move address	0.195	0.153	0.232	0.168
Move up to a higher IMD percentile	0.081	0.065	0.165	0.110
Number of observations	470 136	406 207	51 064	76 284

Note: IMD, Index of Multiple Deprivation.

Table 3. Moves and improvements from lowest quintile locations: owners and employees; marginal effects from logistic regressions

	(1)	(2)	(3)
Variables	*Move*	*Improve*	*Improve, conditional on moving*
Owner	0.0876*** (0.00242)	0.0703*** (0.00206)	0.0565*** (0.00629)
Region (omitted = North)			
South	0.0369*** (0.00369)	0.0449*** (0.00330)	0.0931*** (0.00830)
London	0.0117*** (0.00237)	0.00983*** (0.00201)	0.0106* (0.00638)
Male	−0.00136 (0.00232)	−0.00258 (0.00195)	−0.0105 (0.00639)
Age dummies (years)			
25–34	−0.0312*** (0.00348)	−0.0127*** (0.00299)	0.0358*** (0.00937)
35–44	−0.0955*** (0.00317)	−0.0564*** (0.00272)	0.0346*** (0.00984)
45–54	−0.130*** (0.00278)	−0.0812*** (0.00240)	0.0322*** (0.0111)
55–64	−0.137*** (0.00257)	−0.0859*** (0.00225)	0.0437*** (0.0128)
Number of observations	127 348	127 348	24 622
Nagelkerke R^2	0.0495	0.0410	0.0133

Note: ***$p < 0.01$, **$p < 0.05$ and *$p < 0.1$. Robust standard errors are given in parentheses.

Table 4. Owners and businesses across Index of Multiple Deprivation (IMD) quintiles

		IMD quintile (1 = most deprived)					
		1	2	3	4	5	Total
Number of businesses	1	90.72	89.14	86.58	85.71	85.14	86.87
	2	7.51	8.76	10.07	10.95	11.39	10.13
	3	1.22	1.51	1.86	2.15	2.37	1.94
	4+	0.55	0.59	1.49	1.19	1.10	1.06
Legal form							
Company	1	39.49	43.74	46.11	50.92	56.20	48.84
LLP	1	0.18	0.21	0.27	0.35	0.40	0.30
Partnership	1	21.00	22.82	25.07	24.31	21.77	23.17
Sole trader	1	43.77	38.45	34.63	30.98	28.17	33.67
Firm age band	< 1	21.89	17.32	14.01	12.15	11.67	14.36
	1–2	17.38	14.68	12.67	11.77	11.23	12.93
	2–3	10.93	10.88	10.31	9.90	9.94	10.28
	3–5	12.82	13.44	13.69	13.90	13.87	13.65
	5–10	17.66	18.89	19.87	19.98	20.83	19.74
	10–20	13.77	17.04	19.65	21.31	21.96	19.58
	20+	5.56	7.75	9.79	10.99	10.50	9.46
Sector							
Business services	1	22.32	24.79	25.30	27.64	32.35	27.34
Construction	1	13.68	16.11	16.26	15.12	14.06	15.09
Education and Health	1	2.83	3.32	3.70	3.96	3.96	3.67
Hotels and Catering	1	11.33	7.92	6.81	5.60	4.26	6.52
Manufacturing	1	6.90	7.73	8.75	9.47	8.99	8.61
Other services	1	14.95	14.70	14.15	13.55	13.67	14.06
Property services	1	5.30	5.72	6.75	7.56	7.93	6.92
Retail	1	22.39	20.39	19.78	19.83	18.12	19.74
Transport	1	4.95	4.82	4.82	4.50	4.08	4.56
Annual turnover (£)	< 10 000	25.24	20.90	17.64	15.63	15.03	17.85
	10 000–25 000	17.25	14.80	12.98	11.47	10.82	12.81
	25 000–50 000	14.54	14.15	13.64	12.55	11.74	13.05
	50 000–100 000	12.62	13.06	13.13	12.63	12.55	12.79
	100 000–250 000	13.35	14.54	15.01	15.54	15.09	14.90
	250 000–500 000	6.84	8.30	9.22	9.62	9.84	9.06
	500 000–1 million	4.59	5.80	6.77	7.78	8.08	6.96
	1 million–5 million	4.38	6.34	8.53	10.41	11.49	8.94
	5 million plus	1.18	2.11	3.06	4.37	5.38	3.63

ADDRESSING THE QUESTIONS

Q1: Are business owners living in deprived areas more likely to improve their residential location over time than otherwise similar individuals living in the same area?

The last two columns of Table 2 provide data for the most deprived 20% of areas. These are disproportionately found in London and in the North of England. As elsewhere, business owners in these areas are more likely than non-owners to be male, older, to move address and to move to a more prosperous location. The number of observations in the final row of Table 2 shows that deprived areas have considerably more non-owners than owners of businesses and more youthful populations than the prosperous areas.

Because of the very different populations in these quintiles these demographics have to be taken into account in addressing Q1. Q1 is therefore subdivided, distinguishing firstly between the likelihood of a move and, secondly, if the move occurs, whether by 2011 the mover resides in a more prosperous – higher house price – location than in 2006.

Q1a: Were business owners more likely than non-owners to move their residential location between 2006 and 2011, controlling for other characteristics?

Q1b: If that individual has moved, is a business owner more likely than a non-owner to move to an improved residential location – defined as a higher IMD percentile?

Preliminary answers to these questions are offered in Fig. 2. The left-hand side of the upper graph shows that business owners are more likely to move than non-owners, with the right-hand side showing this for all five quintiles. The lower graph shows the proportion of owners and non-owners who, if they move, do so to a more prosperous address. The format used is the same as in the upper graph. The left-hand side shows the results for both groups, and the right-hand side shows how this varies for each quintile. Two results emerge. First, those in the most deprived quintile are more likely to move to a more prosperous address than those in the least deprived quintile. This is the case for both owners and non-owners. Second, in each quintile a higher proportion of owners than non-owners move to a more prosperous location.[4] This suggests that business owners living in the lowest quintile are more likely than non-owners, if they move, to do so to a more prosperous location. It implies that enterprise is an exit route from disadvantage.

However the picture emerging from Fig. 2 is incomplete since it only examines those moving to a more prosperous location. This could be misleading by failing to take account of the downside risks of enterprise such as bankruptcy which are likely to be more characteristic of business owners than non-owners.

Fig. 3 therefore has three elements: the proportion of owners and non-owners who move to a more prosperous location; those moving, but staying in the same percentile; and the proportion of movers to a less prosperous location. This is shown for each quintile. Owner data are shown in the upper graph and non-owner data in the lower graph. For business owners living in the lowest quintile (upper part of Fig. 3), 71% of all moves were to a more prosperous location compared with 13% to a less prosperous location. The remaining 16% were primarily short-distance moves implying no change in the prosperity of the area. In contrast, non-owners (lower part of Fig. 3) had a lower chance of moving to a more prosperous location (65%) and a higher chance of moving 'down' (17%). The 'downsides' of business ownership are more clearly captured in the pattern of moves of business owners living in the most prosperous quintile in 2006. By 2011, 53% of their moves were to a less prosperous area and 27% were to an equally prosperous area – implying that only 19% of moves were to a more prosperous area. In part this is because there are fewer areas into which those in the highest quintile can move and become classified as more prosperous, whereas there are many more options for those living in the least prosperous quintile – a point to which the paper will return to below.

The valid comparison, however, is with the lower part of Fig. 3. This shows that 60% of non-owners began in the top quintile in 2006 and moved 'down' compared with only 53% of business owners. The proportion of non-owners in the top quintile moving 'up' was marginally lower than for business owners, at 18%, implying that overall the business owners in the top quintile out-performed the non-owners.

The graphs however provide only an aggregate picture and do not take explicit account of the human capital and other characteristics of the individuals in each quintile.

Table 3 shows the results of a binary logistic regression on the likelihood of moving for those living in the lowest IMD quintile. The first column shows the estimated marginal effects. The age effect is clearly present, with the odds of moving being considerably lower for each age category (especially those aged 55–64 years) when compared with the baseline case of those under 25 years. There are also important regional differences. Individuals are more likely to move in the South than London who, in turn, are more likely to move than those living in the baseline North.

However, the key result is that the probability of a business owner moving was 9% higher than for non-owners. This business owner 'effect'[5] is observed even after controlling for regions and age groups, both of which significantly influence the probability of a move. The data therefore point to a positive answer to Q1a: *business owners in deprived locations are more likely than otherwise comparable non-owners to change residential address.*

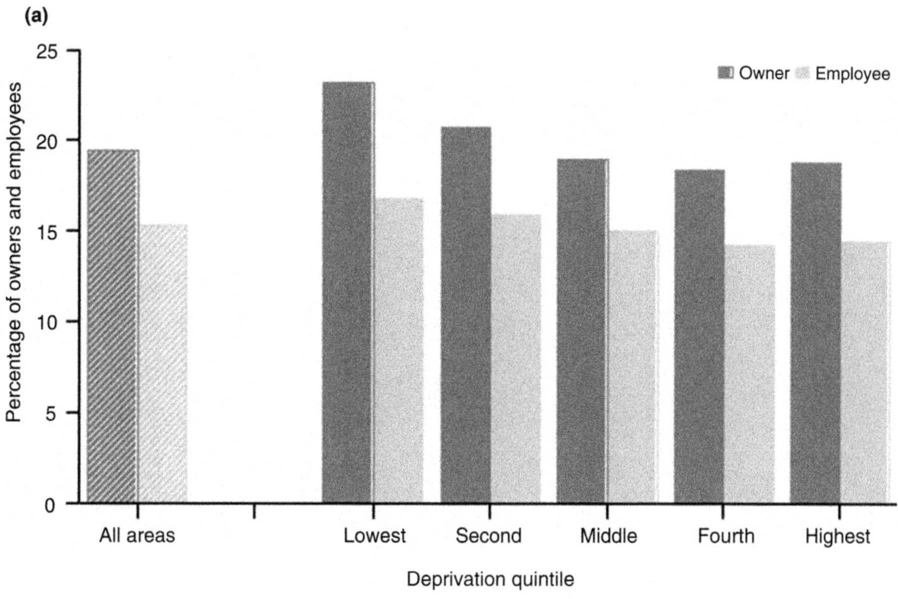

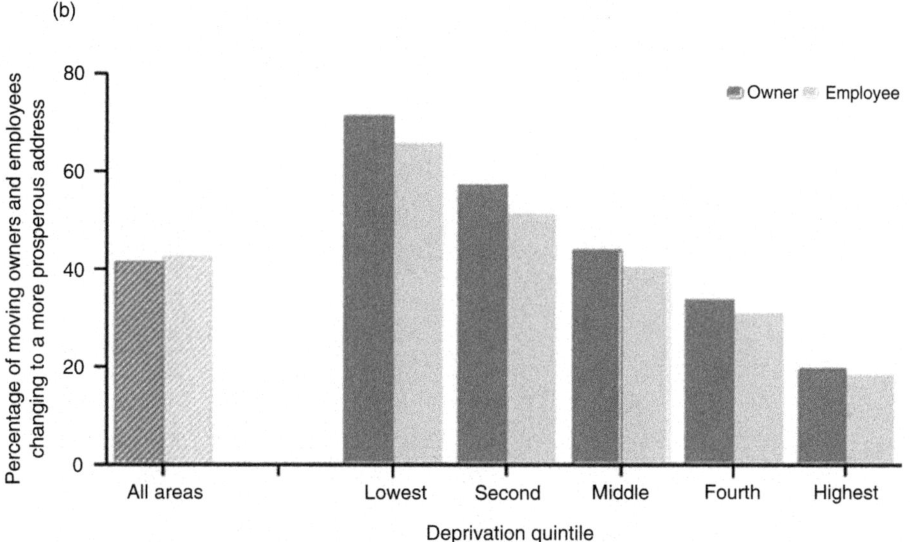

Fig. 2. (a) Probability of address change (percentage of owners and employees); and (b) proportion of individuals moving to a higher percentile in the IMD ranking, conditional on moving (percentage of moving owners and employees changing to a more prosperous address)

The last column of Table 3 shows that, among movers, owners were more likely than non-owners to move to a more prosperous location. Given that all individuals in Table 3 live in the 20% lowest ranked areas, it is unsurprising that the majority who moved did so to a better location, in part because there are more alternatives available.

Table 3 contrasts the factors associated with moving address with those associated with moving up the IMD ranking. Column (1) shows that older individuals are less likely to move, but if they do move they are more likely to move to better area. There is also a regional effect with individuals living in the South being more likely to move to a better area, reflecting the point made above about the distribution of deprived areas across England – there are proportionately more high ranked areas in this region and thus a greater likelihood of moving to one of them. The curiosity is that this logic does not apply to London where there is less strong evidence of movement to a better area than in the baseline 'North'.

Nevertheless, in terms of Q1b, Table 3 shows a significant positive association between business ownership and moving to a more prosperous address for those in the most deprived 20% of areas. Business owners in the most deprived areas are 6% more likely to move to a more prosperous area than otherwise similar non-owners, conditional on moving.[6] The estimates from the two models therefore provide a very clear answer to Q1: *business owners in deprived areas are both more likely to move and, having done so, subsequently to live in a more prosperous location than otherwise comparable non-owners.*

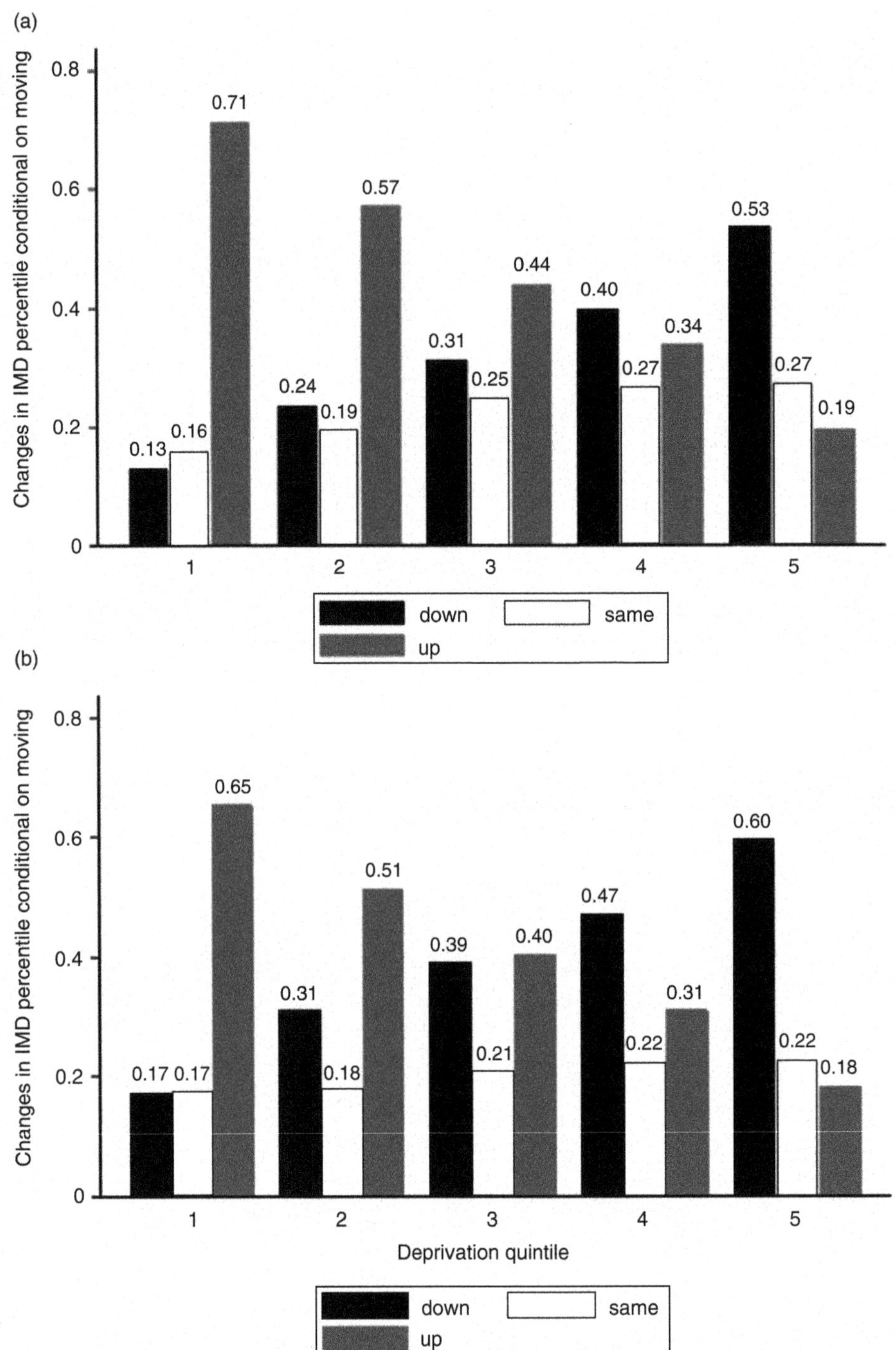

Fig. 3. Changes in the Index of Multiple Deprivation (IMD) percentile conditional on moving, for the five IMD quintiles: (a) owners; and (b) non-owners

As emphasized in the conclusions, these results may be specific to a particular period of time. They also reflect average effects, rather than the effects for marginal entrants, since they examine existing rather than new business owners. Nevertheless, they imply that business owners are more likely to exit from a deprived area to a less deprived area than an otherwise similar non-owner.

Q2: Do business owners living in deprived areas improve their residential location to the same extent as otherwise comparable business owners in other areas?

To address this question one needs to hold constant a range of business characteristics that have been shown (STOREY and GREENE, 2010) to influence new and small firm performance. These are the number of owners of the business, legal form, age, sector, discussed earlier, together with sales turnover as a measure of size.

Table 4 shows these business characteristics vary considerably with the residential location of the business owner in 2006, where quintile 1 is the most deprived 20% of IMDs and quintile 5 is the 20% most prosperous IMDs. The first section of Table 4 shows the number of businesses owned by individuals living in each of the five quintiles. A total of 90.7% of business owners in quintile 1 own only a single business, whereas this is the case for 85.1% in the most prosperous quintile. The second section of Table 4 shows the legal form chosen by the owner also varies by quintile. A total of 56.2% of owners living in prosperous quintile 5 have a business that is a limited company compared with only 39.5% of business owners living in quintile 1. In this latter quintile, business owners are much more likely to have a business that is a sole proprietorship. The third section of Table 4 shows that owners living in quintile 5 are virtually twice as likely to have a long-established business (more than 20 years) compared with those living in deprived quintile 1. The fifth section of Table 4 shows the sectoral composition of businesses owned by individuals varies by quintile. For example, deprived quintile 1 has the lowest proportion of firms in business services at 22.3%. This percentage rises monotonically across the quintiles to reach 32.3% in prosperous quintile 5, complementing the earlier findings of GREENE *et al.* (2008). Conversely, it is also clear that owners living in deprived areas are disproportionately more likely to have retail businesses ('live over the shop') or have a business in sectors such as hotels and catering – primarily the latter. The final section of Table 4 shows the distribution of sales turnover. It shows that owners living in the most prosperous areas typically have considerably larger firms, with 17% of owners living in the highest quintile having (aggregate)[7] annual sales of £1 million or more compared with less than 6% of owners living in the lowest quintile areas.

Table 5. Moves and improvements: owners and employees; marginal effects from logistic regressions, with location-related controls

	(1)	(2)	(3)
Variables	*Move*	*Improve*	*Improve, conditional on moving*
Male	0.00936*** (0.00131)	0.00259*** (0.000786)	−0.00883** (0.00411)
Region (omitted = North)			
South	0.0298*** (0.00134)	0.0278*** (0.000846)	0.103*** (0.00406)
London	0.000221 (0.00165)	−0.000231 (0.000950)	−0.0155*** (0.00501)
IMD quintile			
2	−0.0120*** (0.00205)	−0.0228*** (0.000823)	−0.167*** (0.00536)
3	−0.0210*** (0.00201)	−0.0420*** (0.000754)	−0.286*** (0.00455)
4	−0.0217*** (0.00201)	−0.0570*** (0.000749)	−0.370*** (0.00410)
Highest	−0.0209*** (0.00206)	−0.0844*** (0.000767)	−0.494*** (0.00354)
Age dummies (years)			
25–34	0.0116*** (0.00369)	0.0127*** (0.00232)	0.0512*** (0.0104)
35–44	−0.0691*** (0.00312)	−0.0157*** (0.00188)	0.0535*** (0.0103)
45–54	−0.121*** (0.00286)	−0.0375*** (0.00171)	0.0381*** (0.0107)
55–64	−0.139*** (0.00257)	−0.0455*** (0.00155)	0.0268** (0.0111)
Number of businesses	0.00247** (0.000992)	0.000601 (0.000412)	−0.00155 (0.00342)
Legal form			
Company	0.00267 (0.00284)	0.00739*** (0.00166)	0.0433*** (0.00857)
LLP	−0.00486 (0.0102)	0.000589 (0.00648)	−0.00525 (0.0302)
Partnership	0.00776*** (0.00284)	0.00246 (0.00167)	−0.00258 (0.00841)
Sole trader	0.0299*** (0.00291)	0.00986*** (0.00171)	−0.00287 (0.00843)
Sector dummies			
Business services	0.0129*** (0.00284)	0.00836*** (0.00170)	0.0172** (0.00845)
Construction	0.0106*** (0.00307)	0.000444 (0.00176)	−0.0197** (0.00890)
Education and health	0.0161*** (0.00419)	0.0119*** (0.00266)	0.0292** (0.0123)
Hotels and catering	0.0470*** (0.00384)	0.00784*** (0.00211)	−0.0510*** (0.00951)
Manufacturing	0.00603* (0.00326)	0.00240 (0.00194)	−0.000143 (0.00977)
Other services	0.0171*** (0.00305)	0.00682*** (0.00180)	−0.00262 (0.00879)
Property services	0.0226*** (0.00337)	0.0126*** (0.00208)	0.0288*** (0.00979)
Retail	0.0109*** (0.00292)	0.00215 (0.00170)	−0.0107 (0.00858)
Transport	0.00530 (0.00376)	−0.00321 (0.00212)	−0.0272** (0.0110)
Log turnover	0.00609*** (0.000279)	0.00362*** (0.000171)	0.00831*** (0.000877)
Firm age	−0.00217*** (0.000323)	9.48e−05 (0.000195)	0.00528*** (0.00101)
Firm age^2	−5.34e−06 (1.46e−05)	−3.28e−05*** (8.93e−06)	−0.000179*** (4.56e−05)
Number of observations	470 136	470 136	91 889
Nagelkerke R^2	0.0540	0.0813	0.181

Notes: ***$p < 0.01$, **$p < 0.05$ and *$p < 0.1$. Robust standard errors are given in parentheses.
IMD, Index of Multiple Deprivation.

Table 5 shows the results of modelling the likelihood of an address change taking account of these variables – *Move*. Column 2 shows the probability of improving address; while Column 3 shows the probability of improving, for the subset of individuals who move. As a robustness check, this analysis was repeated using a Heckman probit selection model; similar results were obtained.[8]

The factors influencing *Move* are first that deprived areas are the most dynamic with respect to the movement of population. The probability of a business owner moving are 1.2% lower for business owners in quintile 2 with reference to the baseline case of quintile 1, and 2% lower for business owners in quintile 5 compared with the same baseline, after taking account of firm age, legal form and growth. Of these, it can be seen that owners of younger firms are more likely to move, as are sole traders rather than limited companies.[9] Log sales turnover is positively associated with the odds of the owner moving residential location. It is also found that owners with more than a single business, *No. businesses*, are also more likely to change their residential address.

The right-hand side of Table 5 shows the second step of the analysis for Q2. It examines the factors influencing the residential address changes amongst the 92 000 business owners in the dataset who moved their private residence between 2006 and 2011. Unsurprisingly it shows that business owners initially living in the higher quintiles were less likely to move address, and also less likely to move up – presumably because there are fewer areas into which to move. Again, the paper will return to this issue below.

Differences in the spatial distribution of deprivation are also reflected in the region variable in Table 5, with business owners in the South being more likely to improve, and those in London less likely, compared with the baseline North. The owners of larger businesses are both more likely to move and, if they do so, to move to a higher quintile. Owners of younger firms are also more likely to move, but the relationship between firm age and improving (conditional on moving) is more complicated because of nonlinear effects.

Finally, note the positive association between incorporation and the likelihood of moving to a higher-ranked residential address. This again highlights the important role of the choice of limited company status as a proxy measure for factors and choices made by owners that are not directly visible (FRANKISH *et al.*, 2013).

However, as noted above, the problem with using a simple movement measure is that those in the high quintiles have fewer locations that constitute an improvement than those in the lower quintiles. So, to account for this a relative index is formulated. This assumes that if the initial residential location of a business owner has an IMD ranking of 15, then they have an 85% chance of improving their location when moving, all else being equal. Similarly, those with an IMD ranking of 85 have a 15% chance of an improved move.[10]

Table 6. Owners and businesses: improve performance

(1)	(2)	(3)	(4)	(5)
IMD quintile	Median rank	Percentage above rank 100% – (2)	Percentage improve	Ratio (3)/(4)
1	14.2	85.8	71.3	0.831
2	32.4	67.6	57.1	0.845
3	49.1	50.9	43.9	0.862
4	67.3	32.7	33.7	1.030
5	86.5	13.5	19.5	1.442

Note: IMD, Index of Multiple Deprivation.

This is captured in Table 6, which shows the median IMD ranking for the initial residential address of those business owners who subsequently moved. So, owners who lived in the most deprived areas and subsequently moved typically lived in a location with a ranking of 14. As deprived and prosperous areas are not evenly distributed across England, and the dataset is restricted to those living and moving within a given region, the proportion of locations available to these owners will be higher or lower than this national figure.

The third column of Table 6 shows the proportion of areas above the median ranking in each IMD quintile, weighted for the distribution of owners across the three regions. This shows that for owners in the lowest quintile there were 85.8% of areas above their initial address, 67.6% of areas in the second quintile and so on. The fourth column of Table 6 shows the proportion of owners in each quintile moving to a higher ranked location; the final column shows the ratio of the values of the preceding two columns.

Amongst those in the most deprived quintile, Q1, 71.3% of business owners moved up, a ratio of 0.831, i.e. they were less likely to improve their location than would have been expected given the proportion of areas above them. The ratio for business owners in the next two quintiles is similar, if slightly higher. However, in the fourth, and particularly the highest, quintile the ratios are much higher. Business owners, already in the highest quintile, were more than 40% more likely to move up than might have been expected. In short, although business owners in all quintiles were more likely to move up than non-owners (Table 4), the results from Table 6 (column 5) imply that it is business owners living in the most prosperous area who are most likely to improve.

Q3: Do business owners living in deprived areas improve their residential location to the same extent as business owners in other areas, allowing for business performance?

The answers to Q1 and Q2 took a static view of the business owner and non-owner populations – by only taking account their characteristics in 2006. However, to answer Q3 adequately one has to take account of the performance of the business between 2006 and 2011. For this the two standard metrics are used:

survival/non-survival and changes in sales turnover amongst surviving business.

It is found that 45.5% of business owners in 2006 were no longer business owners in 2011. This was highest at 55% for business owners living in the most deprived areas and fell monotonically for each quintile. Changes in sales turnover are expressed in percentages and grouped in three bands: a fall of more than 25%, an increase of at least one-third, and any change between these two thresholds. The three groups contain broadly equal numbers of businesses.

The first column in Table 7 shows the estimated coefficients in the movement model when the business performance variable is added. The results are clear. They show that compared with the base case of business closure, the business has to survive and grow its sales by at least one-third for its owner to have higher chances of moving residence. When the sales of the business grow less rapidly, or fall, this reduces the likelihood of its owner moving residential location (compared with the base case of business exit). Given that account is taken of sales in 2006, it highlights that residential movement of the owner is powerfully stimulated by sales growth in a surviving business.

This section now turns to the likelihood of improvement – moving to a more prosperous IMD. Column (3)

Table 7. Moves and improvements: owners and employees; marginal effects from logistic regressions, with location-related controls and business performance

	(1)	(2)	(3)
Variables	*Move*	*Improve*	*Improve, conditional on moving*
Male	0.00900*** (0.00130)	0.00233*** (0.000785)	−0.00978** (0.00412)
Region (omitted = North)			
South	0.0297*** (0.00134)	0.0276*** (0.000844)	0.103*** (0.00406)
London	−0.000421 (0.00165)	−0.000505 (0.000945)	−0.0158*** (0.00500)
IMD quintile			
2	−0.0121*** (0.00205)	−0.0229*** (0.000820)	−0.168*** (0.00536)
3	−0.0211*** (0.00201)	−0.0421*** (0.000752)	−0.286*** (0.00455)
4	−0.0220*** (0.00201)	−0.0571*** (0.000746)	−0.370*** (0.00410)
Highest	−0.0214*** (0.00206)	−0.0844*** (0.000765)	−0.494*** (0.00354)
Age dummies (years)			
25–34	0.0114*** (0.00368)	0.0124*** (0.00231)	0.0505*** (0.0104)
35–44	−0.0688*** (0.00312)	−0.0158*** (0.00187)	0.0533*** (0.0103)
45–54	−0.121*** (0.00286)	−0.0372*** (0.00171)	0.0386*** (0.0107)
55–64	−0.138*** (0.00258)	−0.0451*** (0.00155)	0.0284** (0.0112)
Number of businesses	0.00223** (0.000964)	0.000549 (0.000416)	−0.00131 (0.00341)
Legal form			
Company	0.00221 (0.00283)	0.00707*** (0.00166)	0.0429*** (0.00857)
LLP	−0.00475 (0.0102)	0.000618 (0.00645)	−0.00418 (0.0303)
Partnership	0.00847*** (0.00284)	0.00267 (0.00167)	−0.00224 (0.00842)
Sole trader	0.0306*** (0.00291)	0.0101*** (0.00171)	−0.00229 (0.00844)
Sector dummies			
Business services	0.0119*** (0.00282)	0.00798*** (0.00169)	0.0172** (0.00846)
Construction	0.0108*** (0.00307)	0.000514 (0.00176)	−0.0192** (0.00891)
Education and health	0.0163*** (0.00418)	0.0117*** (0.00265)	0.0282** (0.0123)
Hotels and catering	0.0476*** (0.00384)	0.00829*** (0.00212)	−0.0497*** (0.00953)
Manufacturing	0.00525 (0.00325)	0.00208 (0.00193)	−0.000629 (0.00977)
Other services	0.0170*** (0.00304)	0.00675*** (0.00180)	−0.00234 (0.00879)
Property services	0.0212*** (0.00336)	0.0120*** (0.00207)	0.0286*** (0.00980)
Retail	0.0106*** (0.00291)	0.00210 (0.00169)	−0.0105 (0.00858)
Transport	0.00441 (0.00374)	−0.00349* (0.00210)	−0.0271** (0.0110)
Log turnover	0.00666*** (0.000280)	0.00380*** (0.000172)	0.00851*** (0.000892)
Firm age	−0.00161*** (0.000326)	0.000275 (0.000197)	0.00545*** (0.00102)
Firm age^2	−1.99e−05 (1.46e−05)	−3.72e−05*** (8.93e−06)	−0.000184*** (4.58e−05)
Business performance (omitted = died)			
−25% or lower	−0.00309* (0.00158)	−0.00125 (0.000954)	−0.00597 (0.00491)
−25% to +33%	−0.0245*** (0.00162)	−0.00743*** (0.000985)	−0.000638 (0.00542)
+33% or more	0.0192*** (0.00165)	0.0119*** (0.00103)	0.0208*** (0.00483)
Number of observations	470 133	470 133	91 889
Nagelkerke R^2	0.0556	0.0826	0.181

of Table 7 shows that owners of high growth businesses (+33%) are 2% more likely to improve their residential location than otherwise comparable owners that also move.

It might have been expected that exit from business ownership – reflecting failure or even bankruptcy – would considerably lower the proportion of business owners moving to a more prosperous location. However this is not the case. Instead there was no significant difference in the likelihood of their owners moving residence to an improved location between an exiting and a surviving, but slow-growing, business. This is probably because exits are a 'mixed bag'. They comprise a minority where the founder sells ownership and may obtain a substantial capital sum; others who choose no longer to run a business because of better opportunities as an employee; and those where the financial and emotional costs of closure are considerable. These data do not enable these groups to be identified separately.

CONCLUSION

This paper asks whether entrepreneurship constitutes a route out of disadvantage for those living in deprived areas. Three central findings from the paper are highlighted and their implications are then considered.

The first finding is that business owners in the most deprived areas of England are both more likely to move than otherwise comparable non-owners and, if they do, significantly more likely to see an improvement in their residential address than non-owners living in those areas. This result is robust to taking into account that 55% of business owners living in the most deprived areas of England in 2006 were not a business owner five years later. It appears to support the concept of entrepreneurship being a route out of disadvantage.

However, its implications for policy are not straightforward. This is because most, but not all, owners of businesses in deprived areas also live in that area. If their business prospers the owner(s) become more likely to change their residence, so removing from the area this consumer spending. This is of less importance in prosperous areas where fewer business owners 'live above the shop'. The implications for deprived areas of this out-migration of business owners are open to differing interpretations. FENTON *et al.* (2010) emphasize that many residents in deprived areas are transitional, and that although deprived areas never appear to improve, this is because the out-movers are replaced by others moving into the area attracted by low living costs. The alternative interpretation (HOLDEN and FRANKAL, 2012) of why deprived areas never appear to improve is simply that job creation rates are lower. The findings offer some (limited) insight by pointing to movement out amongst the more successful business owners – but only in comparison with those already in employment. What cannot be done is to demonstrate that *entry into* business ownership is beneficial for the unemployed or economically inactive living in deprived areas.

The second key finding is that movement to a more prosperous location is not limited to business owners living in disadvantaged areas. Instead, it is found that successful business owners throughout the IMD spectrum are more likely to have moved to a more prosperous area than otherwise comparable non-owners during 2006–11. Indeed, it appears that it is business owners living in prosperous areas in 2006 who are the prime beneficiaries of enterprise.

The third key finding was that business ownership was not a guarantee of improvement, since it only led to movement to a more prosperous area for the owner when the business survived and exhibited significant sales growth. Closure or contraction reduced the likelihood of a move – although it did not seem to lead to a move to a less prosperous area.

This section concludes by highlighting the limitations of the paper and by counselling the importance of drawing only valid inferences from the results. The definitions used in this paper are both its strength and its limitation. The strength is in providing clarity about the form of entrepreneurship that is being examined and in comparing the 'returns' to an individual with those from being an employee. But it can be recognized that business ownership may not be a perfect proxy for entrepreneurship. The use of housing as a measure of wealth, although it has the key strength of minimizing the under-reporting so characteristic of other indicators of entrepreneurial 'returns', nevertheless remains a proxy for wealth. It is also acknowledged that the range of controls available is not extensive.

Finally, and perhaps most importantly from a policy perspective, one is limited to observing changes over time amongst business owners and non-owners. Government policy, however, seeks to shift individuals into business ownership. The ideal test would be to examine whether those who actually make the shift perform better than a comparable control group who do not. Currently such work cannot be carried out and so the test of policy, although it offers unique insights, is not ideal.

Acknowledgements – This article was presented at staff seminars in the UK at Sussex and the Work Foundation. The authors are grateful to Neil Lee, Rebecca Liu and two anonymous referees for many helpful comments. J. S. F. and R. G. R. wrote only in a personal capacity and do not necessarily reflect the views of Barclays Bank. Any remaining errors are the authors' alone.

Funding – A. C. gratefully acknowledges financial support from the Economic and Social Research Council (ESRC), Technology Strategy Board (TSB), Department for Business, Innovation & Skills (BIS) and the National Endowment for Science, Technology and the Arts (NESTA) [grant numbers ES/H008705/1 and ES/J008427/1] as part of the Innovation Research Centre (IRC) distributed projects initiative, as well as

APPENDIX A

Table A1. Variables relating to owners and employees

Variable	Description
Gender	Male = 1 and female = 0
Age	Age of owner or employee (years): under 25, 25–34, 35–44, 45–54 and 55–64
Region	Region grouping of England, 2006 residential address of business owner or employee: NORTH (North East, North West, Yorkshire, East Midlands, West Midlands), SOUTH (East of England, South East, South West), and LONDON
IMD_quintile	Quintile of the national Index of Multiple Deprivation (IMD), 2006 residential address of the business owner or employee: most deprived = 1 and least deprived = 5
Move	Is the 2011 residential address of the business owner or employee different in 2011 from 2006?: Yes = 1 and No = 0
Up	Is the 2011 residential address of the business owner or employee in a higher percentile of the IMD ranking than in 2006?: Yes = 1 and No = 0
Owner	Was the individual a business owner in 2006: Yes = 1 and No = 0

Table A2. Variables relating to businesses of owners

Variable	Description
No. businesses	Number of businesses owned
Owner in 2011	Individual remains an owner in 2011
Legal form dummies	Dummies for: company; limited liability partnership; partnership; and sole trader
Firm age	Number of years the business has been a bank customer. Maximum value if more than one business is owned
Firm age squared	Squared value of *Firm age*
Log turnover	Natural log of business turnover. Aggregate turnover if more than one business is owned
Business performance	Change in business turnover (aggregate turnover if multiple businesses are owned), 2006–11: No longer an owner = 1; −25% or less = 2; −25% to +33% = 3; and +33% or more = 4. 'No longer an owner' is the base case
Industry dummies	Dummies for: business services; construction; education and health; hotels and catering; manufacturing; other services; property services; retail; and transport

Note: Individuals can own multiple businesses. Hence, they may be associated with more than one legal form and with more than one industry group.

from the Arts & Humanities Research Council (AHRC) as part of the FUSE project.

NOTES

1. 'Since 2006 around £150 million has been committed to implement proposals from England's most deprived local authorities to support enterprise initiatives. A further £280 million will be committed between 2008 and 2011' (BERR, 2008, p. 89).
2. There are 150 steps up the ranking here ordered in integer steps, corresponding to the 150 local areas.
3. The IMD ranking used is for 2010. Focus is on the period 2006–11, comprising both an economic boom and the subsequent crisis. This may affect the generality of the findings.
4. The aggregate findings for 'All areas' (with employees slightly more likely to move up than owners) do not match the results found for each quintile taken individually. This is a sample composition effect – business owners are more numerous in the highest quintiles where the proportion moving up is lower.
5. One possible explanation for this could be income differences, which cannot be controlled. This is recognized here, but it should be emphasized that those with very low incomes are excluded because only those known to be in employment are included amongst the non-owners. To have included the unemployed and the economically inactive would have widened the differences between business owners and all other residents.
6. As with the model for change of residential address, there is no accounting for incomes.
7. Recall that owners in quintile 5 are also more likely to have multiple businesses, hence the use of the term 'aggregate'.
8. It was not easy finding an instrument for the selection equation because many of the variables that predicted 'move' also predicted 'up'. Furthermore, Heckman models make a number of other assumptions that can be problematic, such as the assumption of bivariate normality. However, taking the number of businesses as the instrument, a Heckman probit was estimated and similar results were obtained.
9. Some individuals are associated with more than one legal form by virtue of owning multiple businesses, and so there is no need for an omitted baseline legal form.
10. Other options include comparisons with, for example, two possible random process benchmarks – the 'dartboard' approach, and the random walk. The dartboard model is where there is an equal chance of landing in each part of the 'dartboard' or region, hence an implicit uniform distribution. So, if there are 80% of regions above, there is an 80% chance of moving up. Alternatively, according to the random walk model,

there is the same probability of moving up as moving down – hence, a 50% chance of moving up and 50% chance of moving down – irrespective of the starting point. It is suspected that the true process governing the dynamics of moving up has characteristics of both processes and is an issue requiring further work.

REFERENCES

BERR (2008) *Enterprise: Unlocking the UK's Talent.* March. Department of Business Enterprise and Regulatory Reform (BERR), London.

Blackburn R. and Ram M. (2006) Fix or fixation? The contributions and limitations of entrepreneurship and small firms to combating social exclusion, *Entrepreneurship and Regional Development* **18(1)**, 73–89.

Blanchflower D. and Oswald A. J. (1998) What makes an entrepreneur?, *Journal of Labor Economics* **16(1)**, 26–60.

Cheshire P., Monastiriotis V. and Sheppard S. (2003) Income inequality and residential segregation: labour market sorting and demand for positional goods, in Martin R. and Morrison P. (Eds) *Geographies of Labour Market Inequalities*, pp. 83–109. Routledge, London.

Coad A., Frankish J. S., Roberts R. G. and Storey D. J. (2013) Growth paths and survival chances: an application of Gambler's Ruin theory, *Journal of Business Venturing* **28(5)**, 615–632.

Cowling M. and Mitchell P. (1997) The evolution of UK self-employment: a study of government policy and the role of the macroeconomy, *Manchester School* **65(4)**, 427–442.

Engstrom P. and Holmlund B. (2009) Tax evasion and self-employment in a high-tax country: evidence from Sweden, *Applied Economics* **41(19)**, 2419–2430.

Fenton A., Tyler P., Markkanen S., Clark A. and Whitehead C. (2010) *Why Do Neighbourhoods Stay Poor? People: Place and Deprivation in Birmingham.* Barrow Cadbury Trust, London.

Frankish J. S., Roberts R. G. and Storey D. J. (2011) Enterprise: a route out of deprivation and disadvantage?, in Southern A. (Ed.) *Enterprise, Deprivation and Social Exclusion: The Role of Small Business in Addressing Social and Economic Inequalities*, pp. 16–38. Routledge, London.

Frankish J. S., Roberts R. G., Spears T. C., Coad A. and Storey D. J. (2013) Do entrepreneurs really learn? Or do they just tell us that they do?, *Industrial and Corporate Change* **22(1)**, 73–106.

Greene F. J., Mole K. M. and Storey D. J. (2008) *Three Decades of Enterprise Culture: Economic Regeneration and Public Policy.* Macmillan, London.

Henley A. (2000) Residential mobility, housing wealth and the labour market, *Economic Journal* **108(447)**, 414–427.

HMT (1999) *Enterprise and Social Exclusion.* HM Treasury (HMT), London.

HOC All Party Urban Development Group (2007) *Business Matters: Understanding the Role of Business in Regeneration.* All Party Urban Development Group, London.

Holden J. and Frankal B. (2012) A new perspective on the success of public sector worklessness interventions in the UK's most deprived areas, *Local Economy* **27(5–6)**, 1–10.

Hurst E., Li G. and Pugsley B. (2010) *Are Household Surveys Like Tax Forms? Evidence of Income Self-Reporting of the Self-Employed.* NBER Working Paper Number 16527. National Bureau of Economic Research (NBER), Cambridge, MA.

Jarvis R. and Rigby M. (2012) The provision of human resources and employment advice to small and medium-sized enterprises, *International Small Business Journal* **30(8)**, 944–956.

Jayawarna D., Jones O. and MacPherson A. (2011) New business creation and regional development: enhancing resource acquisition in areas of social deprivation, *Entrepreneurship and Regional Development* **23(9–10)**, 735–761.

Johansson E. (2006) An estimate of self-employment income underreporting in Finland, *Nordic Journal of Political Economy* **31**, 99–110.

Kon Y. and Storey D. J. (2003) A theory of discouraged borrowers, *Small Business Economics* **21(1)**, 37–49.

Lee N. and Cowling M. (Forthcoming 2013) Place, sorting effects and barriers to enterprise in deprived areas: different problems or different firms? *International Small Business Journal.*

MacDonald R. F. and Coffield F. (1991) *Risky Business? Youth and the Enterprise Culture.* Falmer, Basingstoke.

Merz J. (2000) *The Income Distribution of Self-Employed Entrepreneurs and Professions as Revealed from Micro Income Tax Statistics in Germany.* FFB Discussion Paper Number 27. Universitat Luneburg, Luneburg.

Moore A. C., Stinson L. L. and Welniak E. J. (2000) Income measurement error in surveys: a review, *Journal of Official Statistics* **16(4)**, 331–361.

ODPM (2003) *Research Report 5: Business-Led Regeneration of Deprived Areas, A Review of the Evidence Base.* Office of the Deputy Prime Minister (ODPM), London.

Parker S. C. (2009) *The Economics of Entrepreneurship.* Cambridge University Press, Cambridge.

Pissarides C. A. and Weber G. (1989) An expenditure-based estimate of Britain's black economy, *Journal of Public Economics* **39(1)**, 17–32.

Van Praag C. M. and Versloot P. H. (2007) What is the value of entrepreneurship? A review of recent research, *Small Business Economics* **29**, 351–382.

Quadrini V. (1999) The importance of entrepreneurship for wealth concentration and mobility, *Review of Income and Wealth* **45(1)**, 1–19.

Roberts E. B. (1991) *Entrepreneurs in High Technology: Lessons from MIT and Beyond.* Oxford University Press, New York, NY.

Robson M. T. (1998) Self-employment in the UK regions, *Applied Economics* **30(3)**, 313–322.

SARIDAKIS G., MOLE K. and HAY G. (2013) Liquidity constraints in the first year of trading and firm performance, *International Small Business Journal* **31(5)**, 520–535.

SMALL BUSINESS SERVICE (2004) *A Government Action Plan for Small Business: Making the UK the Best Place in the World to Start and Grow a Business – The Evidence Base*. Department of Trade and Industry/HMSO, London.

STOREY D. J. and GREENE F. J. (2010) *Small Business and Entrepreneurship*. Pearson, London.

TAYLOR M. P. (1996) Earnings, independence or unemployment: why become self-employed?, *Oxford Bulletin of Economics and Statistics* **58(2)**, 253–266.

TAYLOR M. (2004) Self-employment in Britain: when, who and why?, *Swedish Economic Policy Review* **11**, 139–173.

TIMMERMANS B. (2010) *The Danish Integrated Database for Labor Market Research: Towards Demystification for the English Speaking Audience*. DRUID Working Paper Number 10–16. Danish Research Unit for Industrial Dynamics (DRUID), Copenhagen.

TUROK I. and GORDON I. R. (2005) How urban labour markets matter, in BUCK I., GORDON I., HARDING A. and TUROK I. (Eds) *Changing Cities*, pp. 242–264. Palgrave, London.

WILLIAMS C. C. (2010) Spatial variations in the hidden enterprise culture: some lessons from England, *Entrepreneurship and Regional Development* **22(5)**, 403–423.

WILLIAMS C. C. and NADIN S. (2012) Tackling the hidden enterprise culture: government policies to support the formalization of informal entrepreneurship, *Entrepreneurship and Regional Development* **24(9–10)**, 895–915.

Regional Effect Heterogeneity of Start-up Subsidies for the Unemployed

MARCO CALIENDO* and STEFFEN KÜNN†
*University of Potsdam, IZA Bonn, DIW Berlin and IAB Nuremberg; University of Potsdam, Economics Department, Potsdam, Germany.
†IZA Bonn, Bonn, Germany.

CALIENDO M. and KÜNN S. Regional effect heterogeneity of start-up subsidies for the unemployed, *Regional Studies*. Evaluation studies have shown the high effectiveness of start-up subsidies for unemployed individuals to improve labour market outcomes of participants. What has not been examined yet are the potentially heterogeneous effects of start-up programmes across regional labour markets. Labour demand-side restrictions in deprived areas generally increase entries into start-up programmes as job offers are limited. However, the survival of firms in these areas is also lower, such that the overall effect remains unclear. Based on German data, it is found that the founding process, development of businesses and programme effectiveness are influenced by prevailing economic conditions at start-up.

Start-up subsidies Evaluation Effect heterogeneity Regional effects Self-employment

CALIENDO M. and KÜNN S. 为失业者提供创业补助金的区域效应异质性，*区域研究*。评估研究显示，提供失业者创业补助金，可以有效增进参与者的劳动市场结果。但创业计画在各区域劳动市场中的潜在异质效应，却尚未被检验。一般而言，较为贫困的地区由于就业供给有限，因此劳动需求面的限制促使创业方案参与的增加。但企业在这些区域的存活率却也较低，致使总体效应不甚明确。本研究根据德国的数据，发现创业过程、商业发展以及计画的有效性，受到创业时普遍的经济条件所影响。

创业补助金 评估 效应异质性 区域效应 自雇

CALIENDO M. et KÜNN S. L'effet régional hétérogène des subventions de démarrage en faveur des chômeurs, *Regional Studies*. Des études d'évaluation ont démontré l'efficacité importante des subventions de démarrage en faveur des chômeurs pour améliorer les résultats sur le marché du travail des participants. Ce que l'on n'a pas encore examiné ce sont les effets hétérogènes potentiels des programmes qui favorisent la création d'entreprises dans l'ensemble des marchés du travail régionaux. En règle générale, les contraintes du côté de la demande du travail dans les zones défavorisées augmentent la demande de participer aux programmes qui favorisent la creation d'entreprises parce que les offres d'emploi sont limitées. Cependant, le taux de survie des entreprises dans de telles zones est aussi moins élevé, à tel point que l'effet global reste moins certain. À partir des données pour l'Allemagne, il est constaté que la phase de démarrage, la création d'entreprises et l'efficacité des programmes sont influés par le climat économique actuel au moment du démarrage.

Subventions de démarrage Évaluation Effet hétérogène Effets régionaux Travail indépendant

CALIENDO M. und KÜNN S. Regionale Effektheterogenität von Existenzgründungszuschüssen für Arbeitslose, *Regional Studies*. Bisherige Evaluationsstudien haben gezeigt, dass Existenzgründungszuschüsse für Arbeitslose die Arbeitsmarktchancen der teilnehmenden Personen deutlich verbessern. Es wurde jedoch noch nicht untersucht, inwiefern die Effektivität dieser Programme in verschiedenen regionalen Arbeitsmärkten bzw. Arbeitsmarktlagen variiert. Schlechte Arbeitsmarktbedingungen mit wenigen Jobangeboten führen in der Regel zu einem stärkeren Übergang von arbeitslosen Personen in Existenzgründungsprogramme, wobei gleichzeitig die Überlebenswahrscheinlichkeit der dort gegründeten Unternehmen aufgrund der schlechten Bedingungen niedriger sein kann. Der Gesamteffekt bleibt damit unklar und muss empirisch bestimmt werden. Die vorliegende Studie zeigt für Deutschland, dass der Gründungsprozess, die Unternehmensentwicklung und auch die Programmeffektivität von Existenzgründungsprogrammen stark von den zum Gründungszeitpunkt vorherrschenden ökonomischen Bedingungen beeinflusst wird.

Existenzgründungszuschüsse Bewertung Heterogenität von Effekten Regionale Auswirkungen Selbstständigkeit

CALIENDO M. y KÜNN S. Heterogeneidad del efecto regional en las subvenciones a proyectos empresariales para desempleados, *Regional Studies*. En estudios de evaluación se ha demostrado que las subvenciones a proyectos empresariales para personas en paro son muy eficaces a la hora de mejorar los resultados de los participantes en el mercado laboral. Sin embargo, todavía no se han analizado los efectos potencialmente heterogéneos de los programas para proyectos empresariales en los diferentes mercados laborales de ámbito regional. Las restricciones en la demanda de empleo en áreas más desfavorecidas generalmente hacen aumentar el número de personas que aprovechan estos programas porque las ofertas laborales son limitadas. Sin embargo, la supervivencia de empresas en estas áreas es también más baja, de modo que sigue sin estar claro el efecto general. Basándonos en datos alemanes, observamos que el proceso de creación, el desarrollo de negocios y la eficacia de los programas están influenciados por las condiciones económicas imperantes en el momento de la creación de la empresa.

Subvenciones a proyectos empresariales Evaluación Heterogeneidad del efecto Efectos regionales Empleo autónomo

INTRODUCTION

The promotion of self-employment among unemployed individuals has been shown to be an effective strategy as part of active labour market policies (ALMP). The main idea is to provide unemployed individuals financial assistance in order to set up their own business and therefore to escape unemployment. Furthermore, start-up subsidies in contrast to other programmes of ALMP are potentially associated with a 'double dividend', if the subsidized businesses create additional jobs in the future and hence reducing unemployment further. The justification of start-up subsidies for unemployed individuals is based on the existence of disadvantages for nascent unemployed entrepreneurs. These might arise due to capital constraints, shortages in start-up-specific human capital or the absence of job-related (and social) networks as well as imperfect information or higher shares of necessity start-ups (when compared with 'regular' business start-ups not coming from unemployment). For instance, capital markets are particularly likely to discriminate against unemployed individuals which restricts access to loans (MEAGER, 1996; PERRY, 2006); restricted access to information about business opportunities might lead unemployed individuals to realize less valuable business ideas (SHANE, 2003). The subsidy therefore aims at helping nascent unemployed entrepreneurs to overcome existing barriers due to their unemployment status.

The overall international evidence on the effectiveness of traditional ALMP programmes such as training, job creation schemes or job search assistance with respect to income and employment prospects is rather disappointing, even if occasionally positive effects are identified (for evidence on Organisation for Economic Co-operation and Development (OECD) countries, see MARTIN and GRUBB, 2001; DAR and GILL, 1998; DAR and TZANNATOS, 1999; or FAY, 1996; and for the European experience, see KLUVE and SCHMIDT, 2002). In contrast, start-up subsidies seem to be more promising. A recent study by CALIENDO and KÜNN (2011) shows that such programmes improve long-term employment and income prospects of participants and are particularly effective for disadvantaged groups in the labour market, such as low educated or young individuals who generally face limited job offers as their outside options are very limited. In addition to the positive impact on a participant's labour market prospects, it is also known that firm foundation can be of major importance for regional development as it has a positive impact on the structural change, innovation, job creation and, hence, economic growth (STOREY, 1994; AUDRETSCH and KEILBACH, 2004; FRITSCH, 2008).

However, what has not been yet examined is to what extent prevailing local economic conditions influence the effectiveness of start-up subsidies as an ALMP programme. Existing evidence on the effectiveness of traditional ALMP programmes (e.g. training, wage subsidies) with respect to economic conditions suggests that programmes are generally more effective in regions with unfavourable economic conditions (LECHNER and WUNSCH, 2009; FAHR and SUNDE, 2009; KLUVE, 2010).[1] The question remains, however, if this evidence is adoptable to start-up subsidies as those programmes do not focus on the integration into dependent employment but into self-employment. Labour demand-side restrictions in areas with relatively bad labour market conditions generally increase entries into start-up programmes as job offers are limited and starting an own business is an opportunity to leave unemployment. However, the survival of firms in deprived areas is also lower, such that the overall effect remains an empirical question which this paper aims to answer. To do so, labour market outcomes of participants are compared with those of other unemployed individuals and the effectiveness of start-ups subsidies as an ALMP programme under different economic conditions is assessed. Furthermore, the paper tries to disentangle whether regional effect heterogeneity is primarily driven by labour demand-side restrictions or differences in business performance.

A combination of administrative and survey data from a large sample of participants in two distinct start-up programmes in Germany, i.e. Bridging Allowance (BA) and Start-up Subsidy (SUS), as well as a control group of unemployed who did not enter these programmes are used. These individuals are observed for five years after start-up and not only survival and personal income but also detailed information about the business structure are monitored. Both programmes basically differ in terms of the amount and length of the subsidy payment. While participants of the BA programme received their monthly unemployment benefits (plus a lump-sum payment to cover social security) for the first six months after business start-up, participants of the SUS programme received a lower fixed monthly payment but for a much longer period (€600/€360/€240 per month in the first/second/third year, respectively). Therefore, both programmes attracted different types of individuals. For instance, SUS participants were generally less qualified, had less work experience (in particular in the field of business foundation) and therefore were less likely to receive unemployment benefits and if so at lower levels than BA recipients (cf. CALIENDO and KRITIKOS, 2010). BA participants were more similar to general business founders, while SUS participants were rather 'atypical'. To investigate the influence of prevailing local economic conditions at business start-up on the founding process, business development and effect heterogeneity in terms of employment and income prospects of participants, monthly information on unemployment rates and gross domestic product (GDP) per capita at the labour agency district level were added. Based on the distribution of these economic indicators, six types of regional labour markets were distinguished.

The descriptive evidence shows that businesses founded by SUS and BA participants are differently affected by local economic conditions at start-up. While businesses by BA participants experience slightly larger firm survival, higher income and more job creation in favourable areas, SUS businesses experience a negative relationship between business success and economic conditions. Propensity score (PS)-matching methods are used to compare participants in BA and SUS with other unemployed individuals to calculate causal programme effects. Programme-specific effect heterogeneity with respect to local economic conditions on employment prospects of participants is found. While the BA programme turns out to be generally more effective in regions with disadvantaged economic conditions, no such clear pattern is found for the case of SUS. A detailed analysis on possible mechanisms driving the effect heterogeneity reveals that estimated employment effects are primarily affected by varying labour market performance of non-participants (indicating labour demand-side restrictions) and less by differences in terms of firm survival under different economic circumstances.

The paper is organized as follows. The second section discusses some theoretical considerations and expectations about the impact of local economic conditions on firm characteristics (start-up rates and business development) and on the effectiveness of start-up programmes. The third section explains the institutional setting of the two start-up subsidies under scrutiny. The fourth section, the main part of the paper, contains the empirical analysis including data description, descriptive evidence, and the identification strategy and results of the causal analysis. The fifth section summarizes the main findings and discusses policy conclusions.

THEORETICAL CONSIDERATIONS

The aim of this study is to investigate the effectiveness of SUS programmes to improve labour market prospects of unemployed individuals under different local economic conditions. As these programmes – in contrast to other ALMP programmes – focus on the integration in self-employment, the effectiveness might be affected by two issues: first, the labour market success of non-participants under different local economic conditions; and second, the business development of subsidized start-ups, i.e. the performance of participants under different local economic conditions. Therefore, the following provides a brief discussion of theoretical expectations with respect to both dimensions.

Beside other factors such as population density, the presence of small firms or infrastructure, regional economic conditions such as aggregate demand or unemployment are a main driver determining business formation (e.g. REYNOLDS *et al.*, 1994; HAMILTON, 1989; GEORGELLIS and WALL, 2000; KANGASHARJU, 2000, amongst others). The labour market approach provides an explanation as it states that individuals face an occupational choice and become self-employed if the expected discounted utility of being self-employed exceeds the one of being in dependent employment (KNIGHT, 1921; BLANCHFLOWER and OSWALD, 1998; PARKER, 2009). In such a model economic conditions might push or pull individuals into self-employment as those characteristics are likely to affect the profitability of self-employment and/or the utility of paid work (HAMILTON, 1986; GEORGELLIS and WALL, 2000; WAGNER and STERNBERG, 2004). For instance, rising unemployment increases the risk associated with dependent employment and decreases wages, reducing the expected utility and pushing individuals into self-employment. At the same time, the profitability of self-employment might increase due to higher availability of low-cost business takeovers (higher closure rates) or stronger business promotion by the public sector in such regions. On the other hand, the pull hypothesis predicts a negative correlation between start-ups and unemployment rates. Low unemployment rates indicate high aggregate demand which increases potential income from self-employment and leads to increased firm foundation. Start-up rates might be further raised by easier availability of capital and lower risk of failure in more favourable economic conditions (PARKER, 2009). However, HAMILTON (1989) and GEORGELLIS and WALL (2000) find that both the push and the pull theory apply and provide evidence that the relationship between unemployment and business formation is inversely 'U'-shaped. This suggests that rising unemployment pushes individuals into self-employment only in areas with initially low unemployment rates but reduces start-up rates in regions with already high unemployment rates. They explain this observation by missing pull factors in very depressed areas.

While there is a large literature on economic variation and business foundation, much less research exits on the impact of regional economic conditions on post-entry firm performance. In general, it is assumed that more favourable economic conditions increase business survival due to higher product demand and lower interest rates (PARKER, 2009). Although the estimated effects vary, the empirical evidence confirms this hypothesis and shows that beside firm and industry characteristics, in particular macro-economic conditions (employment growth, GDP, unemployment rate) play an important role in determining post-entry firm performance (e.g. AUDRETSCH and MAHMOOD, 1995; FRITSCH *et al.*, 2006; BRIXY and GROTZ, 2006; FALCK, 2007, amongst others). Overall it seems that more favourable conditions extend firm survival; however, with particular regard to unemployment rates the effects are ambiguous. KEEBLE and WALKER (1994) and AUDRETSCH and MAHMOOD (1995) find a negative relationship between unemployment rates and business survival, while VAN PRAAG (2003) finds a positive but non-significant relationship. FRITSCH *et al.* (2006) argue that unemployment rates reflect different macro-economic dimensions (economic growth, availability of workers, start-up rates out of unemployment) and depending on the individual impact of each factor the overall effect of unemployment rates on business survival might be positive or negative.[2] In addition, when looking at start-ups out of unemployment it has to be taken into account that individuals might have a higher tendency to switch back to dependent employment if the start-up is only used as a temporary solution to exit unemployment. This might lead to higher exit rates out of self-employment for this group of individuals during an economic upswing when the number of (dependent) job opportunities increases. This would then counteract the positive correlation between economic conditions and firm survival.

Given this evidence, it might be concluded that the risk of business failure is generally higher in deprived areas, which would predict higher programme effectiveness in privileged areas. If this is true the question arises if subsidizing business foundation among unemployed individuals in deprived areas is a sensible strategy at all or whether participants return to unemployment immediately once the subsidy expires. Clearly, this is not only a scientifically interesting but also a policy-relevant question. However, programme effectiveness does not solely depend on the labour market performance of programme participants (survival in self-employment) but on their performance relative to non-participants in the same area. Taking this into account brings up a reverse hypothesis, namely that start-up programmes might be more effective in deprived areas as self-employment provides an alternative to dependent employment which is typically limited in such regions. Existing labour demand-side restrictions in deprived areas might lead to lower employment probabilities among non-participants and hence to higher programme effectiveness in these areas compared with privileged areas.[3] As theoretical considerations do not deliver a clear answer about which of the two opposing effects dominates, i.e. higher business survival versus higher employment probabilities among non-participants in regions with favourable economic conditions, this is an empirical question which will be examined henceforth.

INSTITUTIONAL SETTINGS IN GERMANY

This study investigates the effectiveness of two distinct start-up subsidies under different economic conditions. Both programmes mainly differ with respect to the amount and length of the subsidy. The first programme, Bridging Allowance (BA), amounts to the individual unemployment benefits plus a lump sum payment (68.5% of the benefits) for social security and is paid during the first six months of self-employment.[4] To receive the subsidy the unemployed have to be eligible for unemployment benefits and have an externally approved business plan (issued by the regional chamber of commerce). While BA was already introduced in 1986, the second programme, Start-up Subsidy (SUS), was introduced as part of a bigger labour market reform in 2003. The main intention for the introduction of a second programme was to encourage small business start-ups by opening the programme to a larger group of unemployed individuals. Eligibility to SUS was therefore not restricted to unemployed individuals with benefit entitlement but also open to those with means-tested social assistance, i.e. primarily long-term unemployed and individuals with limited labour market experience. SUS consists of a lump-sum payment of €600 per month in the first year, €360 per month in the second year and €240 per month in the third year and it was prolonged on a yearly basis if self-employment income did not exceed €25 000 per year. Furthermore, SUS recipients have to pay into the statutory pension fund and can claim a reduced rate for statutory health insurance. When SUS was introduced in 2003, applicants did not have to submit business plans for prior approval, but they have been required to do so since November 2004.[5] All eligible applicants received the subsidy (by a legal entitlement) but a parallel receipt of BA and SUS was excluded.

CALIENDO and KRITIKOS (2010) investigate the characteristics of participants in both programmes and show that due to the institutional settings both programmes attract a different clientele of individuals. It was rational to choose BA if unemployment benefits were fairly high or if the income generated through the start-up firm was expected to exceed €25 000 per year. Therefore, SUS participants turn out to be on average less qualified, having less work experience (in particular in the field of business foundation) and therefore are less likely to receive unemployment benefits and if they do then at lower levels than BA recipients. It is concluded that BA participants are quite similar to general business founders and SUS participants are rather 'atypical'. As shown below, this selection process turns out to be important with respect to the results.

EMPIRICAL ANALYSIS

Data

The data used consist of random samples of programme entries in SUS and BA from the third quarter of 2003 in Germany (treatment group).[6] As a control group, other unemployed individuals from the third quarter of 2003 who were also eligible to the programmes but who did not participate in this particular quarter are considered.[7] The data combine administrative data from the Federal Employment Agency (FEA) with information from a telephone survey.[8] The survey was conducted in three interview waves, whereby two interviews took place in January–February of 2005 and 2006 and the last interview in May–June 2008. Finally, the data contain detailed information on individual socio-demographics and labour market history before treatment, programme-specific aspects and different labour market outcomes up to five years after start-up. The analysis is restricted to individuals who participated in every interview in order to observe individual labour market outcomes for the entire period of 56 months. The analysis focuses on men only, since start-ups by women differ in their motivation and intensity. While men are represented along the entire distribution of entrepreneurs, female entrepreneurs tend to be concentrated in particular sectors and among low-profit businesses. This can be attributed to a different motivation, e.g. because more women are seeking a work–family balance instead of earning maximization (KLAPPER and PARKER, 2011; BODEN, 1999). This also explains why women are significantly less likely to become full-time self-employed (GURLEY-CALVEZ *et al.*, 2009; LECHMANN and SCHNABEL, 2012). As this paper is interested in the effectiveness of start-up programmes to improve labour market prospects of participants, these issues are circumvented by excluding women from the analysis and avoiding side-effects due to differences driven by labour supply decisions of female participants and non-participants.[9] Finally, the estimation sample consists of 715 male participants in SUS, 1096 male participants in BA and 1343 male non-participants.

To estimate regional effects, regional labour markets (identified by labour agency districts in the sample) are classified by the distribution of different economic indicators. Based on the theoretical considerations and previous empirical evidence, labour agency districts are aggregated by the level of unemployment rates and GDP as these measures reflect the macro-economic conditions for dependent employment (wages, labour market tightness) and self-employment (aggregate demand, productivity) which influence the decision to start a business, its post-entry performance and reflects existing labour demand-side restrictions. Therefore, that aggregate information on labour agency districts in the third quarter 2003 is added to the data.[10] The unemployment rates are obtained from the German Federal Labour Agency, and the gross domestic product from the German Federal Statistical Office. GDP per capita is calculated to take district sizes into account.

Labour agency districts are aggregated by dividing the distribution of the economic measures into three parts reflecting poor, medium and good conditions.[11] The economic conditions are relatively stable within the observation window.[12]

Table 1 shows the distribution of the different economic measures within the full estimation sample and within each of the six stratified subsamples. First, unemployment rates and GDP per capita are not perfectly correlated as they capture different economic conditions (as discussed above). The correlation coefficient is −0.509 and as a consequence the classified subsamples (poor/medium/good) contain partly different individuals using the unemployment rate or GDP metric. For instance, the poor category using the GDP metric contains in total 1048 individuals from which only 724 (69%) are also included in the poor category using the unemployment rate. Moreover, programme entries for five labour market districts in Germany are not observed, so that only 176 instead of 181 existing labour office districts are observed in the data. The figures further suggest that the distribution of both measures is slightly asymmetric within the full estimation sample which is reflected by differences between mean and median and by varying numbers of assigned labour market districts within each stratified subsample. It can be further seen that sufficient variation in terms of the measures exist to classify distinctive regional labour markets. For instance, areas characterized by poor labour market conditions show a relatively low GDP per capita with a mean of €19 203 which is €14 340 lower than in areas characterized by good economic conditions which is quite substantial.

Descriptive analysis

Based on these observations, this subsection considers variables related to the founding decision of individuals and business development in order to deliver descriptive evidence to the theoretical expectation formulated in the second section. All descriptive results presented below are adjusted for selection bias due to panel attrition by using sequential inverse probability weighting (WOOLDRIDGE, 2002).[13]

Description of the founding process. As derived from an occupational choice model, theory does not

Table 1. Distribution of labour market indicators within the estimation sample

	Full sample	Aggregation of labour agency districts conditional on the local economic condition		
		Poor	Medium	Good
Unemployment rate (%)				
Number of labour agency districts	176	40	61	75
Number of individuals	3154	1019	1073	1062
Start-up Subsidy (SUS)	715	237	251	227
Bridging Allowance (BA)	1096	337	361	398
Non-participants	1343	445	461	437
Mean	11.292	17.800	9.690	6.580
Standard deviation (SD)	4.995	2.520	1.150	0.939
Median	9.383	17.974	9.383	6.712
Minimum	4.083	13.193	7.907	4.083
Maximum	24.584	24.584	11.862	7.885
Gross domestic product (GDP) per capita (€, thousands)[a]				
Number of labour agency districts	176	58	57	61
Number of individuals	3154	1048	1056	1050
SUS	715	231	244	240
BA	1096	365	376	355
Non-participants	1343	452	436	455
Mean	25.708	19.203	24.430	33.543
SD	7.258	2.037	1.229	6.904
Median	23.980	19.640	23.980	30.425
Minimum	14.385	14.385	22.300	27.000
Maximum	49.070	22.280	26.870	49.070
Correlation between the unemployment rate and GDP				
Correlation coefficient	–0.509			

Notes: Labour market indicators are measured in the third quarter of 2003 at the level of labour agency districts. In total, 181 labour agency districts exist in Germany.

[a]In year 2005 prices.

unambiguously predict how different economic conditions influence self-employment rates as both push or pull motives might be valid such that empirical evidence is needed. To identify the motivation of individuals in the estimation sample, the distribution of push and pull motives conditional on prevailing local economic conditions at start-up are depicted in Table 1. First, SUS participants are generally more likely to be pushed into self-employment while BA participants are slightly more often motivated by pull items. On average, 84% (53%) of SUS participants report the item 'Termination of unemployment' ('I always wanted to be my own boss') as the motivation to start a business compared with 76% (56%) in the case of BA. This is consistent with the programme-specific selection pattern, i.e. BA participants are more similar to general business founders while SUS are rather atypical business founders. It is also consistent with earlier research by CALIENDO and KRITIKOS (2009) showing that the previous stereotype suggesting that all start-ups by unemployed persons are necessity based does not hold.

The hypothesis that necessity (opportunity) start-ups are overrepresented (underrepresented) in areas with rather poor economic conditions cannot be clearly confirmed by Table 2. While it cannot be seen that the push motive 'Termination of unemployment' has its highest shares mostly in regions with poor economic conditions, the evidence for the pull motive 'I always wanted to be my own boss' is more mixed. This could indicate that pull motives are less influenced by local economic conditions while push motives are more affected. However, since the overall differences between the regions are quite small, such an interpretation needs to be made with caution.

Moreover, Table 2 shows that the subsidized business founders out of unemployment tend to invest less at start-up in areas with unfavourable economic conditions. This confirms the above finding that unemployed individuals are likely to be pulled (pushed) into self-employment if labour market conditions are (un) favourable. Again, the evidence is less clear for the stratified sample by GDP per capita.

Labour market integration and business development. Following theoretical considerations about the influence of economic conditions on business development as well as existing evidence, higher business survival and growth in areas characterized by favourable economic conditions would be expected. However, it has to be kept in mind that this paper considers start-ups out of

Table 2. Founding-related characteristics

	Start-up Subsidy (SUS)			Bridging Allowance (BA)		
	Local economic conditions					
	Poor	Medium	Good	Poor	Medium	Good
Conditional on unemployment rate						
Number of observations	237	251	227	337	361	398
Motivation to become self-employed						
I always wanted to be my own boss	50.0	58.2	51.7	52.3	56.0	58.3
Termination of unemployment	86.2	84.5	81.7	76.3	78.2	74.9
Capital invested at start-up						
≥ €10 000	11.8	14.4	16.4	33.0	34.4	39.9
Conditional on productivity (gross domestic product (GDP) per capita)						
Number of observations	231	244	240	365	376	355
Motivation to become self-employed						
I always wanted to be my own boss	51.7	52.0	56.0	59.3	54.8	53.3
Termination of unemployment	85.4	83.2	83.9	77.0	76.7	75.6
Capital invested at start-up						
≥ €10 000	14.5	14.6	13.3	35.2	33.6	39.0

Note: All numbers are percentages, unless otherwise indicated.

unemployment for which improved economic conditions might partly lead to lower business survival if there is a higher tendency to switch back to dependent employment with increased job opportunities (as discussed in the second section). This might counteract the positive correlation between economic conditions and firm survival. To assess empirically the long-term labour market success of former participants in both programmes as well as business growth, different indicators measured 56 months after start-up are depicted in Table 3.

Considering the labour market status of former programme participants 56 months after start-up, in the case of SUS (BA) about 60% (70%) are still self-employed and approximately 20% are in dependent employment. This indicates a high and persistent integration into employment. The higher shares in self-employment in the case of BA might be explained by the already mentioned selection of individuals into both programmes, where the positive selection of individuals in BA probably increases the probability of surviving in self-employment.

However, large differences in terms of shares in self-employment across areas are hardly detected. It can be seen that the shares in self-employment are slightly higher if labour market conditions (reflected by unemployment rates) are rather unfavourable, which suggests that missing job opportunities might increase the probability to remain self-employed. With respect to dependent employment such a clear pattern is not found. For instance, in the case of SUS higher shares in dependent employment are found if labour market conditions are unfavourable and the reverse for the case of BA.

To assess further the influence of prevailing local economic conditions at start-up on business survival, Kaplan–Meier estimates for the survival probability in the first self-employment spell across the stratified subsamples are additionally provided in Fig. 1. Besides the visual illustration, a Cox regression-based test on the equality of survival curves below is additionally reported (SUCIU *et al.*, 2004). This test compares observed and expected exit probabilities in each regional subgroup, where the expected exit probabilities are calculated under the null hypothesis that the survival curves are the same across those groups. Consistent with the selection into the two programmes, Fig. 1 suggests that more favourable economic conditions at the time of start-up slightly extend firm survival for the case of BA. In the case of SUS the reverse relationship is found, i.e. higher firm survival in deprived areas. This suggests that limited job opportunities in areas characterized by deprived economic conditions probably urge SUS participants to remain self-employed. However, the statistical support is not very strong (only significant in two out of four cases using a critical value of 0.05), which leads to the conclusion that survival of subsidized businesses is only partly affected by local economic conditions at the time of business start-up.[14]

With respect to income, Table 3 shows the individual monthly working income of former participants 56 months after start-up. A clear positive correlation is found between income and prevailing local economic conditions at start-up for the case of BA. For instance, the working income is higher in areas characterized by good economic conditions (low unemployment rates and high GDP) but the evidence is less clear-cut for the participants in SUS.

Table 3. Labour market status and business development 56 months after start-up

	Start-up Subsidy (SUS)			Bridging Allowance (BA)		
	Local economic conditions					
	Poor	Medium	Good	Poor	Medium	Good
Conditional on unemployment rate						
Labour market status (%)						
Self-employed	62.8	58.2	61.9	70.5	67.9	68.1
Employed subject to SSC	20.3	14.8	17.4	20.8	19.9	21.8
Income situation (net, €/month)						
Working income	1386.3	1546.6	1452.2	1601.2	2113.6	2272.5
Employee structure conditional on being self-employed						
Share with at least one employee (%)	21.8	25.8	16.0	35.9	42.3	41.6
Number of employees[a]	2.4	3.0	1.9	3.6	4.0	5.4
Percentage change to 16 months after start-up	41.2	36.4	−9.5	16.1	29.0	28.6
Conditional on productivity (gross domestic product (GDP) per capita)						
Labour market status (%)						
Self-employed	61.0	59.9	61.9	70.5	64.6	71.3
Employed subject to SSC	19.6	20.4	22.0	20.7	20.1	21.7
Income situation (net, €/month)						
Working income	1357.8	1574.1	1458.3	1674.2	2001.9	2358.4
Employee structure conditional on being self-employed						
Share with at least one employee (%)	28.0	15.6	19.4	39.6	36.9	43.4
Number of employees[a]	2.3	3.7	2.0	4.3	3.6	5.2
Percentage change to 16 months after start-up	25.2	35.3	44.1	45.5	8.7	24.3

Notes: The number of observations is reported in Table 2.
SSC, Social Security Contribution.
[a]Conditional on having at least one employee.

Finally, business size is considered in terms of the employee structure. Recalling the discussion in the second section, it would be expected that more favourable economic conditions facilitate business development. The employee structure is depicted in Table 3 by the share with at least one employee and conditional on having at least one employee in the resulting absolute number of employees. With respect to business growth, percentage change is reported in terms of the number of employees compared with the first interview that took place 16 months after start-up. First, for the case of BA the share of firms with at least one employee as well as the absolute number of employees is larger if the firm started under favourable economic conditions. This is in line with the theoretical expectations. However, and consistent with the findings regarding business survival, for the case of SUS the reverse relationship is found, i.e. former SUS recipients create less employment if founded in deprived areas. Looking at business growth from month 16 to month 56, firms indeed experience employment growth (except SUS recipients in areas with low unemployment rates), but no clear pattern is found with respect to the local economic conditions at the time of business start-up. For instance, former SUS recipients who founded a business in areas characterized by poor/medium/good economic conditions based on unemployment rates experience an employment growth of 41%/36%/−10%, respectively. This indicates higher employment growth in deprived areas. However, conditioning on GDP per capita the opposite is observed, i.e. higher employment growth in privileged areas.

In summary, it can be concluded from the descriptive evidence that businesses founded by SUS and BA participants are differently affected by prevailing local economic conditions. While businesses by BA participants experience slightly higher firm survival, larger income and more job creation in favourable areas, SUS businesses experience a negative relationship between business success and economic conditions at start-up. Therefore, it seems that the theoretical expectation that favourable economic conditions facilitate business development is only adoptable to BA participants but not to SUS participants. This might be explained by the positive selection of individuals in the two programmes, with BA participants being more similar to general business founders.

Causal analysis and implementation

After having presented descriptive evidence so far, this section now estimates causal programme effects. To do so, programme participants will be compared with non-participants in order to reveal if the programme causally improved the labour market prospects of

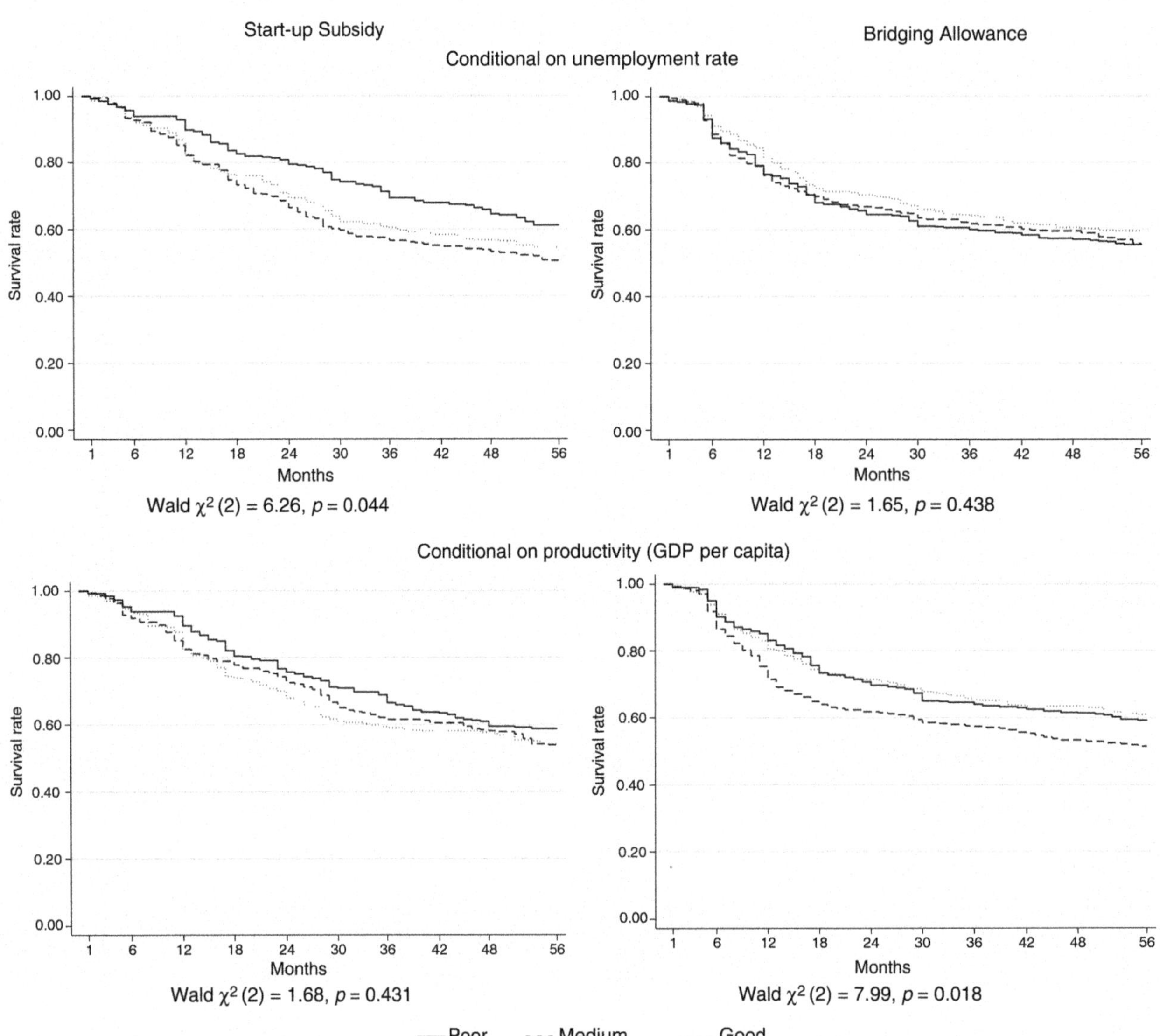

Fig. 1. *Survival in self-employment conditional on local economic conditions*

Note: Kaplan–Meier estimates for the survival probability in the first self-employment spell for programme participants conditional on the prevailing economic conditions at start-up are shown. Test statistics and *p*-values based on a Cox regression-based test on the equality of the depicted survival curves are reported, whereby the underlying null hypothesis states that the survival functions are the same

participants in different regions. Using non-experimental data, it is likely that programme participants differ from non-participants and an unconditional comparison will be biased. To estimate unbiased results, propensity score (PS) matching is used to control for pre-treatment differences between participants and non-participants. The underlying identification strategy is first explained, followed by details on estimation and the matching procedure. Results are then discussed.

Identification strategy. To illustrate the identification strategy, the analysis is based on the potential outcome framework, also known as the Roy–Rubin model (ROY; 1951; RUBIN, 1974). The two potential outcomes are Y^1 (an individual receives treatment, $D = 1$) and Y^0 (an individual does not receive treatment, $D = 0$) whereby the observed outcome for any individual i can be written as:

$$Y_i = Y_i^1 \cdot D_i + (1 - D_i) \cdot Y_i^0$$

As the treatment effect for each individual i is then defined as:

$$\tau_i = Y_i^1 - Y_i^0$$

and both potential outcomes are never observed for the same individual at the same time (referred to as the fundamental evaluation problem), the paper focuses on the most prominent evaluation parameter, which is the average treatment effect on the treated (ATT):

$$\tau_{ATT} = E(Y^1|D=1) - E(Y^0|D=1) \quad (1)$$

The last term on the right-hand side of equation (1) describes the hypothetical outcome without treatment for those individuals who received treatment. Since the condition:

$$E(Y^0|D=1) = E(Y^0|D=0)$$

is usually not satisfied with non-experimental data, estimating ATT by the difference in sub-population means of participants $E(Y^1|D=1)$ and non-participants $E(Y^0|D=0)$ will lead to a selection bias as participants and non-participants are likely to be selected groups in terms of observable and unobservable characteristics with different outcomes, even in the absence of the programme.[15] To correct for this selection bias, PS matching is applied and thus the paper relies on the conditional independence assumption (CIA), which states that conditional on observable characteristics (W) the counterfactual outcome is independent of treatment:

$$Y^0 \coprod D|W$$

where $\coprod$ denotes independence. In addition to the CIA, overlap:

$$Pr(D=1|W) < 1$$

is also assumed for all W, which implies that there are no perfect predictors that determine participation. These assumptions are sufficient for identification of the ATT based on matching (MAT), which can then be written as:

$$\tau_{ATT}^{MAT} = E(Y^1|W, D=1) - E_W[E(Y^0|W, D=0)|D=1] \quad (2)$$

where the first term can be directly estimated from the treatment group and the second term from the matched comparison group. The outer expectation is taken over the distribution of W in the treatment group.

As direct matching on W can become hazardous when W is of high dimension ('curse of dimensionality'), ROSENBAUM and RUBIN (1983) suggest using balancing scores $b(W)$ instead. These are functions of the relevant observed covariates W such that the conditional distribution of W given $b(W)$ is independent of the assignment to treatment, that is:

$$W \coprod D|b(W)$$

The propensity score $P(W)$, i.e. the probability of participating in a programme, is one possible balancing score. For participants and non-participants with the same balancing score, the distributions of the covariates W are the same, i.e. they are balanced across the groups. Hence, the identifying assumption can be rewritten as:

$$Y^0 \coprod D|P(W)$$

and the new overlap condition is given by:

$$Pr(D=1|P(W)) < 1$$

The CIA is clearly a very strong assumption and its justification depends crucially on the availability of informative data which allow one to control for all relevant variables that simultaneously influence the participation decision and the outcome variable. Economic theory, a sound knowledge of previous research and information about the institutional setting should guide the researcher in specifying the model (e.g. SMITH and TODD, 2005; SIANESI, 2004). Although there is no common rule on the set of information necessary, LECHNER and WUNSCH (2013) identify personal and firm characteristics of previous employment as well as labour market history, detailed information on the current unemployment spell and regional characteristics to be most important to include when estimating the programme effects of ALMP. Both administrative and survey information available allow one mostly to reproduce the set of information as suggested by LECHNER and WUNSCH (2013). In addition, information on parental self-employment is included as intergenerational transmission has been shown to influence significantly the start-up decision (CALIENDO and KÜNN, 2011). Although the justification of the CIA is not directly testable with non-experimental data, it is argued that having these informative data makes the CIA likely to hold in the application. Nevertheless, the robustness of the results is tested with respect to unobserved heterogeneity in two directions. First, a conditional difference-in-differences (DID) estimator is implemented to control for time-invariant unobserved differences between participants and non-participants (HECKMAN *et al.*, 1998). Second, a bounding approach is used, as suggested by ROSENBAUM (2002), which introduces an artificial term in the selection equation and tests to which extent of this unobserved factor the results remain significant. This approach does not answer the question whether or not the CIA is fulfilled, but it conveys information on the robustness of the results with respect to unobserved heterogeneity. Applying both tests, the results turn out to be robust with respect to unobserved heterogeneity suggesting that the CIA is a reliable assumption in the study.[16]

Moreover, for the identification of causal effects, any general equilibrium effects need to be excluded, i.e. treatment participation of one individual cannot have an impact on outcomes of other individuals. This assumption is referred to as a stable-unit-treatment-value-assumption (SUTVA). IMBENS and WOOLDRIDGE (2009) argue that the validity of such an assumption depends on the scope of the programme as well as on resulting effects. They infer that for the majority of labour market programmes, SUTVA is potentially fulfilled because such programmes are usually of small scope with rather limited effects on the individual level. Their argumentation is followed and this paper refers to the absolute number entries into SUS and BA which are approximately of the same scope as other ALMP programmes and in relation to the total number of entries into unemployment of 7.6 million in 2003 quite small.[17]

Estimation of treatment propensity. To estimate causal effects of participation in SUS and BA on labour market outcomes of participants, the PS of programme participation are first estimated by applying a non-linear probit estimation. Variations are taken into account in terms of the selection into treatment due to different economic conditions, and the PS within each stratified labour market conditional on unemployment rates and GDP per capita separately are estimated, i.e.:

$$P_{LM}(W) = Pr(D = 1|W, LM = j)$$

where D is the treatment indicator; W is observed covariates; and LM denotes the six different labour markets ($j = 1, \ldots, 6$) characterized by poor, medium and good economic conditions based on unemployment rates and GDP per capita. The informative data at hand allow the inclusion of individual information on socio-demographics, education, past employment, working experience, income situation as well as regional information in the estimation of PS. Different specifications are tested following economic theory and previous empirical findings as outlined above. In addition, econometric indicators such as the significance of parameters or pseudo-R^2 are checked finally to determine one preferred specification.[18] Results of the probit-estimation are depicted in Tables A1–A4 in Appendix A.

As expected from theoretical considerations and descriptive evidence, varying selection patterns into programmes conditional on prevailing local economic conditions are found. For instance, comparing the coefficients of the PS estimations for the BA programme in areas characterized by poor and good economic conditions based on GDP per capita reveals that nearly one-third of the coefficients show different signs. This confirms the hypothesis that local economic conditions affect the selection of unemployed individuals into start-up programmes. As each PS estimation contains individual selection patterns and the discussion is beyond the scope of this paper, the paper focuses on two interesting and common findings with regard to the selection process. First, in particular individuals with an entrepreneurial family background are likely to start a business in deprived areas. This is consistent with findings by TERVO (2006) who argues that those individuals are more likely to be pushed into self-employment as they possess latent entrepreneurial human capital. Second, the higher the remaining individual unemployment benefit entitlement the less likely they are to start a business in areas characterized by favourable economic conditions as opportunity costs are higher (e.g. higher expected wages). Individuals remain longer unemployed and search for better jobs if the labour market offers adequate job opportunities, which is more likely under favourable economic conditions.

Figs A1 and A2 in Appendix A show the distribution of the estimated PS for all regions and both programmes. The distribution of the PS are biased towards the tails, i.e. participants have a higher average probability to become self-employed than non-participants. Nevertheless, participant's and non-participant's PS distributions overlap to a large extent, such that only very few treated observations are lost due to the minima–maxima common support condition (see the numbers below each graph).

Details on matching procedure. Based on the estimated PS, kernel matching is applied and the ATT is estimated, as depicted in equation (2) for each stratified labour market separately, i.e.:

$$\tau_{ATT}^{MAT}|LM = j, \quad j = 1, \ldots, 6$$

The resulting matching quality is assessed, i.e. whether the matching procedure sufficiently balances the distribution of observable characteristics between participants and non-participants, within each stratified subsample with three different criteria: (1) a simple comparison of means (t-test); (2) the mean standardized bias (MSB); and (3) the pseudo-R^2 of the probit estimation in the matched and unmatched samples, respectively.[19] While the t-test on equal means and the pseudo-R^2 indicate a successful matching for both programmes, the mean standardized bias for SUS is after matching within some cells still above the critical value of 5%, as suggested by CALIENDO and KOPEINIG (2008). However, the remaining bias after matching does not have a substantial influence on the selection into treatment (very low pseudo-R^2), so that it can be concluded that the PS matching procedure sufficiently created a control group within each subsample that is very similar to the respective treatment group at the point of entry into treatment. Additionally, it is tested if the matching procedure sufficiently balances differences between both groups in terms of pre-treatment outcome variables such as months in employment and average income in the year before programme entry. The results show no significant differences for almost all variables after matching took place. This reinforces the success of the matching procedure in removing pre-treatment differences between participants and non-participants.[20]

Results

The effectiveness of the two programmes to improve labour market prospects of participants is assessed with respect to two labour market outcomes: integration into the first labour market and earnings. To measure the integration into the first labour market, the binary outcome variable 'self-employed or regular employed' is used, which is 1 for individuals who are either employed subject to social security contribution or self-employed and 0 otherwise. This variable (and not survival in self-employment) is used for two reasons: First, non-participants are less likely to become self-employed than participants; hence, comparing participants and non-participants with respect to self-employment only would bias the causal effects upwards. Second, as the main objective of ALMP is to integrate individuals into the first labour market, this justifies categorizing being regular employed as a success (even if it means that the self-employment spell was terminated). It should be clear that the definition of this outcome variable does not imply that self-employment and wage employment are equally desirable from a programme perspective, but rather that it is an appropriate measure that reflects the degree of labour market integration within both the treatment and control groups. As a second outcome variable the impact on individual monthly working income is assessed. Table 4 contains a summary of the estimated ATT for defined outcome variables within each stratified labour market. The employment effects are depicted at different points in time and cumulated over the entire observation period of 56 months. Since there is no longitudinal information about income, the income effects in Table 4 refer to the end of the observation period.

First, both programmes lead throughout to positive and significant employment effects. Programme participation significantly increases the employment probability of participants compared with non-participants. Positive effects on working income are also found, although they are not always statistically significant. Therefore, independent of the effect heterogeneity with respect to local economic conditions (as will be shown below) both start-up subsidies are effective ALMP tools.

Now, as regards employment effects, some programme-specific patterns are detected. For the case of BA the results suggest that it is more effective in disadvantaged areas as indicated by increasing employment effects with decreasing local economic conditions. For instance, the total cumulated employment effect within regions characterized by poor economic conditions based on unemployment rates (GDP) is 20.7 (19.8) months for BA, but amounts to only 14.6 (14.2) months in regions with good economic conditions. Such a clear pattern is not detected in the case of SUS. Conditioning on unemployment rates, employment effects tend to be slightly higher in areas characterized by poor economic conditions. Although this pattern is much weaker, it is still consistent with the pattern for the BA programme.

Table 4. Causal effects of the Start-up Subsidy (SUS) and Bridging Allowance (BA) conditional on local economic conditions

	SUS versus non-participation			BA versus non-participation		
	Local economic conditions					
	Poor	Medium	Good	Poor	Medium	Good
Conditional on unemployment rate						
Number treated	226	234	210	329	348	375
Number of controls	414	413	406	408	419	406
Outcome variable: 'Self-employed or regular employed'						
After 36 months (percentage points)	37.5	27.3	32.8	29.5	15.3	15.2
After 56 months (percentage points)	20.2	21.5	23.1	23.7	14.1	13.9
Total cumulated effect ($\sum_{t=1}^{56}$, months)	26.4	22.4	24.1	20.7	14.7	14.6
Outcome variable: 'Income 56 months after start-up' (net, €/month)						
Working income	602	(248)	(259)	566	481	448
Conditional on productivity (gross domestic product (GDP) per capita)						
Number treated	220	233	220	347	369	319
Number of controls	412	407	415	417	407	415
Outcome variable: 'Self-employed or regular employed'						
After 36 months (percentage points)	29.1	31.3	33.3	26.6	18.7	14.0
After 56 months (percentage points)	22.7	22.0	24.4	24.3	15.3	13.3
Total cumulated effect ($\sum_{t=1}^{56}$, months)	22.3	24.7	24.6	19.8	15.4	14.2
Outcome variable: 'Income 56 months after start-up' (net, €/month)						
Working income	590	374	(38)	481	683	522

Note: Average treatment effects on the treated as the difference in outcome variables between participants and non-participants are shown. Effects that are not significantly different from zero at the 5% level are given in parentheses; standard errors are based on bootstrapping with 200 replications.

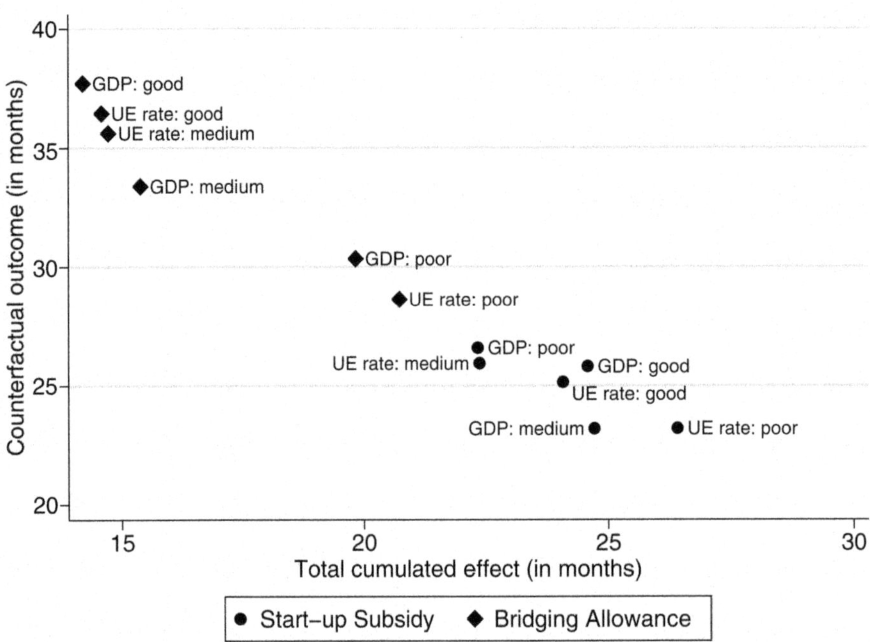

Fig. 2. Regional effect heterogeneity conditional on labour market perspectives among matched non-participants

Note: The horizontal axis shows the cumulated average treatment effects on the treated consistent with Table 4 for the outcome variable 'Self-employment or regular employment'. The vertical axis shows the average months spent in 'Self-employment or regular employment' within the observation period of 56 months for the matched non-participants

However, based on the GDP per capita comparison, the employment effects turn out to be higher in areas characterized by good economic conditions and lower in areas characterized by poor conditions.[21] This is opposite to the finding for the BA programme. The paper highlight, though, that the differences in point estimates are much smaller for the SUS than the BA programme.

To investigate further the mechanism behind the programme-specific pattern, Fig. A3 in Appendix A shows corresponding employment probability levels among treated and matched control individuals over time. As the ATT in Table 4 depicts the difference between participants and matched non-participants, Fig. A3 reveals one possible explanation for the effect heterogeneity. The varying employment effects are primarily attributable to labour market performance among the non-participants under different economic conditions. While the black lines (treated within different regions) almost overlap, the gray lines (matched controls within different regions) show partly substantial differences. For the case of BA, non-participants in disadvantaged regions face lower employment probabilities than in privileged regions leading to the clear pattern that programmes are more effective in disadvantaged areas. It seems that BA with its integration into self-employment counteracts the limited job opportunities for these groups (higher educated with higher earnings in the past) in disadvantaged areas. Again, for SUS no such clear pattern is found. Non-participants in areas characterized by poor economic conditions (solid gray lines) face on average no clear disadvantage in terms of employment probabilities compared with non-participants in other areas. However, for both programmes that effect heterogeneity is primarily driven by labour market performance of non-participants.

Fig. 2 illustrates this negative relationship between labour market performance of matched non-participants and programme effectiveness. Therefore, the ATT for the total cumulated employment outcome (x-axis) is scattered against the estimated counterfactual outcome (y-axis) which reflects the labour market performance of matched non-participants. For both programmes the lower the counterfactual outcome (probably due to limited job opportunities in the labour market) the higher the ATT. This supports the hypothesis that employment effects are primarily driven by the labour market performance of non-participants under different economic conditions and less by differences in terms of firm survival. This is in line with the above Kaplan–Meier estimates, which show that survival of subsidized businesses is only partly significantly affected by economic conditions at the time of business start-up.

CONCLUSION

This paper studies the effectiveness of two different start-up subsidies for unemployed individuals in Germany under different economic conditions. To do so, labour market outcomes of programme participants were compared with those of other unemployed individuals in order to assess in which areas start-up programmes are particularly effective. Moreover, the influence of local economic conditions at the time of start-up on the founding process and development of businesses over time is investigated. A combination of administrative and survey data from a large sample of participants in two distinct programmes, i.e. Bridging Allowance (BA) and Start-up Subsidy (SUS), as well as a control group of unemployed who did not enter these programmes were used. Both programmes differ in terms of the amount and length of the subsidy, where the BA programme consists of a higher monthly payment but runs for a shorter period compared with the SUS programme. These data are enriched with aggregate information on unemployment rates and GDP per capita at the labour agency district level to distinguish six types of regional labour markets.

The descriptive evidence shows that subsidized business founders located in regions with rather favourable economic conditions are more likely to be pulled into self-employment and invest more capital at start-up. With respect to business development a programme-specific pattern arises. While businesses by BA participants experience slightly longer firm survival, higher income and more job creation in favourable areas, SUS businesses experience a negative relationship between business success and economic conditions. This suggests that limited job opportunities in areas characterized by deprived economic conditions probably urge SUS participants to remain self-employed. It seems that the theoretical expectation that favourable economic conditions facilitate business development is only adoptable to BA participants but not to SUS participants. This might be explained by the selection of individuals in the two programmes, where BA participants are quite similar to general business founders while SUS participants are rather atypical.

Based on PS-matching methods to calculate causal programme effects, it is found that both programmes are effective policy tools and increase prospective employment probabilities and working income (although not always statistically significant) of participants. Programme-specific effect heterogeneity with respect to local economic conditions is further shown. This regional effect heterogeneity has not been examined so far and shows that the BA programme turns out to be generally more effective in regions with disadvantaged economic conditions. For participants in SUS a much weaker pattern conditional on unemployment rates is found, and an opposite relationship between programme effectiveness and local economic conditions based on GDP per capita. A detailed analysis on possible mechanisms driving this regional effect heterogeneity reveals that estimated employment effects are primarily affected by varying labour market performance of non-participants (indicating labour demand-side restrictions) and less by differences in terms of firm survival under different economic circumstances.

Overall, the results confirm the promising evidence on the effectiveness of start-up programmes to improve employment and income prospects of participants. It has often been argued that these programmes are especially successful as they provide an alternative to limited job offers in the labour market. In this regard, CALIENDO and KÜNN (2011) show that both start-up programmes – SUS and BA – are particularly effective for disadvantaged groups in the labour market such as low educated or young individuals who generally face limited job offers. The results now add the insight that SUS and BA are also effective under different economic conditions, whereby the degree of effectiveness primarily depends on the labour market performance of non-participants which reflects labour market tightness within different regions. This supports the hypothesis that start-up programmes are a promising tool to augment traditional active labour market policies (ALMP) programmes as they depict an alternative to existing labour demand-side restrictions across subgroups and regions.

Finally, some policy conclusions and limitations of the study must be emphasized. From an ALMP perspective, the study shows that providing unemployed individuals the possibility to become self-employed (and hence escape unemployment) by offering the two programmes has been a successful strategy. It effectively helped participants (especially in areas with poor economic conditions) to overcome labour demand restrictions and to integrate them in the labour market in the long-run. Policy-makers should therefore continue this strategy and provide such programmes to unemployed individuals in future. To increase further the effectiveness of the programmes, it might be worth thinking about the provision of accompanying counselling or coaching programmes. However, policy-makers should be cautious in expanding the scale of such start-up programmes (e.g. by increasing the amount/duration of the subsidy or lowering the entry criteria) due to three reasons. First, this might attract lower ability individuals who would actually not become self-employed under the current circumstances, which might reduce the overall effectiveness of the programmes. Second, subsidy programmes are relatively costly and bear the risk of deadweight effects, i.e. nascent entrepreneurs intentionally register as being unemployed to receive the subsidy. Third, although slightly better business performance is found in good areas (at least for the BA programme), a causal statement cannot be made if subsidized start-ups out of unemployment are successful businesses yet. To make such a statement one would need to compare programme participants with other business start-ups out of non-unemployment. Unfortunately this is not possible with the data at hand. However, this is an important question and future research should provide evidence on the empirical relevance of these three concerns.

Acknowledgements – The authors thank the special issue Editors, Michael Fritsch and David Storey, and two anonymous referees for valuable comments.

APPENDIX A

Table A1. Propensity score (PS) estimation conditional on local unemployment rates: Start-up Subsidy (SUS) versus non-participation

	Local economic conditions		
	Poor	Medium	Good
Age bracket (Reference: 18–24 years)			
25–29 years	0.067	0.218	0.390
30–34 years	0.417	0.092	0.661**
35–39 years	0.133	0.074	0.165
40–44 years	0.290	0.116	0.315
45–49 years	0.447	0.300	0.320
50–64 years	0.781**	0.801**	0.836***
Marital status (Reference: Single)			
Married	–0.065	0.043	–0.188
Number of children in the household (Reference: No children)			
One child	0.116	0.198	0.260
Two or more children	0.286	0.059	0.133
Health restriction that affects job placement (Reference: No)			
Yes	–0.188	–0.210	0.037
Nationality (Reference: German)			
Non-German	0.123	0.067	0.199
Desired working time (Reference: Part-time)			
Full-time	0.608	–0.076	0.126
School-leaving certificate (Reference: No degree)			
Lower secondary school	0.430	0.323	–0.208
Middle secondary school	0.440	0.512	–0.092
Specialized upper secondary school	0.784	0.072	0.030
Upper secondary school	0.468	0.466	–0.164
Occupational group (Reference: Manufacturing)			
Agriculture	–0.085	–0.412	0.021
Technical occupations	0.166	–0.785*	–0.646
Services	0.069	–0.350	–0.379
Others	–0.402	–0.670	–0.425
Professional qualification (Reference: Workers with a tertiary education)			
Workers with a technical college education	0.271	0.110	–0.051
Skilled workers	0.047	0.188	–0.105
Unskilled workers	0.200	0.288	–0.118
Duration of previous unemployment (Reference: Less than one month)			
≥ 1 to 3 months	–1.390***	–1.560***	–1.737***
≥ 3 to < 6 months	–1.632***	–1.529***	–1.473***
≥ 6 months to < 1 year	–1.426***	–1.700***	–1.648***
≥ 1 to < 2 years	–1.446***	–2.005***	–1.659***
≥ 2 years	–1.324***	–1.086***	–1.800***
Professional experience (Reference: Without professional experience)			
With professional experience	0.024	–0.128	–0.164
Last employment			
Duration of last employment	0.002	0.0006	0.003*
Placement propositions			
Number of placement propositions	–0.024**	0.005	–0.015**

Table A1. *Continued*

	Local economic conditions		
	Poor	Medium	Good
Employment status before job-seeking (Reference: Employment)			
Self-employed	0.886***	0.089	0.566**
School attendance/never employed before/apprenticeship	0.326*	0.293	0.378
Unemployable	0.272	−0.015	0.360
Others, but at least once employed before	0.730***	0.474**	0.352*
Regional cluster (Reference: II a)			
II b			
III a	0.012	0.015	
III b		−0.416	
III c		−0.199	−0.722*
IV		0.247	−0.416
V a			−0.574
V b			−0.654
V c			−0.712
Benefits/previous earnings			
Remaining unemployment benefit entitlement (months)	−0.014	−0.032**	−0.035***
Unemployment benefit level (€)	−0.039***	−0.025***	−0.032***
Average daily income from regular employment in first half of 2003	−0.002	−0.002	−0.004
Intergenerational transmission			
Parents are/were self-employed	0.367**	0.784***	0.175
Regional macroeconomic conditions			
Unemployment rate	0.096**	−0.106	−0.160*
Vacancy rate[a]	0.120**	−0.079***	−0.001
Gross domestic product (GDP) per capita	0.072*	0.006	0.003
Constant	−3.338**	3.183**	3.897***
Number of observations	646	656	627
Pseudo-R^2	0.166	0.224	0.224
Log-likelihood	−351.911	−335.623	−315.679

Notes: *10%, **5% and ***1% significance level. Differences in numbers of observations compared with Table 1 are due to missing values for some variables.

[a]Available vacancies as the share of the stock in unemployment.

Table A2. *Propensity score (PS) estimation conditional on local gross domestic product (GDP) per capita: Start-up Subsidy (SUS) versus non-participation*

	Local economic conditions		
	Poor	Medium	Good
Age bracket (Reference: 18–24 years)			
25–29 years	0.001	0.425	0.558*
30–34 years	0.361	0.453	0.639**
35–39 years	−0.087	0.344	0.284
40–44 years	0.358	0.449	0.199
45–49 years	0.497	0.459	0.512
50–64 years	0.952***	0.8255**	0.913***
Marital status (Reference: Single)			
Married	−0.115	−0.132	−0.057
Number of children in the household (Reference: No children)			
One child	0.101	0.337*	0.049
Two or more children	0.381**	−0.054	0.223
Health restriction that affects job placement (Reference: No)			
Yes	−0.124	−0.054	−0.167

(*Continued*)

Table A2. Continued

	Local economic conditions		
	Poor	Medium	Good
Nationality (Reference: German)			
Non-German	0.178	0.366***	−0.134
Desired working time (Reference: Part-time)			
Full-time	1.409**	−0.405	−0.143
School-leaving certificate (Reference: No degree)			
Lower secondary school	−0.258	0.301	0.017
Middle secondary school	−0.146	0.258	0.315
Specialized upper secondary school	−0.038	0.100	0.324
Upper secondary school	−0.047	0.070	0.336
Occupational group (Reference: Manufacturing)			
Agriculture	−0.048	−0.174	−0.293
Technical occupations	0.114	−0.219	−0.834*
Services	0.015	−0.046	−0.566
Others	−0.459	−0.440	−0.706
Professional qualification (Reference: Workers with a tertiary education)			
Workers with a technical college education	0.321	0.188	−0.111
Skilled workers	0.371	−0.252	0.065
Unskilled workers	0.444*	−0.002	0.043
Duration of previous unemployment (Reference: Less than one month)			
≥ 1 to 3 months	−1.342***	−1.656***	−1.748***
≥ 3 to < 6 months	−1.524***	−1.443***	−1.768***
≥ 6 months to < 1 year	−1.212***	−1.423***	−2.030***
≥ 1 to < 2 years	−1.443***	−1.573***	−2.019***
≥ 2 years	−0.825**	−1.426***	−1.714***
Professional experience (Reference: Without professional experience)			
With professional experience	0.173	−0.291*	−0.140
Last employment			
Duration of last employment	0.0005	0.002	0.002
Placement propositions			
Number of placement propositions	−0.041***	−0.007	−0.0007
Employment status before job-seeking (Reference: Employment)			
Self-employed	0.899***	0.593**	0.096
School attendance/never employed before/apprenticeship	0.642***	0.328	0.213
Unemployable	0.038	0.413*	0.449*
Others, but at least once employed before	0.756***	0.568***	0.398**
Regional cluster (Reference: II a)			
II b	−0.219	0.164	0.053
III a	0.418	−0.061	0.662
III b	0.174	0.255	−0.627
III c	−0.347	−0.178	−0.439
IV			−0.002
V a		−0.236	−0.201
V b	−0.333	−0.234	−0.295
V c		−0.304	−0.159
Benefits/previous earnings			
Remaining unemployment benefit entitlement (months)	−0.009	−0.019	−0.048***
Unemployment benefit level (€)	−0.042***	−0.029***	−0.028***
Average daily income from regular employment in first half of 2003	0.002	−0.005	−0.003
Intergenerational transmission			
Parents are/were self-employed	0.559***	0.353**	0.39***

Table A2. Continued

	Local economic conditions		
	Poor	Medium	Good
Regional macroeconomic conditions			
Unemployment rate	0.039	0.005	–0.105
Vacancy rate[a]	0.099***	0.005	–0.024
GDP per capita	0.041	0.165***	0.004
Constant	–2.149	–2.130	3.474**
Number of observations	636	646	648
Pseudo-R^2	0.209	0.205	0.218
Log-likelihood	–326.257	–338.403	–331.188

Notes: *10%, **5% and ***1% significance level. Differences in numbers of observations compared with Table 1 are due to missing values for some variables.

[a]Available vacancies as the share of the stock in unemployment.

Table A3. Propensity score (PS) estimation conditional on local unemployment rates: Bridging Allowance (BA) versus non-participation

	Local economic conditions		
	Poor	Medium	High
Age bracket (Reference: 18–24 years)			
25–29 years	–0.142	0.704**	0.151
30–34 years	0.343	0.571*	0.113
35–39 years	0.246	0.531	0.232
40–44 years	0.206	0.267	0.131
45–49 years	0.035	0.370	0.160
50–64 years	–0.108	0.486	0.317
Marital status (Reference: Single)			
Married	–0.231*	0.060	–0.056
Number of children in the household (Reference: No children)			
One child	–0.107	–0.054	–0.125
Two or more children	–0.049	–0.234	–0.130
Health restriction that affects job placement (Reference: No)			
Yes	0.213	–0.221	–0.141
Nationality (Reference: German)			
Non-German	0.103	0.121	0.240**
Desired working time (Reference: Part-time)			
Full-time		0.982	–0.434
School-leaving certificate (Reference: No degree)			
Lower secondary school	0.394	0.296	0.097
Middle secondary school	0.512	0.355	0.122
Specialized upper secondary school	0.688	0.329	0.212
Upper secondary school	0.680	0.190	0.233
Occupational group (Reference: Manufacturing)			
Agriculture	0.274	0.242	0.063
Technical occupations	0.449	0.590	0.052
Services	0.310	0.432	–0.130
Others	–0.091	–0.004	–0.518
Professional qualification (Reference: Workers with a tertiary education)			
Workers with a technical college education	0.114	–0.298	0.110
Skilled workers	0.147	–0.104	0.136
Unskilled workers	0.275	–0.148	0.154

(Continued)

Table A3. *Continued*

	Local economic conditions		
	Poor	Medium	High
Duration of previous unemployment (Reference: Less than one month)			
≥ 1 to 3 months	–0.985***	–0.980***	–1.052***
≥ 3 to < 6 months	–1.002***	–1.172***	–0.985***
≥ 6 months to < 1 year	–0.795***	–1.309***	–1.134***
≥ 1 to < 2 years	–0.958***	–1.251***	–1.182***
≥ 2 years	–1.104***	–0.937*	–1.576***
Professional experience (Reference: Without professional experience)			
With professional experience	–0.141	–0.214	–0.348**
Last employment			
Duration of last employment	0.003**	0.001	0.003**
Placement propositions			
Number of placement propositions	–0.006	–0.011	–0.014**
Employment status before job-seeking (Reference: Employment)			
Self-employed	–0.463	–0.406	–0.263
School attendance/never employed before/apprenticeship	0.304*	0.051	0.371
Unemployable	0.083	–0.099	–0.027
Others, but at least once employed before	0.242	0.615***	0.025
Regional cluster (Reference: II a)			
II b			
III a	–1.440*	–0.197	
III b		–0.223	
III c		–0.393*	–0.003
IV		–0.237	–0.076
V a		–0.039	0.049
V b			–0.394
V c			–0.236
Benefits/previous earnings			
Remaining unemployment benefit entitlement (months)	–0.012	–0.004	–0.044***
Unemployment benefit level (€)	0.025***	0.022***	0.026***
Average daily income from regular employment in first half of 2003	–0.001	–0.004**	–0.0007
Intergenerational transmission			
Parents are/were self-employed	0.515***	0.704***	0.254**
Regional macroeconomic conditions			
Unemployment rate	–0.069*	–0.108	–0.152**
Vacancy rate[a]	–0.035	–0.041*	0.0002
Gross domestic product (GDP) per capita	0.018	–0.0003	0.003
Constant	0.585	–0.079	1.729
Number of observations	743	771	791
Pseudo-R^2	0.108	0.136	0.124
Log-likelihood	–456.142	–459.37	–480.303

Notes: *10%, **5% and ***1% significance level. Differences in numbers of observations compared with Table 1 are due to missing values for some variables.

[a]Available vacancies as the share of the stock in unemployment.

Table A4. Propensity score (PS) estimation conditional on local gross domestic product (GDP) per capita: Bridging Allowance (BA) versus non-participation

	Local economic conditions		
	Poor	Medium	Good
Age bracket (Reference: 18–24 years)			
25–29 years	0.014	0.010	0.559
30–34 years	0.436	0.029	0.399
35–39 years	0.039	0.263	0.397
40–44 years	0.283	0.038	0.108
45–49 years	−0.064	0.074	0.319
50–64 years	−0.149	0.236	0.213
Marital status (Reference: Single)			
Married	−0.085	−0.184	0.056
Number of children in the household (Reference: No children)			
One child	−0.044	0.024	−0.299*
Two or more children	−0.120	−0.085	−0.298*
Health restriction that affects job placement (Reference: No)			
Yes	−0.159	0.205	−0.127
Nationality (Reference: German)			
Non-German	0.032	0.255**	0.097
Desired working time (Reference: Part-time)			
Full-time	1.241**	0.272	−0.248
School-leaving certificate (Reference: No degree)			
Lower secondary school	−0.208	0.943	0.347
Middle secondary school	−0.297	1.151*	0.344
Specialized upper secondary school	0.027	1.002	0.530
Upper secondary school	−0.200	1.163*	0.273
Occupational group (Reference: Manufacturing)			
Agriculture	0.027	0.330	−0.115
Technical occupations	0.070	0.472	0.147
Services	−0.028	0.412	−0.144
Others	−0.446	−0.178	−0.327
Professional qualification (Reference: Workers with a tertiary education)			
Workers with a technical college education	−0.237	0.050	0.050
Skilled workers	−0.025	0.028	0.122
Unskilled workers	−0.032	0.210	0.067
Duration of previous unemployment (Reference: Less than one month)			
≥ 1 to 3 months	−0.856***	−0.927***	−1.080***
≥ 3 to < 6 months	−0.962***	−0.871***	−1.359***
≥ 6 months to < 1 year	−0.683**	−0.838**	−1.549***
≥ 1 to < 2 years	−0.794***	−1.062***	−1.422***
≥ 2 years	−0.713*	−1.505***	−1.187**
Professional experience (Reference: Without professional experience)			
With professional experience	−0.101	−0.331**	−0.231
Last employment			
Duration of last employment	0.004***	0.002*	0.002*
Placement propositions			
Number of placement propositions	−0.010	−0.007	−0.019**
Employment status before job-seeking (Reference: Employment)			
Self-employed	−0.709	−0.612*	−0.079

(*Continued*)

Table A4. *Continued*

	Local economic conditions		
	Poor	Medium	Good
School attendance/never employed before/apprenticeship	0.372**	0.072	0.166
Unemployable	–0.180	0.115	0.240
Others, but at least once employed before	0.491**	0.292	0.002
Regional cluster (Reference: II a)			
II b	–0.907	–0.054	–0.223
III a	–1.582***	–0.298	–0.401
III b	–1.466**	–0.212	–0.964*
III c	–1.568**	–0.517	–0.528
IV			–0.602
V a		0.145	–0.372
V b	–1.578**	–0.533	–0.966*
V c		–0.274	–0.675
Benefits/previous earnings			
Remaining unemployment benefit entitlement (months)	–0.017	–0.018*	–0.020*
Unemployment benefit level (€)	0.021***	0.023***	0.031***
Average daily income from regular employment in first half of 2003	0.001	–0.001	–0.005***
Intergenerational transmission			
Parents are/were self-employed	0.581***	0.493***	0.354***
Regional macroeconomic conditions			
Unemployment rate	–0.073*	–0.047	–0.109*
Vacancy rate[a]	0.020	0.002	0.004
GDP per capita	0.030	–0.005	0.023**
Constant	0.233	–0.642	0.713
Number of observations	775	777	759
Pseudo-R^2	0.127	0.117	0.157
Log-likelihood	–466.97	–474.72	–440.738

Notes: *10%, **5% and ***1% significance level. Differences in numbers of observations compared with Table 1 are due to missing values for some variables.

[a]Available vacancies as the share of the stock in unemployment.

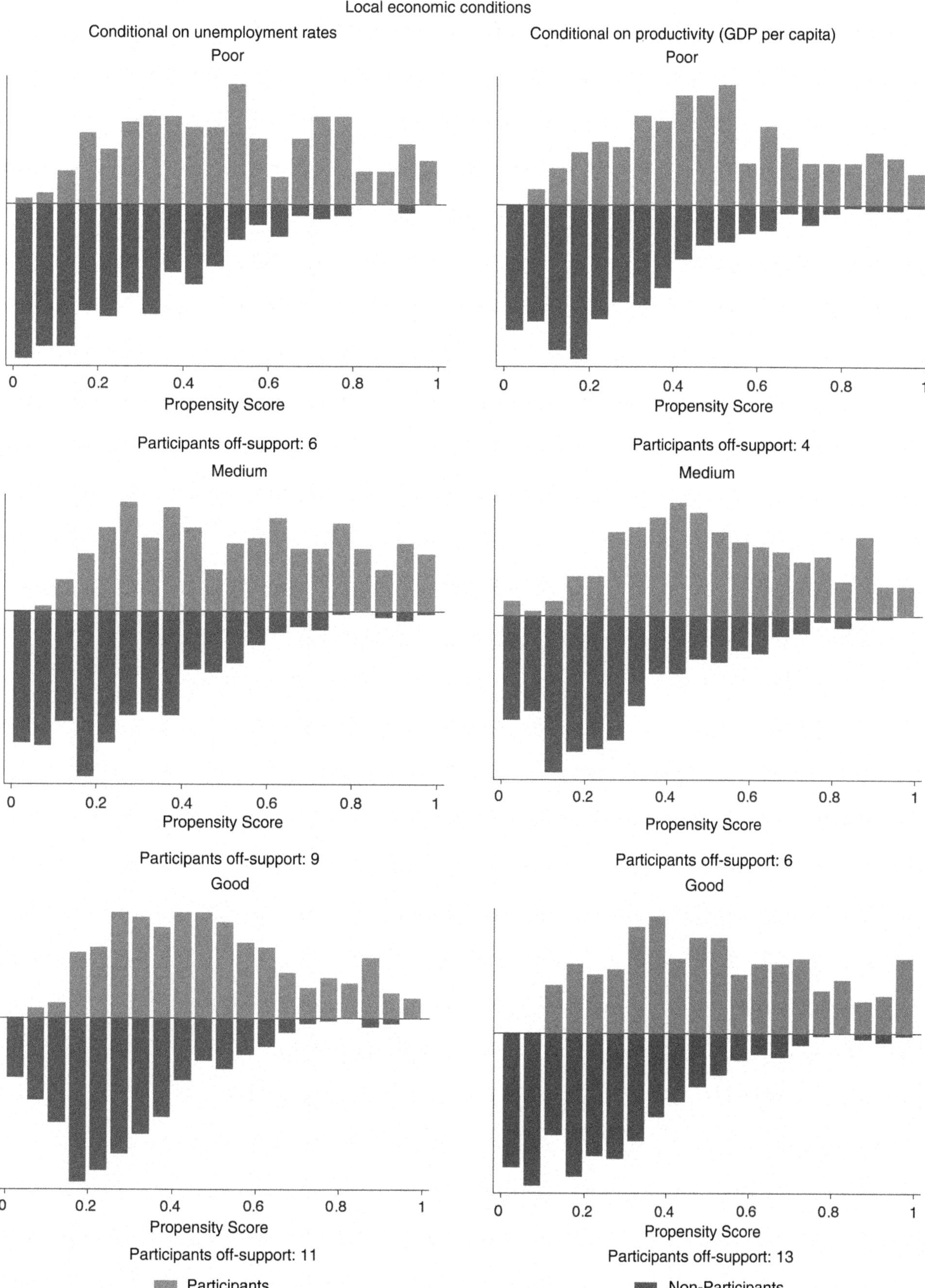

Fig. A1. *Distribution of estimated propensity scores (PS): Start-up Subsidy (SUS)*

Note: Distributions of estimated PS for participants (light grey bars) and non-participants (dark grey bars) are shown. Results are based on probit estimations as shown in Tables A1 and A2. In addition, below each figure the number of participants outside the range of non-participants is shown; those are excluded for the calculation of the ATT (as depicted in Table 4 and Fig. 2)

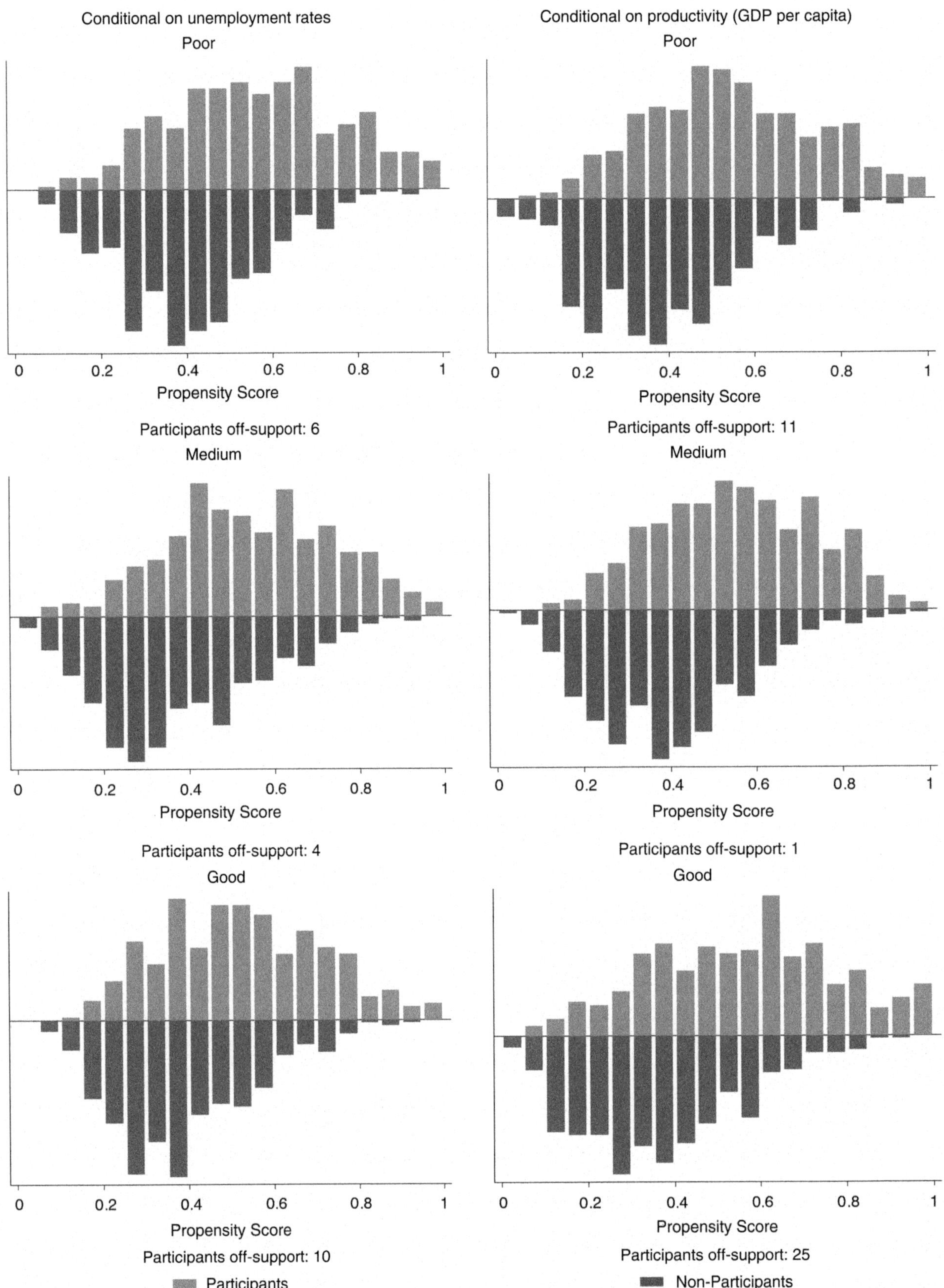

Fig. A2. Distribution of estimated propensity scores (PS): Bridging Allowance (BA)

Note: Distributions of estimated PS for participants (light grey bars) and non-participants (dark grey bars) are shown. Results are based on probit estimations as shown in Tables A3 and A4. In addition, below each figure the number of participants outside the range of non-participants is shown; those are excluded for the calculation of the ATT (as depicted in Table 4 and Fig. 2)

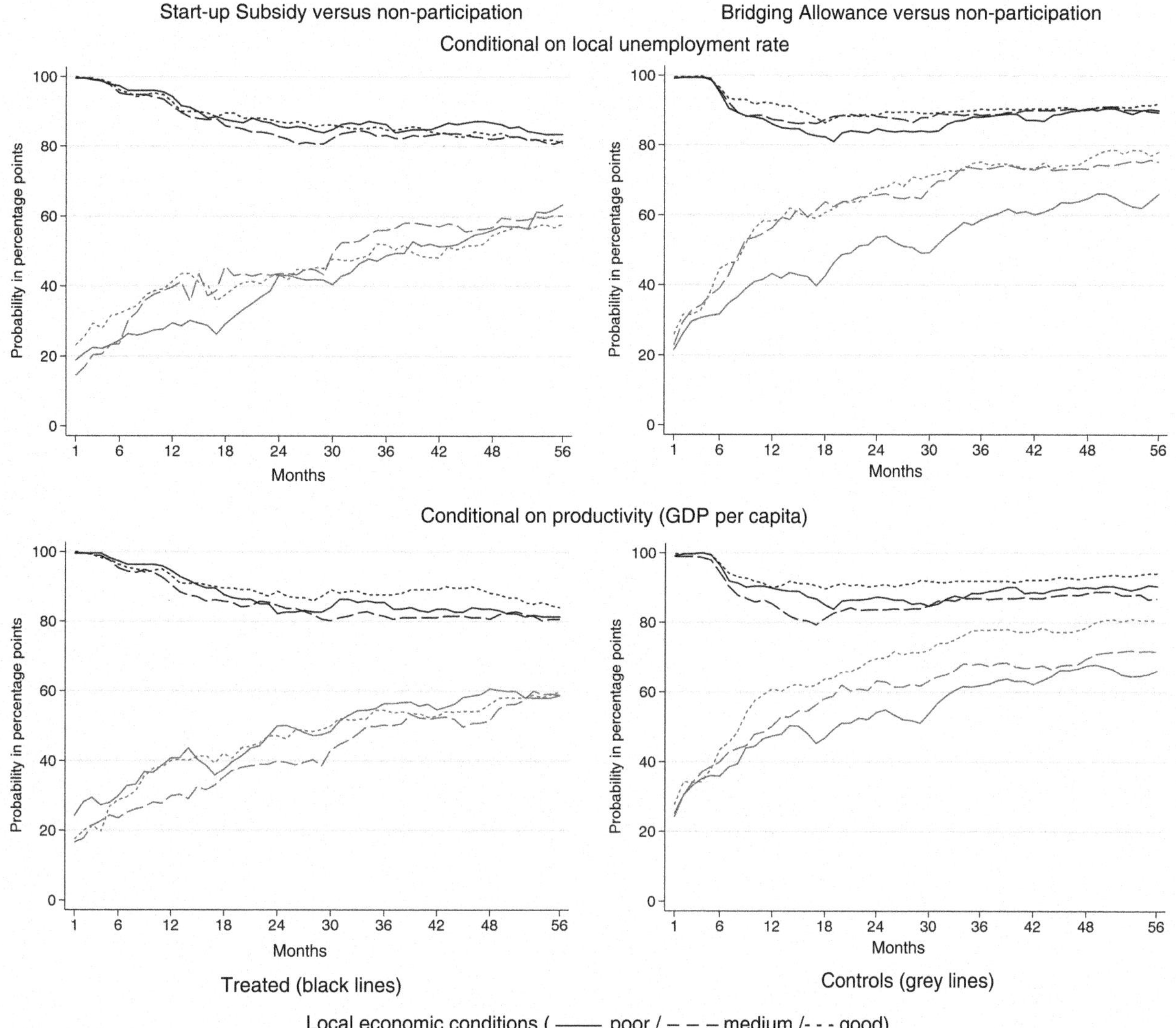

Fig. A3. *Probability levels among participants and matched non-participants*

Note: Probability levels are shown for the outcome variable 'Self-employment or regular employment' among participants and non-participants within the matched sample, i.e. the difference between the solid and dashed lines is the average treatment effect on the treated (ATT). For instance, consider the case of Start-up Subsidy (SUS) versus non-participation. A total of 83.6% (63.4%) of participants (matched non-participants) who were located in an area with poor economic conditions in terms of unemployment rates in the third quarter 2003 are in self-employment or regular employment 56 months after start-up; this applies to 81.0% (57.9%) of participants (matched non-participants) who were located in areas with good economic conditions

Funding – Financial support by the Institute for Employment Research (IAB) in Nuremberg [research grant number 1007] is gratefully acknowledged.

NOTES

1. This is not necessarily true for subgroups of the workforce. For instance, when McVicar and Podivinsky (2010) consider unemployed youths and investigate the effect of the New Deal for Young People in Britain, they find an inverse 'U'-shaped relationship between programme effectiveness and unemployment rates.
2. While the availability of workers to new firms predicts a clear positive impact on firm survival, the effect of economic growth and start-up rates out of unemployment is ambiguous. For a detailed discussion on how economic factors might affect business survival, see Fritsch *et al.* (2006) and Falck (2007).
3. This is in line with findings by Lechner and Wunsch (2009) who show that training programmes in Germany lead to larger employment effects if unemployment is high in terms of both periods and regions. The authors

argue that non-participants are less likely to find a job during periods of high unemployment and if then probably worse jobs. In contrast, participants are locked into the programme when unemployment is high and might face better search and economic conditions if the programme elapses.

4. On average, BA male participants in the sample received €1077 of unemployment benefits per month during their unemployment spell. Given the additional lump sum payment for social security of 68.5%, this corresponds to an average BA payment of €1814 per month.
5. In practice the burden to get such a business plan is quite low so that the impact on the quality of business start-ups is rather ambiguous. Public institutions such as chambers of commerce and industry implemented a standardized procedure to provide individuals with such documents. However, there are no data on subsidized business start-ups after November 2004 so that its impact cannot be empirically evaluated.
6. Having access to only one particular quarter of entrants bears the risk of a selective sample. However, comparing the distribution of certain characteristics (e.g. age and educational background) across different quarters does not show any significant differences.
7. However, individuals in the control group are allowed to participate in ALMP programmes afterwards. The actual number of non-participants who participated in ALMP programmes after the third quarter of 2003 is rather low. Approximately 29% of all non-participants were assigned to programmes of ALMP and only 3% participated in SUS or BA within the observation period.
8. For a more extensive discussion of data construction, see CALIENDO and KÜNN (2011).
9. CALIENDO and KÜNN (2012) provide evidence on the effectiveness of start-up programmes for unemployed women by taking female-specific needs into account.
10. Although business formation influences economic development on the aggregate level (STOREY, 1994; AUDRETSCH and KEILBACH, 2004; FRITSCH, 2008), the prevailing local economic conditions are assumed to be exogenous to new entries into self-employment.
11. The sample is additionally stratified by dividing the respective distributions into four equal parts. Results are similar and lead to the same conclusion. However, lower numbers of observation in each cell result in poor matching quality, which is why it was decided to take three categories as the preferred strategy.
12. The sample was also categorized based on the distribution of unemployment rates and GDP measured at the end of the observation window, i.e. May–June 2008, and it was compared with the initial categorization. It was found that 82% of individuals were assigned to the same category in terms of unemployment rates and 95% in terms of GDP per capita.
13. The willingness of individuals to participate in the survey decreased over time. On average, 46% of all participants and 37% of all non-participants were observed for the entire period of 56 months. The attrition induced a positive selection, i.e. individuals who perform relatively well in terms of labour market outcomes are more likely to respond. Therefore, sequential inverse probability weighting was used to adjust for selective attrition. However, the causal analysis relies on unweighted outcome variables as participants and non-participants are similarly affected by selection due to panel attrition.
14. This is in line with findings by TOKILA (2009) who ran a survival analysis on subsidized start-ups out of unemployment in Finland and found that regional characteristics have only a minor impact on the exit rate.
15. For further discussion, see, for example CALIENDO and HUJER (2006).
16. Only the main findings of the robustness tests are stated here. Detailed results are available from the authors upon request.
17. In 2003, 254 000 individuals participated in SUS or BA compared with 183 000 (295 000) entries in wage subsidies (vocational training) in Germany.
18. For a more extensive discussion of the estimation of propensity scores, see HECKMAN *et al.* (1998) and CALIENDO and KOPEINIG (2008), among others.
19. For a more detailed discussion of matching quality issues, see CALIENDO and KOPEINIG (2008).
20. All results are available from the authors upon request.
21. Keep in mind that unemployment rates and GDP are not perfectly correlated so that the subsamples (poor/medium/good) contain partly different individuals using the unemployment rate or GDP metric (see the fourth section). This explains the slightly different results.

REFERENCES

AUDRETSCH D. and KEILBACH M. (2004) Entrepreneurship capital and economic performance, *Regional Studies* **38**, 949–959.

AUDRETSCH D. and MAHMOOD T. (1995) New firm survival: new results using a hazard function, *Review of Economics and Statistics* **77(1)**, 97–103.

BLANCHFLOWER D. and OSWALD A. (1998) What makes an entrepreneur?, *Journal of Labor Economics* **16**, 26–60.

BODEN R. J. (1999) Flexible working hours, family responsibilities, and female self-employment: gender differences in self-employment selection, *American Journal of Economics and Sociology* **58(1)**, 71–83.

BRIXY U. and GROTZ R. (2006) *Regional Patterns and Determinants of New Firm Formation and Survival in Western Germany*. Discussion Paper Number 5/2006. Institute for Employment Research (IAB), Nuremberg.

CALIENDO M. and HUJER R. (2006) The microeconometric estimation of treatment effects – an overview, *Allgemeines Statistisches Archiv* **90(1)**, 197–212.

CALIENDO M. and KOPEINIG S. (2008) Some practical guidance for the implementation of propensity score matching, *Journal of Economic Surveys* **22(1)**, 31–72.

CALIENDO M. and KRITIKOS A. (2009) *'I Want To, But I Also Need To': Start-ups Resulting from Opportunity and Necessity*. Discussion Paper Number 4661. Institute for the Study of Labor (IZA), Bonn.

CALIENDO M. and KRITIKOS A. (2010) Start-ups by the unemployed: characteristics, survival and direct employment effects, *Small Business Economics* **35(1)**, 71–92.

CALIENDO M. and KÜNN S. (2011) Start-up subsidies for the unemployed: long-term evidence and effect heterogeneity, *Journal of Public Economics* **95(3–4)**, 311–331.

CALIENDO M. and KÜNN S. (2012) *Getting Back into the Labor Market: The Effects of Start-up Subsidies for Unemployed Females*. Discussion Paper Number 6830. Institute for the Study of Labor (IZA), Bonn.

DAR A. and GILL I. S. (1998) Evaluating retraining programs in OECD countries: lessons learned, *World Bank Research Observer* **13(1)**, 79–101.

DAR A. and TZANNATOS Z. (1999) *Active Labor Market Programs: A Review of the Evidence from Evaluations*. SP Discussion Paper Number 9901. The World Bank, Washington, DC.

FAHR R. and SUNDE U. (2009) Did the Hartz reforms speed-up the matching process? A macro-evaluation using empirical matching functions, *German Economic Review* **10(3)**, 284–316.

FALCK O. (2007) Survival chances of new businesses: do regional conditions matter?, *Applied Economics* **39**, 2039–2048.

FAY R. (1996) *Enhancing the Effectiveness of Active Labor Market Policies: Evidence from Programme Evaluations in OECD Countries*. Labour Market and Social Policy Occasional Papers Number 18. Organisation for Economic Co-operation and Development (OECD), Paris.

FRITSCH M. (2008) How does new business development affect regional development? Introduction to the special issue, *Small Business Economics* **30**, 1–14.

FRITSCH M., BRIXY U. and FALCK O. (2006) The effect of industry, region and time on new business survival – a multi-dimensional analysis, *Review of Industrial Organization* **28**, 285–306.

GEORGELLIS Y. and WALL H. J. (2000) What makes a region entrepreneurial? Evidence from Britain, *Annals of Regional Science* **34(3)**, 385–403.

GURLEY-CALVEZ T., BIEHL A. and HARPER K. (2009) Time–use patterns and women entrepreneurs, *American Economic Review: Papers and Proceedings* **99(2)**, 139–144.

HAMILTON R. T. (1986) The influence of unemployment on the level and rate of company formation in Scotland, 1950–1984, *Environment and Planning A* **18**, 1401–1404.

HAMILTON R. T. (1989) Unemployment and business formation rates: reconciling time-series and cross-section evidence, *Environment and Planning A* **21**, 249–255.

HECKMAN J., ICHIMURA H., SMITH J. and TODD P. (1998) Characterizing selection bias using experimental data, *Econometrica* **66(5)**, 1017–1098.

IMBENS G. and WOOLDRIDGE J. M. (2009) Recent developments in the econometrics of program evaluation, *Journal of Economic Literature* **47(1)**, 5–86.

KANGASHARJU A. (2000) Regional variations in firm formation: panel and cross-section data evidence from Finland, *Papers in Regional Science* **79**, 355–373.

KEEBLE D. and WALKER S. (1994) New firms, small firms and dead firms: spatial patterns and determinants in the United Kingdom, *Regional Studies* **28(4)**, 411–427.

KLAPPER L. F. and PARKER S. C. (2011) Gender and the business environment for new firm creation, *World Bank Research Observer* **26(2)**, 237–257.

KLUVE J. (2010) The effectiveness of European active labor market programs, *Labour Economics* **16(6)**, 904–918.

KLUVE J. and SCHMIDT C. M. (2002) Can training and employment subsidies combat European unemployment?, *Economic Policy* **17(35)**, 409–448.

KNIGHT F. H. (1921) *Risk, Uncertainty, and Profit*. Houghton-Mifflin, New York, NY.

LECHMANN D. and SCHNABEL C. (2012) Why is there a gender earnings gap in self-employment? A decomposition analysis with German data, *IZA Journal of European Labor Studies* **1(6)**.

LECHNER M. and WUNSCH C. (2009) Are training programs more effective when unemployment is high?, *Journal of Labor Economics* **27(4)**, 653–692.

LECHNER M. and WUNSCH C. (2013) Sensitivity of matching-based program evaluations to the availability of control variables, *Labour Economics* **21**, 111–121.

MARTIN P. and GRUBB D. (2001) What works and for whom: a review of OECD countries' experiences with active labour market policies, *Swedish Economic Policy Review* **8**, 9–56.

MCVICAR D. and PODIVINSKY J. M. (2010) *Are Active Labour Market Programmes Least Effective Where They Are Most Needed? The Case of the British New Deal for Young People*. Working Paper Number 16/10. Melbourne Institute of Applied Economic and Social Affairs, Melbourne, VIC.

MEAGER N. (1996) From unemployment to self-employment: labour market policies for business start-up, in SCHMIDT G., O'REILLY J. and SCHÖMANN K. (Eds) *International Handbook of Labour Market Policy and Evaluation*, pp. 489–519. Edward Elgar, Cheltenham.

PARKER S. C. (2009) *The Economics of Entrepreneurship*. Cambridge University Press, New York, NY.

PERRY G. (2006) *Are Business Start-up Subsidies Effective for the Unemployed?: Evaluation of Enterprise Allowance*. Working Paper. Auckland University of Technology, Auckland.

REYNOLDS P., STOREY D. and WESTHEAD P. (1994) Cross-national comparisons of the variation in new firm formation rates: an editorial overview, *Regional Studies* **28(4)**, 343–346.

Rosenbaum P. R. (2002) *Observational Studies.* Springer, New York, NY.

Rosenbaum P. and Rubin D. (1983) The central role of the propensity score in observational studies for causal effects, *Biometrika* **70(1)**, 41–50.

Roy A. (1951) Some thoughts on the distribution of earnings, *Oxford Economic Papers* **3(2)**, 135–145.

Rubin D. (1974) Estimating causal effects of treatments in randomised and nonrandomised studies, *Journal of Educational Psychology* **66**, 688–701.

Shane S. (2003) *A General Theory of Entrepreneurship: The Individual–Opportunity Nexus.* Edward Elgar, Cheltenham.

Sianesi B. (2004) An evaluation of the Swedish system of active labour market programmes in the 1990s, *Review of Economics and Statistics* **86(1)**, 133–155.

Smith J. and Todd P. (2005) Does matching overcome LaLonde's critique of nonexperimental estimators?, *Journal of Econometrics* **125(1–2)**, 305–353.

Storey D. (1994) *Understanding the Small Business Sector.* Routledge, London.

Suciu G. P., Lemeshow S. and Moeschberger M. (2004) Statistical tests of the equality of survival curves: reconsidering the options, in Balakrishnan N. and Rao C. R. (Eds) *Handbook of Statistics*, Vol. 23, pp. 251–262. North-Holland, Amsterdam.

Tervo H. (2006) Regional unemployment, self-employment and family background, *Applied Economics* **38**, 1055–1062.

Tokila A. (2009) *Start-up Grants and Self-Employment Duration.* Working Paper. School of Business and Economics, University of Jyväskylä, Jyväskylä.

Van Praag C. M. (2003) Business survival and success of young small business owners, *Small Business Economics* **21(1)**, 1–17.

Wagner J. and Sternberg R. (2004) Start-up activities, individual characteristics, and the regional milieu: lessons for entrepreneurship support policies from German micro data, *Annals of Regional Science* **38**, 219–240.

Wooldridge J. M. (2002) *Econometric Analysis of Cross Section and Panel Data.* MIT Press, Cambridge, MA.

Index

Note: Page numbers followed by 'f' refer to figures, followed by 'n' refer to notes and followed by 't' refer to tables.

Table 2. Effect of past start-up rates on the current start-up rate in West Germany, 1984–2005[a]

	I	II	III
	1984–2005		2000–2005
Start-up rate ($t-1$)	0.432*** (0.0213)	–	0.656*** (0.0461)
Start-up rate ($t-2$)	0.0972*** (0.00774)	–	–
Start-up rate ($t-3$)	0.113*** (0.00992)	0.243*** (0.0236)	–
Population density (log) ($t-1$)	−0.0408* (0.0222)	−0.107*** (0.0382)	−0.154*** (0.0394)
Share of R&D personnel ($t-1$)	0.0425** (0.0197)	0.129*** (0.0285)	0.128*** (0.0281)
Unemployment rate ($t-1$)	0.0276* (0.0154)	0.0660** (0.0286)	0.170*** (0.0474)
Federal state dummies	**	**	**
Constant	−0.238*** (0.0601)	−0.264** (0.110)	−0.0396 (0.118)
Number of observations	1349	1349	355
F-value	274.38***	114.32***	38.97***
Adjusted R^2	0.793	0.592	0.459

Notes: Dependent variable: regional start-up rate in t_0. Pooled ordinary least squares (OLS) regressions. Newey–West standard errors are given in parentheses. ***Statistically significant at the 1% level; and **statistically significant at the 5% level. Newey–West standard errors were used to control for potential autocorrelation of the lagged dependent values with the residuals. A lag of 3 was specified. Running the models with the Huber–Sandwich–White procedure leads only to rather small changes of the standard errors. Potential effects of changes in the reporting system in the years 1999 and 2003 are controlled for by year dummies. Running models I and II only for the 1984–1998 period does not qualitatively change the effect of lagged start-up rates.

[a]Lagrange Multiplier tests indicate some remaining spatial autocorrelation in some of the models of the first and second scenarios even when the federal state dummies are included. The results are, however, robust when running spatial lag and spatial error models. The results are presented with federal state dummies because this model is also used for the quantile regressions (see Fig. 4). Performing the analysis with different control variables suggests that the spatial autocorrelation does not pertain to the start-up or the self-employment rates but is caused by some of the control variables. Accordingly, the Lagrange Multiplier test does not indicate any spatial autocorrelation if the model is run without the control variables. In alternative specifications, the stock of start-ups in past years was used and average start-up rates were lagged as independent variables. Both indicators significantly affect start-up activity.

Table 3. Effect of past self-employment rates on the current start-up rate in West Germany, 1984–2005

	I	II	III
	1984–2005		2000–2005
Self-employment rate ($t-1$)	1.118*** (0.0815)	–	0.606*** (0.0413)
Self-employment rate ($t-2$)	−0.811*** (0.0772)	–	–
Self-employment rate ($t-3$)	0.251*** (0.0520)	0.539*** (0.0339)	–
Population density (log) ($t-1$)	−0.0126 (0.0327)	−0.0274 (0.0430)	−0.0511 (0.0444)
Share of R&D personnel ($t-1$)	0.220*** (0.0272)	0.300*** (0.0324)	0.182*** (0.0321)
Unemployment rate ($t-1$)	0.206*** (0.0294)	0.273*** (0.0349)	0.360*** (0.0521)
Federal state dummies	n.s.	n.s.	n.s.
Constant	−0.107 (0.115)	−0.175 (0.149)	−0.0298 (0.113)
Number of observations	1349	1349	355
F-value	112.01***	55.31***	35.76***
Adjusted R^2	0.381	0.296	0.560

Note: Dependent variable: regional start-up rate in t_0. Pooled ordinary least squares (OLS) regressions. Newey–West standard errors are given in parentheses. ***Statistically significant at the 1% level; and **statistically significant at the 5% level. Newey–West standard errors were used to control for potential autocorrelation of the lagged dependent values with the residuals. A lag of 3 was specified. Running the models in accordance with the Huber–Sandwich–White procedure leads only to rather small changes of the standard errors. Potential effects of change in the reporting system in the years 1999 and 2003 are controlled for by year dummies. Running models I and II only for the 1984–1998 period does not qualitatively change the effect of lagged self-employment rates.

Since the historical data used in the analyses of Scenarios II and III provide only information about self-employment but not on start-up rates, the regressions for the past self-employment rate (Table 3) are also performed in order to be compatible with these scenarios. As could have been expected, it is found that the past regional self-employment rate has a strongly significant effect on the current level of start-ups. This effect is particularly pronounced for the self-employment rate lagged by one year. While population density is not statistically significant, a strong relationship between the start-up rate and the regional level of R&D employment is again found. Also, the unemployment rate proves to be statistically significant.

In a further step, the work of ANDERSSON and KOSTER (2011) is followed and quantile regressions are run. The idea behind this analysis is that the effect of a culture of entrepreneurship that leads to persistence of start-up rates should be particularly strong in regions with relatively high levels of new business formation. Due to the extremely high correlation between start-up rates in successive years, the model is restricted to the start-up rate in $t-3$ and the control variables (Tables 2 and 3).[15] It is indeed found that the estimated marginal effect of previous levels of new business formation tends to be the stronger the higher is the past level of new business formation (Fig. 4) and self-employment (Fig. 5). This relationship is considerably more pronounced if the start-up rate is used as indicator for the past level of entrepreneurial activity (Fig. 4). All in all, the results indicate that persistence of start-up activity is especially reinforced in those regions that have experienced high levels of self-employment and new business formation in the past.[16] Whether this

Table 6. Regression results: probability being involved in (necessity/opportunity motivated) early-stage entrepreneurial activity (base: 18–64 population)

	Type of early-stage entrepreneurial activity								
	Total early-stage entrepreneurial activity			Necessity early-stage entrepreneurial activity			Opportunity early-stage entrepreneurial activity		
	Estimated	SE	*p*	Estimated	SE	*p*	Estimated	SE	*p*
Individual level determinants									
Age	0.15	(0.01)	***	0.19	(0.03)	***	0.13	(0.01)	***
Age squared	−0.02	(0.00)	***	−0.02	(0.00)	***	−0.02	(0.00)	***
Gender (female)	−0.74	(0.04)	***	−0.51	(0.10)	***	−0.79	(0.05)	***
Education									
Some secondary	0.04	(0.06)		0.05	(0.14)		0.06	(0.07)	
Secondary degree	0.29	(0.06)	***	−0.17	(0.14)		0.40	(0.07)	***
Post-secondary	0.39	(0.06)	***	0.13	(0.14)		0.46	(0.07)	***
Household income									
Medium	0.13	(0.07)	*	−0.12	(0.16)		0.19	(0.08)	**
High	0.38	(0.07)	***	−0.36	(0.17)	**	0.51	(0.08)	***
Unknown	0.25	(0.08)	***	−0.16	(0.18)		0.35	(0.09)	***
Year (Reference 2001)									
2002	0.08	(0.12)		0.22	(0.26)		0.27	(0.14)	*
2003	0.07	(0.12)		0.55	(0.26)	**	0.23	(0.14)	*
2004	−0.16	(0.11)		0.15	(0.26)		0.04	(0.13)	
2005	0.10	(0.11)		0.33	(0.25)		0.26	(0.13)	*
2006	0.17	(0.11)	*	0.26	(0.24)		0.39	(0.13)	***
2007	0.20	(0.13)		−0.35	(0.36)		0.36	(0.15)	**
2008	0.09	(0.14)		0.07	(0.33)		0.22	(0.16)	
Urban area level determinants									
GDP per capita (ln)	0.09	(0.13)		0.12	(0.21)		0.07	(0.13)	
GDP growth 2001–06	3.73	(0.88)	***	5.38	(1.51)	***	3.25	(0.84)	***
Employment growth	−0.59	(0.58)		−2.35	(0.99)	**	0.03	(0.54)	
Unemployment rate	0.02	(0.01)	*	0.03	(0.02)		0.02	(0.01)	*
Diversity – Specialization	−3.26	(1.03)	***	−7.99	(1.92)	***	−2.39	(0.97)	**
University: top 75	0.09	(0.09)		−0.02	(0.19)		0.12	(0.08)	
Perceived opportunities	0.52	(0.59)		−1.30	(1.01)		0.82	(0.56)	
Know recent start-up entrepreneurs	0.92	(0.67)		2.42	(1.19)	**	0.34	(0.66)	
Constant	−6.86	(0.56)	***	−9.09	(1.05)	***	−6.83	(0.56)	***
SD (GDP per capita effect)	0.03	(0.01)	**				0.03	(0.01)	**
SD (constant)	0.00	(0.15)		0.00	(0.09)		0.00	(0.21)	
Number of observations		44 209			44 209			44 209	
Number of urban areas		23			23			23	
−log*L*		9639			2252			8091	
Intra-class correlation		1.9%			6.2%			2.0%	

Note: Stata command xtmlelogit was used. $^{*}p < 0.10$; $^{**}p < 0.05$; $^{***}p < 0.01$.

proposed by MEESTER and PELLENBARG (2006), 'harder' economic indicators seem to predict opportunity-motivated entrepreneurial activities better than 'softer' indicators. Thus, support is found for hypothesis 3, but not for hypothesis 4.

CONCLUSIONS

This paper has investigated whether urban areas are more entrepreneurial than the other parts of the countries and to what extent the observed regional differences in urban entrepreneurship are caused by differences in individual characteristics and context effects. Hypotheses based on the relevant literature were derived and these were tested by using a new, unique dataset that captures entrepreneurial activity by over 400 000 individuals across 23 urban areas in 12 European countries. It should be pointed out that while the analysis was focused on urban entrepreneurship, this does not imply that other areas are deemed irrelevant. While urban regions are distinguished to some extent from 'the rest of the country', it is acknowledged that the importance of rural entrepreneurship should not be neglected (STATHOPOULOU *et al.*, 2004).

Table A6. Ordinary least squares (OLS) estimates for employment growth manufacturing

	(1)	(2)	(3)	(4)	(5)	(6)
West and East						
Start-up rate (ln)	0.241**	0.234*	0.241*			
	(0.111)	(0.115)	(0.114)			
Turbulence rate (ln)				0.212*	0.202*	0.212*
				(0.102)	(0.105)	(0.105)
Share of firms surviving a minimum of 1 year (ln)	0.535			0.577		
	(0.338)			(0.337)		
Share of firms surviving a minimum of 2 years (ln)		0.259			0.281	
		(0.241)			(0.241)	
Share of firms surviving a minimum of 3 years (ln)			0.260			0.283
			(0.189)			(0.190)
Population density (ln)	−0.010	−0.012	−0.008	−0.015	−0.017	−0.013
	(0.047)	(0.048)	(0.047)	(0.046)	(0.047)	(0.047)
Share of university graduates (ln)	0.062	0.061	0.061	0.059	0.059	0.058
	(0.087)	(0.087)	(0.087)	(0.090)	(0.091)	(0.090)
Dummy: Region in East Germany	−0.619***	−0.618***	−0.609***	−0.604***	−0.602***	−0.594***
	(0.081)	(0.083)	(0.082)	(0.082)	(0.085)	(0.083)
Constant	−0.551	0.687	0.714	−0.898	0.430	0.458
	(1.439)	(0.955)	(0.720)	(1.431)	(0.957)	(0.720)
Number of regions	96	96	96	96	96	96
R^2 (adjusted)	0.654	0.652	0.654	0.650	0.647	0.650
Mean VIF	3.58	3.71	3.74	3.63	3.76	3.78
Only West						
Start-up rate (ln)	0.152	0.157	0.165			
	(0.115)	(0.121)	(0.122)			
Turbulence rate (ln)				0.116	0.121	0.132
				(0.104)	(0.110)	(0.112)
Share of firms surviving a minimum of 1 year (ln)	0.867***			0.862***		
	(0.199)			(0.212)		
Share of firms surviving a minimum of 2 years (ln)		0.592***			0.587***	
		(0.162)			(0.176)	
Share of firms surviving a minimum of 3 years (ln)			0.510***			0.512***
			(0.127)			(0.140)
Population density (ln)	−0.051	−0.048	−0.045	−0.057	−0.054	−0.051
	(0.035)	(0.037)	(0.036)	(0.034)	(0.036)	(0.034)
Share of university graduates (ln)	0.086	0.088	0.088	0.083	0.084	0.085
	(0.080)	(0.079)	(0.077)	(0.083)	(0.081)	(0.080)
Constant	−2.072**	−0.786	−0.375	−2.172**	−0.891	−0.507
	(0.854)	(0.613)	(0.447)	(0.889)	(0.677)	(0.499)
Number of regions	74	74	74	74	74	74
R^2 (adjusted)	0.192	0.194	0.211	0.180	0.181	0.198
Mean VIF	1.97	2.02	2.01	1.95	2.00	2.00

Notes: $*p < 0.05$, $**p < 0.01$, $***p < 0.001$ Standard errors are given in parentheses.
VIF, variance inflation factor.

Table A2. Continued

	Local economic conditions		
	Poor	Medium	Good
Regional macroeconomic conditions			
Unemployment rate	0.039	0.005	−0.105
Vacancy rate[a]	0.099***	0.005	−0.024
GDP per capita	0.041	0.165***	0.004
Constant	−2.149	−2.130	3.474**
Number of observations	636	646	648
Pseudo-R^2	0.209	0.205	0.218
Log-likelihood	−326.257	−338.403	−331.188

Notes: *10%, **5% and ***1% significance level. Differences in numbers of observations compared with Table 1 are due to missing values for some variables.

[a]Available vacancies as the share of the stock in unemployment.

Table A3. Propensity score (PS) estimation conditional on local unemployment rates: Bridging Allowance (BA) versus non-participation

	Local economic conditions		
	Poor	Medium	High
Age bracket (Reference: 18–24 years)			
25–29 years	−0.142	0.704**	0.151
30–34 years	0.343	0.571*	0.113
35–39 years	0.246	0.531	0.232
40–44 years	0.206	0.267	0.131
45–49 years	0.035	0.370	0.160
50–64 years	−0.108	0.486	0.317
Marital status (Reference: Single)			
Married	−0.231*	0.060	−0.056
Number of children in the household (Reference: No children)			
One child	−0.107	−0.054	−0.125
Two or more children	−0.049	−0.234	−0.130
Health restriction that affects job placement (Reference: No)			
Yes	0.213	−0.221	−0.141
Nationality (Reference: German)			
Non-German	0.103	0.121	0.240**
Desired working time (Reference: Part-time)			
Full-time		0.982	−0.434
School-leaving certificate (Reference: No degree)			
Lower secondary school	0.394	0.296	0.097
Middle secondary school	0.512	0.355	0.122
Specialized upper secondary school	0.688	0.329	0.212
Upper secondary school	0.680	0.190	0.233
Occupational group (Reference: Manufacturing)			
Agriculture	0.274	0.242	0.063
Technical occupations	0.449	0.590	0.052
Services	0.310	0.432	−0.130
Others	−0.091	−0.004	−0.518
Professional qualification (Reference: Workers with a tertiary education)			
Workers with a technical college education	0.114	−0.298	0.110
Skilled workers	0.147	−0.104	0.136
Unskilled workers	0.275	−0.148	0.154

(*Continued*)

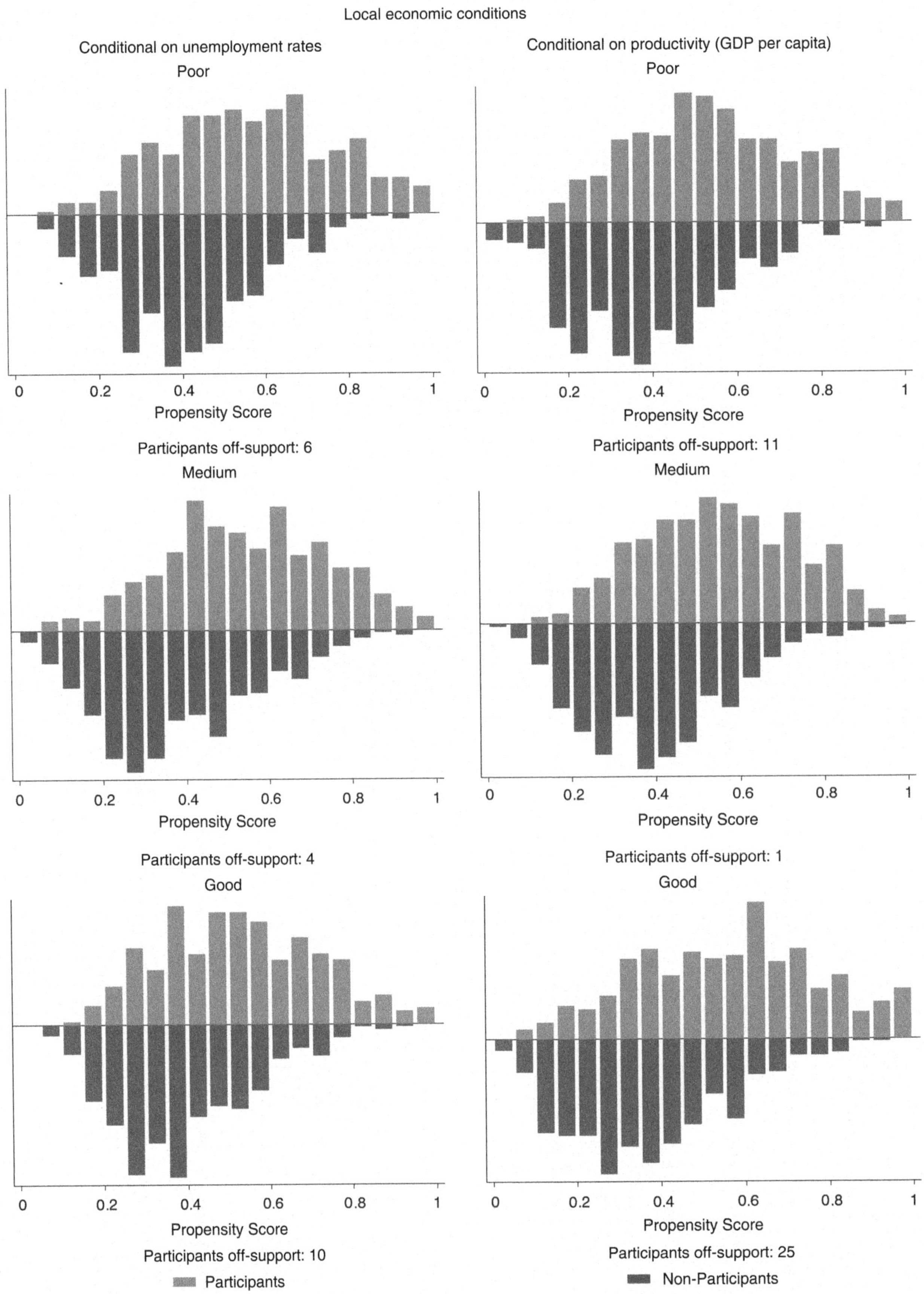

Local economic conditions

Conditional on unemployment rates

Poor

0 0.2 0.4 0.6 0.8 1

Propensity Score

Participants off-support: 6

Medium

0 0.2 0.4 0.6 0.8 1

Propensity Score

Participants off-support: 4

Good

0 0.2 0.4 0.6 0.8 1

Propensity Score

Participants off-support: 10

Conditional on productivity (GDP per capita)

Poor

0 0.2 0.4 0.6 0.8 1

Propensity Score

Participants off-support: 11

Medium

0 0.2 0.4 0.6 0.8 1

Propensity Score

Participants off-support: 1

Good

0 0.2 0.4 0.6 0.8 1

Propensity Score

Participants off-support: 25

Participants

Non-Participants

Fig. A2. Distribution of estimated propensity scores (PS): Bridging Allowance (BA)

Note: Distributions of estimated PS for participants (light grey bars) and non-participants (dark grey bars) are shown. Results are based on probit estimations as shown in Tables A3 and A4. In addition, below each figure the number of participants outside the range of non-participants is shown; those are excluded for the calculation of the ATT (as depicted in Table 4 and Fig. 2)